Training for performance

Training for performance

A meta-disciplinary account

John Matthews

methuen | drama

Methuen Drama

1 3 5 7 9 10 8 6 4 2

First published in 2011

Methuen Drama, an imprint of Bloomsbury Publishing Plc

Methuen Drama
Bloomsbury Publishing Plc
36 Soho Square
London W1D 3QY
www.methuendrama.com

A CIP catalogue record for this book is available from the British Library

ISBN: 978 1 408 12918 0 (hardback)
ISBN: 978 1 408 12917 3 (paperback)

Available in the USA from Bloomsbury Academic & Professional,
175 Fifth Avenue /3rd Floor, New York, NY 10010
www.BloomsburyAcademicUSA.com

Typeset by Country Setting, Kingsdown, Kent CT14 8ES
Printed and bound in Great Britain by Martins The Printers,
Berwick-upon-Tweed

For you, Faith, with all my love

Contents

Illustrations

Figure 1. The author's full name on his Application to Register for a Higher Degree by Research with University of Surrey.

Figure 2. The author's signature on his Application to Register for a Higher Degree by Research with University of Surrey.

Figure 3. Signature of Guido Fawkes on a confession made on 9 November 1605. Guido's name can be seen in a faint hand immediately above the torn bottom right corner of the document. Reprinted by permission from The National Archives, UK.

Figure 4. Signature of Guido Fawkes on a confession made on 17 November 1605. Guido's full name can be seen above 'Her Majesty's State Paper Office' stamp, adjacent to the signatures of the other conspirators. Reprinted by permission from The National Archives, UK.

Figure 5. 'Virtual John'. Photograph by Astor Agustsson. Reprinted by permission and with thanks.

Figure 6. 'Real John'. Photograph by Glen Birchall. Reprinted by permission and with thanks.

Figure 7. 'Tim the Tortoise' by Aardman Animation for Leonard Cheshire Disability 'Creature Discomforts' campaign. Reprinted by permission and with thanks to Leonard Cheshire Disability.

Figure 8. Ian Wilding, voice of 'Tim the Tortoise'. Reprinted by permission and with thanks to Ian Wilding.

Figure 9. Bill Viola, *Six Heads* (2000). Video on wall-mounted plasma display. Artist's proof. Photograph by Kira Perov. Reprinted with thanks to Bill Viola and Kira Perov.

Figure 10. 'Plate III: Joy – High spirits – Love – Tender feelings – Devotion', taken from Charles Darwin's *The Expression of the Emotions in Man and Animals*.

Acknowledgements

First and foremost thanks to my wife, Faith. Without you none of this is possible and none of it would be worthwhile.

Special thanks go to my mother, Marilyn, and my father, Ian, for your loving kindness and support and to my brother, David, for the inspiration and guidance you have provided. My thanks also to my new family, Jef, Jan and Max – I hope this book sheds some light on what I've been up to all this time.

I owe much thanks to Alan, Adrian, Simon and Joe for your patient teaching and continuing advice and a debt of gratitude to Inderjeet Garcha, who has edited this book, for your generosity throughout the process. Martin and Adrian H., for your insightful comments and suggestions I am very grateful.

Introduction

Training has become integral to performance practice in the early twenty-first century. To confirm this, one needs only to open a theatre programme. The archetypal formula of the actor's 'biog' contained therein tells us – the audience – where, and thus how, a given actor has trained. This ubiquity of the actor's 'biog' suggests that there is, for actors as for audience, a premium placed implicitly on training in what have been called 'the big drama schools'[1] – and acronyms such as RADA (Royal Academy of Dramatic Art) or CSSD (Central School of Speech and Drama) carry a particular currency in the semantic field of the biog. For three years, during the time in which I was preparing this book, I taught at one of these 'big drama schools', an institution member of the National Council of Drama Training,[2] an organisation whose very existence confirms Nicholas Ridout's observation that, in a commercial theatre environment today, 'the specialist can best secure his or her livelihood by the acquisition of specialist training'.[3]

Training is not only central to the 'mainstream' theatre, for which the big drama schools provide 'vocational training', but also to a diverse range of performance practices which conduct themselves in opposition to this model of commercial theatre. In performance self-identifying as 'devised', 'physical theatre', 'task-based' or 'durational', an association between the performers and a specific practitioner and his or her approach to training can be seen as intimately associated with the measure of a performer's capabilities and the merit of the work that they produce. In the area of performance often referred to as 'live art', the very aesthetic of training rigour can be seen to comprise a significant component of the artwork, as the lengthy and physically arduous performances of Tehching Hsieh and Marina Abramovic (to give just two examples) demonstrate.[4] The association between training and the value of performance is also in evidence in universities in Britain, America and Europe, wherein methodologies of famed practitioners of the twentieth century are widely taught, and assume a privileged position in the syllabus of theatre and performance degree programmes.

Training has assumed a central role in the organisation of theatre and performance practice, as well as in the study of these arts, as it has done in other areas of social living. Complete an application form for a job and it is likely that you will be required to detail your skills, abilities and experiences and to substantiate these with reference to qualifications and training. Perform a job and you may find that you are required to undertake 'professional development' activities or 'on-the-job training' before you can carry out given tasks, obtain specific responsibilities or operate certain processes and machinery. Attend a trial or study litigation and note how many claims and counter-claims are disputed over grounds of 'adequate training' and the responsibility for ensuring it. Read a newspaper and register how many tragedies and triumphs in politics, medicine, construction, sports, education and any other area of human endeavour issue from a shortage or excess of 'proper training'. Survey the plenitude of professions today which are supported by a requirement for training, from driving instructor to personal trainer, private tutor to 'life coach'. Training for performance is an experience quintessential to social life and yet, despite the significance of training to living, our critical knowledge of this experience in the fields of theatre and performance is profoundly limited.

'Training', according to Ian Watson, a professor of performance and author on the topic of training practice, 'is a generic term that means different things to different people'.[5] Watson points out that the performer training practices of America, France, India and Japan are quite distinct from one another, and yet the practitioners of these diverse disciplines, across this range of settings, all use the term 'training' to describe what they do. Watson's approach to describing what training is or means typifies a common understanding that regards training as a series of exercises undertaken to obtain specific expertise; training, this understanding asserts, is simply those exercises one undertakes before performing in order to prepare oneself for performance or to make oneself a 'better' performer. Watson's observation may be true enough at a superficial level, but to maintain that 'training' has a generic meaning appears increasingly banal as the fuller range of people and practices that interest Performance Studies get involved in the action. If the term 'training' is applied to a diverse range of activities within theatrical practice, this range is even fuller and more varied in the non-theatrical contexts in which the term training is applied, as the above thumbnail sketch of 'social life' illustrates.

Watson's approach to 'defining' training evinces a failure within Theatre and Performance Studies to get to grips with training in the manner in which these disciplines purport to show concern with 'key words'.[6] The taxonomical interests of the discipline of Theatre Studies can be traced back through the output of modern scholars such as Raymond Williams, via his 1976 work, *Key Words: A Vocabulary of Culture and Society*, and to the writings of the earliest critics of theatre, Plato and Aristotle. More recently, Ric Allsopp and David Williams have written about the long-standing interest of *Performance Research*, the flagship journal of Performance Studies, in surveying the way that words, vocabularies and discourses of performance are changing through 'attending to terms that are contested'.[7] Sharing this interest, this book is motivated by the fact that what would seem to be one of the key terms associated with practices of theatre and performance – 'training' – is not under contestation but is understood by Theatre and Performance Studies as having a merely generic usage.

Asking 'What is training?' is in reality a way of asking 'What is *called* training?' – a matter of exploring, analysing, comparing and contrasting the different contexts in which the term is used. This book examines a small selection of such contexts, including theatre, dance, religion and rehabilitation. In the pages that follow, the investigation into training draws upon my participation in actor training, dance training, rehabilitative physiotherapy and monasticism. The periods of participation in these practices range from weekly workshops over the course of a year to seven days and nights spent living in a Benedictine monastery. My own participation in training is not intended to be definitive of each discipline, but the practices in which I have participated are chosen for specific reasons: the three performer-training sites – in Butoh with Katsura Kan and Marie-Gabrielle Rotie, in actor training with Phillip Zarrilli and with the Odin Teatret – introduce the critical imperatives of Performance Studies directly to theatrical training experiences. These imperatives are concerned with philosophical and anthropological enquiry, and relate to a desire to describe and comprehend the processes and experiences associated with performance and performing. Participatory research in rehabilitation on a stroke recovery ward and in a long-stay residential care home takes these imperatives into everyday settings while my encounters with the ancient practices of monasticism, experienced when I was living in a community of Benedictine monks at Worth Abbey, provides a historical perspective on training's interpersonal dynamics, organisational techniques and relationship to work. Throughout this book, research into training in the sites detailed above is complemented by experiences and insights drawn from my ongoing teaching at one of the 'big drama schools' in the UK.

The characteristics of training that emerge through the subsequent chapters of this book provide a movement towards delimiting a field of the study of 'training for performance', as opposed to a series of distinct fields of study dedicated to '*this* training for *this* performance'. The study of training contained within this book offers a vocabulary and framework of analysis for academics and practitioners from diverse fields of training and practice. This book makes an argument for the value of, and need for, a 'meta-disciplinary' understanding of training which identifies the processes that are common in a selection of training practices, tentatively hypothesising that these processes might help to define a category of experience called training.

This book takes a particular approach to investigating embodied practices, an approach developed relative to the approaches currently deployed within a 'field' of knowledge related to actor training. Displacing 'body–mind' rhetoric (and its associated agenda), which has dominated discourse on actor training, this book provides a differently attuned view of embodied practice through a conception of the body as metabolic. This conceptualising approach introduces the interests of the discipline of Performance Studies with 'relational dynamics' to an area of discourse in Theatre Studies, stimulating some novel questions about the purpose of training activities.

Positing *vocation* as one experience common in training, I describe how a sense of a private 'calling' to training can be experienced alongside the more material Althusserian interpellation that takes place in the institutional settings where training comes to be practised. The notion of vocation developed herein can be seen as one of training's unique characteristics, and one which sets it apart from a Foucauldian notion of discipline, which has hitherto provided one dominant framework through which philosophically to conceptualise training practices.[8]

Training for Performance examines not only the experiences of individuals in training but also assesses how a very personal sense of vocation can become modelled within the interpersonal dynamics of a group. In most examples, training can be seen to occur within a social unit, and this book analyses the significance of the unique conditions between individuals in groups of individuals training together. The obedience exhibited by group members to one another, and to the group, is identified as a significant aspect of training for performance. Comparing and contrasting the effects of social organisation in training with the effects of group relations in performance unites training discourse with contemporary concerns in the fields of theatre practice.

A principal aim for me in this book has been to 'decentralise' the exercise in critical discourse around training. The 'generic' understanding of training, evident in Watson's conception, has situated exercises at the centre of accounts of actor training in Theatre Studies. Given that, as Watson rightly observes, the exercises practised in each discipline of training are largely specific to that training practice, it would seem to follow that what constitutes training has little to do with the specificity of each exercise, but more to do with something about exercising itself. Addressing itself to the formation of both group and individual capabilities through training this book explores in detail how the acquisition of skills, which has been seen as a key hallmark of training, relates to the construction of social identities and the self-identification of individuals with ethical and aesthetical paradigms. Asking *a priori* questions about training, such as 'What is an exercise?' and 'What does an exercise do to a trainee?' is the major concern of this book. Through asking such questions about training, and pursuing these with rigour through practice and theorising of that practice, this book generates a coherent though necessarily provisional view of training practices which can account for the experience of training itself.

Askeological investigations

As I have argued above, asking 'What is training?' is, in reality, a matter of asking 'What is *called* training?' And that involves asking about a range of practices – not only theatrical – wherein the term is used. In this respect this book is indebted to Heidegger's well-known work, *What is Called Thinking?* for the realisation that the articulation of a useful answer entails the formulation of an appropriate question.

This chapter, motivated by the possibility that the generic usages of training may evince a *genus* of training, takes a lead from another celebrated philosophical text, Wittgenstein's *Philosophical Investigations* and its insistence that, as Robert Fogelin puts it in his commentary, 'the meaning of a term has not been fixed until its use in a broader setting has been established'.[1] Fogelin points out that the association of meaning and use in Wittgenstein comes via Frege who wrote, 'Never . . . ask for the meaning of a word in isolation, but only in the context of a proposition.'[2] Wittgenstein's extension of Frege's concern for 'propositional context' in his *Tractatus Logico Philosophicus* – 'only propositions have sense; only in a nexus of a proposition does a name have a meaning'[3] – is sometimes seen as a refutation of Frege's claims that expressions have both a sense and a reference (a sense being the meaning or significance of an expression, and reference being the thing that uniquely satisfies the sense of an expression), given that Wittgenstein argues that names have only a reference but no sense, while propositions have a sense but no reference.

I don't intend to pursue any connection between this book and Wittgenstein's too far; the focus of my analysis of training is less concerned with the philosophy of language or the disaggregating of sense and reference than with the tracking of 'meaning' through different contexts of usage. However, the assertion that there is an intimate connection between meaning and use motivates this meta-disciplinary study precisely because it suggests an irreducible connection between *all* usage contexts and the 'meaning' of a term. Wittgenstein showed in his later work, *Philosophical Investigations*, that accepting that a word, such as 'training', might be impossible to define in anything other than a generic sense does not entail accepting that training cannot be *explained* in quite definitive ways.

Wittgenstein invites his reader to find a definition for the word 'game' and then, through systematic analysis of the various approaches he anticipates, he shows that conceptions based on amusement, competition or rule-based action will fail to capture the totality of what is meant in all the contexts in which 'game' is used.[4] The point of the exercise however is not to show that no definition can be found for 'game' but that one is not necessary, because, even without definition the word is *used* effectively to explain specific phenomena. Furthermore, our understanding of 'game' allows us to use the term selectively, even to the extent of explaining new activities as yet undefined as games. Indeed, Barker and Hacker write in their commentary on *Philosophical Investigations*, with reference to Wittgenstein's example of 'game', that this means, 'my understanding of what a game is is *completely* expressed in the explanations I can give of "game"'.[5]

Following this train of thought, what seems interesting and significant to me about training is that the generic usage of the word 'training', rather than simply meaning different things to different people, might actually mean the *same things*, as it is used to describe differently augmented, configured, situated and conceived activities. To do as Ian Watson does in *Performer Training: Developments Across Cultures* and to describe training as a 'generic term'[6] is to overlook the fact that a diverse range of people all use this term to explain and interpret their practices, and this would seem to suggest that, even if there is no essential *meaning* to the term, there may be shared characteristics of any activity or experience that is called training.

My intention in this book is not to *define* what is called training because this would involve a process of identification between meaning and use, which as Donald Gustafson, following Wittgenstein, has shown is quite literally 'nonsense' but to *explain and understand* it by investigating some of the characteristics that occur in instances where it is used.[7] Explaining and understanding the term training will of course produce a certain kind of knowledge about it, which will not be in the form of definition but of *isolation.*

Deleuze has written about isolation as a 'sub-medical process' common to artistic (critical) and medical (clinical) activity whereby concepts are not defined but diagnosed. Writing on this process in *Coldness and Cruelty*, Deleuze later explained in interview his desire to describe the 'articulable relationship between literature and clinical psychiatry'.[8] The idea was not to apply psychiatric concepts to literature but, as Smith and Greco have explained, 'to extract non-preexistent clinical concepts from the works themselves'.[9] As in Wittgenstein's method of arriving at an understanding of terms by showing that the meanings of words are not defined but delimited by their particular use, Deleuze argued that the method of arriving at a coherent concept (for example, in Nietzsche's philosophy, nihilism) is a diagnostic one, whereby symptoms (*ressentiment*, the bad conscience) are isolated in the conditions and forms in which they arise.[10] The 'clinical view' achieved by isolation is coherent in so far as its symptoms or characteristics are irreducibly present in all instances of the application of the concept, and in this respect the sub-medical isolating method resembles Wittgenstein's version of 'meaning is use' insofar as each and every correct use of a term corresponds to a certain explanation of it.[11]

The clinical view of training that will be developed throughout this book will be the product of the isolation of key concerns or processes encountered in the different sites where the term is applied. This kind of knowledge, which is generated through the symptomological practice of observation and analysis, resists (as Allsopp and Williams put it on behalf of Performance Studies) producing 'a summative or in any way definitive'[12] term, but rather assembles a provisional constellation of characteristics to be added to and tested. The framework for this observation and analysis is *askeology.*

What is askeology?

'Askeology' draws on the ancient Greek verb *askeo* and combines it with a familiar suffix applied to those things that we feel driven to know more about, describe, analyse and explain. *Askeo* means 'to train', its literal translation being 'to work with raw materials'.[13] The familiar adjective 'ascetic' derives from the term *askesis*, meaning the practice of training or exercise. Warriors and athletes in Greek society applied the discipline of *askesis* to attain optimal bodily fitness and grace.[14] The manner of life, the doctrine or principles of someone who engages in *askesis*, were referred to as 'ascetic' – a word which, over time, has come to describe persons who practise a renunciation of worldly pleasures or comforts to achieve higher intellectual or spiritual goals. Asceticism now refers in particular to the undergoing of extreme physical and psychological trials of deprivation, often self-inflicted, and is intimately associated with religious training.[15]

Consequently few actors – even the 'holy' ones – would be likely to describe their training as ascetic, and the same could probably be said of trainees in other non-religious contexts.[16] Even a contemporary monk may speak of his 'ascetical life' and yet dissociate himself from practising extreme physical privation, and this is in part because 'asceticism' now describes a particular discipline of training and no longer speaks of the embodying of a meta-disciplinary process of training. It is useful to preserve the association of asceticism with spiritual training, but it would also be useful if one could push backwards through the etymological construction of 'asceticism' and resuscitate the term *askeo* to denote the field of this study of training. If *askeo* could once again refer to the practis*ing* of training, the *working with*, then askeology might describe a field of study which looks to comprehend 'training' at a meta-disciplinary level as well as in its multiple disciplinary manifestations. The word askeology might allow one to state that there are 'trainings' and there is 'training', and that both these things are askeological concerns. Then, perhaps, our actor, monk and all other trainees might be willing to say that their practices are *askeological.*

The very word *askesis,* by virtue of ending with '-sis', expresses an activity and thus describes a mode, or rather modes of training; it speaks of the ways in and by which a meta-disciplinary category underlies or overcodes a range of activities. This thinking about and naming of a meta-disciplinary category manifest in various embodied acts suggests that we might think about training as a process extending before or beyond its actualisation as praxis. This concern for training's disciplinary activities as manifestations of meta-disciplinary processes appears to have been subsumed into different concerns over time. For example, when Alison Hodge argues in her influential collection *Twentieth Century Actor Training* that 'the centrality of actor training is evidenced by the fact that many of the innovators in this field have been responsible for both unique training techniques and for some landmark theatre produc-tions',[17] she is asserting that, in the theatre at least, the significance of 'training' is that it denotes certain technical activities which give rise to performative expressions. The enslaving of the term 'training' to describe specific regimes of activity has produced a silence where a term should speak of the practice of practising them. Just as 'performance' is used to denote that which exists in and during specific performance*s*, and that which survives them, so too a word is needed to describe that which exists in, on, over and beyond the existences of training.

In reviving *askeo* in something akin to its original meaning I do not in-tend to engage in a rewriting of history. I do not know what ancient Greek trainees thought about *askesis,* and this book is not about ancient ascet-icism. The reason I want to extract *askeo* from asceticism, and to reformulate it as 'askeology', is to delimit a field of study which investigates training. I do not want to displace 'training' from this field by dislodging it from its title position in certain fields of study – 'actor training' or 'performer training', for example – for, on the contrary, askeology is *about* training. However, as Hodge has shown, 'training' doesn't describe a field of knowledge, practices, experiences, encounters, but speaks of disciplinary technical activities and we have no way of accounting for the fact that its usage is so widespread other than to simply state that it is.

The proliferation of the term 'training' as a suffix in formulations such as Alison Hodge's 'actor training', or Ian Watson's 'performer training' indicates that it has existences and operations beyond and apart from these things. Conversely, the compounding of 'training' with terms such as 'actor', or 'performer' suggests a coincidence with them. Askeology is a study of this thing called 'training' which seems bound to acting and performance and yet somehow not subsumed or completely contained within them. Askeology asks about diverse disciplinary trainings, and about the meta-disciplinary character of training.[18]

I am not interested in adapting *askeo* into 'askeology' simply to restore currency to obsolete terminology, but rather to be *clear* and *precise* about training, in the most basic way described by Gregory Ulmer in his consideration of word use: 'The most basic way to be clear or precise is to define a word.'[19] I contend that askeology should be (and to some extent already is) a research field, but that its various sites and activities, and their connections to one another, need to be highlighted and conceptualised clearly and with precision. This field is already operational, though unnamed, in the sense that its bibliography already encompasses studies of managerial and organisational efficiency, acting and dancing manuals, practical and theoretical guides to performance, sports science textbooks, medical textbooks, physiotherapy case-studies, educational guidebooks and progress reports, anthropological investigations of cultural rites, narrative accounts of personal experiences, video diaries and photographs from studios, rehearsal rooms, clinics and sports fields, webpages and internet archives and, of course, the very lives of those who train or are trained. The study of askeology is existent and operational by giving it a name – albeit a somewhat idiotic one. I mean to point to that fact.

Is askeology an idiotic name?

Many theatrical characters from the hobbling King Oedipus, to the no less royal Ubu, from the archivist Krapp to the STEWARDESS FORGETTING HER DIVORCE[20] have placed centre stage Alan Read's assertion that 'a certain idiotic quality in a name does not mean that the subject has to be stupid'.[21] If, to a twenty-first-century reader, the name 'Oedipus' is idiotic in the contemporary sense of being 'dumb-sounding', then this subject is the archetypal idiot in the etymological sense of the word, deriving from the Latin *idiota* meaning 'ignorant person'. Ignorant as Oedipus may be of his parentage, the idiot who solved the riddle of the sphinx is not 'stupid', from the Latin *stupidus* meaning 'slow-witted' as used to describe those in a lethargic 'state of stupor'. In his book *Theatre, Intimacy and Engagement: The Last Human Venue*, Read coins the 'idiotic' name of *showciology* for a discipline composed of the prefabricated materials of practices at the borders of theatre: philosophy, sociology and phenomenology. According to Read, showciology is, unlike its progenitors, 'homeless' and 'like all "prefabs" . . . as temporary as one requires and provisional enough not to worry anybody when the time comes for its removal'.[22]

'Askeology' shares several characteristics with 'showciology', not the least of which is the hybridity of its name, but while askeology holds a particular relationship to showciology this book remains a singular work with an agenda all of its own. However, a selection of the contemporary arguments and ideas that prompted *Theatre, Intimacy and Engagement* also inform this book, as one produced at the same historical moment as Read's. Read's rethinking of first questions that undermine the supposed efficacy of political theatre, as they do the proposed benignity of the relational conditions of performance, provides a suitable context for the contemporary concerns that motivate *Training for Performance*. His recognition of the reality that 'appeals to resist defining the shape of a field always serve those in power',[23] limited as that power may be, stimulates this book to trace a field of training and a method for its study. Doing so might provoke a reconsideration of what such a field might include and problematise some well-established assumptions – for example the assumption that training is merely a 'generic' term. As Read has noted, such efforts would not be welcome in an academic environment that had no relevance to the world outside but, because training is thoroughly embedded in the 'outside world', as is acutely evident in the rehabilitative examples that will come into play throughout this book, it provokes an academic imperative to 'stabilise' a field and a discipline for its study.[24]

If *Training for Performance* shares some contemporary concerns with *Theatre, Intimacy and Engagement*, it is also interested in the contemporary performances which appear in Nicholas Ridout's book *Stage Fright: Animals and Other Theatrical Problems* – performances typified by their relational dynamics and by the conditions of the stage-frightened and star-struck within a community of barely differentiated actors and spectators. When both Ridout and Read tag new actors – animals, objects and infants – to the front of a historical conga-line of idiotically named theatrical characters, they site new concerns at the leading edge of Performance Studies. When Read, in a shared contemporary moment, is forced to adopt a term 'in the absence of a discipline',[25] I am, by contrast, compelled to adopt a discipline in search of a name. Thus my project is, unike Read's, in part a taxonomic one of giving names to and descriptions of processes and experiences that have been going on quite happily in their various homes before askeology arrived to make a scene. Drawing together the various scenes of askeology to make a stage for its processes and experiences is in fact the point of this book, and, just as showciology is made of prefabricated materials, so too the discipline of askeology (which is much, much older than its new name) is a combination of disciplinary practices. If askeology can reclaim the concept of *askeo* from asceticism, it might utilise it to speak about training in terms of processes as well as practices.

'Practice' is something of a problematic word for Performance Studies, as Susan Melrose for one has discussed at length.[26] This stems partly from the fact that 'practice' can be used to denote certain *modes* of doing, what Melrose refers to as a qualitative dimension – that allows a distinction to be made between 'practices of everyday life' and those specific to performing arts more generally, for example – as well as that *doing* itself. This project refers to 'practice' in a quite limited sense that Melrose (perhaps fittingly) refers to as belonging to 'etymological enquiry' in which 'practice has been consistently understood to mean the action of doing something . . . anchored in human skills and habits, or routines, or arrays of action ratified by one or another institution'.[27] These routines of skills and habits differ widely in type between different disciplines and so this particular definition of practice conveys the sense that 'practice' might describe the collection and organisation of these within a given setting while also conveying that the collection and organistion of practice could be a common theme. This consistently understood and 'widely used' definition of practice also helps to account for and describe the 'qualitative' differences between modes of practice because it can also 'refer to the *method* of action or work, and to the *outcome* of action or work',[28] and thus I take on this definition in order to engage the 'unique training techniques' that evince for Hodge and others the centrality of training to performance practice.

Alison Knowles gives the definition of working through a 'process' as meaning that 'materials are understood and allowed to develop with intelligence and intuition in every direction'.[29] Knowles's description of what occurs in working through a process helps to tease out the differentiation made in this book between practice and process by focusing on the 'understanding' and 'development' that occurs in encounters with the 'intimation of materiality' in this notion of practice.[30] Taking practice to be these 'material' schemata outlined above necessarily raises the question of what happens when one embodies these (because, of course, a part of their materiality is consituted in the body that embodies them) and so indicates that askeology must investigate 'practice' and 'process' if it is properly to speak about what occurs during training. These terms, so understood, might then enable the conception of training as a process (or rather processes) extending in, through and over its particular manifestations as practice, thus facilitating an investigation of training as disciplinary activity and meta-disciplinary category.

Thinking about training in such a way – as a particular category of experience – requires one to give heed to how these activities fit within other categories of experience, and how these lived experiences should feature in any theoretical treatment. Thompson and Schechner have agreed that 'performance studies recognises all areas of social life as topics for the performance theorist'. However, performance research in any area of social life must not, as Alan Read has observed, subordinate the ecstasies and anguishes of living to the status of mere example, as if 'the veracity of an interpretative tool rather than the suffering that is happening [in living]' were 'the object of the exercise'.[31] Taking the contrary approach, and asking not what living can do for performance theory but what performance can do for living, Read suggests that performance is required 'to think more carefully about its relevance to suffering'.[32] If, as Thompson and Schechner contend, performance is a model for understanding what happens in all areas of social life, it must, as Read argues, bear its own burden within the world and take up its place alongside the subjects it relies on. If performance should think about its relevance to human suffering, one way in which it might do so is to meditate on the experiences of *performing* such suffering.

From suffering in theatre to suffering in performance

In seeking to describe training as a meta-disciplinary category of experience the term 'suffering' is useful in helping to conceptualise how this category might 'overlay' divergent practices. In using *suffering* to act as a placeholder for the meta-disciplinary experience of being 'subject to' which is felt in training, I need to be clear about what it does and does not refer to. As Aristotle wrote, suffering 'is not a simple term'.[33]

A certain definition of suffering may help to describe the ordeals of the (justly or unjustly) convicted, captive-soldiers and patients of all kinds that Thompson and Schechner anticipate in prisons, war zones and hospitals because the word *suffering* has long been used as an 'umbrella term' under which all manner of specific pains, griefs, wants and losses have collected. Suffering, of course, denotes the experience of being *subject to* certain (at least notionally) external 'environmental' factors – in the cases cited above, the range of undesirable, unpleasant and unwanted physical and emotional impositions of conflict, be they social, civil or corporeal.[34]

In this respect suffering has long held a particular relationship to asceticism, where discomforts of almost all magnitudes have been willingly and conspicuously modelled into a way of life.[35] The extreme deprivations of the Founding Fathers of Christian monastic orders – the restriction placed on eating, sleeping and speaking – are examples of suffering because of the physical or emotional pain they cause, but also, and more pertinent to this study of training, because these are instances of purposeful subjection. It is this specific understanding of a meta-disciplinary experience of subjection, denoted by the word *suffering*, that can help to describe a meta-disciplinary experience of *askesis* in training.

Having borrowed that word from ancient Greece and used it to speak about 'suffering' as a form of subjection, I am well aware that I may not be tapping into the most empathetic or inclusive tradition of thinking about suffering. While Aristotle may have reprieved theatre (or more accurately, mimesis) from its Platonic banishment in his *Poetics*, he also made one of the earliest assertions that the suffering of some individuals is more important than the suffering of others. As Earl Miner has shown, suffering, to Aristotle, is the 'most desirable tragic experience',[36] and his codification of *hamartia* issues from what Kenneth McLeish has called a 'hierarchy of the human imagination' in which men are superior to women, good people to bad, and pretty much anything to slaves – for an audience 'is not moved by reversal [of fortunes] in "little" lives'.[37] While Aristotle may have been the first formally to codify the mechanics of tragedy and properly secure a place for theatre alongside philosophy, he may also have implanted in theatrical tradition the belief that certain sufferings outweigh others. I am not referring here to the social status of a tragic character – for all Arthur Miller's stated belief that he had pro-vided a more socially responsible version of the classic tragedy by making Willy Loman a *low man*, he failed to realise that the issue is not who is *allowed* to suffer a tragic fate but who *deserves* one.[38] Central to Aristotle's conception of the tragic hero is the reality that his (predominantly *his*) suffering is of his own choosing; so, if (as I will come to suggest) an ultimately irreducible difference between 'discipline' and 'training' proves to be the degree of choice involved in each, askeology may have unwittingly cast trainees in the tragic role.[39]

The troublesome dimensions of the ethics Aristotle assembles through the management of *ethos* and the stratification of theatrical characters according to the extent to which they are in control of their own suffering is, I would suggest, not to be located in the fictional world of the narrative as such but in the 'real' world of the play. It is in this realm, the realm of the theatre space, where a spectator might be more properly *cleansed* by witnessing the sufferings of some individuals than he is in witnessing the suffering of others.

The attribution of responsibility to character in Aristotle's *Poetics* takes an early (if not the first) step towards what is sometimes called the three-dimensionality of character by equipping theatrical characters with agency and provides a touchstone for later – and still now largely hegemonic – traditions of actor training based on Stanislavski's psychologised actor-training techniques. Heraclitus' 'ethics of ethos' is succinctly expressed in his famous statement *ethos anthropos daimon* or 'character is fate', where 'fate is not governed from elsewhere but is in your character, the way you bear yourself each day';[40] and this pre-empts the historical shift in philosophy of self that can be traced in Aristotle's *Poetics*. In the *Poetics* Aristotle directs this philosophical shift into the aesthetic field of dramatic tragedy, establishing a parallel tradition where the 'will of the gods' is gradually superseded by the autonomy of character in driving theatrical action. It is an uncomfortable thought that 'choice', in its contemporary and frequently parodied relationship to a character's 'objectives', might have arrived in actor training through the codification of hierarchies of theatrical suffering, but no less disconcerting is the knowledge that the research discipline of Performance Studies might reiterate and reinforce such hierarchies. If Performance Studies does, as Thompson and Schechner claim, recognise all areas of social life as topics for the theorist, some of these topics – 'hospitals, prisons and war zones'[41] – have been singled out by virtue of the unique importance of the suffering that occurs within them. If askeology opens a domain in which to speak about a particular kind of suffering associated with *askesis* – with the activity of training – then it does so in a way which, unlike Aristotle's codification of tragedy or the stratification of research areas in Performance Studies, does not impose a hierarchy of suffering because it insists on a quite precise etymological usage of the term.

Relating the two different conceptions of suffering – the 'umbrella term' and the etymologically specific usage – helps to make clear the ways in which askeology's meta-disciplinary concerns are in tune with the conceptualising strategies of particular research themes in Performance

Studies. If the hierarchies of character evident in 'the theatre' organise the various experiences assembling under the umbrella term of 'suffering', then they reflect the hierarchical divisions between topics present in certain theoretical strands of Theatre and Performance Studies – put simply, that a war zone or a hospital is a more 'worthy' investigative site than an amateur dramatics society or a proscenium stage.

Askeology's attention to the shared experience of *being subject to* operative in *all* experiences of training identifies with different traditions of Theatre and Performance Studies, traditions which 'assemble a vast network of discourses and practices'[42] on the grounds of concepts and categories. Marvin Carlson has made clear the dangers of 'seeking some overarching semantic field'[43] to cover seemingly disparate usages of concepts such as 'performance', but as Jon McKenzie has shown meta-disciplinary accounts of these categories can preserve the contested status of such concepts without producing overarching definitions if they locate the 'underwordly stratum' or 'formation upon which all the contesting ... unfolds'.[44]

Reflecting, as askeology does, on a meta-disciplinary category of activity requires a focus on the particular qualities of subjection that relate to the experiences of that activity, rather than the discipline-specific subjections which are unique to the various settings for that activity. This does not mean that askeology is dispassionate or indifferent to the different forms of *seriousness* presumed by or imposed on various examples of training, from the evening class in acting to the residential treatment of stroke; but one of its major strengths, and one which will contribute towards its ability to stimulate novel questions, is its reluctance to hierarchise, and its view of *askesis* as directly related to meta-disciplinary experiences of *suffering alteration*.

Suffering alteration

In the second book of *De anima*, Aristotle differentiates between a 'generic' potential and an 'existing' potential. A child, he notes, is a generic potential in the sense that it has not yet developed certain capacities and yet exhibits the potential to do so. This will, however, involve the child 'becoming other' and in this sense is radically different to an existing potential. Whoever already possesses knowledge, by contrast, is not obliged to become other: she or he is instead potential thanks to a 'hexis' or a 'having' on the basis of which s/he can also *not* bring his/her knowledge or skill into actuality.[45] Agamben observes in his essay 'On Potentiality' that the concept of 'potential' is commonly understood in the generic sense. What Aristotle observed, and what Agamben articulates, is that this generic conception of potential does not properly express or account for the faculty of an expert – of a trained individual. They note that the trained practitioners' potential is partly constituted in their *refusal* to perform their particular skill or their refraining from performing it, a potential closely associated, as Read puts it, with the human ability to 'do less than [we] can'.[46]

The existing potential of the trained person is the potential *not* to perform, a capacity which Agamben describes using the term *impotentiality*. Agamben points out that what Aristotle proposes is quite different to an idea of potentiality that is annulled in actuality. Aristotle writes that 'He who possesses science (in potentiality) become someone who contemplates in actuality, and either this is not an alteration – since here there is the gift of the self to itself and to actuality (*epidosis eis auto*) – or this is an alteration of a different kind.'[47] A process of training is in some way constituted by a transformation in the trainee from generic potential to existing potential rather than from potentiality to actuality – from a 'not having' to a 'having', from potentiality to impotentiality. Agamben calls this a process of 'suffering an alteration', and askeology describes a field of research which asks about the processes of 'suffering an alteration' in the embodied experience of altering generic potential to existing impotentiality through training.

This field of research, which is concerned with the experience of 'suffering an alteration', cuts across disciplines wherein such alteration takes place. In this way, this book provides a meta-disciplinary account. To ask about a meta-disciplinary category is to ask about a great range of practices. Why, one might ask, should one want to collect all these things and peoples together, and what would be useful in so doing? They are after all, in one sense, already superficially grouped together; they group themselves together by talking about, writing about and experiencing 'training'. However, this superficially conglomerated community is characterised by that fact that, on the whole, its members do not recognise their connectedness but rather assume their estrangement. What then might be the value of theorising the already-connectedness of these peoples and practices?

The theorising of already-connectedness has been a central task of Performance Studies since it pointed to the fact that theatre, ritual, everyday lives, art, drag, gender, identity, sexuality, the secular and the religious are already connected. When theorists first began to speak of 'performance studies' they spoke of the possibility of uncovering and describing an already existing, unifying category that would allow seemingly disparate activities to be reconceived and understood accordingly. The word 'performance' was used long before its appropriation by Performance Studies, yet the nuance with which it is now considered and utilised to speak about what was already there has permitted a wholesale reconsideration of human activity. A study of training that sought to connect numerous training practices and develop ways to speak about 'training' can also facilitate such a reconsideration.

In proposing connecting, or highlighting the already-connectedness, of these diverse materials I am of course taking on the task of reading them. As someone who has been trained to locate and produce 'knowledge' by reading certain materials in certain ways how am I, a theatre and performance scholar, to reconcile with the various knowledges in philosophy, theology, pyschology, medicine, and sport science? Happily, I am not alone in confronting this problem and the question it provokes has been more succinctly phrased before me by Phillip Zarrilli when he asks: 'What constitutes "knowledge" in the practice of . . . a long-term training?'[48] Doubly reassuring for me is that Zarrilli, in answering his own question, contended that there are at least three kinds of 'knowledge' gained about training: knowledge 'in'; knowledge 'for' an 'ever-deepening relationship to the art of practice'; and 'knowledge about (this) engagement'.[49] Rebecca Loukes has, in her article for *Performance Research,* codified Zarrilli's categories into three distinct 'areas' of knowledge:

1. My experiences of training, and my own psychophysical development.
2. My reflections on that training (verbal and written).
3. The contexts/languages/discourses surrounding the training (i.e. other materials, interviews, archives etc.).[50]

While Zarrilli and Loukes are concerned with the problems facing a researcher researching *one* specific discipline of performance training, their observations help me to develop a way of engaging a range of materials from a range of disciplines. The texts about which I have expressed anxiety would seem to fit into Loukes's third category/area seeing as they are not really 'mine', but are rather (to me) 'about' training.[51] Zarrilli and Loukes signal the fact that a greater or rather more primary problem than reading diverse texts is selecting them in the first place. In the case of askeology, this problem goes beyond the familiar problem of a 'literature review' because it is tied to the very nature of the project itself. However, the scope Loukes affords to include materials that might be 'about' training (interviews, archives, etc.) suggests that what makes material 'about' something has more to do with the way it is read than the way it is written. It is as texts about a meta-disciplinary notion of training rather than as disciplinary discussions of particular practices that I read theology and philosophy – reading almost 'against the grain' or rather through the lens of my particular project and the knowledge it is seeking to produce.

This is evidently leading towards another problem: the subjectification of the materials I select to my own agenda and the disavowal of their own specificity and uniqueness. The linguist Kenneth Pike's definition of the terms 'emic' and 'etic', which differentiate between forms of knowledge, might helpfully contribute towards reconciling this problem. Pike recognised that an appreciation not only of subjectivity but of its particularly enculturated situation could create a divide between forms of knowledge. Acknowledging that, as a researcher, one must always coordinate one's position according to differently enculturated and situated subjects, he claimed that two kinds of knowledge could be distinguished: first, *emic* constructs, which are accounts, descriptions and analyses of a particular practice expressed in terms of the activities and categories deemed meaningful and appropriate by communities or cultures in which that particular practice operates; second, *etic* constructs, which are accounts, descriptions and analyses of a particular practice expressed in terms of the activities and categories deemed meaningful and appropriate by a community of scientific observers.[52]

Applying these terms to Loukes's three 'areas' of knowledge about training, her first two areas appear to represent 'emic' knowledge of training generated from 'within', while her third area appears to account for the 'etic' constructs of training. Yet perhaps what Pike's terms most pertinently reveal is that to subdivide materials and knowledge, as Zarrilli and Loukes have done, is really to take one's place among *all* forms of subjective knowledge and set about (implicitly) defining one's particularly enculturated position relative to these. This is, of course, doubly effective in researching and theorising training because, as Zarrilli observes, 'training' is not only encountered through literary materials, since 'practices are not things, but an active embodied doing'.[53] So the researcher who sets out to investigate training practices not only assumes a place among the various forms of literature about training, but also among the bodies that generate these knowledges. 'Taking part' is important to all performance theorists (those who take apart critically the taking-of-parts), but Zarrilli's assertion impels a researcher such as myself to participate in the practices he or she seeks to understand and to experience their effects alongside others.

Of course, as Elizabeth Grosz has contended, 'experience cannot be unproblematically taken as a source of truth' because 'experience is not outside the social, political, historical and cultural forces'[54] which help to formulate the 'enculturated position' described by Pike. Interestingly, Loukes draws together the problems of 'reading' (as a mode of encounter in both the literal sense and the sense adopted by semiotics to describe one's encounter with non-literary signs) and 'doing' in her assertion that 'As I attempt to understand these [training] practices (partially) through participation, I could not have learned what I have solely through "reading".'[55] Loukes argues for a methodology that 'allows for an active dialogue between the perceptions and experiences of the researcher and the "perceptual systems" of the informants/practitioners'[56] which avoids becoming what Rhoda Metraux has called a 'generalised account of [the researcher's] own experience'.[57]

Temporarily abating my fear of producing 'generalised' knowledge, and with the reassurance provided by Loukes, I arrive at a way to 'read' and 'do' different training disciplines, borrowing from anthropology the description 'participant-observation' to stand for the ways in which I assume my place among training's forms of knowledge. Tamara Kohn writes of anthropologists teaching their students how a method of participant-observation, 'born out of necessity on a Trobriand Island, became a defining feature of the discipline [of anthropology]'.[58] A necessity to speak 'with' another involved the dissolving of distances between oneself and another, she writes. 'Participant observation is about speaking the body language and hearing people talk about their body practice and the social world it constructs.'[59] Within this dialogue, feeling one's own body and hearing one's own voice allows one to empathise with and understand people for whom meaning and nuance of activity is vital.

Such a method is, of course, not unique to this project, but is already being practised by many performance scholars researching training. As indicated above, Phillip Zarrilli has been something of a pioneer in a form of participatory research in performance training, particularly in his investigations of Kalarippayattu martial arts.[60] Since 1989 Paul Allain has been 'doing' research into training that recognises the imperative of taking part. Most of the research in his book, *Gardzienice: Polish Theatre in Transition*, 'stems from personal contact with the company abroad and in Gardzienice village itself'[61] and the times he spent not only observing but also participating in Gardzienice's training. Allain's subsequent work on the theatre practices of Tadashi Suzuki, as well as his directorship of the British Grotowski Project, operate by an appreciation of the centrality of participation to any project that seeks to engage embodied practice.[62]

The application of an anthropological method within performance research can be traced back at least to the collaborations between Viktor Turner and Richard Schechner in the early 1980s.[63] The collaboration between these two figures excited a more generalised collaboration and a drive within the disciplines of anthropology and performance studies to participate in each other's practices, as literally realised in the title of a posthumous collection of Viktor Turner's work, *The Anthropology of*

Performance. If there is an 'anthropology of performance', there is also, of course, 'a performance of anthropology', and it is in the research-driven participatory practices through which researchers perform anthropology that Zarrilli, Allain and Loukes find their modes of encounter with training. That is where this book takes its inspiration.[64]

My research for this book is based on a most primary assumption – that if anyone seeks to contribute to knowledge, he or she should contribute to the disciplines within which it is produced, recited and sedimentised, and must endeavour to speak *to* and *with* individuals therein not *for* or *about* them. As Zarrilli and Allain have shown, to confine training research to literary investigations of accounts of training is to scratch at the surface of etic structural descriptions – to peer in on them from the 'outside'. As Kohn has shown, one cannot investigate embodied social processes by sitting on the outside looking in, and rearranging descriptions that may not even be recognised by the subjects of an enquiry. Recognising with Kohn the importance of feeling one's own body and hearing one's own voice, I respond to the critical imperative to take part in the trainings I investigate. Though I accept that this book will be read as an etic document, I have endeavoured to allow emic voices (including my own) to speak through it, to it and with it, especially in the limited descriptions of my own research that appear in each chapter.

Participatory research always runs a risk of imposing the implicitly accepted norms of an etic community of researchers on emic practices and experiences that may not recognise these norms. While participant-observation methodologies can purport to produce mutual findings as the result of collaboration or exchange between the researcher and the subjects of his research, if the 'rules of engagement' are solely determined by one or the other the norms and expectations of one community, either emic or etic, are imposed.

During the course of my research for this book, I have initiated contact with training practitioners and made clear my aims – to engage in training practice so as to be able to write something about training. I have invited those practitioners, to whom training practice is not only a research interest but a fundamental part of their lives, to determine the extent of my participation in 'their' training activities. In this way, some of the responsibility for the insights in this book has been devolved to the people whose practices I study.

Perhaps unsurprisingly given my approach, this project has also experienced several 'unsuccessful' negotiations. While I don't undertake to analyse thoroughly the policing of boundaries around training groups, it is important to record my fruitless attempts to conduct research at the Actors Studio London and with the Royal Marines, if only to make explicit the reality that entrance into certain groups is more strictly controlled than in others. That an acting studio should prove more secretive and exclusive than a monastery or that the armed forces have more ethical inhibitions than the health service gives an indication of how many suppositions about training need to be reconsidered.

'Gaining access' is, of course, one important aspect of participatory research, but knowing how to engage the materials and experiences one gains access to is another equally valid concern. John Law, who has devoted a great deal of effort to reimagining investigative ethnographic methodologies and documentary practices, has already laid out what the probable achievements of modes of research that combine knowledge bases and their perspectives will be:

> the overall aim of a multi-voiced form of investigative storytelling
> need not necessarily be to come to a conclusion. Its strength
> might well be in the way it opens questions up.[65]

Here again, in the range of the questions opened up, askeology meets the same challenges as showciology associated with what Alan Read has referred to as 'the analytic scale'. With such a range of literature and participatory experience accessible to askeology, and so many voices in conversation, a certain degree of miniaturisation must occur in order to delimit the scope of this book – that is to say, my research must necessarily start with and work through the localised example when faced by a multiplicity of examples. However, Read has argued that 'the particularity of a given event cannot be grasped by that miniaturising move any more than making a point of study infinitely BIG' [*emphasis in original*],[66] indicating that scale is itself determined not so much by the 'object' of study but by the researcher and theorist's modes of encounter and documentation. His assertion is even more pertinent in the case of askeology, where the object of study is not a single 'event' but an ongoing and changing procession of practices and experiences. The impossibility that Read recognises via Latour, of staying in either the local or global scale too long, is played out in this book not by a shift from the miniature and particular to the expansive and general but in the movement between different disciplinary 'sites' of inquiry.[67]

One site in particular – the monastic – would seem to prompt a special apology partly as a result of its scale and partly because, as Read has written with reference to another archetypal Christian site, the nativity, 'the parameters of a Christian narrative may not appeal'.[68] There are as many good reasons to be wary of knowledge produced in religious settings as there are for knowledge produced anywhere else, but there is with the monastic the danger that information may appear to take on a peculiarly authoritative status simply as a result of the historical depth and breadth of its resource. Read, in his apology for the example of a school nativity, identifies something of a bias in the academy towards 'complex' examples that might privilege the adult, intellectual and secular over the juvenile, irrational or sacred or, in the case of his particular example, the professional-theatrical over the amateur-performative.

Any academic anxiety that a school play might not be sufficiently complex to operate as discursive example becomes inverted in the mammoth complexity of monastic history and ascetic theology where anxiety becomes a fear that the example's multifariousness might destabilise discussion altogether. In the interests of scale, some sort of trickery of perspective might be required such that by positioning the monastic distantly relative to the theatrical and the medical the 'really large' can sit next to the 'really close' and not make it look out of proportion – as in tourist photos where smiling holidaymakers appear to lean against the tower of Pisa, pinch the Coliseum or balance Big Ben on an open palm. In this book, I make something of an equivalent methodological version of this photographic manoeuvre by 'scaling down' the monastic as much as is possible to the small example of the Benedictine community at Worth Abbey, where I lived as part of my research. There is little that can be done to cool the blush of self-recognition on the face of an academy

– whose hierarchical structures, organisational principles and very existence is, in some sense, the result of the monastic institution – as it looks on even this small-scale section of it. The reality that, as Foucault has shown, penal, educational and therapeutic institutions can trace their administrational frameworks to the monastery, has an obvious bearing on the study of the interpersonal conditions of my other training examples, and so challenges askeology to avoid studying the rehabilitation unit, the theatre studio or actor workshop as more than simply the offspring of an institutional parent.[69] But given the history of the monastic institution as perhaps the first organised site of training, it is appropriate that it should have a place in perhaps the first organised attempt to isolate a category of training. The monastic will be, like the other training sites in this book, foregrounded through specific localised events and practices to ensure that its contemporary manifestations are shown to be equivalent to other contemporary settings in which the same range of historical principles and techniques are operative. One thing that Foucault's analysis of prisons assuredly shows is that the present-day monastic enjoys no special claim to historical techniques.

Each written example drawn from my participatory research that appears in this book serves not as the substantiating evidence of the veracity of askeology but as something more like the *ansatzpunkte* first proposed by Erich Auerbach; 'a firmly circumscribed and easily comprehensible set of phenomena, whose interpretation is a radiation out from them, and which orders and interprets a greater region than they themselves occupy'.[70] Auerbach's *ansatzpunkte* or 'points of departure' within his work *Mimesis: The Representation of Reality in Western Literature* serve as launch pads for critical attention, at once situating the 'random particular' example from the text *within* the text and the culture of which it is a product, as well as situating the author within the (particularly enculturated) process of interpretation. Greenblatt and Gallagher have noted that Auerbach's *ansatzpunkte*, which they describe as 'the isolation of a resonant textual fragment that is revealed under the pressure of analysis', can act 'to represent the work from which it is drawn and the particular culture in which that work was produced and consumed'.[71] Thus the 'small-scale' example opens up a vista on (or maybe just a set of questions about) the 'larger scale' whole of which it is a part. In assessing the impact of Auerbach's technique in literary criticism and beyond, Gallagher and Greenblatt conclude, 'the new historicist anecdote as many of us have deployed it is an Auerbachian device'.[72] Indeed, a somewhat 'new historicist anecdote' version of the *ansatzpunkte* has been used to great effect by Steven Mullaney in his book on the development of theatre in sixteenth-century London, *The Place of the Stage: Power, Play and License in Renaissance England.* In this work, at the beginning of Chapter 2, 'The Place of the Stage', Mullaney draws not from literature as such but from historical records to create a 'reverberating' image that offers 'innumerable points of entry'[73] on the culture and society of sixteenth-century England. Taking Auerbach's 'point of departure' literally and metaphorically, his opening paragraph consists of a description of the departure of the last of London's lepers from the city to a hospital in Southwark. From out of this anecdotal, randomly particular description he initiates his analysis of the locale of London's earliest theatre buildings, noting that 'few points of departure could be as radiant as leprosy's final excursion from the city'[74] in helping to interpret and unpack the culture in which the theatre is constructed.[75] Following Mullaney, this project utilises a version of Auerbach's *ansatzpunkte* that draws not on literary example but on description of a set of phenomena. Extending Mullaney's application of this technique, and in an attempt doubly to foreground the situated-ness of the author within the example, my *ansatzpunkte* are descriptions produced from the experiences of my participatory research; they are points of departure that are initiated from my position within the phenomena I observe and describe.

An important consideration for this analysis, drawing as it does on participatory research in the generation of points of departure, is the level of validation of knowledge that any description of research experiences may appear to impose. Descriptions that report to draw, as do Zarrilli's, for example, on 'extended periods of extraordinarily intensive training'[76] implicitly affirm not only the authority of the researcher to speak about certain practices but also the completeness of his or her descriptions and interpretations. Alan Read is clear that the 'well contracted presumption that being there ("in the community") for longer

[is] inherently "better"' is something of a 'worthy rhetorical tactic' that implies a specious presenteeism.[77] Paul Allain, who has written, 'I do not feel that my [*sic*] authority to write about Suzuki training is invalidated because of my lack of direct experience of Suzuki's own teaching',[78] is evidently sensitive to this tactic and the rightful entitlement to speak about certain experiences it entails. Read's particular assessment of 'being there' should be understood in the context of his previous work *Theatre in Everyday Life* (1995), which employed a form of the specious presenteeism that he now rejects. Where Read's earlier work was informed by theatre that 'took place between 1978 and 1991',[79] his later text is supported by 'weak examples' that act in the 'spirit of "keeping things in play" [rather] than the explanatory hierarchy of ordering by exclusion'.[80] It is the latter of these two approaches that informs my descriptions, but my concern is less with the worthiness of such an approach or the entitlements of authorship it evokes and more with the monopoly on interpretation it implies.

My descriptions, which are limited in scope and scale, recognise, with Auerbach, that ethnographic descriptions must remain localised and focused if they are to attain any form of completeness because, 'he who represents the course of a human life, or a sequence of events extending over a long period of time . . . must prune and isolate arbitrarily'.[81] It is precisely because training is an often lifelong undertaking that it cannot be handled in the same way as other episodic experiences that interest Theatre and Performance Studies, but which often have the limits of their completeness firmly circumscribed by the dimming of lights and the sounds of applause. Life, Auerbach wrote, unlike theatre's interruptions within it, 'has always long since begun, and it is always still going on'.[82] The everyday-ness of much of training activity in monasteries, rehabilitation wards and conservatoires means that a trainee experiences much more than a researcher can ever hope to document; so producing the kinds of descriptions that appear to report the completeness of training experiences because of the breadth of data they seek to represent may obscure this reality.

Rather than attempt to write about lengthy periods of 'being there' in training, my descriptions of my participatory research document small things and brief events because, 'the things that happen to a few individuals in the course of a few minutes, or hours, or possibly even days – these one can hope to represent with reasonable completeness'.[83] It is this level of completeness, within firmly circumscribed moments drawn from my participatory research, that my examples attain, and this does not entail the imposition of exhaustive interpretation of the events described but rather the representation of experience that remains fundamentally open to interpretation.

Though each point of departure is situated within my participatory research in a given discipline of training, the chapters themselves can also be read as points of departure within performance training as a meta-disciplinary phenomenon. As Auerbach realised when faced with six thousand years' worth of 'world literature' in over fifty languages, 'because of the superabundance of materials, of methods and of points of view'[84] mastery of such a meta-discipline is impossible, and thus it can only be investigated and debated through situating a self at various points within it. John Law, in a 'Post-Structuralist Detour' during his paper on methodology, *Making a Mess with Method*, arrives at a similar conclusion to Auerbach's through different (though equally pragmatic) reasoning and from a more contemporary vantage, concluding that, 'As we seek to know the world not everything can be brought to presence . . . because bringing to presence is necessarily incomplete because if things are made present (for instance representations) then at the same time things are also being made absent'.[85] In *Mimesis* Auerbach tells his reader that in selecting *ansatzpunkte* he simply 'open[s] a volume of Shakespeare at random';[86] and here his attempt to deal with enormity and diversity through 'randomness' meets Law's attempt to account for those sites from which we *do not* depart by upholding the 'mess' of the world and reflecting it in our interpretations. René Wellek's assertion that *Mimesis* 'must be judged as something of a work of art'[87] because of the creativity of the selection performed can be heard echoing in Law's arguments for the use of allegory as a research tool, not so much to select but to hold the mutually exclusive together: 'Allegory is the art of meaning something other than, or in addition to what is being said . . . It is the craft of making several not necessarily very consistent things at once.'[88]

Law settles on allegory as a useful investigative storytelling device because of its capacity to represent, if not disrupt, the othering that occurs whenever a researcher sets out to describe phenomena. Law argues that most research undertaken in Europe and the USA is predicated upon certain philosophical notions of realism that seek to present the 'real' world as logically (and preferably simplistically) ordered by producing it as such. In place of the logical and simplistic descriptive 'conclusions' of such research projects, Law proposes allegory that 'brings to presence an out-there that is multiple, vague, shifting and non-coherent'.[89] Of course Law's 'intuition . . . that the world is largely messy'[90] and so warrants a concomitantly messy method of description also imposes an order (of messiness) on the 'real', constructing or rather producing it as 'really messy' in favour of being 'really simple'. However, his notion of allegory does achieve a disavowal of the 'premium of singularity'[91] in method and description. The various descriptions offered in this book, drawn from my participatory experience of diverse forms of training, have the same limitations as any other descriptive method but aim, as do Law's allegories, to disavow the 'premium of singularity' in description of performance training in order at least to open questions up.

Each chapter in this book begins with an allegory, in the Lawsian sense, that functions as a point of departure situated within askeology as it is located in the experiences of performance or training practice. These points of departure open on to small sets of allegories arising out of my research experiences and help to open out the specific concerns that dominate each chapter. This selection of allegories arising out of my research experiences help to map out the meta-disciplinary terrain of training through the identification of vocation, obedience, formation and automatisation as leylines that run through the practices of theatre, dance, rehabilitation and monasticism. Discussion of this small range of features of a meta-disciplinary category of training develop out of the allegories in play precisely because my awareness of the importance of such processes to the training practices of patients, monks, dancers and actors developed in my encounters with these individuals.

Training for what performance?

Askeology, composed of the great range of materials, methods and perspectives I have already pointed to, must rely on allegory and points of departure, and investigate by departing from (and describing) situated points within the broadest category of 'performance training'. Auerbach showed that defining the 'world' that would partner 'literature' in his meta-discipline was a crucial concern, and he argued that such a notion would have to include not only geography and topology but also 'take into account religion, philosophy, politics, economics, fine arts and music'[92] in the development of texts. Just as Auerbach sought to describe the concerns contained within the scope of a 'world' that produced and was produced by 'literature', so too investigating 'training' necessarily entails describing and defining what performance could stand (in) for.

Since Performance Studies has already mobilised meta-disciplinary conceptions of performance as something extending beyond particular performances, it is necessary to understand 'performance' as a meta-disciplinary category in order to investigate the meta-disciplinary forces of training that relate to it. It is quite proper that we have no agreed definition of 'performance' seeing as it is our 'object' of study, and also appropriate that our definitions, descriptions and conceptions of performance should remain 'in development'. From Herbert Blau's near-paradoxical approach, that 'what is universal in performance is the consciousness of performance'[93] (which, as Ridout has shown, may well only be consciousness in the audience[94]) to Schechner's appreciation of this same spectatorial dimension and addition of an equally slippery '"quality" that can occur in any situation',[95] notions of 'performance' within Theatre and Performance Studies today remain not only contestable but, also and importantly, provisional.

Given that askeology is going to need an (albeit provisional) description of performance that will help to explain some of the connections between the range of practices it investigates, Jon McKenzie's efforts to '*to rehearse a general theory of performance*' [*original emphasis*][96] will act as a point of orientation throughout this book. In *Perform or Else: From Discipline to Performance* McKenzie writes of the possibility that a general theory of what we mean by performance might be called for or indeed long overdue. He approaches 'performance' in much the same way that Foucault conceived 'discipline', by configuring it as an 'onto-historical' formation of power – ontological because it entails a displacement of being that challenges notions of history, historical because this displacement is 'historically inscribed'.[97] McKenzie asserts that performative power draws upon and combines other power forces and its ontological displacements can be investigated by analysing the historical inscriptions of these combinations.

In *Discipline and Punish* Foucault describes 'discipline' as a force operated by the discursive statements of penal law and mechanisms of surveillance. Bentham's panoptican prison is deployed as example of, and metaphor for, the subjectivating apparatus of disciplinary power. 'Discipline' is the name Foucault gives to the meta-disciplinary force operational in the controlled articulations of bodies in time and space and the deterrent and corrective impact of surveillance upon them. Disciplinary power is activated through/by these ordered articulations and monitored and enforced by mechanisms of surveillance. As with his notion of 'discourse', a key concern for studies of discipline is 'inequalities of power': who or what is mobilising this onto-historical force, why and against whom? Foucault notes that disciplinary power always accomplishes something on global, national, institutional or interpersonal levels at the cost of prohibiting something else. As Foucault equated the disciplinary mechanisms of schools, barracks and prisons to ask about the operations of disciplinary power, McKenzie connects the performances of artists, activists, workers, executives and computers to ask about 'performance' as a force overcoding performances. He observes that, like discipline, performance produces a new subject of knowledge and one quite different from that produced under the regime of panoptic surveillance. Unlike the unified, centred and actual subjects of panoptical surveillance the subjects of performative power are fragmented, decentred and virtual as well as actual.

Performative subjects do not occupy a 'proper place' in knowledge but are produced and maintained (or not) by a variety of socio-technical systems: 'The desire produced by performative power and knowledge is not modelled on repression . . . it is instead "excessive".'[98] Where disciplinary power seeks to normalise deviation, performative power stimulates norms to transform themselves through their own deviation and transgression. This is because the mechanisms of performative power are neither rigid nor sedentary but flexible and nomadic, governed only by the imperative 'Perform – or else.' Mckenzie suggests that performance is a *challenge*. 'Perform' is a challenge to do something, to do something better, consistently, for the first time or just again. The normalising force of this challenge is operated and modulated by the demand that what is brought forth by the challenge *performs*. *How* it performs, how it *continues* to perform, or how it might *regulate* this performance is secondary to the concern that it *does*. Should what is brought forth fail to satisfy the challenge to perform it will be discontinued, immobilised, marginalised, rejected or made obsolete.

'Performance', for McKenzie, is a standard to be attained; something to be done, carrying within it its own consequences for failure. Unlike discipline (modelled on repression) whose machinery will not be abated by deviation or transgression, whose processes seek it out and correct it, 'performance' (modelled on satisfaction) permits and encourages variation up to the point at which it fails to satisfy. In this respect performance is radically different from discipline – it is excessive and wasteful, more apt to 'decommission' than 'discipline'. Performance then, for McKenzie, is the response to the demand to *do something* (by any means). This notion of performance can be seen operating in the range of practices that appear in this book which give a selection of human performances straddling a range of embodied activity. McKenzie himself explicitly states that even his general theory is in *rehearsal*, is training getting ready to perform, and so if to 'perform' is to *do something* against the threat of failure, what is involved in training for this performance – or perhaps more appositely, *who* is involved?

When conducting participatory research it is vital to consider who one can, or should, participate with. I can 'suffer' with a range of people and under a diversity of training regimes but, as a participant-researcher, despite the best efforts of contemporary thinkers in diverse fields to break down the distinctions between 'man' and 'animal', I simply can't dance with those interesting new actors who now join the conga-line of performance I referred to earlier. Una Chaudhuri has written of current attempts in disciplines of geography, literature, philosophy and performance to 'take animals seriously',[99] and evidence of one of these attempts can be found in Brooman and Legge's book on *Law Relating to Animals*. Here it is shown that animals train, in a strict legal sense at least, and the principles of this legal category cascade down and fine away into the practices of domestication, laboratorial experimentation and big-top routines where the rules and regulations of 'The Performing Animals Acts' (1925 and 1968) are enforced. While the frameworks provided by the acts order and organise the performance of ducks and horses in the work of Societas Raffaello Sanzio and Theatre Razi which occupy Nicholas Ridout's work, as well as the appearance of lions and other 'wild' creatures in circus tents, they also regulate the training of these and other performing animals.[100] That animal rights organisations contest the ethical status of the practices that are included in this legislation suggests that a line between animal training and animal torture might be difficult to draw while the reality that invertebrates are not protected by the acts indicates that 'animal' cannot simply be understood as 'not-human'.

Children also train, in a certain sense of the word, as is demonstrated in sporting academies and athletic clubs and evinced by the accomplished performances of child actors on stage and screen. This territory of childhood training also has problematic ethical dimensions, as is evident in the ambivalent accounts of a 'sheltered life . . . [spent] interviewing, training, working',[101] documented by Tom Goldrup in his interviews with thirty-nine former child actors. Within Goldrup's collection the account given by Diana Carey (famous in America as the child star 'Baby Peggy') of the child actor Bobs Watson and his eight siblings who were all trained to cry on cue, 'making them popular with every director in Hollywood',[102] is one example of the troubled and troubling rights and wrongs of childhood training.

Even if these concerns can or should be negotiated, the primary obstacle to undertaking participatory askeological research into animal or childhood training is that it is not possible to mutually determine with them what these research experiences will involve. In the case of animals, if they are truly to be taken seriously, this entails a problem of research ethics, because, as Roger Scruton has categorically stated, 'there is no conceivable process whereby this [animal] consent could be delivered or withheld'.[103] Consenting to take part is not in and of itself the ethical issue – in Chapter 5 I will undertake to analyse surrogate consent in the training of non-communicative rehabilitation patients – but rather that taking animals seriously in a way that affords them consenting powers would, as Scruton points out, be a 'gross and callous abuse of them'.[104] Treating animals as though they posses powers of consent would mean holding them responsible for their own ethical judgement – a responsibility that 'would weigh so heavy on the predators as to drive them to extinction'.[105]

In the case of both children and animals attempting collaborative participatory research would also pose a methodological problem, since the research data produced in animal or childhood case studies would not be co-produced in interaction between emic and etic perspectives on training, but would be the product of two 'outside' perspectives – my perspective and the perspective of the child's guardian or the animal's keeper. The impetus given to appreciations of the performance of children and animals by the Actor Network Theory (ANT) of Latour (1987 and 2005), Callon (1986) and Law (1987 and 1992) could no doubt provide the basis of a material-semiotic analysis of agency and action within training, but this approach would, despite its best ethnomethodological intentions, necessarily have to speak *for* certain 'actants'.[106]

The complete absence from this book of two of the more surprising actors in contemporary performance would be regrettable, and so I will open a small discussion on juvenile and animal agency in performance to help to explore the operations of training groups in Chapter 4. But *I* can't do their training *with them*, or *speak with them* and I am not willing to merely write *about them*. For this reason, askeology, for now, cannot follow showciology's particular expansion of 'the collective' developing out of Bruno Latour's notion of 'the social' in which actors, audience and 'other entities, beings and non-human things' will be given 'equal consideration'.[107] Instead this book takes a model of the collective from Hannah Arendt's notion of a public 'space' or 'realm of appearance' which comes into being only when humans act together.

For Arendt, the 'state of appearance' is a space of political freedom that comes into being whenever humans act together through the medium of speech. The veracity or 'reality' of the public realm owes

> not to the mere fact of appearance, but to the fact that what receives this reality appears simultaneously to, and is spoken about by, many persons each of whom occupies a different position and looks upon the phenomenon from a different perspective. A differential of position and perspective thus correlates with human plurality.[108]

The 'political' imagined by Read's assertion that there is no such thing as an 'empty space' for theatre is commensurate with Arendt's notion of a 'state of appearance' as a 'space' for political action defined by the complex of relations that operate within it.[109] This book expands Arendt's conception of such a realm of appearance to include activities other than the singular act of speech. Recognising, with Read, the need to consider the relations between performance and politics, askeology (as a limited study of humans) looks to Arendt's notion of 'action', a particular conception of agency that will be tied into the activities of trainees throughout this book, as 'the *only activity that goes on directly between men without the intermediary of things, or matter*' [*emphasis added*].[110]

Managing who can and cannot, or should or should not be included in this book is a concern related to deciding who, or what, should 'come first'. Chapters 3, 4, 5 and 6 explore meta-disciplinary processes of training – vocation; obedience; formation; and automatisation. These chapter headings do not impose a linear structure on the experience of training. The nature of a book, neatly described in the microcosmic example of the contents page, demands that they appear in some form of order, but from this an 'order' of training should not be inferred. Each chapter offers a unique perspective on the experiences of training opened up by my observation of training practices and my participation in them.

Training's most seductive command to trainees is to participate, to enter into its processes and to let them enter in. This book is both 'meta' and 'inter' disciplinary; meta-disciplinary because it asks about forces that shape disciplines of training and which exceed boundaries between disciplines, and inter-disciplinary because it is *among* disciplines.

It is something of a commonplace now to call any project that inves-tigates more than one 'discipline' of knowledge inter-disciplinary, and Performance Studies provides something of an archetypal model for this. However, as I have already suggested, askeology lies across other disci-plines and enters on to their stages precisely because the forces that shape its processes do not respect the current cartographic boundaries of the academy. A study of these processes cannot simply position itself above disciplines, since training itself does not, but rather the meta-disciplinary forces of training infiltrate disciplines, shaping their processes and the experiences of embodying them. In seeking to *do* these embodied experi-ences and start to understand these processes, askeological investigations must lead through disciplines and must by necessity be *among* them. Thus askeology is inter-disciplinary not because it seeks to describe the spaces *between* disciplines but because it investigates what passes through these spaces and what happens in them.

As a performer and a trainer of performers working within the parti-cular discipline of theatre the next chapter is positioned within Theatre Studies and the askeological investigations that unfold throughout the book begin in and return to this site.

The wholly actor

What comes after body–mind discourse is what comes first

This chapter, unlike the chapters that follow it, does not focus on a meta-disciplinary process of training but rather reflects on some key concerns in discourse on training in the field of Theatre Studies, and situates the meta-disciplinary project of askeology within its contemporary moment. This project is as much a part of the current historical moment as the new dynamics of play that typifies its theatre – a theatre where, as Ridout has suggested, 'theatricality' is a key and negative term.[1] Ridout's 'historiography of performance' describes three moments, almost simultaneous in a sense of historical time and thus perhaps more appropriately thought of on the scale of a life span rather than as sequential epochs. The three stages Ridout identifies can be seen to comprise the infancy, adolescence and middle age of performance (and its attendant Performance Studies): the first, the emergence of theatrical practices that reject, oppose or move beyond the framework of the theatre; the second in which these practices connect to definitively non-theatrical practices in a developing (inter)discipline of Performance Studies; and the third postmodern 'antitheatrical' moment.

Ridout's overview of performance in the twentieth century prompts me to consider how askeology might fit within the current moment and how, like the parallel moments in a history of theatre, it might find itself at a juncture seeking to adapt new ideas or discard certain existing theoretical totems. The 'wholly actor' is of course intended to parody the totemic figure of the 'holy actor' and some of what has been written about his/her no less iconic creator Jerzy Grotowski, and to draw attention to the fact that both figurers cast a broad shadow over theatre and performance practice and study today, especially in the field of training. Grotowski displayed a tendency towards presenting himself as a 'direct descendent'[2] of Stanislavski, and the influence of Grotowski's actor-training techniques are probably as prevalent in theatre and performance scholarship as those of his predecessor, even if the Russian's legacy looms larger in conservatoire-fed 'mainstream' theatre, cinema and the popular consciousness.

The reason I employ the parodying term 'wholly actor' – a decidedly 'third moment' postmodern tactic – is in an attempt to highlight some of the concerns of performance's infancy which, in the particular 'field' of training, are intimately associated with Grotowski, and to reflect on how these concerns may or may not concern Theatre and Performance Studies today. If, as Scheer has suggested, 'the characteristic gesture of postmodern performance is parody' then a book such as this can perhaps be best situated in its own cultural-historical moment if it too makes 'a pretence of revelling in the slippage'.[3] Margaret Rose, following Bradbury's notion of the 'Death of the Subject', has shown in her book *Parody: Ancient, Modern and Postmodern* that parody, especially in its current relationship to a 'politics of performance . . . where nothing has a single and unicultural meaning', entails a 'self-knowing' that ensures 'the right to invest ourselves differently tomorrow' is maintained.[4] My parodying of the term 'holy' in this chapter is motivated by the temporal direction that Rose identifies in postmodern parody – the right to do things differently tomorrow – and the control such parodying exerts over the investment of individuals in frameworks of cultural meaning.

This chapter meditates on the prevalence of mind–body or body–mind terminology in discourse on actor training in particular, while also making select connections to monism/dualism debates in theology and medicine and considering why Theatre and Performance Studies have dwelt on, and continue to promote, questions of mind–body integration in training. In assessing the place of mind–body questions in the historiography of performance, I consider the possibility that in performance's third moment, if that is what *now* is, these questions may no longer be the most stimulating or essential ones prompted by encounters in and with training. I propose to open up novel questions in the following chapters by thinking through a different set of critical imperatives and a fresh conception of 'the body' which puts different and (I argue) more relevant concerns at stake.

'I don't talk about the mind–body split'

In an interview with Stelarc published in 2002, Nicholas Zurbrugg asks him if he sees his technological-prosthetic-performances as forms of 'mind–body split, or perhaps as a kind of triangular mind–body–technology split'. Stelarc gives the somewhat tetchy reply,

> I don't talk about the mind–body split . . . when we talk about the body here, we talk about the total physiological, phenomenological, cerebral package – we're not talking about a body opposed to a mind, because I don't want to make those kinds of distinctions. A body for me is a person, and a person is a thinking, moving, aware entity. I don't want to be immersed in those old metaphysical distinctions between the soul and the body, or the mind and the brain.[5]

Stelarc's reluctance, or rather explicit refusal to enter into discussion over mind–body interrelation stands in stark contrast to the propensity of other practitioners and academics to conduct discourse on performer training in the midst of these 'old metaphysical distinctions'.[6] Phillip Zarrilli is an important figure in this trend within theatre and performance training scholarship: he has published several articles and books discussing the 'the body–mind' in training as well as organising an international symposium entitled 'The Changing Body: The Body–Mind in Contemporary Training and Performance' at Exeter University in January 2006.[7] Zarrilli edited something of a 'landmark' collection of articles on performer training published in 1995 as *Acting (re)Considered: Theories and Practices*, revised and published in 2002 under the title *Acting (re)Considered: A Theoretical and Practical Guide*. In the revised version of his 1995 essay, '"On the Edge of a Breath, Looking": Disciplining the Actor's Bodymind through the Martial Arts in Asian/Experimental

Theatre', reprinted under the new 2002 title, '"On the Edge of a Breath, Looking": Cultivating the Actor's Bodymind through Asian Martial/ Meditative Arts', Zarrilli writes about certain Asian martial arts training practices that 'reject the Cartesian body–mind dualism, assuming instead that body–mind is an integrated whole'.[8] The semantic shift from the martial (*discipline*) to the organic (*cultivation*) evident in the essay's new title, as well the disappearance of 'experimental theatre', probably reflects the development of Zarrilli's interest in what he and others have called *psychophysical* or *psychophysiological* methods of performer training.[9] Indeed in Zarrilli's more recent work, *Psychophysical Acting: An Inter-cultural Approach after Stanislavski* (2009), he claims to have arrived at 'a means to overcome the separation between the mind and the body'[10] through training; to unify the 'long-term Western binary dividing mind from body that so problematically crystallized in the mind–body dualism of the seventeenth-century French philosopher René Descartes'.[11]

Zarrilli's characterisation of the Cartesian body–mind as non-integrated would appear to recite the philosophical trope identified by Sarah Patterson and Tim Crane, whereby simplistic notions of 'Descartes' views are introduced only to be refuted by relatively simple argument'.[12] Zarrilli's characterisation of Descartes' theories of mind and body appears to presume that Descartes believed mind and body to be co-existent elements of the self that share no interaction, and not the coherently realised products of a radical scepticism acknowledging that it may 'be the case that these very things which I am supposing to be nothing [the body and the world], because they are unknown to me, are in reality identical with the "I" of which I am aware'.[13] Descartes' distinction between mind and body is not a dualism of 'mind' and 'body' but of 'thinking substance' and 'extended substance', and these can be differentiated because they are conceived through different concepts. As Patterson explains 'his [Descartes'] dualism derives not from the possibility of mind existing without body, but from the claim that thought and extension are attributes of different substances'.[14]

Zarrilli cites Shaner's claim that, 'phenomenologically speaking one can never experience an independent mind or body'[15] as an idea which 'reject[s] the Cartesian body–mind dualism'[16] and supports his notion of body–mind cultivated through training. Yet, as Burnyeat claims, thanks to Descartes 'the subjective truth has arrived to stay, constituting one's own experience as an object for description'.[17] And McDowell argues the subjective sensory experience of individuals integral to post-Merleau-Ponty phenomenology – where 'how things seem to a subject [is taken] as a cause of how things are'[18] – arrives in philosophy through Descartes. So although Cartesian body–mind philosophy is at the root of pheno-menology, Zarrilli mobilises this to demonstrate Descartes' irrelevance.

The opposition between phenomenology and Cartesian philosophy of mind is false. Addressing his reader, Zarrilli laments, 'how unimagin-atively *we* have conceived of the imagination' [*emphasis added*].[19] The only example of this lack of imagination he provides is of an imaginary actor visualising the image of a seagull in Chekhov's play, warning that this 'means much more than seeing the gull projected onto the screen of one's mind'.[20] I would respectfully suggest that his characterisation of this kind of imagination seems to involve little more than projecting its image on to the screen of *my* mind. Returning to an imaginative image of Descartes, he asserts, 'Under the influence of the Cartesian dualism, the imagination is too often considered to be an "image" conceived of a something *in* the mind.'[21] He argues that the actor who has been 'training *through the body*' [*emphasis in original*] should be able to 'actualise a full-bodied connection' to an imaginative image which is 'palpable' through the actor's body.[22] Here, again Zarrilli's description of imagining ('properly' understood) as a 'psychophysiological act'[23] misconstrues Descartes, who himself described something similar in his often over-looked assessment of the role of the pineal gland in imagination and sensation:

> It is not [the figures] imprinted on the external sense organs,
> or on the internal surface of the brain, which should be taken to
> be ideas – but only those which are traced in the spirits on the
> surface of the gland H [the pineal gland] (where the seat of the
> imagination and the common sense is located).[24]

Zarrilli's notion of imagination as a 'thinking with the body' finds itself quite literally *seated* in the body by Descartes' assessment of the pineal gland. Descartes' conception of the complex interplay between mind and body has always been subtler and more anatomically nuanced than critics such as Zarrilli have been willing to acknowledge. Indeed, Descartes' devotion to anatomy and physiology in helping to explain the complex interplay between thought and action has prompted Richard Watson to conclude, 'if Descartes were alive today he would be in charge of the CAT and PET scan machines in a major research hospital'.[25] Zarrilli's assertion that a Cartesian 'mind–body dichotomy' can be 'overcome' in certain training practices[26] by 'activating "a mediating system that links the mind and the body"',[27] and the claim that a state of body–mind unification is what 'training through martial arts has the potential to *accomplish*' [*emphasis added*],[28] establishes a false conflict between a philosophical 'Cartesian' notion of embodiment and Zarrilli's own experiences of an 'optimal' state of embodiment: 'the aim [of training] is psychophysical integration – reaching an alternative state in which body–mind dualism is transcended'.[29]

Asian martial arts training is afforded a peculiar status in Zarrilli's writing because it doesn't so much *contradict* the philosophical tenets of 'Cartesian' dualism but rather *heals* them, transforming a dualistic existence of mind and body into an integrated experience of body–mind. A philosophical paradox is therapeutically resolved, and in this respect Zarrilli blurs the distinction between 'thinking' and 'doing' as activities in the process of training with philosophical conceptualisations of 'mind' and 'body' as substances. Paradoxically, Zarrilli's training practice *assumes* the existence of a dualism between mind and body in order to perform an interweaving of the processes of thinking and doing – thus producing the optimal state of 'standing still while not standing still'.[30] This 'state', as described by Zarrilli, is brought about by psychophysical training 'that transforms not only the practitioner's relationship to his body and mind in practice but also how one conceptualises that relationship'.[31] This bears many of the hallmarks of the 'zone' or 'flow' states described in sports science; and it seems particularly pertinent that the 'essential elements' of the flow state according to sports scientists Jackson and Csikszentmihalyi, such as 'complete absorption in the activity', 'merging action and awareness', 'a sense of control', 'transformation of time',[32] are evident in Zarrilli's descriptions of the state of 'standing still while not standing still': 'giving oneself over completely in the moment to an action', 'enter[ing] a state of heightened awareness', 'gradually [becoming] able to control and modulate [physical and vocal capabilities]', 'engag[ing] in the present moment' while developing 'a new awareness of [one's own] bod[y] in and through time'.[33] The 'effortless movement'[34] wherein practitioners feel themselves to be paradoxically exerting great force with minimal effort, reported to be typical in experiences of 'flow', also resonates with Zarrilli's description of his own experiences of 'standing still while not standing still': 'My tensions and inattentions gradually gave way to sensing myself simultaneously as "flowing" yet "powerful", "centred" yet "free", "released" yet "controlled".'[35] Drawing from the same semantic field as sport science, Zarrilli describes 'standing still while not standing still' as being 'in a state of released/fluid "flow"'.[36]

It would perhaps be unwise to read too much into the fact that Zarrilli's mentor, Govindankutty Nayar, uses the phrase 'flowed like a river'[37] to describe particularly efficacious body practice, but it is nonetheless surprising that Zarrilli makes scant reference to the body of sports psychology literature on the phenomenon of 'flow' in his descriptions of such optimal states. For example, the clinical psychologist Dr R.A. Carlstedt draws on a body of sports-based research into 'zone' or 'flow' states in which individuals report trance-like feelings of practising with an altered state of focus: 'he or she dissociates and becomes deeply focused on some other internal or external stimuli' than the 'task' they are practising.[38] While there is debate over whether such a state involves an increase or decrease in focus, it is generally agreed that 'these unconscious lapses or episodes of intense absorption have obvious consequences for performance, both in the positive and negative sense',[39] and that the 'mediating of mind–body processes is associated with peak performance in zone, or flow states'.[40]

It seems reasonable to assume that sports science and clinical psychology are associated for Zarrilli with what he calls his 'sports body'[41] – the product of American sport and health pursuits – which is 'gradually . . . [and] "positively" disciplined' through precisely non-Western training practice.[42] This perhaps explains why Zarrilli cites writers such as Yuasa

Yasuo and his translator Shigenori Nagatomo, who have published on 'an Eastern Body–Mind Theory' and draws on a decisively non-Western frame of reference for the 'state' he describes.[43] Carlstedt's observations of the mediating between mind and body processes in 'flow' state performance directly echo Zarrilli's citation of Nagatomo, though through a more 'Western-medical' rhetoric, suggesting that the kind of training Zarrilli describes doesn't so much *overcome* a Cartesian mind–body dichotomy, but rather *constructs* it and uses this construction to give a philosophical and inter-cultural focus to what might otherwise be a description of neurological phenomena.

Zarrilli's notion of Descartes' metaphysics is perhaps only what Patterson and Crane have called a 'Cartesian interpretation of Descartes',[44] and his conception of practice that 'accomplishes' body–mind integration is perhaps better understood as practices that induce a 'flow-state'. The example of the 'Cartesian' approach to Descartes in Zarrilli's writing typifies a widespread commitment in theatre and performance practice and scholarship, particularly discourse on training, to body–mind discourse. Robert Gordon recently claimed in his book on theories of acting, 'all modern approaches to training assume the unity of the performer's body–mind'.[45] If this is so, askeology must be responsible for asking, *why* is it so? If, as Joseph Roach has so eloquently demonstrated, all theories of acting operate by social, cultural and scientific models of the self, it needs to be asked *why* modern theatre training practice makes this assumption. If there is, or has been, a general cultural trend towards holism in the twentieth century, as Campbell has argued,[46] one is tempted, as Roach might be, to place Gordon's observation in the context of such a tendency. To see the assumption of body–mind unity in the modern performing arts as a part of a more generalised Anglo-American or Anglo-European trend towards holism is problematic largely because such a 'generalised' trend is not as explicitly evident in other non-performing arts training disciplines. The fact that holistic conceptions of the individual in religious training, for example, are by no means modern would suggest that theatre plays a particular role in this current trend.

Gregson, Drees and Gorman make the point that 'the Judeo-Christian tradition is not as dualist as is sometimes supposed' and that there is a strong 'holistic strand of Christian thinking' that dates back at least to Aquinas.[47] Esther de Waal also observes in her commentary on the *Rule of St Benedict* that, in Benedictine training, 'it is the whole person that is addressed',[48] and elsewhere in her writing that Benedictine spiritual anthropology has always operated a conception of the 'unity of the whole person'.[49] One might make the case that religious training is always likely to non-conform with secular cultural trends and thus represent something of an anomaly within Campbell's general cultural tendency. It is certainly true that rehabilitation training has been part of this trend in precisely the same way as Zarrilli. As Grant Duncan explains,

> Recent attempts by medical thinkers to *overcome* organic reductionism in favour of a more holistic representation of disease and health routinely begin by attacking Cartesian dualism. [*Emphasis added.*][50]

The particular problem with viewing the trend towards holism in performing arts as part of a broad cultural drift is that the emergence of holistic body–mind discourse in theatre training would appear to coincide with increased interest in Indian and Asian training practices in Britain, Europe and America. The increased interest shown by British, European and American scholars and practitioners in Butoh,[51] Suzuki[52] and kalarippayattu[53] trainings, for example, might lead one to conclude that the tendency towards holism in the performing arts is perhaps more accurately described as a tendency *towards performance and training practices that operate a rhetoric of holism* within performing arts. This would seem to suggest that within this historical trend there has been something at stake for 'Western' theatre in particular in making holistic assumptions.

Thinking through what this might be must necessarily begin *within* this trend, and necessarily coordinate theatre with other social and cultural sites; so, as an *ansatzpunkt* or *allegory,* I offer three events from this cultural moment, occurring within a three-year period: the production of Christopher Hampton's play *Savages* at the Royal Court in 1973; the debate conducted between the anthropologists Stephen Corry and Lucy Mair in successive articles in the journal *Anthropology Today* in 1975; and the departure of Phillip Zarrilli to India to study performance training for the first time in 1976.

In *Savages* the British government official Alan West is kidnapped by the MRB (Movimento Revolucionario Brasileiro) in Brazil and held as a bargaining chip to exchange for political prisoners. The bargain never goes ahead and instead West is shot shortly before the Cintas people are exterminated when their Quarup celebrations are bombed.[54] Before Alan West (*the* West?) is shot by his captor and guard Carlos, they debate, among other things, the plight of the indigenous Indians of South America, and West shows himself to be a knowledgeable ethnographer. West appeals to Carlos to act on the systematic termination of indigenous beliefs and practices before diverting his efforts into a military coup that will only succeed in replacing one authoritarian government with another. To this Carlos responds:

> All this crap about Indians, it's just romantic bourgeois sentimentality . . . All your liberal hearts bleed at the thought of those poor naked savages fading away, but it never crosses your apology for a mind that half a million children under five starved to death in Brazil last year.[55]

It seems fitting that at about the same time as Carlos (played by one of 'the West's' more famous actors, Tom Conti, in his London debut) stages the theme of the West's well-meaning but condescending, and perhaps dangerously negligent, ethnographic fascination with 'primitive' culture, two British ethnographers should be conducting a public debate about South American 'ethnocide' in the pages of *Anthropology Today*.

Stephen Corry's article 'Ethnocide: A Report from Columbia', published in early 1975, describes the plight of 'the Indian' under the 'Casa Arana' (British Peruvian Rubber Company Co. Ltd). As 'forced' workers, the indigenous Indians were reportedly maltreated, beaten, tortured and murdered. 'The Indian' for Corry refers to the broadest indigenous population, a heterogeneous grouping made up of numerous different 'tribes', and he observes that under the influence of the Casa Arana, 'many groups were completely annihilated, others merely decimated'.[56] Corry concludes his report by noting 'a slow and seemingly inexorable movement towards a loss of tribal and ethnic identity' which will mean that 'over the next generation some groups will cease to exist'.[57] By way of optimism he opines that 'against this trend, the reassertion of group/tribal/ethnic feeling is coming from all areas of the world'.[58] It is precisely the national geography implied in this assertion that Lucy Mair targets in her article, 'Ethnocide', in a contemporaneous issue of *Anthropology Today*.

Challenging Corry's description of ethnocide as 'the destruction of an ethnic group by a dominant ethnic group by means other than deliberate killing',[59] Mair retools the term, turning it on Corry and 'the people who use the word to condemn a kind of destruction [but who] have not made up their minds what it is they are condemning'.[60] She claims that 'some people speak of "ethnocide" when what they mean is the abandonment of their previous way of life by populations which have continued to live and to reproduce themselves through the generations'.[61] Mair concedes that when a population is exterminated either by negligence or deliberately, as is described by Corry, we can agree that ethnocide has taken place, in a certain sense of the term. On the other hand, Corry's description of the erosion of indigenous culture is a form of the ethnocentric 'pristinism' that denies marginalised cultures access to technology, industrialisation or democratisation – or, as she more succinctly puts it, like telling non-dominant ethnic groups, 'the party's over before you have even had a bun'.[62]

Jonathon Benthall, the editor of a collection of *Anthropology Today* articles that includes both Corry's and Mair's, describes 'pristinism' as a trend in Western anthropology that not only fetishises the 'primitive' but also essentialises cultural identities in ways that dislocate ethnic groups from the modern world and prevent them from engaging with it.[63] Thus the assumption that 'primitive' peoples are primordially linked to their environment, or that they are guardians of physical or spiritual truths unknown or lost to the West, which he sees as a thematic strand of popular anthropology in the 1970s, has gradually waned, so that some now even hold the position that the 'pre-modern' primitive is actually a modern construction. The meaning of the term 'ethnocide', for Mair, becomes inverted, being used to describe the paternalist movement by ethnographers such as Corry who deny marginal ethnic groups access to the modern and, by upholding their otherness, effectively prohibit their social and cultural reproduction.

If Phillip Zarrilli's departure for India in 1976 places his research into kalarippayattu in the historical context of the debates between West and Carlos, Corry and Mair, it also places his subsequent writing on Asian martial arts and meditation practices in the critical context of ethnocide. Zarrilli is very conscious of the burden on him in writing about these practices, and admits, 'I found it difficult to describe my experiences in language that neither objectified nor . . . romantically subjectified and/or reified my own experience, applying to it a thin gloss of self-congratulation.'[64] It would be harsh to judge Zarrilli's writing as ethnocidal, in Mair's sense of the word, but his focus on body–mind interrelation and the subsequent centrality of such a focus in theatre and performance research on training is a legacy of a phase of 'inter-cultural' and anthropological research. Thus, the centrality to Theatre and Performance Studies of performance practices in which body–mind discourse holds sway needs to be seen as part of a particular historical moment.

It is perhaps not surprising that the publication of Richard Schechner's article 'Actuals' in *Performance Theory* (2003) under its original title in *Essays on Performance Theory 1970–1976* (1977) should trace the same anthropological thematic through the identical historical period I have outlined above. Schechner's exploration of performance initiated through a description of Tiwi rituals arrives, like Mair, at the conclusion that 'the hot interests in anthropology over the past generation or so have not been all good'.[65] It seems safe to assume that Zarrilli is not one of the 'soft-headed artists' whom Schechner accuses of looking for 'a field hoping to find in the Other a finer version of what their own self might be' and in the process constructing 'neo-Rousseaurian fantasies of "primitive" people', but it seems equally safe to assume that he is one who responded to (or perhaps anticipated) Schechner's call for 'wholeness', for 'therapies which start from the one-ness of mind/body feeling' as a performance 'actual'.[66] The 'end to dichotomies' announced by Schechner – so that

'a whole person   *not* mind/body'[67]

is presumed by performance – appears to be accomplished by Zarrilli's description of Asian martial arts practice and the transposition of a particular body–mind model into 'Western' theatre and performance.

Within this historical period Zarrilli is by no means alone in answering, or pre-empting, Schechner's rallying call: Jane Blocker, in her book *What the Body Cost: Desire, History and Performance*, argues that 'more damage has been done to "woman" with the simple theoretical divide between mind and body than anyone can adequately calculate or ever fully explain', and because of this she contends that 'we should not be surprised . . . that the mind/body division was much in evidence at the time of performance art's popularisation in the sixties'.[68] Schneider, in her *The Explicit Body in Performance*, makes a similar observation, noting that female and non-dominant 'ethnic' bodies have been 'aligned with the infinitely splintering, visceral and tactile "body" side of the Cartesian mind/body split',[69] and it is this that, in the 1960s, performance began to assail.

Given the political significance of a certain Cartesian interpretation of mind and body in the oppression of women and other groups, it is perhaps not surprising that Schechner, Zarrilli and other artists and theorists should seek practices of wholeness for performance, or that cultural conceptions of the individual said to oppose such a Cartesian model should assume a privileged place in performance and training practice and theorisation. What is slightly more difficult to understand is why, as Campbell has noted, three decades on 'it can be argued that Richard Schechner's assertion of the need to accept "body thought alongside cerebral cortex thinking" is being realised both within the performing arts and the more general cultural tendency towards holism'.[70]

Within the particular case of Performance Studies, the tendency towards holism of *thinking* and *doing* can perhaps be seen as contingent upon the tendency towards dismantling the presumed divide between *theory* and *practice* which has been so valuable to the discipline. Zarrilli's preface to his 1995 edited collection speaks directly to this division and signals the imperative to reconcile; 'this book was prompted', he tells his late-twentieth-century reader, 'by a growing recognition of the need for a collection of essays which would speak to students of acting *and* students of theory' [*emphasis as original*].[71] The project of askeology, with its participant-observer approach, is a grateful inheritor of a research climate made habitable by the mobilisation of rhetorics and paradigms of holism in an earlier moment of performance studies. Alan Read's idea 'that theory and practice ... are interdependent',[72] published in another preface to another landmark publication, situates Zarrilli's sense of growing recognition in its historical moment; and Read's fifth axiom of showciology – 'No practice without theory, no theory without practice, and neither in context'[73] (in the sense that such an underlying notion has been transformed from *assumption* to *axiom*) – puts this project in its own. While it may be naive to assume that the fratricidal relationship between theory and practice has been made properly fraternal by Theatre and Performance Studies, if one can take Read's fifth axiom as not only a signal of intent but also a report on the state of affairs 'on the ground', the insistence on continuing to conduct a discourse of holism on 'the body–mind' in theatre and performance scholarship seems at best redundant and at worst a kind of disciplinary parapraxis. If Read's assessment of the relationship between thinking and doing does in some way report the current 'thought' in theatre and performance studies, could the seeming anomaly of body–mind discourse be the result of some disciplinary conditions more serious than a collective Freudian slip? Could it be that the reason for the persistence, or rather the *persistent insistence on* wholeness in theatre body discourse today is not so much tied into the gender and race politics of the 1960s and 1970s, or the project to reconcile practice with theory, as in the recalcitrant anxiety since at least this time of performance about its own essential inequalities?

Performance, in its various forms as 'ritual', 'art', 'happening' etc., has (arguably not just since the 1960s but as far back as the Dadaists and beyond) sought to remove itself from what Patrick Campbell has called *the theatron* – an 'institution of active blindness and inactive embodied actor[s]'.[74] In this movement the theatre audience has been atomised and undergone various reconfigurations from *spectator* to *spect-actor*[75] and more recently *witness*,[76] and the apportionment of agency between 'doer' and 'watcher' gradually has been made more equable. It is not surprising, I would suggest, that within this broad movement the mind–body 'split'

– which, as Campbell has noticed, 'looks significantly like the theatron's division between disembodied seer and blind embodied actor'[77] – has become a *bodied* focus for dissatisfaction with the terms of the ephemeral contract of theatre. Might then the presence of mind–body discourse in performance, that Blocker first noticed emerging in the 1960s but is *evidently* still with us today in theories of training, be the less-than-fully-conscious forestalling, frustrating or punishing-by-proxy of theatre's own apparent insistence on a certain un-equable form?

If, along with Stelarc, I am able in this book to avoid the 'old metaphysical' issue of mind–body interrelation and assume that 'person' can account for any and all aspects of the individual, it is because of, not in spite of, the work done by Zarrilli and others in arguing for a *wholeness* in the conception of the individual. If analyses of body–mind models in training disciplines of the present and recent past complement and rehearse audience–actor models of theatre, any project that seeks either to emphasise or de-emphasise the wholeness of the individual in performance training will unavoidably confront the agenda of a contemporary theatre and performance that still enjoys a troubled relationship with the politics of the theatron and which remains disquieted over the terms of the 'theatrical contract'. In this context, to do as Stelarc does and avoid body–mind debates is no less a political manoeuvre than Zarrilli's insistence on conducting them in any and all sites. If Stelarc's performance practice is exemplary in imagining a theatre wherein agency is in a sense radically redistributed not only among 'doers' and 'watchers', but over space and time as well as throughout his body; and if this theatre is in any way 'prefigurative',[78] as Chris Hables Gray has called it (an image in the present of possible future constellations of not only relations within theatre but in a wider political realm), his refusal to talk about a body–mind might *prefigure* an emerging cultural trend – one that is self-consciously capable of assuming that beyond the theatron what *makes a body* has become impossible or unnecessary to define.

If the conditions of obsolescence 'beyond the theatron' seem to be recalling the state of affairs 'Beyond the Thunderdome', perhaps I should say that a deliberate silencing of body–mind discourse should not be expected to precipitate the kind of collapse that ensues around Max 'Mad'

Rockatansky in the iconic movie. Moving this historical account forward in time, the emergence of a dystopian *mise-en-scène* in 1980s movies such as *Mad Max 3: Beyond Thunderdome* (1985) provides the cinematic environment into which steps the infamous cyborg T1000, played by an actor arguably more influential then Stelarc in prefiguring future political conditions (at the time of writing the incumbent 'Governator' of California) – one who not only accepts Schechner's contemporaneous proposition of the need to reckon 'body thought alongside cerebral cortex thinking' but expands its terms. If, as John Appelby has argued, the 'one theoretical claim with which Stelarc is particularly associated . . . is that the body is obsolete',[79] it is not this assertion, but his apparent insistence on the obsolescence of body–mind discourse in theatre and performance studies that is more relevant here, because what Stelarc proposes is not that 'body–mind' be decommissioned but that it be overwritten, souped-up and superseded by a self-conscious silencing of these 'old metaphysical' distinctions. This would of course be a silencing that entailed hushing, but only as a *stage whisper* that is precisely calculated to let the listener hear what is being left unsaid.

In this askeological project I do not propose to silence body–mind discourse just because it is tied into the political battles fought in an earlier moment of performance, the spoils of which are now being enjoyed, but because to move away from these discussions – as Stelarc proposes – is to ventilate a new set of questions. Schechner's call for wholeness –

a whole person	*not* a mind/body
families	*not* fragmented individuals
communities	*not* governments[80]

– now seems somewhat anachronistic, in the climate claimed by postmodernity where, as Sarup and Raja have identified, the *alienation* once experienced in families, societies and individual subjects has been displaced by *fragmentation*.[81] If, as Eagleton has argued, such postmodern conditions are the environs of the world's rich – that the rich have *mobility* while the poor have *locality*[82] – then it is also the thematic territory of some of the theatre companies that have recently enjoyed time in the limelight of Performance Studies.[83] In this climate of 'Certain Fragments' where, according to Elinor Fuchs, 'the character' has died a death, theatre has somewhat ironically inherited a certain wholeness where the dichotomy of 'real' and 'represented' has given way to the 'really represented' and the responsibility for producing meaning has been thoroughly dispersed and democratised.[84] The questions that seem to need raising about body practice in this particular moment seem to have less to do with *how a person fits together* and more to do with *how persons interrelate* not only with one another but with the varied objects of the world. In body–mind discourse on training, the 'neutral' body 'observable from the outside'[85] that apparently caused Zarrilli so many problems is made to square up against the intra-sensing body of subjective experience in accounts of wholeness; and as a result training discourse is bound to recite the conflicts between *thinking* and *doing* and rail against the poetics of the theatron and . . . meanwhile . . . in another part of town . . . contemporary performance practice seems to have released itself from the narrow politics of a 'Cartesian' divide and engaged a politics that is the *means* by which the conditions of cooperation are organised.[86]

What *now*?

Having embarked from one 'point of departure' in the recent twentieth-century past, it now seems like a good time to arrive at one in the twenty-first-century present.[87] In a paper co-written with Annemarie Mol, *Embodied Action, Enacted Bodies: The Example of Hypoglycaemia*, John Law cites the following extract from an interview with Miriam T—, a diabetic,

> Me, well, I know my body pretty well, and if I were to prick and measure myself right now, I know that I'm fairly low [in blood sugar], for I feel kind of, eh, I've got to eat something extra, because I've injected too much [insulin]. That is, we were having chilli tonight and that's with beans and that's a lot of carbohydrates, and then I tend to inject two or three units more so that it [blood sugar] doesn't go up too much, but now I've been doing things in the garden, so, hmm, I have to eat an extra something because

otherwise I won't do well. But now we can have nuts, so I do allow myself that, hah, nut.[88]

Miriam T—'s account of managing hypoglycaemia helps to draw out the ongoing preoccupations of performance and theatre scholarship working in the area of training under discussion here, and to propose a way out from underneath these. In her opening statements Miriam T— acknowledges that there are at least two kinds of knowledge about her body – her own intra-subjective knowledge ('I know my body') and the knowledge of her body as the object of medical measurement ('if I were to prick and measure myself right now'). These forms of knowledge account for Miriam T—'s two bodies – the one that she *has* and the one that she *is*. This, in itself, is not startling. In fact, we all know this, according to John Law, and it is where any contemporary consideration of embodiment begins – with the simple fact that I have a public object-body and a private subject-body.

According to Mark Sullivan, this particular dualism underlies and troubles modern medicine because, 'the body known and healed by modern medicine is not self-aware'.[89] This dualism relates to the 'Cartesian' dualism between body and mind and reverberates in neuropsychiatry just as the placebo pill 'allegorically' represents it. In contemporary health discourse, as in Theatre and Performance Studies, the term 'body–mind' becomes embroiled in a conflict between simplistically characterised 'Western' notions of embodiment and what are characterised as more properly sensitised 'Eastern' ideas about the self. Regrettably, this conflict has somewhat disabled the term 'body–mind' as a descriptor of cultural-theological-philosophical paradigms of self and aligned it with a particular privileged cultural paradigm which is notionally Eastern. In the case of theatre, there is more to be said about the construction of such a paradigm as 'Eastern' by 'Western' theorists and practitioners and the 'Orientalising' manoeuvre this implies than space here allows; but perhaps we can situate all this within Zarrilli's observation and take him at his word when he claims, '*all* languages of acting are highly metaphorical . . . We should not mistake a discourse *about* acting as a representation of the thing that the discourse attempts to describe.'[90] Perhaps more problematic than the cultural politics at play is the rhetoric of integration and unity implied by Zarrilli's own body–mind paradigm, for as Mol and Law indicate, 'to say that a body is a whole . . . skips over a lot of work'.[91]

Acknowledging that these dualisms of subject–object and mind–body are prevalent concerns for training theorists and practitioners in medicine, theatre, performance and beyond, I follow Mol and Law in asking if it might be possible to leave these commonplaces and attend to the way we *do* our bodies, because this might move 'us to a place where gathering knowledge – whether objective or subjective – is no longer idolized as the most important way of relating to being in the world'.[92] Looking at Miriam T—'s account again, it is apparent that she is not only subject and object, but also *actor*, because, in various ways and in relation to the world, she *does* her body. As well as feeling or knowing the level of her blood sugar and being able to measure and record it, Miriam T— also *enacts* hypoglycaemia, as well as *acting* to counter it. In the consumption of chilli, the work she does in the garden, the insulin she injects and the promise of nuts she may get to eat, she enacts her own body incorporating what surrounds her. Her surroundings, like her 'proper' body, must be 'prepared for action' because 'while a body-in-practice may incorporate some of its surroundings it may also . . . excorporate some of its actions'.[93] Thus this body that Miriam T— does is not whole and the paradigmatic activity of a body-in-action is not *observation* that belongs to the object-body, or *intra-sensing* that produces the subject-body, but *metabolism*.

For the 'metabolic body' the skin is permeable and inside and outside is not stable, and this metabolic body is actively engaged in enacting itself. Such a conception of a body-in-action is not restricted to diabetic bodies; as Mol and Law point out every-body, whether in practising yoga, exercising in the gym or walking down the street, is enacted as a metabolic system, and suggesting that we have a coherent body or are a proper whole hides from us one of the tasks of living: 'Keeping yourself whole is one of the tasks of life. It is not given but must be achieved, both beneath the skin and beyond, in practice.'[94]

This notion of metabolism entails a particularly sensitised understanding of embodiment. Deriving from the Greek word *metabole*, meaning 'change' – a compound of *meta*, meaning 'over' in common usage, and *bollein*, meaning 'to throw' – metabolism describes processes of active change between states. As a medical term, metabolism literally describes the continual 'overthrow' of fixed relations in a body's interaction with its environment and encompasses both anabolic processes whereby matter is assimilated into an organism at a molecular level and catabolic processes by which complex molecules are broken down and excreted.[95] It represents an understanding of a body as inherently linked to its environment via continually changing relations, the maintenance of which are fundamental to its biological existence and central to its continued survival.

The particular 'metabolic' conception of bodies I am proposing is motivated by phenomenological notions of embodiment which have been developed via a critique of perception that grounds the individual body in the world, a grounded relationship that enables each individual's knowledge of the world. For Maurice Merleau-Ponty, a body is always in the world and 'I' am never separate from that body because, 'I am not in front of my body, I am in it, or rather I am it.'[96] It is not possible to transcend my bodily involvement in the world because I am primarily related to it, and this has led Margaret Betz Hull, in her reading of Merleau-Ponty, to note that because of this primary relation 'my body yields knowledge as, "I can", as a set of possibilities for me'[97] in the world. Despite, or rather because of its grounding of the individual in the world as the primary source of knowledge about the world, these phenomenological investigations have stimulated philosophers to explore the knowledge I, as an individual, possess of *other individuals*.

Before Merleau-Ponty, Edmund Husserl in *Formal and Transcendental Logic* (1929) accepted that we belong to an inter-subjective world: others give me my name, teach me my language and help me to negotiate my position within my own society. This is what Husserl called 'communalisation' (*Vergemeinschaftigung*) – whereas, for Husserl, this 'communalised [sic] transcendental life first constitutes the world as an *objective* world, as a *world that is identical for everyone*' [emphasis as original],[98] and for his followers, Hans-Georg Gadamer and Emmanuel Levinas, subjective differences and 'otherness', as it is encountered in conversation, dialogue and face–face encounters, assume a central place in phenomenological considerations of embodiment. For Gadamer, language, especially in the context of the kind of speech which occurs with others in conversation (*Sprache*), is the essential constitutive medium of our understanding of the world because, as he claims, the 'things themselves' reveal themselves only in and through language: 'in truth . . . the illusion that the things themselves precede their manifestation in language conceals the fundamentally linguistic character of our experience of the world'.[99] For Levinas, the inter-subjective character of knowledge and our experiences in the world necessitates an ethical consideration of our existence with others because my being-in-the-world entails being in a world of others, or perhaps of *alterity* itself, and because all social interaction is already in some sense taking place within the sphere of the other. For Levinas 'things' are 'not the quintessence of all the relations that constitute our presence on the earth' – rather 'the relationship between the same and the other . . . is the ultimate fact',[100] and consequently my responsibility to the other is the fundamental structure upon which all other social structures rest.

The constitutive operations of embodied perception in and among a world of others and other objects, and especially Merleau-Ponty's attention to what Betz Hull calls the 'I can' of an individual's relationship to these, influenced J.J. Gibson's psychological theories of an 'ecological' model of perception, and these are especially pertinent to the notion of metabolism in training being developed here. Gibson's theories of 'environmental affordances' situate perception within each individual person's 'lifeworld' where objects achieve definition for an individual via the determining of what 'action' they might afford him or her.[101] Speaking of the particular example of theatrical acting, but in terms which might transpose on to an analysis of being an 'actor' in one's own 'lifeworld', Martin Welton has observed that the primary relationship between perception and the utility of the thing perceived in Gibson's 'affordances' raises concerns over the structuration of a lifeworld, since here we are talking about not only 'an actor's embodiment as an existential condition of "being-in-the-world" but also the extent to which such an act of being is constitutive of that world'.[102] Welton describes this particular act of constitutive perception of theatrical habitats as a 'tuning up' of self in relation to environment on the basis of what that environment affords in terms of (theatrical) action. Anthony Chemero suggests that affordances need to be understood as relations between things that 'exist in the environment and are just as real as the things in the relationship'[103] – in Miriam T—'s case, for example, her dependency on insulin every bit as real as the hypodermic that transports it, her relationship to the other with whom she will dine tonight as real as the beans on her plate.

More recently other scholars, including Zarrilli, have taken up an 'enactive view' of perception where 'experience is a process of engaging the dynamic possibilities of [a] particular form or structure as it happens'.[104] Regrettably, this enactive view does not supplant body–mind discourse in training but becomes embroiled within it, so that the redundant equation concerning the unity of body and mind acquires a temporal and spatial dimension: 'body and mind at work together as one in the moment' wherein 'space-time unfolds'.[105] The 'problem of the actor *not* understanding what it means to inhabit one's "whole body", and therefore *not* being able to access and utilize . . . in-depth body–mind awareness'[106] remains a difficulty in many accounts of training, despite the more pressing concerns about remaining 'whole' stimulated by an ecological understanding of lived experience.

While an anxiety about the interrelation of body and mind might still linger in some current thinking on embodiment, 'enactive' accounts, such as Zarrilli's and especially Welton's, position my notion of metabolism in training in relation to a certain contemporary discourse on the body. What Dermot Moran has called the 'circular causation' of individual and environment purported in the Gestalt psychology of Wolfgang Kohler, Kurt Koffka, A. Gelb and K. Goldstein – where 'stimuli are always perceived and interpreted in a rich and complex environment'[107] – is, Moran writes, taken up by Merleau-Ponty in his *Phenomenology of Perception*, and has produced an understanding of the body in relation to its environment via the senses. Expanding the epidermal boundaries of an organistic metaphor in much the same way I have proposed to do with metabolism, Merleau-Ponty wrote: 'Our own body (*le corps propre*) is in the world as the heart is in the organism; it keeps visible spectacle constantly alive, it breathes life into it and sustains it inwardly, and with it forms a system.'[108] The necessarily anthropocentric focus of a study of human perception perhaps inevitably arrives at this view where 'I' am at the centre of all things such that even 'time is not a real process' but is constituted by my embodying of it and 'arises from my relation to things'.[109]

Clearly, in the case of the individual, embodied perception is, as Welton writes, constitutive of the 'lifeworld' and perhaps even the time in which that lifeworld takes place, but the utility and necessity of affordances in the example of hypoglycaemia reveal that the world and its objects are also constitutive of the lives that can or *must* be lived within it. In the context of disability, the 'enactive' view of perception, where 'experience is a process of engaging the dynamic possibilities of the particular form or structure as it happens',[110] seems somewhat deficient; the multivalent agency entailed by accessing *possibilities* belies what Miriam T— shows to be the *necessity* of acting.

Embodiment entails 'doing' the body in ways that, as Chemero might argue, will involve the co-constituting of very real relationships, which are, of course, constitutive of the organism. With these concerns in place, training will emerge throughout this book as an organised and motivated engagement in the structuring of a lifeworld that, rather than being aligned to an optimal state of integration, might act to counter particular centrifugal forces of disintegration, against the pull of which we work to remain 'whole'. While there might be rather more at stake for Miriam T— in her own lifeworld than in the theatrical ecologies of Welton's actor, 'the corpse' might, in a certain sense, haunt the *corps propre* of both: the breakdown attendant upon 'corpsing' when one, in theatrical parlance, 'falls to pieces out there' might provide yet another theatrical metaphor to be productively co-opted into everyday English usage – since, whether acting in theatrical spaces or the socio-cultural, bio-political ones in which they are embedded, 'one does not hang together as a matter of course: keeping oneself together is something the embodied person needs to do. The person who fails to do so dies.'[111]

Stelarc's *PING BODY* performance (1996), where he is hooked up to the web through sensors and via computer, and his movements controlled by an audience logged on to other computers elsewhere, seems to provide a fitting allegory for the conditions of metabolism that Mol and Law have argued are essential to body practices, quite literally excorporating the responsibility for action over perhaps the largest terrain humankind has successfully mapped and at the same time incorporating spaces, prostheses and other people into this moment of theatre.[112] If Stelarc's *PING BODY* is too literal a realisation of Mol and Law's assertion that 'keeping yourself whole is one of the tasks of life . . . it is not given but must be achieved, both beneath the skin and beyond, in practice',[113] it is the hope of askeology that descriptions of the various lives held together in different trainings can avoid being held up by body–mind debates and that these concerns can be overwritten (and thus incorporated) by a concern for how bodies metabolise in training, or how training metabolises bodies.

Knitting and holes

If training discourse in the present moment is to be conducted on different terms, and especially if it is to be askeological and engage the broadest range of (theatrical and non-theatrical) performance training, it will need to extend out of the concerns of the theatron and into the relational dynamics that characterise performance. While this chapter historicises some key concerns in the field of training within Theatre Studies, it also situates askeology historically among some contemporary developments. In this respect the 'wholly actor' could become the 'woolly actor' not only by the exchange of a single character but because contemporary performance, as Read (2008) has explained and Ridout (2006) has witnessed, is characterised by the increasing appearance of fur-covered characters on stage.[114] The woolly nature of performance prompts different but related concerns to those stimulated by the furry skins of performers because, while wool might be to fur what meat is to flesh or handbags to alligator hide, animal actors such as the mouse Nicholas Ridout watches scurrying across the stage of a presumably infested West End theatre are figuratively *knitted* into the action as they are matrixed by performance.[115] As animals progressively break down barriers between themselves and humans and increasingly push through the 'fourth wall' of theatre – which was rendered thoroughly permeable in the first moment of performance – to appear on stage, barriers between categories such as human and animal, actor and non-actor are unravelled by the knitting 'linking element'[116] of performance. Theatre and Performance Studies now shows a keen interest in the 'confusion between the sign and the thing, acting and matrixed behaviour',[117] and the example of the animal suggests that in performance, now conceptualised through a relational aesthetics, the politics and binary dynamics of the theatron have been superseded by the proxemics of more complicated matrixes of relations and the 'wholesome' imperatives of mind–body holism replaced by the 'woolly' view of actors as ecological.

It is not the collapse of high and low categories in the latest moments of performance as such that provides the environment for askeology but the re-determination of boundaries and classifications enabled by such a collapse (*collapsus* from *collabi*) or falling (*labi*) together (*cum*), with things which were previously distinct becoming merely different.[118] If the hierarchies of modernism still lurking in the theatron have mostly given in under the strains of postmodernity, they have not given rise to undifferentiated knowledge but to the knowledge of *differance* where nothing is outside 'the text'.[119] The project of reconceptualising categories of 'actor' and 'spectator', 'theory' and 'practice' in this environ of differ-ence where neither has absolute meaning has been well under way in Performance Studies for some time now, and any, even rhetorical, notion of an empty *unwritten* space of appearance has been thoroughly problematised.[120] Yet, despite these developments in the study of perfor-mance and its participants, a relational view has not yet been brought to bear on the phenomena of training that (in one sense at least) precede it.

In a historical moment where Ridout has suggested that the antitheat-ricality of much contemporary performance art is an expression of artists' fears that they cannot be untheatrical enough, it is perhaps unsur-prising that training discourse is fixated with railing against an outmoded notion of theatricality. In an artistic climate where Bourriaud's much quoted *Relational Aesthetics* has firmly secured the importance of 'forms which do not establish any sort of precedence, *a priori*, of the producer over the beholder',[121] the recitation of the political battles of the theatron in training studies are an anachronism. If Theatre and Performance Studies now embraces a range of performative activities identified by their relational dynamics and aesthetics and is able to think about acting in various 'non-theatrical' senses, training discourse has an imperative to decentralise 'the actor' of the modern stage and open up analysis in stages beyond 'the stage'.[122]

To take this wordplay of the wholly actor and properly return it to the contemporary stage I should perhaps not only be thinking in terms of knitting but also of *openings* – not only in the 'void' that Simon Bayly identifies 'at the heart of appearing',[123] and which Read relates to the 'gap' between differentiated genres of discourse,[124] but also in the *hole* in theatre and performance discourse where a 'first philosophy' of training should be. The 'holy actor' on the stage of training discourse finds him- or herself hemmed in at the wings by first philosophies of performance which, according to Janelle Reinelt, are a key identifying feature of Theatre and Performance Studies in the UK today.[125] These philosophies, as Bayly writes, are 'generated with a concern for what was originally overlooked or forgotten'.[126] In this historical moment the 'holy actor' of theatre training is a 'holey actor', and askeology arrives alongside other first philosophies of performance to ask the first questions about what is called training and fill the hole by illuminating what seems to have fallen into it: the overlooked connections between theatrical and non-theatrical training and the neglected question about a meta-disciplinary activity of training.

As Bayly indicates, any such philosophy, in concerning itself with what was forgotten, will become locked in the construction and deconstruction of the very idea of an origin, and askeology bears this out as its etymology appeals – like much of European theatre history – to the 'Greek site', while resisting what Levinas called 'Greek' thinking. Where, for Derrida, nothing is outside the text, for Levinas no thought is outside language – Greek to be precise, since 'when we think we speak in Greek, even if we do not know this language'.[127] 'Greek' and 'Hebrew', in Levinas each refers to a sub-textual way of thinking and speaking, in which the former is the 'ontological mode that seeks to describe the whole' and the latter the 'dialogical that is never complete and preserves dissent'.[128] The movements towards first philosophies which Reinelt identifies are definitively contemporary and decisively askeological because commitments to thinking on the overlooked and forgotten in dialogical ways that resist describing the whole are not only a theatrical concern – for example, the theologian Kevin Vanhoozer's efforts to produce a *First Theology* that, like Levinas, wants to resist the 'Greek-thinking' that takes 'texts captive with a "totalising" method that acknowledges only what conforms to its categorical scheme';[129] or Kathryn Montgomery's efforts to think about *How Doctors Think* and realign the practice of clinical judgement with hermeneutics as opposed to scientific enquiry. Both evince the efforts of respectively religious and medical communities to go back to the first questions about their practices.

Apart from Theatre Studies' myopia of the theatrical actor and the comparative blind spot in training discourse for actors in the relational–performative, the focus on *what-makes-an-actor*, as a psycho-physical being, in one sense harks back even to a pre-modern stage and the 'Greek' thinking that wants to describe the wholeness of the whole. Askeology, equipped with the critical imperatives of Performance Studies, wants to sit among contemporary interests in performance, its social qualities and spaces where 'a feature of much contemporary criticism and art practice has been a shift towards understanding art as relational and dialogical'.[130]

With an interest in the performers of theatrical and non-theatrical spaces rather than a pious commitment to the sanctified (or sanctimonious) *actor*, askeology extends actor training discourse into the knitted action of performances. If the concerns of performance are situated, as Campbell suggests, among the concerns of other disciplines of knowledge and within a broad cultural trend, this is not only a trend towards presuming holism – that no longer bears the responsibility to presuppose its non-existence – but one wherein the first questions come first.

The political projects of the early moments of performance and Performance Studies have been overcoded by the dialogical concerns of its latest stages, and the holy actor who appeared from the disciplinary regime of theatrical training on to an empty stage will now have to play a supporting role to the relational and ecological dynamics of wool and the first philosophies of training in the hole into which askeology is summoned to look.

 Vocation

During my time researching monastic training at Worth Abbey in Sussex, living with its community of Benedictine monks, I spent two days pulling dock plants from an acre of field by hand. I should say here that this non-chemical method of weed-killing was not a penitential invention of a sadistic abbot, but the eco-friendly initiative of Felton, the groundskeeper at Worth. I should also be clear that it was I who asked to be put to work, or rather I who asked to experience some of what an aspiring monk would undergo during the early stages of their training, and so I accompanied Joshua and Damian, two postulants at Worth who had been sent by the Abbot and Novice Master to help Felton in this task.[1]

I am noting all this to be clear that the uprooting of thousands of dock plants from an acre of field was an agrarian necessity and not an exercise specifically designed to test patience or commitment; rather, given that this necessity existed, it was co-opted to contribute to the experience of two individuals aspiring to become monks. These two days were quite unusual in comparison with much of the time I spent at Worth. Working as we were in a field on the furthest reaches of the Abbey estate, far from the rest of the community, and comprised as our group was of two non-monks (Felton and I) and two not-yet-fully-monks (Joshua and Damian), conversation flowed quite freely. In direct contrast to the encompassing silence experienced during most of the days I spent in the Abbey, these two days were characterised by the volume, range and everydayness of our communication. Given the unusual licence to converse afforded by our task, I took the opportunity to try to ascertain from the two aspiring monks what it was that had led them to Worth and what it felt like to be called to monastic training.

Both Joshua and Damian were obliging, though at the time I found their inability to pinpoint a specific event or sensation surprising. Damian alluded to an incident in which he came close to drowning while swimming in the sea as something like a turning point, but his description of his own experience of a calling was not the revelatory 'road-to-Damascus' moment I was naively expecting. Instead, the shared characteristic of Joshua and Damian's response to my questioning about their sense of 'calling' was a certain open-endedness. Both seemed assured that something was directing them to Worth and both expressed a strong drive towards the life of religious formation that lay ahead, but neither was willing to assume complete authority over their own experience of calling. Instead their attitude towards their own sense of vocation appeared to be investigatory and exploratory – almost as if they were trying to locate this calling and trying to decipher its sound.

A vocation to monastic training has a quite definitive character. The belief that a calling comes from God puts the trainees in a dependent position even in relation to their own experience of vocation. This is because such a vocation is not simply the product of the will of the trainees, not solely a product of their own agency, but also of the will or agency of a divine power. As such, monastic callings demand to be searched for, explored and amplified – they require an effort to be 'heard' and thus more fully experienced. This is unambiguously expressed in the opening word of St Benedict's Rule[2] for monks, 'Listen', and the ensuing command to 'attend to the message you hear'.[3] The early stages of monastic training spent in the postulancy and later in the noviciate are principally characterised by an attempt to identify and comprehend the forces driving a trainee to monastic training. This process is called 'discernment' because its aim is to discern if there truly is a divine calling to monastic life or if the impelling forces to monastic training are purely 'personal' – pragmatic, psychological etc.

Although discernment is especially associated with the early stages of monastic training, it is an enduring part of monastic life. To pursue, explore, expand and feed one's vocation and similarly to be alert to its diminishment or complete disappearance are all part of Benedict's command to attend to the message one hears. The process of discernment undergoes a certain transmogrification after the profession of solemn monastic vows. The process of 'ongoing formation' displaces discernment by refocusing the task of searching for and exploring one's calling to ensuring one's development through responding to the nature of the vocation that has been discerned. In a section entitled 'Ongoing Formation of Solemnly Professed Monks' in *School for the Lord's Service: Stages of Monastic Growth*, an internal publication of the Benedictine Congregation used as something like a regulation and best-practice handbook, all monks are reminded that

> None are exempt from the obligation to grow humanly and as religious; by the same token, no one can be overconfident and live in self-sufficient isolation. At no stage of life can monks feel so secure and committed that they do not need to give careful attention to ensuring perseverance in faithfulness; just as there is no age at which a monk has completely achieved maturity.[4]

Though 'ongoing formation' is an explicit task of monastic training, it is particularly configured in the early stages of training as concerned with the testing of a calling. Indeed, Benedict devotes an entire chapter of his Rule to 'The Reception of Candidates for the Community'. In it he advises that entry into monastic training 'should not be made too easy, but we should follow St John's precept and make trial of the spirits to see if they are from God'.[5] 'Trial' is something of a watchword in the early stages of monastic training. In order to discern whether the calling to monastic work comes from God, Benedict advises that 'rebuffs and difficulties' be put in the way of aspirants and postulants and that they should not be shielded from the 'trials of monastic life which can *appear* to us to be hard and even harsh' [*emphasis as original*].[6]

While the accounts the postulants gave of their experience of vocation as we dug up dock roots indicate something about the specificity of a monastic calling, they also provide an insight into the meta-disciplinary qualities of vocation. The everydayness of our exchanges while working in the fields distinctly contrasted with the exchanges I experienced most of the time at Worth. Our conversation in the fields was characterised by the range and volume and also, most interestingly for me, by the style of our singing. Felton and I soon discovered a mutual interest in popular and folk music, and to some amusement we passed much of the time by swapping songs. Unlike the psalm-singing of the daily office, modelled on the eight tones of Gregorian chants,[7] our singing was syncopated, urgent, often up-tempo and comparatively imprecise. The subjects of our songs were quite distinct from the Old Testament characters of the psalmody, and over the course of several hours we ran through numerous folk ballads of murders, adulterers, thieves, lovers and addicts. In a memorable detour from the profane I recall our discussion of gospel tunes and our inspiration to sing one in particular. Joking as we were about the seemingly punitive nature of our task and our appearance to those who passed by down the adjacent country lane, we imagined ourselves to be sharecroppers or chain-gang labourers as we sang 'In the Highways', a tune made famous by the American folk matriarch Maybelle Carter. One verse of this song in particular has come to help me conceptualise and describe the essential characteristics of vocation, as a meta-disciplinary process:

> If he calls me, I will answer
> If he calls me, I will answer
> If he calls me, I will answer
> I'll be somewhere working for my Lord

It is in this instance of singing to two men undergoing religious callings and in the early stages of monastic training, and particularly in the singing of this verse of this song, that two of the most significant defining characteristics of vocation as a meta-disciplinary process of training can be drawn out and explored. These are *vocality* – or the communal, interdependent and relational nature of vocal exchange – and *work*. My focus on vocality comes not so much from the fact that we were *singing* this song, though this is of course part of it, but more from the sentiment expressed within the verse and what it stands for within Christian spirituality: from the fact that 'he calls me'. Likewise the focus on work is wrapped up in the facts that not only were we working pulling up weeds, but also that according to the lyric we were answering a call; we were 'somewhere working'.

The root of vocation

It is apposite to start with an allegory that literally gets to the root in this chapter, which will navigate through the historical germination of a concept of vocation as well as the significance of the meanings at the root of the word itself. This particular allegorical point of departure will enable me to explore the various characteristics of vocation that afford it a status as meta-disciplinary process by opening out a view on vocation that does not start with but rather arrives at work.

The secular world has become quite accustomed to regarding vocation as a particular kind of work that appears to transcend the realities of capitalist labour even as it may function within them. In Larry Cochran's humanist psychology study of *The Sense of Vocation*, conducted by analysing twenty life-stories of individuals who felt they had pursued a vocation, he gives a somewhat problematic description of vocation as a life-story the narrative of which is understood as profoundly meaningful by its author: 'For those with a sense of vocation, life is shaped in a way that lights up one's existence in an elevated story the person lives.'[8] This profundity, its character and precisely how it affects living prove difficult for Cochran to identify from anything other than the humanist perspectives of those who experience vocation. In his introduction he saddles himself with a very narrow version of vocation as a moral premium by citing John Stuart Mill's attainment of 'what might truly be called an object in life; to be a reformer in the world',[9] which Mill purports to have acquired as a result of reading the works of Bentham at the age of fifteen. Cochran's assertion that Mill achieved a sense of vocation that would endure throughout his life seems to base this sense of vocation on an intellectual commitment to a just or moral cause and propose a conception of vocation that is synonymous with having a moral or ethical purpose or goal. Cochran's rather more straightforward efforts to describe rather than explain vocation produce a conception which is both more stimulating and accurate in that it brackets moral value and focuses on the exclusiveness of vocation because while everyone might have a work position – and a morally 'good' one at that – not everyone has a vocation.

The specific ethical standards implied by Mill's notion of being a reformer and Cochran's assertion that commitment to such an ideal might constitute a vocation don't sit well with accounts such as Lazreg's reports of the French army's professional training in coercive tactics during the Algerian war (1954–62). Lazreg explains that the inclusion of torture in soldiers' training curriculum and the 'subsequent profession-alisation did not diminish the brutality of the practice or its indiscriminate use; nor did it improve the attitude of the torturer towards his victim', but rather it identified and supported those who, like one soldier in particular, 'found himself a vocation as an efficient torturer'.[10] While Cochran successfully identifies a popular association of vocation with certain meritorious work, it is perhaps disconcerting how this highly moral commitment to social reformation and the repugnant practice of torture can so easily convene in Cochran's description of the difference between a professional role and a vocation.

Throughout this chapter I will explore vocation's association with work through the monastic allegory I have offered and a select example from my research into stroke rehabilitation, but this won't be done by thinking through the ethical value of the work that is undertaken (Lazreg's torturer renders that avenue obsolete) but through the *form* of work that might be unique to all experiences of vocation. I won't be starting with the association of work with vocation, but with a consideration of what Cochran has referred to as a 'sense' of vocation, such as Joshua and Damian experience it during training. Given the widely acknowledged reality of the subjectivating effects of labour, the explanation of this 'sense' will aim to clarify the characteristics of vocation that reportedly transform one's experience of work and try to outline, through the rehabilitative example in particular, the quality of an *imperative* to training. To start, my allegory is brought into contact with perhaps the most complex assembly of allegories mankind has produced – the religious narrative – as the dock plants prompt me to think about the root of vocation.

Vocality

Of course getting to the root of a word doesn't tell us what it really means, but rather how it has been *used*, and this might enable the interpretation of what 'vocation' entails via investigating what it is *used* to describe. It is probably no surprise to you to know that the words 'vocation' and 'vocality' share the same Latin roots, in *vocare* and *vocalis*, meaning 'of the voice', and *vocatio*, meaning 'a call'.[11] There are several histories of the linguistic development of the word 'vocation' but for centuries it has had a distinctly Christian tenor. It would appear that Tertullian was the first to translate the Greek *klesis* (literally meaning 'call'[12]) into *vocatio* in his third-century translations of Pauline and Johannine Biblical literature.[13] The concept of 'a call' to live as a Christian in the writings of St Paul and St John gave the Christian a special destiny; but perhaps most importantly the idea that Christians were specially called to live a certain life helped to foster a sense of communal identity within Greco-Roman and Hebrew contexts. While the notion of a calling set Christians apart from society in general, it also connected them to one another and bound them into a community. Although baptism was a key process in the embryonic stages of development of Christian communities, as time passed and baptism was largely displaced by christening, 'calling' would assume a more central position in the construction and sustaining of these communities.[14]

As Esler explains, the experience of being Christian in the first three centuries A.D. was characterised by the threat of persecution, often in the form of martyrdom as well as the exclusive right of the baptised to celebrate the Eucharist. These factors helped groups of early Christians to define themselves in antagonism and contradistinction to Roman society, and bind together as an exclusive community. As Christianity not only came to be tolerated by the Roman state but eventually adopted as its official religion, the exclusive sense of Christian identity radically changed and from the fourth century, when St Anthony – often regarded as the 'first monk' – and Pachomius began the development of anchoritic communities, Christians were forced to reformulate their sense of identity, or rather drastically adapt the organs of identity they had developed.[15] It is of particular importance to askeological investigations of religious training to note that the growth and development of these fourth-century Christian communities and especially of their monastic groups was in part affected by the experience of 'calling', and thus through something akin to a quality of voice.

'Vocation' is a word used within the Christian monastic tradition to denote the experience of beginning, the moment when an aspirant becomes aware of their calling to religious life. It also describes the undertaking of that religious life over time, and the sustaining of one's calling to it. Thus a calling to monastic training, a 'vocation', describes both the impulse and the implementation – the call and the response. When writing about vocation it is almost impossible to disentangle the matter of a calling to a particular undertaking from the matter of undertaking the thing itself. For the purpose of analysis, though, it is necessary to impose a certain division and imagine that it is possible to separate the call from the response. With such an imagined division in place, it is possible to address the quality of the calling and the particular kind of work involved in vocation.

If he calls me ...

The Bible is one of humankind's greatest storehouses of allegories and, as its theology may produce one grand or meta-narrative, so too the narrated events in its Old and New Testament books might also contribute parts towards one grand meta-allegory.[16] If, as Law suggests, an allegory invites a reader to interpret beyond the literal, then the Acts of the Apostles, the prophecies of the Old Testament and especially the parables narrated by Jesus are exemplary of the allegorical form. The Bible is replete with stories of callings and these individual narrative events ask to be read a number of ways just as they describe a number of different voiced encounters: Samuel heard a call and mistook it for the voice of a priest.[17] In his case it was an audible voice, just like a human voice, but when Elijah heard a voice on Mount Horeb it came in a whisper.[18] Paul heard a voice at his baptism in a vision and so did Jesus. Using a favoured allegorical image of Christ as a good shepherd, John wrote: 'He calls his own sheep by name and leads them out . . . and his sheep follow him because they recognise the sound of his voice.'[19] John's image is a useful one to help identify the particular attributes of vocality being mobilised within Christian discourses by the word 'vocation'. Clearly John is not documenting a particular instance of human–animal communication, but trying to give an allegorical or metaphorical shape to callings *in general* (that could encompass the mistaken voice, the whispered voice, the voice from a vision etc.), and thus represent what is going on in vocation.

It may be safe to assume that John's image of a shepherd conversing with sheep was more affecting at a time historically closer to man's withdrawal from other animal species, via his naming of them, than it is now, at a time when philosopher-men and philosopher-women have all but completed mankind's return and where the anthropomorphy of Disney in particular has successfully rendered the strange, familiar. Indeed, John Stokes, in his consideration of the wild animal act in theatre, has observed that our present historical moment is characterised by an inverse proportion between the total number of animals and the volume of species we are willing to claim as possessing human characteristics: 'Wild animals are on the decrease at the same time as the boundaries between human and non-human are being eroded by philosophers.'[20] The fact that, as the biblical commentator Greenslade has observed, the Bible and the Christian thought that accompanies it resist the 'poetical anthropomorphy of the Olympic gods or the symbols of Hinduism'[21] which give animals human form in making them divine, and instead persist in an anthropomorphic presentation of God that renders the divine human even as it renders the human animal, is significant because it provides a counterpoint to the fundamental assertion that God created man *in his own image*. It may be important in the interpretation of this image of calling to observe that the anthropomorphy of divinity (even as it animalises the human) runs parallel with the central theological anthropomorphising thread wherein a Christian God is rendered human-father and the dominant anthropomorphising forms of church architecture where St Paul's image of Christ as 'the head of the body; the Church'[22] is played out in literal representations.[23] The image of Christ – himself perhaps the ultimate in anthropomorphy – as the Shepherd is usually interpreted as representing the benevolent covenant between the Holy Trinity and mankind. This image, which refers us to an early Middle Eastern soundscape of shepherding whoops and whistles, places man-the-sheep in proximity to Christ-the-shepherd, just as in the biblical narrative man himself sent Jesus to become properly anthropoid via human birth among the animals.

Vocatio, being a call, has the quality of being voiced, and so this call is not just a sound produced by natural forces or contact between inert objects. It is issued forth from someone (or some entity), by another to which and by which it becomes possible to orient oneself. The essential element of John's image is that the sheep *recognise* the sound of the shepherd's voice. This posits the (metaphorical) sheep and shepherd as constituent parts of a community (of at least two, but by inference, more) who are able meaningfully to communicate with one another. It is evident that John is attributing some of the qualities of linguistic speech to his notion of a calling, and this probably explains why Tertullian translated John's notion of calling (*klesis*) into 'vocation', thereby attributing to it, as did John, some of the qualities of speech.

It would appear that in the case of a Johannine conception of calling, it is the vocal quality of linguistic speech operative within the metaphor that is intended to represent the interrelation and interaction taking place between God and his followers. To suggest that sheep and shepherd share a language is perhaps just as problematic as to suggest that God and humankind share one, but this is of course not what the non-literal reading proposes. Rather, this metaphor is intending to take what is known about language and associate it with a non-linguistic conception of calling. But exactly what quality of vocal utterance or meaningful speech is being attributed by John (and translated by Tertullian) to the metaphysical calling of Christian vocation?

There is perhaps limited value in reading a metaphor or allegory literally in searching for a reason why an image of linguistic communication has been historically used to describe vocation. Apart from the dehistoricising effects of interpreting this communicative image through a Saussurean concept of *langue* as a single collective organisational structure of both human speech and reason, the overly literal interpretation of 'calling' it would impose would be insufficient to operate in the range of calls reported in the Bible.[24] The existence and operation of a linguistic community posited by such a semiology might help to explain the interpersonal relatedness invoked by John's use of 'calling', but instead I look to historically contemporaneous conceptions of 'calling' to try to understand the use of such a metaphor in the writings of John and Tertullian.

There seem to be two important facts. First, as I have stated, there are numerous recorded instances of vocal communication between human and God in the Bible; and second, there are multiple parables, metaphors and allegories of calling in the Old and New Testaments.[25] The accumulating images in John of Christ as a shepherd would suggest that John is trying to invoke some of the qualities of shepherding to represent the relationship between God and humans. Among the various qualities of shepherding transferred on to the relationship between God and humans is, as is demonstrated in this particular version of the image, the act of communication by which a shepherd commands and his sheep respond. John extends his usage of the Greek *klesis*, which literally translates as 'call', beyond this metaphor to describe and denote the kind of interaction that takes place between God and human and it is surely significant that both Paul and John use 'calling' to represent the interaction that occurs when individuals experience a divine directive to undertake something in particular. I want to be clear here that the notion of vocality I am identifying within early Christian notions of vocation does not impose linguistic semiology upon metaphysical callings. I am observing that for centuries Christian trainees have been working with the concept of vocality to 'metaphoricalise' the interpersonal relationships affected by religious calling and in so doing attribute to them some of the qualities of voice.

What kind of voice, what kind of speech?

To return to the present-day monastic, in certain instances a trainee may describe their experience of a call as very literal, but this is not to say that all monastic vocations are literal callings or that, because they are not, a communal or relational quality of vocality is not present within them.

There are, as I have already illustrated, many kinds of 'calls' recorded in the Bible, because there are many kinds of 'speech' operative in Christian discourse and practice. Robert Llewelyn, in his book *A Doorway to Silence: The Contemplative Use of the Rosary*, provides a consideration of the different ways of 'speaking' during prayer. He notes that words of prayer 'may be said aloud, or whispered, or framed by the lips and said silently, or "said" in complete silence with the lips closed and tongue still'.[26] Just as with John's use of 'call' to describe the experience of communication *from* God, Llewelyn uses the same associated qualities of voice in his definitions of 'speech' to represent what is going on in communications *to* God. Seeing as there are different ways of speaking associated with and practised in prayer, it should not be surprising that there are quite different experiences of 'calling' collected within vocation. Just as Llewelyn extends the qualities of speech to acts that occur in silence, it is possible to extend the quality of vocality to 'calls' that are not literal within the process of vocation because the relevant quality of vocation is not linguistic per se, but rather *shares a quality of communality and relationality with language.*

John's image of the shepherd collecting together his sheep is a useful one by which to interpret monastic vocation and its subsequent secular manifestations. A call in this sense is a directive, an *imperative*; it is not just a sound but a vocal command. It says 'follow'. This command or request is intelligible to listeners because they recognise it and understand it, because it possesses a quality of shared or collective meaning. For the call to be fully articulated as directive, it is necessary for the called to recognise the caller and *respond*. The good shepherd calls his sheep: they *follow* because they *recognise* the sound of *his voice*. In this respect vocation is relational because its vocality positions the called within a communal context, developing subjectivity as one in relation to another, one who is not alone. Importantly though, the calling of a vocation is not just relational but instructive and purposeful, seeing as individuals experiencing vocation feel themselves to be called *to do something*.

I will answer ... or 'worldly' calling

The conditions of relatedness assembled by vocational calling are, in the monastic example, directly mapped on to a hierachy of human inter-personal roles. The 'relatedness' that is initiated between the trainee and a divine other becomes increasingly overcoded by human relationships as the training progresses, drawing the monk into a more rigorously ordered community and situating them within social networks. It is important to bear in mind that a calling to a monastic training in the metaphysical sense is also a calling to a monastery and a group of monks in a physical sense. The imperative to monastic training experienced as a spiritual command also entails an imperative to a group of individuals and to the undertaking of quite practical tasks. St Benedict is careful to integrate the calling experienced to God's work thoroughly into the worldly work of the monastery, and in this way the process of vocation begins to diffuse into the process of obedience that I will be examining in the next chapter: as Benedict states (again using the example of a vocal command) an order from a superior should be treated 'as though it came from God himself'.[27]

The development of a monk through monastic training initially instigated by a divine calling progresses through a number of formal phases in which the conditions of relatedness between trainee and God (between called and caller) become superimposed upon interpersonal interactions with other monks. The first and principal movement in this process (and one that endures throughout training) is that which superimposes the relatedness between aspiring monk and the divine on the relationship between aspiring monk (as well as the fully professed monk he will become) and abbot. This superimposition is manifest even in the title given to an abbot, and the question of an abbot or abbess's authority is tackled early in Benedict's Rule.

> Anyone who aspires as abbot or abbess to be superior of a
> monastery should always remember what is really meant by the
> title ... For it is the place of Christ that the superior is understood
> to hold in the monastery by having a name which belongs to

Christ, as St Paul suggests when he writes: You have received the spirit of adopted children whereby we cry *abba*, Father.[28]

From the superimposition of this divine personage the transposition of relatedness to all other individuals is affected.

The earliest phases of the transposition of the conditions of relatedness on to human relationships occur during the postulancy and noviciate where the aspiring monk's relationship to monastic work comes under the formal influence of the abbot and novice master. *The School for the Lord's Service: Stages of Monastic Growth* records in its regulations and directives pertaining to the postulancy that, 'the length of the postulancy is determined by the abbot, who decides when the purpose . . . has been achieved'. Furthermore the postulant 'may be told to leave by the abbot' at any time.[29] During the postulancy the abbot appoints a novice master from the ranks of solemnly professed monks to be responsible for 'the supervision and guidance'[30] of aspiring monks. If postulants proceed to become novices they come more fully under the control of the novice master, who defines the channels by which novices interact with other community members and importantly also defines the terms on which novices interact with the 'outside world'. The extent to which the experience of relatedness to a divine authority assembled in vocation is mapped on to and played out in interactions with others is explicitly accomplished by the noviciate, as is explained in directives 28 and 29 of *The School for the Lord's Service.*

28. The novice master is to give clear guidance to the novices about contacts with those who are not members of the community, correspondence and the use of the means of social interaction.

29. The abbot is to determine, in consultation with the novice master, the policy of the community as regards contacts between the novices and professed monks; putting this policy into practice is the responsibility of the novice master. No one except the abbot and novice master may impose offices or tasks on a novice, or correct a novice.[31]

The relationships between a novice and other individuals both within and outside the monastic community are in part defined by the holding (and performing) of roles and associated responsibilities. During a novice's progress through the phases of monastic training his relationship to others and the channels by which he can interact with them are re-negotiated and reordered. A key practice in the redefining of interrelat-edness is the ceremonial professing of temporary vows and later, solemn vows, but the earliest phases of monastic training are in part concerned with transposing the interpersonal relationships between novice and novice master and between novice and abbot upon the relationships between trainee and 'caller', thus inscribing a trainee's vocation within a worldly and human community. In this way the communal quality of vocality first experienced in the divine call is translated into the aspirant's interactions with other members of a community and the call to *do something* is shaped and configured into a call to fulfil certain tasks *as enabled by definitive relationships to others.*

The transposition of vocation's conditions of relatedness into a very worldly context of organisation might tempt some commentators to begin to see such training as the kind of process that produces a certain disciplined subject. However, if askeology is to take the emic seriously, as I have proposed, it can't gloss over the 'sense' of vocation as experienced by trainees in favour of developing purely post-structuralist accounts of their subjectivation or psychological apologies for an individual's con-tinued sense of vocation during hard and potentially alienating labour. Any etic conceptualisation of the interpersonal organisation of training's communities must acknowledge the fact that the level of coercion is much lower in training than in discipline, and thus must ask what a vocational imperative might fully entail.

The notion of vocation as a spoken call is distinctive to religious tradi-tions of training. This is almost certainly because it is thought that the one who is calling in religious contexts is a transcendent or divine other whose call is quite different to the call of a worldly other. In secular con-texts no such being is acknowledged, and therefore no such call possible. Accordingly it would be inaccurate to suggest that the concept of vocation operational within Christain monastic training could be extended into other secular training contexts unexpurgated of some of its decisively

Christian characteristics. However, as I have tried to demonstrate through a focus on the etymology of the word 'vocation' and the nuance of its application to religious experience, the relational and communal quality of linguistic communication entailed by 'vocation' may well serve as a meta-disciplinary description of the experience of initiating training. To say that a meta-disciplinary notion of vocation is concerned with inter-relation and communication is not sufficient to differentiate this kind of calling from other linguistic acts or exchanges, and thus mark it out as uniquely embroiled in training practice, but, as is evidenced in John's image of the sheep and in Maybelle Carter's Gospel lyric, vocation is not *just* relational but rather it is directional and responsive. It is an *imperative* to someone or some duty – 'He *calls* his own sheep . . . his sheep *follow* Him'; 'If He calls me, I will *answer*'.

In thinking about vocation as a training process, it is important to remember that the vocal call is not just a sound by which one can position oneself and one which can be overlayed on to institutional hierarchies, but it is also an imperative. Vocation denotes the vocal qualities of speech shared by callings and describes these callings as personally experienced imperatives *to others* and to *undertake specific activities with others*. The imperative to undertake certain things with certain others is a crucial quality of vocation, as also are the relational networks it begins to assemble through the qualities it shares with vocal communication. To describe more thickly what 'imperative' means in the experience of vocation as well as to demonstrate the operation of calling in other training practices, it is necessary to leave the monastic example for now and explore vocation in other training contexts.

To examine just how an imperative to do something could operate outside religious doctrine and begin more fully to describe the meta-disciplinary application of a nuanced understanding of vocation in studies of training, I turn now to my experiences with those undergoing rehabilitative training. The medical narratives of patient case histories are, unlike parables, designed to clearly disambiguate the literal from the allegorical, and they ask to be read in definitely non-metaphorical ways. Subsequently, in looking at what is said and not said in the case history of a rehabilitation patient I will not be looking to infer the allegorical but rather to interpret the narrative of his recovery to try to clarify just what an imperative to training could entail outside of the rhetoric of Christian spirituality.

Imperatives

It is evident that at a certain level of analysis what drives a stroke patient to a rehabilitation ward is quite different from what sends an aspirant to a monastery. The difference is often *painfully* evident, and the understanding of vocation I am developing certainly does not seek to overlook this difference or simplistically to equate religious revelation with cerebrovascular injury. As I have been explaining so far, 'vocation' in its Christian usage refers less to distinct events and more to an individual's perception of a certain imperative to do something. It is the precise character of a vocational imperative, and the specificity of what it directs one to experience, that I need to clarify; and in order to do so I offer the example of a documented case study of a stroke patient named in medical literature only as 'JD'.

T. David Punt documented the case of the patient 'JD' in his article for the journal *Physiotherapy*, 'No Success Like Failure: Walking Late after Stroke', published in 2000. JD's recovery of walking after a stroke will here serve as an illustrative example of the operation of vocational imperatives within a secular training context. JD is a seventy-five-year-old man who was admitted to hospital with a sudden onset of right-sided weakness and diagnosed as having suffered a left cerebrovascular accident. He was classified as having had a severe stroke because he was unable to maintain sitting balance during the first seven days of his admission. As an in-patient, JD was initially rehabilitated on a general ward and then in a reabilitation unit until his discharge six months later. At the time of his discharge JD had regained sitting balance, but was unable to walk and forced to rely on an attendant-propelled wheelchair. He was advised by his physiotherapists that walking was now an unrealistic goal and that his rehabilitation had reached a 'plateau'. However, eight months after his discharge and fourteen after his stroke JD was treated by a physio-therapist as an out-patient at his local hospital and within two sessions had walked ten metres (a landmark distance in physiotherapy) with the assistance of a tripod. After a three-month period during which JD was seen twice a week he had halved the time it took him to walk this distance.

There are certain important aspects of physiotherapy as a particular training discipline that must be understood before it is possible to interpret this case study. First, it is a consensus among physiotherapists that most recovery occurs within the first three months after stroke and many argue that little further functional recovery will occur after this time.[32] Second, the physiotherapists who treated JD as an in-patient were adhering closely to the principles of the Bobath method of rehabilitation.[33] It is not feasible to explain this method here fully, but it is necessary to outline a few key features. Bobath therapy was the form of physiotherapy most widely practised in the British Isles at the time of JD's treatment,[34] and its emphasis is on correct procedure. It asserts that problems with gait are primary and should be attended to before functional problems. In other words to encourage walking (functional) before proper gait had been developed will not lead to positive recovery but to further motor problems. This being so, proponents of the Bobath method discourage the use of walking aids such as tripods because they can ingrain improper gait, bringing about further disability in the long run.

Noticing that JD could maintain balance while standing unaided, the physiotherapist who treated him as an out-patient, though Bobath-trained, decided to encourage the use of a walking aid. His choice caused some degree of controversy among his colleagues, the fallout of which is interpreted in Punt's paper. Some contend that the retrograde effect of his methods will be felt by JD in time and others maintain that there will be no such effect. Others still contend that there may be retrograde effects in terms of gait and general neuroplasticity (interrelation of cognitive processes and bodily action in achieving physical movement), but these will be outweighed by the functional gains JD has made. Importantly, at the time Punt wrote the report the physiotherapist treating JD had tried to move him on to a walking stick, but JD declined, informing him that he was content with the current level of mobility he had achieved. So, what does this case study indicate about JD's calling to rehabilitation?

The word 'imperative' is particularly appropriate to describe the attraction towards training experienced in training because it conveys something of the quality of voice I have identified as present in vocation. Denoting an ' "expressing command" (*Come here!*) '[35] in its common usage, it is particularly apt to stand for the nature of a calling *to do something* contained with vocation. To dwell on roots a bit longer, its etymological origin in the Latin *parare*, meaning 'to make ready', also helps to define the pregnancy inherent in a calling-to-do-something.[36] As well as these apsects of the word 'imperative' that make it suitable to describe that which is experienced in vocation, its indifference to intellectual agency should also be noted. To say that an individual experienced a 'desire' to train or a 'want' would be to assign their motivation to the intellect and to choice, and this would undermine the accounts of Joshua and Damian who are unambiguously clear that the monastic way of life is not solely a *choice* made in the sense of conscious decision-making. To contend that a physical injury is synonymous with a spiritual awakening would be inaccurate, but to assert that both instances might contain, or produce what Eugenio Barba has called (with specific reference to theatrical training) 'an imperative to change oneself'[37] is to suggest that both can be viewed as involved in the experience of vocation.

It might be tempting to view the relationships between JD and the Bobath practitioners on the in-patient physiotherapy ward, and subsequently between JD and the out-patient therapists, as a result of National Health Service treatment policy and not his own vocation to rehabilitation. Certainly, official protocol in referral processes plays a part, and it would be easy to detour away from the terms of vocation being defined here and to ask about institutional structures – to ask if the same agency can be attributed to JD in his defining of his own relationships to others as can Joshua or Damian in their aspiration to enter the noviciate. As I have explained through the example of the interpersonal relationships assembled and ordered in the postulancy and noviciate at Worth, the imperative to *do something* (which possesses a quality of relatedness) is articulated and given a practical existence by its transposition on to and into interpersonal group structures. This does not mean that doing the body-in-action becomes a circumscribed task of performing all those duties, obligations and activities prescribed by a subject position within a organisational procedure. As Deborah Lupton has explained, Foucault's assertion that 'the imperative of health [is] *at once* the duty of each and the objective of all' [*emphasis added*],[38] reminds us that the epidemiological imperative (that which occurs in the collective) is *simultaneous* with the individual imperative – one does not proceed from the other but rather the same imperative is manifest at the level of both the individual and the collective.

In the preface to his book *The Imperative*, Alphonso Lingis explains that he is concerned with elaborating two strikingly simple theses. The first is that sensibility, sensuality and perception are not reactions or adjustment to the physical world and its causality or the ordering of amorphous data of the physical world, but *responses to directives*. The second thesis is that the directives encountered throughout the physical world, 'in the night, the elements, the home, the alien spaces, the carpentry of things, the halos and reflections of things, the face of fellow humans and death *have to be described separately*' [*emphasis added*].[39] Lingis's list is by no means exhaustive, and his elegant description of the command of the imperative, on those who contemplate the imperative, to describe directives separately incites me to add 'in training' to his growing list.

Lingis observes that the more baffling the 'problem' one encounters in the physical world, 'the more there arise, exultant and proud, people who find in it a summons for their minds, their feelings and their skills'.[40] Lingis's understanding of our responses to directives recalls the commanding quality of a vocation evoked in Johannine callings by utilising a concept of 'summons'. The subtlety with which Lingis unpicks human encounters with the imperative and sets about separately describing the directives within them shows that the 'command laid on human thought and human intervention' which summons our minds, feelings and skill is 'met with at once'.[41] In his consideration of the directives within one of his favourite forms of encounter – the face-to-face – Lingis is summoned to describe speech. He observes that the activity of speech mimics our response to directives encountered in, through and with others and auralises them because 'to speak is to respond to someone who has presented him or herself'.[42] In the opening line of four successive paragraphs that contemplate the imperative through speech he asserts,

When we speak, we speak to others . . .

When we speak, we speak for others . . .

When we speak, we speak in place of others . . .

We speak for the silent and for the silenced. (*Layout as original.*)[43]

In these considerations of speech, an other or others are always present, such that speech is depicted as a communal, or at least interpersonal, activity. Lingis's descriptions of the ways we speak to, for and in place of others situates interpersonal encounter at the centre of speaking and recalls the relationships to others implicit in the notion of vocation as calling. Thus, for Lingis, the conditions of interrelation present in speech *issue from* the imperative we encounter in others; and so too, in training, the organisational structures do not define the interaction between individuals as such but rather are produced by, and proceed from, each individual's calling to training. The experiences of trainees and their own expression of these experiences can help to display the particular organisation of the relationships between individuals, the terms which define their interactions with each other and what the practices that they practise together are designed to accomplish. This in turn can help to bring into relief the particular qualities of a vocational imperative.

Independent walking

Staying with the physiotherapeutic, in their article 'Recovery of Walking Function in Stroke Patients after Minimal Rehabilitation' for the journal *Physiotherapy Research International,* Hale and Eales note that, 'Independent walking function is a highly desired goal among stroke victims, and has been well reported in Western literature.'[44] According to these researchers, the recovery of walking function is one of the goals most desired by stroke patients because it increases their independence. If an imperative to do something is mapped into and defines organised interpersonal interactive structures and practices, what is enabled because of these structures (or rather the experiences of undertaking what is enabled by a given interpersonal structure) can help to define the particular qualities of the *something* in an imperative 'to do something'.

It would appear from JD's case history and the attitudes he expressed towards his rehabilitation as documented by Punt that JD's imperative, as he experienced it, like so many others after stroke, was to attain functional mobility – to walk independently. Evidently, the interpersonal structures and interactive practices he experienced on a Bobath in-patient treatment programme could not facilitate and enable this. By contrast, the interactive practices and interpersonal structures in the out-patient treatment allowed JD to recover walking ability. Punt summarises the difference between JD's experiences of the two different rehabilitative methods:

> The argument here is that JD achieved his goal of walking because of a *fundamental change in his physiotheraphy management* . . . [This change] . . . led to a very important change in JD's physical performance and – perhaps more significantly – allowed him to achieve his goal. [*Emphasis added.*][45]

It would be easy to see JD's case history as a story of the relative success of two training procedures, but interestingly this is not the focus of Punt's argument. He writes in his conclusion, 'it is surely possible that different approaches can meet with varying success for different patients', and goes on to argue that 'the willingness of therapists to empower patients by engaging them in *true partnership of their management* is perhaps so crucial' [*emphasis added*].[46] It is telling that Punt uses JD's case history not as an opportunity to debate the competing virtues of different training methods but to raise the question of the 'management' of rehabilitation training and to imply that each patient might have uniquely experienced needs that will not necessarily conform with the generic normalised goals of organised treatment programmes. He argues that it is not the methods in themselves that determine the outcome of rehabilitation training but the climate in which they are practised, which is itself determined by the interrelation between therapist and patient. The fact that, as Punt points out, it was not just a certain set of exercises that enabled JD to recover walking ability, but that the design of these treatments was produced by the particular interpersonal interaction between JD and therapist. Furthermore, that JD resisted efforts to help him to walk without a tripod suggest that JD experienced a particular imperative to independence, rather than the ergonomic and aesthetic imperatives to correct gait associated with Bobath or the 'normalised' imperatives to unaided walking imposed by his out-patient treatment. What JD's case history shows is his unwillingness to be wholly subjectivated by either of the rehabilitative discourses in which he was trained – that his training involved more than becoming the subject of a certain set of practices because he himself brought a uniquely experienced imperative to the training and was able to modify the treatments to conform to his own imperative to independence.

In focusing on therapist–patient interaction and definitions of the terms in which they *work together* to pursue a patient's vocational imperative, Punt indicates the importance of social relationships in training. It is important to observe here that the social context of physiotherapy in both in-patient and out-patient settings is quite different from the context of monastic training. The community formed of various social interactions and interrelations in Worth Abbey is self-evidently different from the social networks of patients and therapists operating in rehabilitation wards. I have already explained through discussion of the monastic example that part of the experience of vocation as a meta-disciplinary process entails the transposition of certain imperatives on to and into social networks, and I am here contending that JD's imperative to walk independently is also articulated within interpersonal relationships in the social experience of rehabilitation. It is however necessary to ask *what kind* of social networks are operating in training and what aspects of these networks are intimately associated with the meta-disciplinary experience of training?

Training communities

In writing about the communal and relational qualities of voice inherent in vocation I have already begun to speak about individuals together;

about groups, about communities. Accordingly I need to be clear about just what I am employing 'community' to mean for askeology. I do not suggest that all trainees are consciously working with the same notion of community, or even that they are all consciously working with an idea of community to the same degree. I am simply noting that the trainees I worked with, across disciplines, trained together and maintained social relationships through their practice: that *they all collected to do things together.*

To conclude that groups of people who undertake training together constitute a community because of their physical proximity would be a very limited interpretation of the concept of community. This is not to say that their being close to one another is not significant, but to recognise that the physical interactions between trainees is not, in and of itself, sufficient to produce a community. After all, we all regularly (and sometimes perpetually) share spaces with certain people – neighbours, colleagues and shoppers, for example – without necessarily feeling any communal bonds with these people. This would seem to suggest that *the way we engage* with the people we interact with is important and that this might have something to do with the particular interactions enabled by group organisation and that this in turn might have an effect on what we *do* together.

I would like to be quite clear at this point that training communities are not politico-philosophical communities, such as those defined by Jean Luc Nancy, as 'primordial, ontological condition[s] of being-with or being-together',[47] in which we are always-already a 'we' because, as is quite obvious, at a practical level training communities are *exclusive.* This exclusivity is integrally linked to vocation because the uniqueness of an individual calling to a particular training acts not only to introduce a trainee into a pre-existing group but also to (re)assemble a community by including some and excluding others. Training communities are groups to which a trainee is impelled and into which a trainee is initiated or from which they are rejected. Community, in the sense that is applicable to askeology, is defined at the level of group social interaction rather than at the level of 'primordial' human togetherness. Training communities collect together to share practices and are defined at the level of their *organisation.* In this way, the notion of community important to askeology has less to do with being together (in a Heideggerian sense of *Dasein,* taken up by Nancy in *Being, Singular, Plural*) and much more to do with the ways individuals *act together.*[48]

Illuminating an understanding of community more appropriate to askeology, Durkheim proposed an idea of community based upon social solidarity and a commitment to a set of shared values, which he called 'collective conscience'.[49] According to his contention, community might be determined by the commitment of individuals to values or objectives shared by others rather than by their spatial proximity to one another. These commitments might, of course, be produced in or inflected by (or even guide and determine) spatial relationships. The sociologist Robert Nisbet has attempted to give a formal definition of community which could incorporate physical proximity into Durkheim's nuanced defini-tion, stating that community 'encompasses all forms of relationship which are characterised by a high degree of personal intimacy, emotional, moral commitment, social cohesion and continuity in time'.[50] An important factor to draw from these two ideas is that 'sharing' is fun-damental to community, in the sense relevant to askeology. Thus, central to this form of community is the existence of certain forms of relation-ships between individuals that allow them to conduct this sharing, and that these go beyond existing close to one another and into the realms of *acting together.*

Amit has done much to show that the practice of applying, or 'ascrib-ing' as Sally Mackey calls it, the term community to a group can be dangerous and even violent if it lays 'primordial' claims on what is shared as being part of an essential collective identity, determined by factors of ethnicity or gender, for instance.[51] The extent to which a claim on human *being* is dangerous is perhaps to be debated, especially during a time where, according to John Stokes, 'the boundaries between human and non-human are being eroded'.[52] Such a claim is however undoubtedly violent in the sense that it forcibly produces a powerful (human) effect.

At a meta-disciplinary level, that which is shared in training com-munities does not rely primarily upon primordial sharing; rather, the community is the expression of the negotiation and interrelation of individuals.[53] This means that the notion of community I am associating with training groups is more akin to what Mackey calls 'consociations': 'a form of community where face-to-face interactions are still an essential part of being-in-the-world although these interactions need not be well-established historically or all-inclusive'.[54] This notion of community is much more in keeping with the metabolic body described by Mol and Law, where part of the action required for keeping the body together is excorporated into the interpersonal environment of the individual. It is sufficiently congruous with the metabolic body to account for the tension that Mol and Law identify in the task of living metabolically because 'you will be part of many consociations . . . at any time of your life'.[55]

Mackey contends, along with Rapport and Amit, that in the exclusive and localised cases of consociations, community 'becomes a matter of choice'.[56] The form of agency implicit in this notion of 'individual choice'[57] seems incapable of properly accounting for the organisation and endurance of such consociations. Indeed the two examples of consociations offered by Mackey, parent–teacher associations and socialising with work colleagues, evince the potency of imperatives experienced by community members (to provide effective learning environments for the young, or to ensure stable and enjoyable working conditions with their peers) that cannot be reduced to mere individual choice to consociate. Thus the organisation of consociations, particularly those in training groups, is 'voluntary', as Mackey suggests, but is not simply a matter or rational decision-making. As Gerard Delanty argues, 'the vitality of community . . . is found . . . in the *search* and *desire* for it'.[58] The organising process that is associated with such a form of community is 'communication'. It is the means by which social relationships are activated and organised. Both 'community' and 'communication' stem from the Latin root word *communis*, which means 'common'. *Communis* is a paired formation of Latin etymons for 'together' (*cum*) and 'obligation' (*munis*).[59] This perhaps explains why communication and community are often used to denote means to, or instances of, 'naturalised' togetherness that transcend societal order and why, as Shane Phelan puts it, 'we see the continuing appeal of community as a vision of human relations that resists the advance of the modern state'.[60]

Communication might, in some circles, still be treated as the encoded transfer of information between 'sender' and 'receiver' in a particular medium. Despite the recalcitrance of this sender–receiver/actor–audience model in certain sections of 'the arts', Rudi Learmans, and others, have effectively argued that Roland Barthes's version of 'the text' as a space of interpretative productivity wherein the reader or receiver assumes the role (and obligations) of the writer or sender, has done much to influence postmodern performance's 'open-ended, multi-layered "texts"'.[61] This model of communication 'still bet[s] on the validity of the dominant view of communication',[62] according to Learmans, because such post-modern performance work still presupposes a deal of cultural capital for it to be understood as just that. The form of communication presupposed by both the dominant 'transfer' model of communication and the post-modern (and post-structuralist) twist it receives does not properly account for the kind of communication that organises community in the sense being developed here because of their focus (respectively) on the temporarily isolated 'message' or the socially isolated 'reader–writer'.

Learmans, utilising Niklas Luhmann's social systems theory, notes that communication may be 'purely private', as postmodern performance asserts, but can still acquire a 'social relevance, even social existence, when the uttered information *elicits one or more new communications*' [*emphasis added*].[63] This notion of communication is inherently social and reliant upon developing (metabolic) conditions of interpersonal related-ness over time because 'the enchainment of communications that refer to each other, [. . .] also co-produce [. . .] each other'.[64] Such a model of communication is not only reliant upon social conditions, but serves to produce and negotiate them over time as meaningful 'messages' are exchanged, reinforcing accepted understandings and provoking new ones. Such a model of social communication serves to organise consoci-ative communities where the community members simultaneously represent and negotiate the sharing that occurs between them. The experi-ence of relatedness within vocation organises human relationships modelled upon its 'communicational' function and creates conditions in which individuals are able to *act together* to do what they could not do alone. Only now, with an understanding of the relational qualities of vocation and how these are transposed on to social networks – or rather how these produce interpersonal networks without being totally subordinated to their organisational structures, and with a conceptualisation of the uniqueness of vocation and its personally experienced reality – are we finally able to arrive, as it were, where we started – with the allegory of labouring in a field and at what might otherwise be considered the start point for any consideration of vocation: work.[65]

Work

I am, of course, not original in calling attention to the impact of monastic notions of vocation on secular attitudes towards, and practices of, work. In the conclusion of his *The Protestant Ethic and the Spirit of Capitalism*, Max Weber reflects on the slippage between what I am defining as a *directive* to work in religious vocation and the *incentive* (or series of *disincentives to not-work*) in mechanised labour.[66]

> The Puritan wanted to work in calling; we are forced to do so. For when asceticism was carried out of monastic cells into everyday life, and began to dominate worldly morality, it did its part in building the tremendous cosmos of the modern economic order. This order is now bound to the technical and economic conditions of machine production which today determine the lives of all the individuals who are born into this mechanism, not only those directly concerned with economic acquisition, with irresistible force. Perhaps it will so determine them until the last ton of fossilized coal is burnt.[67]

Weber traces the development of certain attitudes and trends in the practising of work in capitalist societies back to the sixteenth-century Reformation and in particular the development of Calvinistic Protestantism. According to Weber the gradual transposition of vocation as a particular kind of work from monastic to secular contexts was begun by a thirteenth-century German theologian and famously consolidated by a fellow countryman three centuries later.[68] Until the mystic Johannes 'Meister' Eckhardt wrestled the notion of vocation as a call from God away from monasteries and asserted that God could, and did, call lay people to secular work through which they could 'experience the highest ideal of the nearness to God',[69] it was widely thought throughout Christian cultures, right up until the sixteenth century, that only monks could do 'work' because work was 'God's work'.

By the end of the sixteenth century, the idea that a monk alone could experience a vocation was on the wane and with the dramatic intervention of Martin Luther it would come to be all but extinguished in Protestant Europe. In his translations of the Bible, and other biblical texts, Luther introduced the conception of a calling (*Beruf* in his translation) as two-dimensional. On the one hand one could experience a *spiritual calling* to eternal salvation in Heaven and on the other an *external vocation* to serve one another and the world, in short one's profession. Luther's conception of vocation had very important consequences for the development of vocation and its transposition into secular practices because it effectively transplanted an ancient tension within asceticism into non-religious work.

Two competing biblical images of work

The first image of work in the Bible (which within the biblical narrative is *the* first work) is of God creating heaven and earth over six days until 'God ended his work which he had made; and he rested on the seventh day from all his work'.[70] As a part of this work, 'God created man in his own image, in the image of God created he him; male and female created he them.'[71] Lingis assesses the extent to which this narrative produces an imperative, met with by early Christians noting,

> The [early] Christians had located [the imperative] in the creative
> origin of humans and of external nature; for them the dictum
> with which, according to the first chapter of Genesis, the divine
> will creates functioned as a command laid on human thought and
> human intervention in creation.[72]

This biblical image of work as a divine occupation is soon contradicted in Chapter 3 of Genesis where God inflicts work on man as a punishment for eating fruit from the tree of knowledge:

And unto Adam he said, because thou hast harkened to thy wife, and hast eaten of the tree . . . cursed is the ground for thy sake; in sorrow shalt thou eat of it all the days of thy life . . . in the sweat of thy face shalt thou eat bread, till thou return unto the ground.[73]

Contained within these two successive biblical images of work is a paradox of asceticism that runs through notions of vocation as a particular kind of work. The first image of work appears to suggest that there is a holiness to work, since God undertook work to make men and women in his own likeness. So human work recalls divine work and expresses the connection between humanity and divinity. In contrast, the second image depicts work as a punishment, since it is now tied to the processes of living in the world and becomes a necessary condition of earthly life. This seemingly paradoxical conception is at the root of asceticism and the reconciliation of the two images in ascetic practice is performed by focusing on the redemptive capacity of human labour, as succinctly explained by Laurence McTaggart, a monk at Ampleforth Abbey: what we might be tempted to see as a necessary evil or as punishment is in fact the means used by God for our Salvation.[74] Martin Luther initiated the translation of this paradox from theology to philosophy, but given that the existence of a redemptive God does not survive the transplantation of vocation into secular practice, the possibility for the realisation of the first image of work must undergo a transformation.[75] However, it is the second image of work as a 'necessary evil' that tends to define nineteenth- and twentieth-century debates of secular work in the guise of 'alienation'.

Pinning down alienation

The influential economist Adam Smith contended in *An Inquiry into the Nature and Causes of the Wealth of Nations* that the division of labour produced the required conditions for profitable work and the inevitable alienating character of work helped to form the basis of his economic system. Book 1, Chapter 1, begins:

The greatest improvement in the productive powers of labour, and the greater part of the skill, dexterity and judgement with which it is anywhere directed, or applied, seem to have been the effects of the division of labour.[76]

His description of the divided labour in a pin-making factory acts as a 'trifling' example of the division of labour, which would come to be the target of Marxist economic theory:

> One man draws out the wire, another straights it, a third cuts it, a fourth points it, a fifth grinds it at the top for receiving the head; to make the head requires two or three distinct operations; to put it on is a peculiar business, to whiten the pins is another; it is even a trade by itself to put them into the paper; and the important business of making a pin is, in this manner, divided into about eighteen distinct operations.[77]

Smith's conception of divided work seems congruous with the image of labour as a necessary and arduous adjunct to life, and he is willing to accept that its function, though profitable for some, is neither pleasurable nor edifying for those who undertake it. As well as being alienating for this class, divided labour, according to Smith, acts to bring people together only through their opposition and self-interest, because it causes them to interact in occasion of barter and exchange. He points out that

> man has almost constant occasion for the help of his brethren, and it is in vain for him to expect it from their benevolence. He will be more likely to prevail if he can interest their self-love in his favour ... Whoever offers another a bargain of any kind, proposes to do this.[78]

When we undertake to exchange that which we have acquired through divided labour with someone else 'we address ourselves, not to their humanity but to their self-love, and never talk to them of our own necessities but of their advantages'.[79] Smith's endorsement of such an estranging system is founded upon his conclusion that it leads to the greatest generation of national wealth. Marx, who perceived the great inequalities in the generation and distribution of 'national' wealth and the oppressive effect of such a divided labour system on workers, would of course go on to attack this. In contrast to the oft-cited aspects of

Marx's theory of alienating labour that would seem to resonate with Smith's assessment (while disagreeing vehemently with him over the ethics of such a reality) is his much less frequently recited assertion that work can be an act of self-creation and is therefore not just a means to an end, such as production, but an end in itself. Through work, a person is able to reproduce him- or herself and see a reflection of him- or herself in that work when it is placed in the world.

The obstacle to such a form of human happiness for Marx is not work itself, but *the interpersonal conditions under which it is practised* – in short, the division of labour within societies of private property ownership. In his critique of James Mill's *Elements of Political Economy*, Marx notes that, were it not for the phenomenon of private property, 'My work would be a *free manifestation of life*, hence an *enjoyment of life*.'[80] What is more, Marx concludes that beyond the confines of private property and commodity exchange, work undertaken by individuals could fulfil not only individual human happiness but affirm mutual qualities of humanity; 'Our products would be so many mirrors in which we saw reflected our essential nature. This relationship would moreover be reciprocal; what occurs on my side has also to occur on yours.'[81] He imagines the conditions in which 'we' (two human beings) carry out 'our' work not as alienated labourers in capitalist society but as 'human beings' and contends that, in such conditions,

> Each of us would have *in two ways* affirmed himself and the other person. 1) In my *production* I would have objectified my *individuality, its specific character*, and therefore enjoyed not only an individual *manifestation of my life* during the activity, but also when looking at the object I would have the individual pleasure of knowing my personality to be *objective, visible to the senses* and hence a power *beyond all doubt*.[82]

Marx goes on to explain that in the enjoyment of another human being in the product 'he' had created, 'he' 'would have the *direct* enjoyment both of being conscious of having satisfied a *human* need by my work, that is, of having objectified *man's* essential nature, and of having thus created an object corresponding to the need of another *man's* essential nature'.[83]

Linking individual activity to collective human experience, Marx notes that in so doing

> I would have been for you the *mediator* between you and the species, and therefore would become recognised and felt by you yourself as a completion of your own essential nature and as a necessary part of yourself, and consequently would know myself to be confirmed both in your thought and your love.[84]

In a decisive conclusion to a theorised appreciation of the collective experience of work in a group *not* defined by commodity exchange networks but by something more like human togetherness, Marx states, 'In the individual expression of my life I would have directly created your expression of your life, and therefore in my individual activity I would have directly *confirmed* and *realised* my true nature, my *human* nature, my *communal nature*'.[85]

In conceiving of secular work in this way, Marx effectively recuperates some of the edifying quality of work inherent in Book 1's image of work while replacing a redeeming God with 'humanity'. This is done by focusing not on the task of work itself, *but on the conditions in which it is undertaken and what these conditions enable workers to experience and express together.*[86] We can see in the competing ideas of Smith and Marx the recitation of the competing images of work in the first two books of Genesis. It is Marx's assertion that work can perform a function beyond what is necessary and that *in the experience of working* there is the potential for self-expression and a fuller realisation of one's own humanity, which is particularly pertinent to askeology. The faculty of a task to enable individuals to experience, express and realise aspects of their own personality or humanity is vitally important to training.[87] However this requires a focus on the individual experience of work, and for now I wish to maintain focus on the communal quality of work identified by Marx and the social elements of training communities I have been discussing in order to demonstrate how the conditions for such activities of togetherness are neither dependent upon divinity, in an ascetical tradition of work, nor precluded, as Marx would have it, within and by private-property ownership in society.

Three species of work

Hannah Arendt, in her book *The Human Condition*, introduces a useful set of distinctions concerning work by analysing human activities in terms of *labour, work* and *action*. By drawing these distinctions she enables askeology to identify with precision the specific human activities going on in training communities by looking closely at the productive processes they engage. 'Labour', Arendt contended, is cyclical and repetitive. It is connected to the processes of life, growth and death. Labour and labouring leave nothing behind because the materials produced through labour are consumed as soon as they are produced. The cyclical and repetitive qualities of labour reflect the biological processes of life and, in this sense at least, labour has no end. Examples of labour include food preparation, gardening, cleaning and other subsistence activities. The work of many traditional artisans (masons, cobblers etc.) might also fit within this category. In a consumer society we are intended to labour to make a living, and the biological processes of living are extended into our lives in society by our labour.

'Work', by contrast, is teleological. It has a beginning and an end and moves us into the realm of material goods. Through work we produce artificial things that we use but that are also capable of outlasting us. Through fabrication we engage in the process of reification whereby that which is created takes on a life of its own. Labour supports daily life and as such is inherently constructive. Work by contrast has a violent and destruction dimension. Human beings produced tools not only to support life but also to construct the world. Fabrication has a definite beginning and a predictable end. In the utilitarian world of work, things made through work tend to be (or become) both useless and permanent: they take on a particular immortality because they outlast their creators and often even the purpose for which they were created. For this reason, products of work may possess destructive capabilities; as Arendt notes, 'the question therefore is not so much whether we are masters or the slaves of our machines, but whether machines still serve the world and its things',[88] or if they have come to rule and even destroy the world and its things. Unlike labour, whose products are consumed almost as they are created, the products of work linger and resist absorption back into productive processes.

In contrast to both *labour* and *work, action* does not necessarily produce or use materials. Action is unpredictable, irreversible and anonymous. It does not construct, as such, but rather names the transactions that take place between people, in matrices of relationships based on human plurality. Through action we assert ourselves in the world and set in motion that which was not there before. Action takes place in a complex context of already existing relationships. For Arendt, action is never possible in isolation because it involves the presence of another. Work depends upon the materials of nature to produce an object and upon a physical world in which to insert it. Action, however, is not contingent upon nature or the world as such but upon other persons sharing (in) those things. Unlike labour or work it is difficult to define or confine its results. Action essentially describes a species of work which is to be understood as interaction.

Arendt, like Lingis, situates her conception of action in human experience and the images of work in Gensis, drawing out the plurality (and inferred subsequent relationality) on which action relies: 'in its elementary form the human condition of action is implicit in Genesis ("Male and Female created He *them*")' and thus 'the multitude of human beings comes to be the rest of multiplication'.[89] Here Arendt focuses less on the redemptive–punitive dichotomy of work in Genesis, than on the fact that action arises out of the elementary or given conditions of togetherness because of 'the fact that men, not Man, live on earth and inhabit the world'.[90] Arendt refers to the 'miracle of giveness' and calls for the political acceptance of plurality, arguing that the acceptance of difference is not a cause for resignation but the very condition for the uniquely human condition of action.[91] For Arendt, 'life' is the activity that corresponds to labour, and 'wordliness' the condition that corresponds to work. The corresponding condition of action however is 'plurality' – the fact that 'we are all the same, that is, human in such a way that nobody is ever the same as anyone else who ever lived, lives or will live'.[92] This given condition of plurality enables webs of human relationships to be assembled and sustained based on the unique contributions each individual can make within a whole, thus providing the networks required for action. Arendt repeatedly confirms that these webs of human relation-ships are sustained by communicative interaction,[93] and it is this empha-sis on togetherness, interrelatedness and communicative interaction that returns me to the account I gave at the outset of this chapter.

Acting

With the aid of Arendt's descriptive categories it is tempting to describe the time Felton, Joshua, Damian and I spent uprooting dock plants as labour, as a necessary process in the sustaining of life in the monastery. This would have been more obviously so in early Benedictine monasteries that were mostly or entirely self-sufficient, but the fields of Worth are not used to grow food for the community but to stable horses and harvest wood for sale. In spite of this, the labour of uprooting dock plants remains connected to the continued survival of the monks, since the use of the weeded field enables the activities that sustain life to continue. Labour, in Arendt's sense, has a well-established legacy in Christian monasticism, which tends to co-opt and configure labouring practices as ascetic exercises in order to deliver philosophical and spiritual insights. This was, in part, what was occurring when the abbot dispatched Joshua and Damian to the fields; but again it would be easy to fall into the debate over the alienating or enriching quality of toil here, between the two images of work and a consideration of individual rather than interpersonal experience. What an abbot may see as a valuable ascetic practice an observer may perceive as a dehumanising imposition. Although the extent to which the ascetic dimension of such training exercises is to be found in non-religious trainings is not to be underestimated, and will be more completely explored in the chapters that follow, for now Arendt's categories enable me to analyse this activity at a different level and to suggest that the meta-disciplinary form of work overcoding such 'labour' during training is action.

In setting the postulants to work in the fields, while professed monks attend to different tasks about the abbey, the abbot establishes (or rather reaffirms) relationships between postulants and monks, as well as between postulants and monks (and himself) and the outside commu-nity, by defining what they undertake and with whom. In this way the 'unorganised' togetherness produced in the experience of vocational imperatives is given organisation as its conditions of relatedness are mapped into interpersonal relationships. Indeed, action is perhaps the conception of work best suited to describe what occurs because of the relatedness inherent in vocation: as Arendt explains, action, like calling, has a 'linguistic structure'.[94] Her claim that 'most deeds are in the form of words'[95] does not assert, as Seyla Benhabib explains, that speech is a form of action but rather that 'she is claiming that human action is linguistically structured'[96] because communication structures the plural 'public space' in which action occurs.[97] Thus the task of uprooting dock plants is predicated upon and also activates a matrix of interpersonal relationships based on duties by focusing the plurality of individual responsibilities within the monastery. The various tasks that are assigned to community members, which range from keeping the bees, serving the food, cleaning, attending to guests etc., draw into relief the web of interdependent relations between individuals within the community and *the action the group can undertake as a whole by virtue of the interaction of its members.*

Accepting that a certain public space may be operational within the decisively private, exclusive and excluding space of the monastery, as it is within the broad and inclusive territories of a National Health Service, requires an understanding that these public spaces are organised by the unique and personal imperatives experienced by the individuals who constitute them. The case history of JD suggests that the action occurring within these spaces is able to produce effects that could not be produced by the individuals acting alone, and that, while this action is necessarily collective, it may have a specific impact on individuals within the group. Where the action occurring in a field on the outskirts of a monastic estate may give rise to rather intangible effects in the spiritual development of monks, the action occurring on in-patient and out-patient wards where victims of stroke undergo rehabilitation may produce, or fail to produce, rather more dramatically evident effects. If the production of such effects is related to the organisation of interpersonal relationships, then stroke provides the next chapter with an impetus to explore the ways in which communication processes operate to organise, manage and perpetuate the interrelational networks through which action occurs.

4 Obedience

If training assumes its own particular 'public space', this space, or spaces, are always embedded within other broader spaces of a *polis*, where social relations are constructed and reassembled. The 'theatre event' is, of course, thoroughly instituted within the *polis*-space just as 'performance' may, in a certain sense, be the means by which all social relations are conducted. This chapter will describe the 'public space' of training brought about by the action of its members by considering it alongside very *public* situations of theatre and performance – situations we have become accustomed to thinking about through a concept of relationality – and via legal, medical, psychological and ethical frameworks. That training's public spaces are, like the sites of theatre, embedded within other organs and institutions of the *polis* is perhaps nowhere more starkly evident that in the example of stroke, where injury radically disrupts social relations and recovery redetermines them.

In *Ash on a Young Man's Sleeve*, Dannie Abse's part autobiographical novel, Abse tells of how his childhood friend Keith Thomas acquired 'The Black Curse' after being touched by a stranger. The young Abse warns Keith that, should he see the stranger again, the black curse will take effect and tragedy will befall Keith at every turn. After they coincide with the stranger at a rugby international Abse taunts Keith mercilessly for several days, revelling in playing at all kinds of games that have now become too dangerous for the ill-fated Keith even to contemplate partaking in. The pleasure in his role as Keith's tormentor is short-lived and, after reporting his particular delight in splashing in a swimming pool until the skin of his toes and fingers wrinkles, all the while shouting about the dangers of chlorine to a forlorn Keith waiting for his friend in the spectators' gallery, Abse bathetically asks his reader: 'How was I to know that the very next week Mrs Thomas would have a stroke?'[1]

Abse's description of the state Keith's mother is left in after her attack manages to convey some of the defining characteristics of the ordeals of stroke patients from the cruel deficit between the two sides of the body to the limb paralysis and loss of speech:

> Keith's mother, only forty years of age, lay grasping, propped up in one side of her bed with one side of her face and one side of her body paralysed. Her eyes were pulled over so that she was for ever looking towards her right, where normally Mr Thomas slept. She couldn't speak, they said, though she could hear everything. The doctor reported that she had had a large thrombosis in her brain.[2]

The treatment available to Mrs Thomas in the Cardiff of the early 1930s was comparatively minimal and, the following morning at three o'clock, Keith's mother died.

Abse charts the fallout from Mrs Thomas's death through the behaviour of Mr Thomas, his neighbours and his son Keith. The night of her death, Mr Thomas comes through the road drunk and screaming and the whole street locks its doors and pulls down its blinds and 'for as long as two minutes each person thought of his own death and in their hearts it was five-to-three in the morning'.[3] After several weeks of no contact between Keith and Abse, Keith approaches him as he plays in the park:

> 'You killed my mother,' he said.
> 'I did not.'
> 'You did.'
> 'I didn't.'
> 'You did.'
> And then with great effort he added, 'The Black Curse.'[4]

This chapter begins with Abse's account of stroke for several reasons. First, because in it Abse manages to convey some of the key characteristics of stroke that I encountered during my time researching rehabilitation training on a residential stroke recovery ward in Cardiff approximately three miles and seventy-seven years in distance from Mrs Thomas's attack. Statistics suggest that in the UK alone around 130,000 people a year suffer a stroke, and though most are over sixty-five, stroke can and does affect people of all ages and, of those on the ward at Rookwood Hospital where I conducted much of my research, none was older than Mrs Thomas.[5]

It's hard to be prepared for the experience of seeing the physical effects of stroke on someone, particularly someone the same age as you, and Abse's account of his visit to the bedside of (the elderly to him) Mrs Thomas conveys something of my experience of interacting with stroke sufferers in their twenties and thirties. A crucial difference between Abse's account and my own experiences is that, unlike the patients at Rookwood, Mrs Thomas did not receive rehabilitation treatment and did not survive to undergo processes of recovery. Despite this, Abse's account powerfully portrays the wider ramifications of stroke in the sense that the effects of Mrs Thomas's stroke play out in the lives of her husband, son, friends and neighbours. Here, of course, these effects are associated with grieving rather than with recovery, but Abse does convey the radical and wide-reaching effects of stroke on the lives of individual suffers as well as their friends and family.

Abse conveys the inescapable fact that both the cause and the effect of a stroke is *rupture* – the localised rupture occurring in the brain of the stroke sufferer as a result of either a blockage in the blood vessels that supply oxygen and nutrients to the brain (ischaemic stroke) or a bleed from burst blood vessels into brain tissue (haemorrphragic stroke), setting in motion a sequence of ruptures like the epicentre of a seismic shock. The rupture occurring in the brain of Mrs Thomas acts for Abse as a model for rendering the disruptions and interruptions that occur in his local Cardiff community. Through his account he shows how the interpersonal networks of human relations in his Cardiff street – the relationships between neighbours, wives and husbands, children, and friends – are disrupted and reaugmented by the rupture in Mrs Thomas's brain. Abse's awareness of the effect of stroke on interpersonal relations helps me to think through the example of rehabilitation training in stroke recovery in terms of the interpersonal conditions associated with injury.

In addition to these reasons for opening this chapter with Abse's account is the fact that Abse, himself a medical doctor, perhaps due to his evident sensitivity to the ways in which unknown and unanticipated forces affect the lives of individuals, was intimately involved in a conflict over probably the most famous piece of experimental research into obedience, the so called 'Milgram Experiment', which has been so important in shaping contemporary understandings of obedience and which by its very design is tied in to both the theatrical and the askeological.

Abse's 1973 play, *The Dogs of Pavlov*, was written in response to and as direct provocation of Dr Stanley Milgram and his famous social experiments that sought to find the causes for obedience. These started in 1961, three months after the trial of Nazi war criminal Adolf Eichmann began. The experiments were devised to answer the question, 'Could it be that Eichmann and his million accomplices in the holocaust were just following orders?'[6]

Though the design of Milgram's experiment is well-known, its theatrical premise and the particular relevance it has to training warrant special attention. Milgram devised an experiment in which paid volunteers would be asked to administer increasing voltages of electrical current to another volunteer (in fact an actor and member of the experiment team) as and when they failed a simple task. As if the imperative of training was itself an unquestionable incentive, Milgram informed the volunteers that the experiment was designed to test the thesis that humans were able to learn more effectively through punishment, but in reality it was testing the willingness of the volunteer to cooperate with authority when its demands contravened their own stated moral and ethical codes. The surprising results showed that the overwhelming majority administered what they knew to be fatal shocks of 400 volts even when they could hear the screams of the volunteer/actor suffering them. Milgram noted that 'with numbing regularity good people were seen to knuckle under to the demands of authority and perform actions that were callous and severe'.[7] As a piece of 'invisible theatre' par excellence, the screams of an actor have now become enshrined in the history of social experimentation and still, in an exemplary Boalian effect, stimulate discussion today.

In light of his findings, Milgram advanced what he called the 'Agentic State Theory'. He argued that, 'The essence of obedience consists in the fact that a person comes to view himself as the instrument for carrying out another person's wishes, and he therefore no longer regards himself as responsible for his actions.'[8] Further, 'Once an individual conceives his [*sic*] action in this light, profound alterations occur in his behaviour and his internal functioning. These are so pronounced that one may say that this altered attitude places the individual in a different state from the one he was in prior to integration into the hierarchy.'[9] Milgram contended that this shift in state was the consequence of an imbalance in the distribution of authority in organised interpersonal groups.

Abse's play *The Dogs of Pavlov* was published with an introduction by the author entitled 'The Experiment', in which he explains Milgram's obedience experiment and argues that such 'human guinea pig experiment[s]'[10] are unethical because they rely on the volunteer being 'had, hoaxed, fooled'.[11] The central grounds on which Abse challenges the ethical justification of Milgram's experiment is that the 'other volunteer' was 'in on the secret. He was an actor' and his role as the participant who receives rather than administers electric shocks 'was bullshit, a cover story'.[12]

In the 1973 edition of *The Dogs of Pavlov* Abse reprints two letters from Professor Milgram, the first in response to a copy of Abse's critical introduction and the second in response to the play text itself, effectively playing out a dialogue between the two doctors, with Abse's introduction followed by Milgram's first response, and Abse's play by Milgram's second response. This makes the 1973 text a quite rare and interesting document in that it gives each man the chance to respond to the other's position, with Abse (perhaps charitably) giving Milgram the last word – unless, of course, one considers the dramatic statement to be the body of the text, in which case the play really would be 'the thing' and would have, if not the last laugh, then the last scream and the final word on the matter. One of the most fascinating elements in this debate, and the one most relevant to this project, is that both Abse and Milgram stage their conflict on the territory of theatrical illusion and role-playing such that the attitudes we might expect them to hold (as dramatist and scientist) seem to be reversed. Abse challenges the ethical justification for Milgram's experiment on the grounds that it exploits theatrical illusion to put volunteers under moral stress, and Milgram defends his methods with the assertion that, in the theatre, no one would condemn the use of theatrical illusion to bring about intellectual enrichment or revelation. Milgram concedes that there is a difference between the illusion practised in his experiment and that practised in Abse's theatre, observing 'those exposed to your [Abse's] theatrical illusions expect to confront them, while my subjects are not forewarned'.[13] He goes on to contend that the ultimate test of the ethical justification of the deception is to be found in the personal responses of those who were deceived, and to this end he cites 'innumerable conversations'[14] with volunteers in which they expressed to him their pleasure and satisfaction with the experiment. Milgram cites one case in particular, of a volunteer turned Conscientious Objector who wrote to him to express his 'sincere thanks for [Milgram's] contribution to [his] life'.[15] Milgram succinctly states in terms he himself underlines for impact,

> The central moral justification for allowing a procedure of the sort used in my experiment is that it is judged acceptable by those who have taken part in it.[16]

The very fact that an influential artist and an influential social psychologist should conduct a debate over acts of theatrical role-playing is in itself interesting for many reasons, not the least of which is their foregrounding of the ethical responsibilities of the purveyors of illusion. However, the aspect which is of greatest interest to an askeological consideration of obedience is that, while they debate the proper ethical conduct with respect to theatrical illusion, both implicitly assert the capacity of role-playing *itself* to induce certain, potentially harmful conditions.

Milgram and Abse appear ultimately to disagree over the proper ethical use of role-playing and theatrical illusion but implicitly agree on the effectiveness of these elements of performance in producing certain social conditions. While Milgram chooses to focus on the operations of authority and the status of individuals within hierarchies of role-holding individuals to explain the compliance of his volunteers, Abse alerts him (and us) to the effects of role-playing *itself* in inducing certain social conditions, since the conditions of authority and hierarchy cherished by Milgram are not 'really' present, or rather are only really present because they are in fact performed.

Abse's anguish at Milgram's treatment of his volunteers as 'human guinea pigs' is directed at Milgram's synthesising of the forces of stress that have their 'real' counterpart in 'honest' human interaction and at his failure to disclose to those involved the synthetic nature of their lived social conditions. In focusing Milgram's question about why humans behave the way they do in certain circumstances around the fulcrum of 'real' and 'synthetic' situations, Abse calls attention to the theatricality of social experimentation and asserts that the 'real' relationships between individuals are really only those defined by each individual's role performed within a social unit constructed of role-playing individuals. To understand how this will help me to delineate what obedience means in training contexts it is necessary to explain a little of the history of obedience experimentation and theorisation and how more recent thinking on the phenomenon of group-based behaviour has confronted the dispute between Milgram and Abse.

Deindividuation – from disinhibited behaviour to group action

Though Milgram was responding to the immediate events of the Second World War, his concerns can be seen to be part of an established tradition of social-psychology research that looks at the ways individuals act in group situations. In Gustave LeBon's 1895 text, *The Crowd*, regarded as one of the earliest works of social psychology,[17] he proposed that individuals suffered radical alterations to their powers of autonomy when acting as part of a crowd. LeBon proposed that a process occurs when an individual is situated within a crowd which brings about a psychological state of reduced self-evaluation induced by an individual's relationship to and within a crowd. He argued that this state is characterised by a reduction in self-restraint and an increase in 'anti-normative' behaviour, and this has been used to explain the actions of lynch mobs and violent riots.[18] As the discipline of social psychology developed, it extended LeBon's ideas to attempt to explain the seemingly inexplicable actions of men and women when operating en masse. In 1952, Festinger, Pepitone and Newcomb were the first to apply the scientific-sounding term 'deindividuation' to the phenomena that LeBon witnessed in the actions of individuals in crowds. They argued that deindividuation was the consequence of individuals not being treated *as individuals* in crowd situations. Because of this anonymity it was argued that individuals are likely to feel less accountable for their actions and more prone to irrational and disinhibited behaviour.

Later studies, such as Milgram's and Zimbardo's equally infamous Stamford Prison Experiment (conducted in 1969, results published in 1971) attempted to investigate non-crowd-based situations as sources of deindividuation, and looked instead at more formally controlled situations involving interpersonal interaction such as prisons, and scientific experiments themselves. Though deindividuation was a popular focus of scientific research throughout the 1970s, empirical support confirming the effects of anonymity in group situations was not forthcoming and, according to Diener there was virtually no evidence for a *psychological state* whatsoever.[19] In consequence of this lack of evidence, those social psychologists working on group-based behaviour have come to refine the terms of deindividuation, contesting the early claims that a lack of accountability is the key cause of deindividuation, as well as extending Milgram and Zimbardo's assertions about authority. Instead of focusing on anonymity in group-based encounters, studies tended to emphasise a reduction of self-awareness experienced by individuals when in groups.[20]

The extent to which 'disinhibited' behaviour is anti-normative has become a matter of dispute: the disorderly view of crowd behaviour, for instance, stands in contrast to historical analyses of crowd behaviour. George Rudé in his book, *The Crowd in History: 1730–1848*, records that in numerous examples of crowd situations the crowd demonstrates capacity for restraint and orderly behaviour. Ralph Turner and Lewis

Killian's work *Collective Behaviour* shows, also through historical analysis, that crowds often act according to popular principles and consensus. LeBon's view of a hysterical crowd in which individuals act as isolated, disinhibited destructors has now largely given way to the view that individuals in groups *tend to shift from self-directed and autonomous behaviour towards group-defined and guided behaviour*. In contrast to Milgram's claim that the effect of the organisation of a group on individual members is to disinvest them of their inhibitions and enable them to undertake action they would not normally consider undertaking, Tom Postmes and Russell Spears contend that the opposite is true. In their 'Social Identity Model' of deindividuation they assert that deindividuation leads not to a loss of self but to a decreased focus on personal identity, and that deindividuation actually increases responsiveness to group 'norms' which produce controlled rather than disinhibited behaviour. They conclude that the interpersonal organisation of groups leads not to anti-normative and disinhibited behaviour but to structured and purposeful collective action:

> Thus the factors that social psychologists have identified as playing
> a crucial role in the formation of collective behaviour appeared
> to lead to a specific form of social regulation rather than its
> breakdown.[21]

In reaching this conclusion they appear to contend that Milgram's volunteers obeyed the scientist/experimenter not because they had come to conceive themselves as conduits for authority but because, at a certain level, the social unit constructed in the experiment (of which they were part) directed and enabled them to do so. They did not suffer a loss of personal agency as Milgram concluded, but acquired a part in a collective agency as a result of playing a role within an organised interpersonal network.[22] It is the conditions of interrelation and interaction that bring about deindividuation in this sense of social identity, and these conditions are, in this instance, based on theatrically prescribed roles; this is to say that, at a certain level, each volunteer performs a role as 'volunteer' and the particular duties attendant upon the performance of this role, a performance which in turn enables the performance of the other roles within the group. Thus the reason that Milgram's volunteers 'obey' is because the social unit constructed in/by the experiment as it appeared to them (comprised of volunteer, scientist and other volunteer) requires that each member 'play' according to their role in order for the whole to function and to be maintained. It is not so much a case of the volunteer overriding their moral codes or acquiescing to authority as of playing the role of volunteer, whose performance is necessary for the whole unit to act collectively and perform the experiment.

It is evident that this form of obedience in social identity deindividuation is quite different to the obedience one might encounter in conflict situations, in the military, or even at work. In these contexts, 'obedience' affected by coercion, punishment or physical harm is far closer to the realm of 'discipline' Foucault identifies in penal institutions that impose upon the bodies of involuntary prisoners. Obedience, in the sense invoked by deindividuation, arises in contexts that are precisely defined by the voluntary participation of individuals and by the absence of the explicit threat of punishment in the case of a failure to obey.

Obedience, or 'listening to others'

As I have begun to suggest above, 'obedience' is a troublesome word to use because of the range of connotations and associations that situate 'obedience' in a context of discipline and coercion. Obedience would appear to be associated with ethically justifiable coercive action only in the case of children or animals, whose behaviour is determined by obedience to their guardians. A certain sense of 'obedience' is of course tied in with categories of personal choice and the tension between voluntary participation and coercion, categories that are configured in the cases of children, and particularly animals, in contradistinction to adults. For this reason, attitudes about the obedience of animals to humans often exhibit an underlying commitment to a benevolent covenant between 'man' and 'beast'. Examples can be found in discourse on animal training. Steve Lindsay, in his *Handbook of Applied Dog Behaviour and Training*, suggests that 'a coevolutionary process . . . appears to have prepared a biological bond between people and dogs . . . [and] the training process helps to perfect and intensify this evolutionary bond'.[23] Despite the unsubstantiated claims to a coevolutionary process, within the framework established by such an idea Lindsay is able to assert that 'training serves the obligatory role of improving canine life . . . [because] by learning to follow rules happily and obediently, social conflicts are reduced and a leader–follower bond based on affection, communication and trust is allowed to form'.[24] Here, of course, Lindsay is referring to 'canine life' as a socialised existence in which adherence to (adult human) norms and standards reduces conflict, ergo 'improving' things for Rover.

Sociology does not make such wide-ranging value-based claims of improvement in the life of children through societal imposed norms, but it does assert the necessity of leader–follower relationships between adult and 'helpless infant'[25] in its conception of 'socialisation'. Anthony Giddens explains:

> Socialisation amongst the young allows for the more general phenomenon of social reproduction . . . [because] . . . in the early years of life children learn the ways of their elders thereby perpetuating their values, norms and social practices.[26]

The socially reproductive effects of such socialisation mark the co-operative and conformist attitudes and behaviour of children as positive and commendable, thereby rendering 'obedience' as a largely positive or more simply 'good' phenomenon when exhibited by the young. Once the individual personality is developed to adulthood, 'obedience' takes on a new set of connotations, and attitudes towards adult human obedience tend to be uneasy, as is evidenced by Abse's response to Milgram's experiment. However, despite the problems of using such a loaded word as 'obedience' in askeological study, because of the degree to which it can precisely delineate what is going on in the networks of interpersonal interactions assembled in training, I intend to try to define what it could be used to mean to training.

It will probably not be a surprise, given the close attention I have paid so far to the etymology of words in producing some key terms for (and including) askeology, that I am interested in the forms of meaning that might adhere to particular uses of 'obedience'. Obedience would appear to have entered the English language in the fourteenth century, and has at its root the Latin *oboedire* meaning 'to hear and heed' or literally 'listen to', being a compound of *ob* meaning 'to' and *audire* meaning 'listen'.[27] It is this precise etymology of obedience that helps me to describe what occurs as a consequence and continuation of vocation in experiences of training, because obedience is always about individuals within interpersonal networks. The use of 'obedience' to describe a process of 'listening to' recalls the conditions of vocation outlined in the previous chapter but adds to them a quality of agency. As I have already contended, a calling to training contains within it certain conditions of relatedness that can become mapped on to interpersonal networks, thereby conducting a 'personal' experience into a group context. Allied to this is a process of 'listening to' that instates the agency of the individual within the group because it is this *voluntary response* to the networked interrelations within a group that brings about the social identity deindividuation as outlined by Postmes. The social psychological perspective on interpersonal organisation in groups suggests that training's public spaces may give rise to a 'collective' in which individual agencies are invested and within which trainees might suffer a certain deindividuation. The effects of 'listening to' a 'calling' entail *actively* relating oneself within a group and practically responding to the demands of one's role within a given collective. The effect of such deindividuation of group members is perhaps to enable the group to act collectively.

Alphonso Lingis, whose writings on the imperative I discussed in the previous chapter, reminds his reader that, 'in the philosophy of mind no one doubts that thought is subject to an imperative'.[28] He explains that, in thinking, this imperative commands one to reason rightly and to conceive of concepts correctly so that, properly understood 'thought *is* obedience' [*emphasis added*],[29] because as soon as thought begins, 'it does so in subjection to the imperative'.[30] In an expression of the absolute primacy of Kant's Categorical Imperative, and to demonstrate the inadequacy of a treatment that might try to derive the imperative from principles such as the law, he writes, 'The force of the imperative is the command one obeys before one formulates the law'.[31] Lingis's illustrative use of the particular example of the law is particularly relevant to the examples I use in this chapter to help develop the notion of obedience I am proposing. The inadequacy of legal formulations of agency and responsibility properly to account for the kind of 'acting' operational in training, and the necessity instead to ask about the response of individuals to directives set by others in the experience of vocation, will be themes of this chapter.

As has already been noted, Lingis's contention is that lived experience is not a set of reactions to physical causality or the impositions of order on amorphous data, but responses to the directives found in the world and its things. In a depiction of these responses that characterises them as strikingly didactic, he observes that,

> Hang gliders *learn* from the winds and the thermals and from materials the right way to make and to fly a hang glider, as the composer *learns* from the symphony emerging before him which are not yet the right notes. [*Emphases added.*]³²

Extending his examples of response to directives to encompass artistic activity, he draws on the semantics of exploration:

> As for performers there are the right feelings to *find* for every turn in the concerto and dance, there are the right feelings to *find* for an ancient ritual in a sacred space. [*Emphases added.*]³³

In the 'learning from' and the 'finding in', Lingis asserts the relational conditions inherent in one's response to a directive – the ways in which one is compelled to relate to materials, sounds, spaces and others by virtue of the commands a directive places on the individual. The relationships (and the ways for maintaining and engaging these relationships) that an encounter with training forces on a trainee are at the heart of the notion of obedience I am assembling because, as Lingis observes, each directive commands a certain kind of response.

Having worked through psychological perspectives of the effects of acting in groups, and in order to open out the allegorical example of stroke and continue this explanation of a notion of obedience in training, I now move towards the theatrical and performative interests and concerns from which this project was initiated – in this way mirroring the historiographic passage of 'performance' from the theatrical outwards until 'the return of theatre', as forecast by Ridout.[34] This will allow me to incorporate specifically theatrical experiences of training into this developing notion of obedience as a collective response to imperatives and will bridge towards a consideration of the askeological through the conditions of the explicitly theatrical and the implicitly performative.

The example of the workshop: the group

To help explain how such a notion of obedience functions in training I will be drawing on an example from my participatory research: a four-day Butoh dance workshop series with Katsura Kan, organised by Fran Barbe for the Theatre Training Initiative.[35] This disciplinary example will help to show that, in training, there is something going on for an individual that is brought about by their position within a group and that, at a meta-disciplinary level, the experience of training is intimately linked to 'collective action'. The idea of collective action extends what I have already said about Arendt's notion of *work* within interrelated pluralities to show how such work acts to produce an interrelated collective capable of acting as a single entity.[36] This four-day workshop series followed a format with which I was already very familiar – indeed, a format with which most actors, dancers, theatre students, businesspeople and probably countless others are already familiar: the workshop. I don't want to expend too many words on an analysis of the spatial-proximical relationship of individuals within workshops, although I'm sure that this would be very fruitful, but rather I want to focus more keenly on how the relationships within the workshop format organise interpersonal interactions – how they provide the conditions for obedience.

It would not be in keeping with the terms of obedience I am developing simply to look at how I, as a workshop participant, followed Katsura Kan's 'orders', or how Kan delimits the possibilities of what we might do during the workshop by setting certain tasks. Such an analysis would be looking at the levels of discipline within workshop and would likely arrive at similar conclusions as Milgram, but as Postmes and Spears suggest, to understand an individual's experience within particular groups we must remain cognisant of the voluntary nature of their participation, and not assume that they will simply 'do as they are told'. The idea of obedience being developed for askeology here is something quite different from simply doing what one is told to do. In order to show how obedience brings about a process of deindividuation within a training group, and what such deindividuation enables a group to do, it is necessary to describe what occurred over the four days in question. In my description I pay close attention to the main focus of the workshop series, which is the same as *a* main focus of Butoh dance itself: walking.

Hokohtai, the impersonal (universalised) 'walking body', is at the root of Butoh.[37] Sondra Horton Fraleigh, in her book *Dancing into Darkness: Butoh, Zen and Japan*, explains that this uniquely Butoh-ian walk, the *hokohtai*, is central to the dance form. She writes, 'When I perform this Butoh walk, I experience a meditative movement manner of entering the Zen question: What is *mu*? (What is emptiness?).'[38] Precisely what this Butoh walk entails, or even if it *entails* anything, is beyond the scope of this chapter. I do not seek to define it, or impose Fraleigh's definition of Butoh walking on any other Butoh practitioners' notion of their own practice, I simply quote her here to indicate that, just as walking is at the root of her Butoh, so too it formed the basis of Kan's workshop series.[39]

During the four intensive days with Kan, I, along with approximately ten fellow participants, worked to develop a choreographic score essentially consisting of a slowed-down performance of my 'everyday' gait. Each day was book-ended by extensive group warm-up and warm-down exercises, consisting mainly of yoga positions but also of more general stretches and martial arts exercises; but the time in between was primarily spent walking. Kan put us in pairs on each day of the series to help each other master the performance of a 'slowed-down' version of our own walk. The first day started with observation and after each partner was comfortable that they were familiar with their partner's 'everyday', 'real-time' walk we were told to take it in turns to slow down our performance of our own walking gait, with the assistance of our partner. We slowed the walk to half-pace, quarter-pace and eventually about one-tenth of our normal pace. Each person was responsible for correcting any errors in their partner's walking – any movement that deviated from the pattern of his or her 'everyday' walking – either by verbal command or physical touching; and Kan would support this by moving from pair to pair observing first the full-pace everyday walking and then by offering suggestions verbally and by physical contact.

After an hour or so working with a partner, trying to capture the qualities of one's own walk when it was slowed down, the group re-gathered to show our progress. One partner from each pair stood at the back of the studio with all other participants seated at the opposite end. Slowly each standing participant walked from the back of the studio to the front. When all had finished, Kan invited those sitting to comment on what they had seen. Kan asked the sitting participants to pick out who was most 'natural' – that is, who provided the most verisimilar expression of their own real-time gait – and make comments on the success and failures of the walking group. After this was done, the sitting group stood and repeated the walking exercise. After feedback from those observing, all were invited to comment on either the experience of watching or the experience of walking. The subsequent three days followed the same format, although as our mastery of the slow walk improved additional elements were added such that this walk formed the compositional basis of small, improvised choreographies. These choreographies ranged from the inclusion of the activity of 'catching a stone' into our slowed-down walking score to 'imaginatively' incorporating environmental sounds from within the space into our walking – for example, when I hear a car pass by outside the wall to my right as I walk, this might have the effect of pulling my left shoulder backwards, behind me as it were, as I walk to bring it closer to the sound, or I might transform the car sound into an accelerated movement of my fingers.

So what was happening here? It is evident that at a certain level each individual is attempting to master the performance of a slowed-down walk, but this is not all that is happening. The partnering of participants, Kan's guidance and the group feedback periods all point to the fact that the accomplishment of each individual's effort to master their own walk and develop this into a choreographic score was tied into the efforts of the whole group, seeing as each individual was both reliant upon others and relied upon by others in the workshop. The framework of the partnering, and of Kan's interventions within this framework, as well as the group feedback activities, all served to encourage each individual to attune to the efforts of others and to situate their own efforts within the context of a working group. The 'work' of each day and of the series of workshops as a whole is not simply for each individual to master the performance of walking but also for each individual to aid others in their mastery, to respond to them and exchange with them and thus to *play a part in the walking of the whole group.*

Walking together

An entire group is challenged to stomp as firmly as possible on the floor for approximately five minutes in a common rhythm to a set piece of music. At the end of the stomping, the ensemble falls to the ground to lie still, containing mounting exhaustion and gasping for breath, until a second music cue signals a slow rise and steady walk downstage with calm energy.[40]

Above is the academic and theatre director Julia Whitworth's description of the 'stomping and *shakuhachi*' performed in the Suzuki method of performance training. The development of Suzuki's methods has some cultural and historical parallels with the development of Butoh as a performance form – both occurred in twentieth-century Japan and both draw on Noh and Kabuki aesthetics – but it is not these similarities that I am focusing on here.[41] I am more concerned with the relationships between individuals, and between an individual and the group in the performance of training exercises, particularly those that involve 'walking'. It is significant that (as Whitworth notes) Ellen Lauren, a member of the company Saratoga International Theatre Institute (SITI), with whom Whitworth collaborated in the exercise described above, defines training as nothing more than the interpersonal dynamics and shared experiences of individual members; 'Lauren identifies training *as* the infrastructure of the ensemble, the language they share' [*emphasis added*].[42] In her article on the training practice of SITI for *Performance Research*, Whitworth contends that training companies develop, through the organised interactions of individual trainees, 'incorporate identities'.[43] She writes that the conditions for Suzuki's notion of 'personal metamorphosis' attained through his training practice 'ha[ve] to do with the relationship between the individual and the training [understood as a framework of exercises], as well as the individual and the group'.[44] Whitworth explains how the collectivity of the exercise and the relationship between the group and the individual enable the individual participant to accomplish things that they simply could not accomplish alone:

> That which keeps the participant going, even during the greatest moments of extreme trauma, is the collectivity of the exercise . . . Just when the individual cannot continue further, a collective death occurs, as, instantaneously, everyone in the room falls on the ground. Out of this death an impossible new strength is reborn as the challenge to stay together propels the individual past her exhaustion.[45]

Succinctly, she explains that 'as an individual, one could not do it alone; one would not do it alone. In the context of training, of the ensemble, the impossible is achieved.'[46] It is this collectivity of training that forges what Whitworth calls 'incorporate identities' out of the 'intensely relational'[47] conditions of training.

Whitworth is of course not alone in acknowledging the relational conditions of training, or in her appreciation of quite how they operate within ensemble exercises in workshop. Jonathon Pitches's consideration of Meyerhold's biomechanics in an edition of *Performance Research*, 'On Objects', also deals with collectivity in training. Rather than focusing on what is achieved by, or for, the individual within such intensely relational conditions, Pitches is concerned with the collective experiences of the group in Meyerhold's stick-throwing exercises, noting that the ensemble exercise 'absolutely depends on *common understandings*' [*emphasis added*].[48] He concludes that rhythm provides 'the means by which direct and unarticulated understandings are communicated'[49] during ensemble exercises.[50] In so doing, he signals the possibility that task-based exercises, in addition to developing the 'skills' of the trainee, also provide the relational framework for the communication of understandings.

Performance Studies has become accustomed to isolating its objects of study through application of a framework of relational form. Nicolas Bourriaud's *Relational Aesthetics* has provided impetus in this approach as well as a semantic field of terminology for delimiting and discussing interpersonal situations occurring within other broader and more complex interpersonal contexts. As Bourriaud puts it, an artwork is 'the principle acting as a trajectory . . . a linking element, a principle of dynamic agglutination'.[51] Ric Allsopp points out in his editorial 'On Form/Yet to Come' in *Performance Research* that Bourriaud's conceptualisation of the artwork is not altogether 'contemporary' but 'is of course inscribed through a large part of the twentieth century in strategies of art and performance making'.[52] Allsopp goes on to discuss the idea of 'form' in performance, and to situate the articles that follow in that edition of the journal as a matter of *non-matter*. The 'form' of performance, he argues, has undergone a 'dematerialisation' and 'materials and contexts of performance [are] sets of relational processes that reflect the intensities, differences, transformations and translations that constitute the work of performance'.[53] Alan Read, in his more recent writing, has done much to show that such a notion of performance plays a necessary part in 'the social' that looks beyond performance's conditions of relatedness and towards their association with(in) other networks. The social, so understood, 'is the work of 'the tracing of associations',[54] not the goal-oriented work of 'social' theatre and performance that 'announces a premature end to the constant process of collective performative politics'.[55]

Though Theatre and Performance Studies have become accustomed to conceptualising performance as a particularly highlighted and defined network of relational connections, the disciplines have not so thoroughly sought to look at training through such a conceptual framework. Those same relational conditions of the performance object, or more appropriately *performance situation*, structure and delimit training situations but their effects in training situations are crucially different to those in performance. Alain Badiou's 'extraordinarily vague' definition of 'situation' as that which is constituted only by the fact that it possesses an infinite number of distinct components which might include 'words, gestures, violences, silences, expressions, groupings etc.,[56] is especially suitable for describing the *performance situation* which, in all its various styles and genres, might be understood as that which 'presents these elements and not those'.[57] Badiou's 'situation' is concerned with the structure or *organisation* of this infinite number of components and how they relate to one another, because 'the structure of a situation is what specifies it as a particular situation'.[58]

In this sense 'situation' is a particularly appropriate term to describe the kind of artistic practice in question because 'a situation is simply the result of such a structuring'.[59] The 'work of performance', as defined by Bourriaud, would appear to be nothing other than that 'linking element', the defining, delimiting, describing and naming of a relational network – a definition that seems strikingly congruous with Lauren's description of training. Part of the performance situation might also be the articulating of the relational structure conducted by the inhabitation of its related positions by 'actors' over a given period of time. The instating, inhabiting and articulating of a relational network in performance can induce a certain deindividuation, as will become clear, but *only during the performance situation*. The uniqueness of deindividuation in training contexts exists in the sustained and repeated aggregation of the individual agency of group members into the collective agency of the group; as Whitworth explains with respect to the walking of the *shakuhachi*, 'one does not lead the way based on an individual idea or isolated impulse. Instead one *is subject to the will of the group itself*'[*emphasis added*].[60]

Alerting us to the particular character of incorporate identities in training, it is significant that Whitworth should focus on the issue of 'collective will'. Whitworth is vague in her descriptions of the operation of such a collective will, or precisely how it comes into being, offering only a description of it as 'an organic, ever-shifting, non-articulated will'.[61] Her notion of a 'non-articulated will' seems almost contradictory and requires more precise development and description, but her notion of collective willing and collective action provides a way of approaching individual–group experience in training. What is most surprising about her invocation of incorporate identities (and their contingent wills) is the spatial and temporal scope she assigns to them:

> In New York City as well as in other parts of the world . . . there exist communities of theatre artists . . . [that] . . . although not themselves members of the SITI company . . . are also *linked, by their collective experience* and dedication to the training, to the corporeal, even corporate culture of the SITI company. [*Emphasis added.*][62]

The acknowledgement of a global corporate culture is not particularly striking, and Whitworth very briefly unpacks this aspect of incorporate identity noting the necessity of marketing in keeping non-profit experimental theatre alive.[63] What is more unusual and provocative about Whitworth's notion of incorporate identity is that these separate communities are linked by 'collective experience' to a 'corporeal' culture of SITI training. Indeed the penultimate sentence of her article concludes, 'I am, by virtue of even my novice training and subsequent use of it as a director, an initiate to the SITI incorporate identity'.[64] Whitworth's notion that the collective experience of training produces and sustains corporeal cultures – incorporate identities that extend beyond the spatio-temporal confines of a given group exercise – proposes a radical way of thinking about the experience of training.

Precisely how the agglutination of individuals into a single collective, and the corresponding transference of individual agencies to a collective agency, occur in training can be understood through examination of the relational conditions of performance. The process of deindividuation occurring in training extends, recites and repeats forms of related interaction present in the performance situation and in so doing affects its participants at the levels of individual autonomy and generates a collective capable of acting (and being held responsible for action) as a single entity. To explain how this occurs, I refer back to the development of social identity deindividuation theory through the lens of two performances of riot, because a consideration of how legal ascriptions of agency operate with respect to relational phenomena will help to explain how individual agency plays a part in the production of incorporate identities.

The criminal crowd

Book III of LeBon's 1895 text *The Crowd* is concerned with 'The Classification and Description of Different Kinds of Crowds', one such kind being 'Crowds Termed Criminal Crowds'. LeBon appears reluctant to qualify crowds as 'criminal' but 'retain[s] this erroneous qualification because it has been definitely brought into vogue by recent psychological investigations'.[65] For LeBon the qualification 'criminal' is logically tied to individual agency and in this way 'A crowd may be legally yet not psychologically criminal.'[66] In a slightly mystifying analogy intended to illuminate the difference between psychological criminality and criminality in the eyes of the judicial system, LeBon argues that:

> Certain acts of crowds are assuredly criminal, if considered merely in themselves, but criminal in that case in the same way as the act of a tiger devouring a Hindu, after allowing its young to maul him for their amusement.[67]

Although LeBon doesn't explain the precise terms of this analogy, it seems significant that the two members he selects to stand in for a notion of non-psychological criminality in crowds are an animal and a juvenile. In superimposing a legal framework on nature, LeBon appears to suggest that three things strain the boundaries of legal categories of criminality – animals, the young and crowds. LeBon argues for a certain exemption for these three, or if not this then a recalibration of what it means for an entity without developed individual agency to act criminally. LeBon implicitly acknowledges that there is a tension within Western legal frameworks predicated on particular notions of juvenility, animality and collectivity. These frameworks suggest that groups, like animals and juveniles, cannot properly form psychological intentions thought to be necessary for actions (as distinct from behaviours) and thus, though they may be found legally accountable, they cannot be held morally responsible for any harm they cause.[68] Those same conceptions of animals, juveniles and groups that make their 'obedience' productive and virtuous also disinvest them of individual responsibility.

LeBon, in his dissatisfaction with the 'erroneous' qualification applied by his peers to crowds, alludes to the legal reality that crowds *are* frequently held legally accountable, or rather that individuals possessing of individual agency are held accountable for the actions of, or for their actions within, crowds.[69] LeBon's observation of the juridical procedures taken against (adult) individuals acting in crowd-based situations has a stark relevance to the related conditions of performance. Taking as an example the two group-based events of the clash between striking miners at Orgreave coking plant on 17 June 1984 and the artist Jeremy Deller's re-enactment of the 'battle' in 2001 as two different situations of performance, it is possible to see how LeBon's anxiety over moral responsibility and collective action plays itself out in related conditions of performance.

'The miners: united'

> An arm grabbed me around the neck from behind and I was smashed in the face with a riot shield. He encircled my neck with his other arm, took his truncheon in both hands and squeezed . . . My possessions were removed and recorded and I was escorted out to a transit van . . . Eventually we were put into a pig bus and taken to Rotherham. So successful had been their haul that all the cells in Rotherham were full and the twenty or thirty of us from Sheffield were placed in an outside compound . . . The prosecuting solicitor took off his half-glasses, placed them on the desk and read out the charge. I was a Rioter.[70]

Above is the miner Bernard Jackson's account of his arrest at Orgreave on 18 June 1984 and subsequent charging at Rotherham court. Jackson explains that a catalogue of offences for which the group was responsible (and according to Jackson were not perpetrated until after his arrest) such as creating barricades, stretching wires across roads and starting fires was cited against him as an individual before he was remanded to jail. Ninety-five picketers were charged in total with a range of offences including riot and unlawful assembly, and although a number of these were put on trial in 1987 the trial collapsed and charges were dropped. The level of organisation within the picketing group, as could be defined by their membership of the National Union of Mineworkers or simply by their gathering in one place with a 'unified' aim, led to individuals being charged with offences that could only be committed by a group. There seems to be a certain absurdity to the spectacle of the lone Bernard Jackson standing in the dock and hearing a charge of 'unlawful assembly' read against him, yet such an apparent oxymoron has precedent in law.

In Jeremy Deller's 2001 're-enactment' of the riot, often referred to as *The Battle of Orgreave*, similar levels of organisation operate such that the conditions of relation between individuals serve to interconnect individual actions in the production of group action. The re-enactment however operates under a kind of legal dispensation, almost like a Bakhtinian notion carnival, wherein the conditions of relatedness as well as the occurrences of the historical event are dislocated from their political context, and within a discourse of imitation can be played out harmlessly within certain spatial and temporal boundaries. The scope of the dispensation is realised in a quite literal boundary placed around the event, as explained by an event organiser recorded in Michael Figgis's film of the battle, when he announces to the crowd over a PA, 'There are in fact two rope barriers that have been placed in front of you.'[71]

As with Bakhtin's carnival, in spite of the temporary dispensation from normative societal order and the status of the event as performance, or art, the same legal codes that can hold individuals responsible for collective harm continue to operate and apply to the activities of the actors and participants in/during Deller's battle.[72] The aggregation of individual agencies within the collective, but also crucially the assignation of collective agency within the individual, continues to operate. The operation of the same legal jurisdiction (and the relative anxiety about it) within both the 1984 and 2001 battles is evidenced by the statements to camera in Figgis's film of the re-enactment made by an event organiser and a participant playing the role of a miner, respectively

'If anything gets out of hand and it goes over the top, the thing will be stopped.'

'Fuck 160 quid [the fee paid to participants], we're goin' for it! If they throw us off they throw us off.'[73]

The legal status of the 1984 clash between miners and police, as well as the status of the 2001 *Battle of Orgreave*, ensures that an individual can be held legally responsible for action taken by a collective. Crucially though, the legalistic 'deindividuation' in which the agency of the individual actor is related to the agency of a group is restricted to the spatial and temporal boundaries of both these relational situations. The degree to which individual and group agencies are aggregated, in the eyes of the law at least, does not extend beyond the spatio-temporal framework of the event; beyond the ropes placed around the event and the duration of time during which the action unfolds. What is most striking about Figgis's film of the re-enactment is the contrast between the sedate and orderly preparations for 'the big day' and the anticipation, excitement and anxiety that things might 'get out of hand' once the re-enactment begins – a contrast produced, perhaps, by the realisation that once the re-enactment does begin, each individual will become a part of something they cannot individually control and yet may be held personally accountable for.

In contradistinction to this, the status of training as a sustained and repeated enacting of conditions of relatedness results in a more enduring sense of deindividuation and the production of a more lasting aggregation of individual and collective agency in what Whitworth calls 'incorporate identities'. This is affected not only by relational conditions as such but through the self-engagement of individual executive function in interpersonal exercises. The qualities of self-engagement and their dependence upon executive function is perhaps best described through the example of physiotherapy, because in this example legalistic models of individual agency blend into psychological and physiological ones and help to develop a more detailed account of what is required to bring about deindividuation and its conditions of collective action. If the legal culpability of an individual for actions undertaken by a group tells us something about the conditions of relatedness and the distribution of responsibility in performance situations, then the legal process of surrogate consent in medical therapeutics indicates the level of individual agency that is required by the organisation of groups in situations of training. If askeology has any residual anxiety at this stage about those who don't have a voice within it, or those who don't have a 'right of reply', such anxiety can see itself reflected in rehabilitative training in the experiences of those who literally cannot speak for themselves.

Surrogate consent

James is a young man resident at Rookwood who has suffered a severe cerebrovascular accident that has resulted in surgery to remove part of his brain.[74] It is not clear exactly what caused James's stroke, mainly because he was found alone, collapsed in his home. As a consequence of his accident he is now almost completely unable to move his body and suffers significant muscle tightness which, if left untreated, would result in tissue atrophy. As a result, like most stroke patients, James practises a series of stretching exercises first thing in the morning and at periodic intervals during the day in order to lengthen his tightened muscles, arrest the onset of paralysis and attempt to produce movement and mobility gains.

It is possible that though James (like Mrs Thomas) cannot speak, he can hear everything. He is responsive to an extent (he has been observed yawning, and he occasionally groans during uncomfortable treatments), but the therapists working with James have not yet found a way to properly communicate with him. In the conviction that he may 'have sound' even if he doesn't 'have speech' they keep up a constant monologue in which they inform James of what they are doing and why. Given the extent of James's disability, he is unable to practise what therapists call 'active movements', meaning that, in the practising of his stretching exercises he must be manipulated and supported by a therapist and a technician.[75] The fact that James has to be treated through 'passive movements' (movements supported by a therapist) and the fact that he cannot communicate his relative discomfort during these painful exercises means that the rehabilitation routine designed for him has had to be the product of 'surrogate consent'. Surrogate consent is the medical term used to describe consent given by a patient's guardian or guardians in cases where an individual is incapable, because of a lack of executive function, of giving consent directly.[76]

> Executive function is a concept meant to capture the highest
> function of cognitive abilities. The type of cognitive operations
> thought to be 'executive' in nature allow us to act and control the
> enormous number of internal and external representations available
> to us that are necessary to guide our behaviour in time.[77]

Mark D'Esposito gives the above definition of executive function in the conclusion of his article 'Executive Function and Frontal Systems' in *Neuropsychiatry*, though he arrives at this after debating the 'wide range of cognitive processes, such as focused and sustained attention, fluency and flexibility of thought . . . in planning and regulating goal-directed behaviour'[78] included under the rubric of 'executive function' in neuropsychological literature. These 'highest levels' are of course routinely denied to animals and minors in cases where veterinarians and paediatricians locate these functions in people who are, in a legal sense, their 'owners'. If modern humans are reluctant in assigning agency to children, or animals, then they are also indisposed to withdraw it, and the sovereignty attendant upon it, from adults.

Though the bioethical question about the 'right to die' places the medical tenet of the right to refuse treatment under strain, the attempts of the medical profession to give voice to those without speech have endeavoured, via somewhat Stanislavskian-dramaturgical modes of 'building a character', to uphold the sovereignty of the individual in the right of refusal even if not in the right of annihilation. While the character built has this one key element of a will to live (or rather, not die) determined for them by the authors of their treatment, in other respects the characterisation of the silenced patient can, within certain parameters, resemble the pre-accident self. The procedures of surrogate consent invite relatives, guardians, spouses and medical specialists to respond to distressing articulations of 'magic if'-type questioning and to provide answers that will have decidedly 'real' consequences in determining the intensity and frequency of the stretching exercises as well as other equally formative but unequally painful activities such as day trips and music or drama therapy.

If, in the theatrical and more broadly performative examples of rioting, the individual is understood to be a stakeholder in an albeit transiently assembled group, then in rehabilitative training the group requires the continued expression of the will of the individual even if, in the surrogate-consensual example, elaboration of theatrical modes is required to support this. Where the temporary involvement of individuals with one another in a group might characterise the relational aesthetic of a theatrical or performative event, the continued investment of the individual will in the activities of the collective could characterise an experience of training – and the importance of this experience may be testified to by the lengths to which groups will go to give voice to each member.

To reflect on the less dramatic even if no more theatrical, Whitworth's notion of incorporate identities incorporating individuals who do not come into direct physical contact but are corporeally linked through a collective experience of practice, suggests that training collectives do not suffer the same spatio-temporal constraints placed on performance. Pitches adds some weight to Whitworth's hypothesis by analysing how the 'common understandings' fostered in biomechanical exercises are evidenced beyond instances of training in performance situations. Citing contemporary reviews of Meyerhold's productions, he observes that 'connection[s] between the training and the productions remain largely implicit in the production analyses'.[79]

After citing how the critic Alexei Gvozdev 'marvelled at the sympathetic unity of the collective movement of the three actors, which was completely synchronised',[80] Pitches takes on the task of explaining quite how such 'collective movement' is transposed from the relational conditions of training exercises into the relational framework of performance, and he suggests that the synchronised action results from training exercises 'demanding the kind of collective responsibility'[81] he describes. When a stick is dropped in training the whole group stop and regroup, gathering up any dropped sticks so that the whole group can recommence. From this observation, Pitches's idea of 'collective responsibility' extends Whitworth's assertions for collective will in noting that any such form of agency must necessarily bear a contingent responsibility: 'the *responsibility* for accurate throwing and catching thus becomes collective' [*emphasis added*].[82]

Whitworth's assertions about incorporate identities possessing collective will and Pitches's observation that with will comes responsibility, pose interesting questions for Performance Studies, with its concern for relation form: what forms of 'acting' operate in performance – understood as a relational aesthetics – and in what ways can we describe acting relationally? The 'dematerialisation of performance object'[83] occurring in areas of contemporary practice has not only challenged our formal conceptualisations of theatre, but undermined previously stable understandings of the acting that has long been its paradigmatic practice. This perhaps enables us to understand why Nic Ridout's attention, while seated in the audience of a production of Pinter's *The Caretaker* in 2001, is arrested not by the 'actorly' performances of Douglas Hodge and Michael Gambon, but by their 'non-human performer' co-star: the mouse that makes 'an entrance from downstage left'.[84] Ridout holds back, perhaps because of the negative connotation of 'theatricality' he identifies, from calling this mouse a non-human *actor*, but nonetheless sets about describing how 'its *activity* was matrixed' [*emphasis added*][85] within both the fictional setting of the play and the deep mythology of acting, such that ironical hypotheses about the Equity status of the mouse and its forthcoming Broadway tour are stimulated.[86]

If accounting for the various objects and situations of 'performance' in the age of relational aesthetics has become a challenge, then taking account of the variety of acting in/for/by such an aesthetic has become a necessity. This challenge was faced in 2009 at 'The Centre for Excellence in Training for Theatre' at Central School of Speech and Drama, during a conference appropriately called 'How to Act',[87] during which theatre makers, thinkers and writers assembled to talk about what acting means at this historical moment. Recognising that understanding acting is not a matter of *defining* what it is, but of *describing* what it is in any given context – and as Bruno Latour has made clear, 'if a description remains in need of an explanation, it means that it is a bad description'[88] – askeology is faced with the challenge (and necessity) of describing the acting within and of a group.[89] If the medical example of surrogate consent and its proximity to bioethical questions about the right of refusal highlights the agency required for an individual to matrix themselves within the action of a group, in the same way that spatio-temporal situations of performance matrix actors, then it also draws our attention to the need for a discussion of the ethics of the distribution of responsibility within groups. Where 'collective' offences such as rioting or unlawful assembly might have their boundaries firmly located by the law, the perimeters and parameters of responsibility and its distribution in the action of groups assembled as non-temporary consociations might be less clearly defined.

Collective acting

Accounting for the ways groups act and for individuals acting within groups has proved to be a problem not just for Theatre and Performance Studies, or for the juridical system, but also for philosophy. The apparent paradox in the image of the lone individual being charged with riot is at the heart of several philosophical controversies surrounding collective acting. As with legalistic conceptions of responsibility and blameworthiness, philosophical debates about collective action focus on causality and morality. However, unlike the personal responsibility evoked in certain notions of theatrical acting as well as in the juridical processes named above, collective action does not associate either causality or responsibility with discrete persons or the free will of individual agents.[90] Instead, blameworthiness and causal responsibility are associated with groups and the responsibility accorded to collective actions is located in them as collectives.[91]

I have taken pains to state in this chapter that the notion of obedience I am developing should not be thought of as the kind of obedience evoked in penal institutions and in other contexts that operate by coercion and punishment, and this is because the voluntariness (as a thing bound up with executive function) is contingent with collective acting. In his generally sceptical article 'Collective Responsibility' in the *Journal of Ethics*, Jan Naverson proposes that a consideration of voluntariness of membership is required in assigning responsibility for actions taken by groups. He distinguishes between four different types of groups: fully voluntary groups; groups that are involuntary in entrance but voluntary in exit; groups that are voluntary in entrance but involuntary in exit; and those groups that are involuntary in both respects. Naverson contends that responsibility is diminished, and perhaps altogether eradicated, as one moves down this list. Naverson's list provides useful criteria by which to define the conditions of 'incorporate identities', criteria that also help to describe the forms of groups that could be named as such. To help to contribute to the definition of obedience in training contexts I note that all the disciplinary examples of training I analyse in this book are voluntary in entrance and exit, and as such qualify in Naverson's terms as 'fully voluntary groups', even though the monastic and the rehabilitative suggests that these categories might require a little more definition.

Philosophers such as May (1987), Bratman (1993), Velleman (1997), Gilbert (2000) and Corlett (2001) have contributed to a developing definition of the conditions in the kind of groups Whitworth suggests by her 'incorporate identities' and these thinkers have produced descriptions of the conditions and qualities of a group with a collective will. Confronting the classical methodological individualism first properly articulated by Max Weber in 1914, and by H.D. Lewis in 1948, and its rejection of collective responsibility on the grounds that groups cannot think as groups and thus cannot be said to formulate intentions traditionally thought to be necessary for actions (as distinct from behaviours), May, Bratman, Velleman and Gilbert set about defining how collective intentions are formulated and how they enable group action.[92] Angela Corlett also sets out to describe how intentionality needs to be understood in relation to groups, and how it relates to a notion of collective agency:

> [A] collective (intentional) action is an act the subject of which is a collective intentional agent. A collective behaviour is a doing or behaviour that is the result of a collective, though not the result of its intentions. A collective action is caused by the beliefs and desires (wants) of the collective itself.[93]

In her consideration of intentions and behaviours, Corlett is explicit in her argument for genuine collective will, which she depicts as bound up in 'beliefs and desires' held by the collective itself. She thus echoes

Whitworth's assertion that collective will can be 'organic' and 'ever-shifting' in accordance with the evolving wants of a group, but shows that collective will must necessarily be articulated to be intentional.

Margaret Gilbert, in her consideration of collective action, utilises Durkeim's theory of 'social facts' to develop what she calls a 'plural subject account' of shared intentions to justify group actions as intentional, not behavioural.[94] Like Michael Bratman, she does this by looking at joint commitments, arguing that group intentional actions occur when two or more persons constitute a plural subject of an intention to carry out an action; 'they are jointly committed to intending as a body to do A'.[95] Being 'jointly committed as a body' is quite literally manifested in the passive stretching exercises performed by James, his physiotherapist and technician. In these exercises the commitment of each individual to a collective body (assembled not only with but *by* an intention to do something) is manifestly played out on the actual body of one of its members.

This kind of collective subjectivity manifest in rehabilitation is congruous with the notion of a 'truly plural' subject that David Velleman describes as '[involving] two or more subjects who combine in such a way to make one subject',[96] particularly when one considers the stretching exercise from the point of view of consent discussed earlier – in the case of James's surrogate consent, his family, as well as his physiotherapists, combine with him to produce a single collective subject which recuperates the loss of executive function suffered by James. Like Velleman and Gilbert, Larry May employs social theory (Jean-Paul Sartre's existential relational theory) to argue that groups can perform actions in cases where individuals are related to one another and act in ways together that would not be possible if they were to act alone. For him, groups that are so organised are not trans-individual but relational, and as such can be said to act collectively. His description of the facility of relational acting appears to account for both the passive nature of James's stretching exercises as well as his surrogate consent by considering group experience in terms of what it activates and enables rather than what it precludes or delimits. Furthermore, his focus on the enabling qualities of particularly related groups helps to explain Whitworth's astonishment at the 'impossible new strength reborn' out of the collective death in Suzuki training, and informs her claim that, in the context of a relational ensemble, the impossible is achieved.[97]

May also asserts that a condition of groups that are capable of collective action could be that some individuals be authorised to represent their own actions as the actions of the group as a whole.[98] An analysis of the prevalence of this condition in training case studies could be valuable to askeology, provided it could circumvent the tendency to see groups as 'institutions', because by focusing on 'action' taken by an individual May asserts the necessity of thinking in terms of what people do – the roles they play rather than what they are (i.e. the roles they hold).[99] The necessity of avoiding focusing on institutional roles is suggested by Whitworth in her observation that the 'intensely relational' conditions of SITI's training are particularly evident in regard to the 'teacher/master/leader [conducting the training exercise] in the room – a leader who is not, significantly for SITI, the company's director'.[100] Here Whitworth observes that the hierarchically organised institutional roles of a (professional) company such as SITI are not necessarily enacted in all or any of the experiences of training exercises, which may draw different 'leaders' from within a group, or operate an ensemble structure. In this observation, Whitworth invites her reader to think about the 'collective physical experience'[101] of training which forges incorporate identities in distinction to the holding of professional roles with a more literally understood (business) corporation.

Raimo Tuomela makes a defence of collective responsibility in his 'we intentions', although, unlike Gilbert, he does not propose the subject in question to be pluralistic: in fact the opposite. Instead he argues that collective intentional agency supervenes on individual intentional agency in ways that justify talking about both collective intentions and collective actions. He argues that collective intentions supervene on individual intentions to the extent that the intentions, beliefs and desires of particular collectives are 'embodied in' and 'determined by'[102] intentional actions, beliefs and desires of individual members of the collective in question.[103] In this statement, Tuomela gives an account of the individual with respect to the group and contends that the collective action (though genuinely collective) is embodied in the individual, which perhaps helps to explain quite how spatially and temporally separated individuals, such as students of SITI Whitworth describes as being spread across the globe, can be 'linked by their collective physical experiences . . . to the corporeal'[104] incorporate identity of the collective.

These forms of collective acting in training groups cannot be described by recourse to a purely aesthetic relationality assembling under the sign of a benign 'linking element' because not only are the conditions of relation voluntarily and intentionally assembled, but because the kind of acting made possible by these conditions has – as Corlett et al. have shown – a moral dimension. Alan Read's use of 'plasma' to represent the medium in which conditions of relations are assembled is perhaps more useful here, recognising as it does the productive capabilities of relationality – that relations do not just link pre-existing entities but can 'give rise' to new things.[105]

John Law and Michael Callon in a paper 'On Qualculation, Agency and Otherness' propose that the assembling of relations makes certain action, or rather agency, possible and thus raises the possibility of newness, and crucially for them this agency is necessarily collective. The assembling and operation of situation-specific productive relational conditions, which they call qualculation, can be 'understood as a process in which entities are detached from other contexts, reworked, displayed, related, manipulated, transformed and summed in a single space',[106] and the action that takes place 'within' such qualculative spaces 'is a function of the material arrangements, including bodies, in which they are produced'.[107] This idea of 'space' is compatible with the spatio-temporal scope assigned by Whitworth to incorporate identities, because the space and time 'frame' of a given qualculative situation is equally broad. One example of a qualculative space given by Law and Callon is the 'telethon' that runs for a whole weekend through 'a whole lot of . . . events around France'.[108] Even accepting the durational nature of much performance work, Law and Callon's notion of space would seem to transcend a merely *aesthetic* relationality, referring instead to genuinely co-dependent relations with much more at stake, because in such a space relations proliferate – 'everything is being connected with – and made dependent upon – everything else',[109] such that 'what's happening is that a *collective actor* is being created out of a motley crowd (of now visible) individual actors' [*emphasis added*].[110]

If these motley crowds resemble in one way or another the criminal crowds that first occupied social psychology, they may produce an actor in a sense evoked in the traditions of impersonation that have persisted through Milgram's social experimentation. The techno-organisation of the contemporary mob that now appears not to lynch but rather in a *flash* still, as Facebook-organised 'parties' have shown, has the potential to stimulate criminal activity even if it is legally restricted and eminently containable.[111] While organised and orchestrated group phenomena such as Deller's *Battle of Orgreave* may matrix the activities of numerous actors, the strictly patrolled border of their matrices highlights a certain *mise en scène* within the spaces of a *polis*, and their spatio-temporal restrictions may prevent them from constructing a rather more enduring 'stage set' without which, according to Arendt, 'man cannot live'.[112]

Arendt makes use of what might seem like a rather old-fashioned theatrical metaphor of a stage set to describe the kinds of conditions in which human beings act together and produce new things, but her notion of public space, like Law and Callon's qualculative space, properly de-territorialises space as we might now expect performance to dematerialise the art object. Even given our reluctance to endow animals or children with proper agency, we can see that, as actors within a relational aesthetics, they may be – as is the case with Ridout's *Caretaker* mouse – matrixed within a situation in a way that simultaneously empowers them as purposeful or meaningful while remaining largely indifferent to their will. The legal perils haunting Deller's re-enactment suggest that within such a matrixed situation individual actors are invested with a responsibility (which is usually attendant upon agency) that perhaps overdetermines their influence on or within the group. While these individual actors may accrue agency and responsibility within the situation that goes beyond that which they possess outside it (especially in the cases of the perennially excluded animal and infantile), their matrixing within theatrical spaces of the *polis* does not produce a collective actor in the way that the public space of action can. For where the theatrical may outline a set within the biopolitical stages of the *polis*, action constructs a new stage set wherein groups themselves can act.

Taking on some of Law and Callon's assertions about qualculation, in a limited sense of a networked space that focuses on humans and their relationship to one another, Arendt's idea of action and *natality* can help to explain the formation of a collective actor through obedience and the agency unique to such an entity.[113] In her biography of Rachel Varnhagen, Arendt writes that human life requires a stage set and that the world 'is only too ready to provide another if a person decides to toss the natural one, given him at birth, into the lumber room'.[114] The 'natural' stage set to which Arendt refers is the given conditions of plurality caused by human birth wherein she locates the 'human condition' and which provides the model for the other stage sets provided by the world, perhaps best understood as various bio-political domains.[115] Within these bio-political domains 'public spaces' can open out. As with Law and Callon's notion of space, these are not, as Benhabib explains, spaces in any topographical or institutional sense, but rather emerge 'whenever and wherever men act together in concert'.[116] These spaces are not given, but rather arise because of the presence of a common action, and like qual-culative space they are both the object and the location of an 'action in concert'[117] and also, like them, can produce new things. The assembling of such public spaces in and by training – their *form*atting – makes acting, in the finest tradition of mimesis – a process of producing something new – possible,[118] and this leaves askeology with the task of describing how a *collective actor* is '*form*atted', to use Read's televisual rhetoric of plasma, in performance training.

 Formation

The 'form' of an exercise, understood as the organisation of bodies and body parts, through time and space, has dominated accounts of actor training since at least as early as Stanislavski's chapbooks and arguably as far back as Quintillian's first-century treatise on rhetoric, *Institutio Oratoria*.[1] In this chapter, more contemporary concerns about the 'formatting' of social spaces, stimulated by a relational view of performance and of the body, are interwoven with the prevalent interests in form as a 'structural' phenomenon through an account of the meta-disciplinary process of 'formation'. That it is only now, in its fifth chapter, that this book arrives at exercises, which have provided flesh and bones to training discourse and bread-and-butter to theatre scholarship, is testament to askeology's commitment to asking the *first* questions about training in much the same way that today's 'ethical consumers' seek after the origins of their food. The analogy of consumption might not be an altogether flippant one, seeing as askeology's concern for the meta-disciplinary processes of training might be performing a certain 'ethical sourcing' in going to the roots of our usage of the word 'training' and inviting practitioners and theorists to consider what they have on their plates.

Where a preoccupation with 'sourcing' may have become a ubiquitous concern for the developed world and compelled those of us who live in it to trace the passage of our food and clothing back to their origins, perhaps the time is also right now for a sourcing of the ideas in circulation in Performance Studies which has, like Western economies at large,

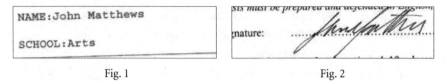

<table>
<tr><td>NAME:John Matthews</td><td>sis must be prepared and defended in English</td></tr>
<tr><td>SCHOOL:Arts</td><td>nature: ....</td></tr>
</table>

Fig. 1   Fig. 2

made a great deal of product from other people's raw materials. Going 'back to the roots' in theory, as in other aspects of culture, does not of course entail 'getting to the truth' but rather getting closer to a beginning which might put where we are at now in a certain context. So this chapter attempts to put first-things-first by taking an allegorical example from the earliest stages of the professionalisation of my own expertise and thus from the beginning of the gradual acquisition of the specialist training which, as a fellow professional has observed, is necessary to secure a live-lihood in the modern world. This example comes from my doctoral training which, because of its pedagogical context, allows a meditation on a quite literally *primary* exercise: handwriting.

The images in Figures 1 and 2 show my full name, typed and signed on my application to register for a PhD with the University of Surrey. If primary school was the site wherein I learned to write my name and developed the skills to manipulate a primary site of meaning – the page – then these skills have accrued new potency for me working in a discip-line that, as Ric Allsopp has put it, sees 'the page as a site of performance'.[2] That the site of language's inscription may be viewed *as* performance rather than *for* performance, as Allsopp suggests, evinces the concerns of a contemporary moment of performance, but askeology's concern with the example of writing, characteristic of its *a priori* questioning, is some-what older or *before.*

Heidegger commented on the bond between writing and the hand, foregrounding man in the word and the word in man in much the same way as the biblical narrative; when 'in the beginning was the word'[3] and the world was *transformed*, having been 'without form'.[4] That, within this narrative, *form* emerges as elements that are produced as distinct from one another – heaven, earth, wetness, dryness, day, night, the seasons – provides one (albeit problematically creationist) model through which to think about forming, just as the 'formal' regulations of the PhD thesis provide another.[5]

The hand is, together with the word, the essential distinction of man . . . Man does not 'have' hands, but the hand holds the essence of man, because the word as the essential realm of the hand is the ground of the essence of man.[6]

If words invite interpretation then Heidegger's *man who does not have hands*, in today's culture of the mediatised image, puts me in mind of various images of men who, partly because of their lack of hands and partly because what this has in Platonian readings of appearance been taken to mean, will not be considered *proper men*. The ostracising of such a group has been traced historically by Erving Goffman who tracked the notion that bodily signs 'expose something unusual or bad about the moral status of the signifier'[7] back to the ancient Greeks through the concept of 'stigma' and its association with Platonic claims that 'it doesn't appear . . . that a sound body makes a good soul, but on the contrary, a good soul by its own virtue provides the best possible body'.[8] The cinematic terrorisers of *The Fugitive* and *Peter Pan* – 'the man with one arm' and Captain Hook – share a space with the altogether more 'real' villains of global terrorism such as the silhouetted 'Detainee P' or the animated Abu Hamza who gesticulate on the flat screens that simultaneously bring terror and entertainment into the home.[9] That these men find themselves without hands implies that they find themselves without language and, like the other beasts who are without words, cannot pass as properly human. The plasmatic quality of these images directs Heidegger's concern for an ecology of the word – 'the essential realm of the hand' – towards a very contemporary notion of writing, where the simple forms of letters operate not within 'a static body of convention, but a nexus between large areas of contemporary practice'.[10]

The relationship between the simple forms of letters and the complex formatting of plasmatic space provide ways to gain some traction on the relationship between the 'structural' forms of exercises and the organisation of public spaces in training. The metabolic and ecological view of writing – that notation entails an 'active and material engagement of the reader in the writing of the page'[11] – helps one to think through the meaningful communicative and hermeneutic functions of training exercises in structurating (or *formatting*, as Read would have it) public space. Handwriting exercises also call our attention to the complex question of materiality because written language takes the form of marks on a surface, while the materiality of spoken language takes the form of modulated and interrupted breathing and is even conducted across the material of the body.[12] Plasma is, as Read suggests, a richly descriptive term for the environment in which relational conditions take form because it already 'carries with it the implication of a moulded or formed thing'.[13] Unlike the idealised empty space, presumed by theatre since Brook, into which elements are *introduced* – 'I can take an empty space . . . a man walks across this empty space'[14] – in plasma, all the elements are already present and particularly configured, already *formed*. The empty space and plasma do not represent observable or measurable phenomena but rather two different conceptualisations of *how things happen*; and if, as Read suggests, plasma is only an updated version of the 'ether' that once accounted for the effective milieu in which phenomena occur, then Brook's 'empty space' becomes the vacuum of the same scientific tradition that nature reputedly so abhors and that the actor, being at first evacuated from it, is somehow called to fill again, rushing in like air.

Addressing this debate between what he sees as the 'formalism' associated with 1970s structuralism and 'contemporary performance' practice 'informed by a relational view of performance as a shared moment of becoming, an event within an always wider and more complex set of associated processes', Ric Allsopp argues that 'form . . . is perhaps no longer to be used in its more conventional association with the imposition of fixed organisational frameworks . . . but in an active sense of processes of formation'.[15] Nicholas Ridout, echoing Allsopp's perceptions of the current 'state' of theatre, argues that 'modern work' such as Handke's *Offending the Audience* (1966) and Forced Entertainment's *First Night* (2001) takes 'articulating anxiety about its own form as its central subject matter'.[16] In the context of this 'modern' experience, Ridout reads Alison Hodge's assertion that the schools, academies, laboratories and theatres, wherein actor training becomes situated in the twentieth century, 'ultimately prepare the actor for work'[17] as an acknowledgement of the alienating working conditions of 'the actor in the modern city'.[18]

Drawing on Arendt's notion of action as a particular formation of work, this chapter asks if Hodge's assertion may be rethought so that the work to which it refers is not the straightforwardly alienated labour of the 'modern actor', or tied exclusively to the schools, academies and laboratories in which actor training has reportedly found its twentieth-century home. Given what has been discussed in the previous chapter, askeology is challenged to describe both the formatting of group relations that constitutes a collective actor, while also taking account of the fact that (theatre) training also forms the individual actor. Re-formations within plasma are not only productive at the level of the network or collective, but also effective at the level of the individual: in forming a collective actor, performance training (and theatre training in particular, and most literally) also forms individual actors.

The poet and literary theorist Lyn Hejinian goes some way towards unscrambling the formation of individual and collective in contending that 'form . . . is an activity'.[19] The active dimension of form suggests not only the formatting activity occurring around the collective, but also the activity of bodies-in-action, active within such a relational network. Despite all post-structuralism's assaults on 'formalist' meaning-making and semiotics, it is particularly pertinent that a literary theorist should join this discussion, since literary theory, and writing in general (including its 'performative' attempts) still relies on written form. As grammatology from Gelb through Derrida to Ulmer has attempted to differently connect and unpick the correlation between speech, writing and knowledge, it has been, and still remains beholden to 'the word' as both its critical focus as well as its modus operandi.[20] The interpersonal and individual experience of written language helps to show how form, as an activity, is involved in the 'task', to recall Mol and Law's terms, of holding oneself together, incorporating as well as excorporating certain elements and activities.

Shortly after the extract cited above, taken from his *Parmenides*, Heidegger goes on to lament that the typewriter tears writing from the realm of the hand and turns it instead into something 'typed'. Steven Connor, in his paper 'Modernism and the Writing Hand' observes that Heidegger's despair at the disruption of the stylus by the typeset has proved decisively authoritative in subsequent considerations of the technology of writing. Connor himself expresses confusion that typewriting should be perceived as so alien in a culture that also contains piano music, and writes that 'one of the ways that one might interpret this new writing technology is as a new modality of music'.[21] Without wishing to enter into the debate about the different qualities of interplay between the meaning-maker and the writing surface in the examples of handwritten and hand-typed language, I would like to take on board Connor's assertion that these technologies are ultimately different modes of the same practice and that, in writing a letter by hand, for example 'o', or striking the 'o' key on a typewriter or keyboard, one is still engaging in the *activity* of forming 'o'. This activity has, as Heidegger and Connor discuss, itself evidently been trans*formed*, but something of the task of forming demanded by 'o' endures such that the (literal) form of the letter on the page in both the typewritten and handwritten example is apprehensible to a reader as 'o'.

Taking the example in Figure 2 of my name, printed on my application to doctoral study and alongside it my handwritten signature, without wishing to open up a discussion of the *efficacy* of these two modes of writing (given that it appears that only my handwritten signature can actually stand in for me, represent me, or represent on my behalf) I would like to focus on the form of the 'o' in both of these images. My experience of forming the typewritten 'o' is different, though not completely distinct from my experience of writing 'o' by hand: in the first I reach with the second finger of my right hand across the keyboard, and with my palm resting on the table depress the key that easily yields to my touch. In the latter, I take a pen between my thumb and index finger bracing it against my second, and, with palm rested on the page, move my thumb and index finger together through a small partnered pirouette. Despite these differences, in both cases I am engaging in the activity of forming an 'o': my actions are intentional and efficacious in each modality to produce the same (or perhaps only equivocal) effect.[22] The alterations that so vexed Heidegger brought about in the formation of letters by the typewriter are, of course, as Connor has shown, not unprecedented. However, even Connor's focus on parallel examples of mechanical extensions of the hand ignore the rather more obvious, and rather more extensive modal differences in the formation of letters.

The two images shown in Figures 3 and 4 depict two rather more famous 'o's in an altogether more notorious name than my own, Guy or Guido Fawkes. Like the two images of my own signature, there is a certain modal difference between the performances of these two signatures, although here the different modes are not the result of mechanical intervention (in the act of writing at least) but of an altered metabolic state. The two images above show the signature of Guy Fawkes signed on two separate confessions made eight days apart. The image on the left (signed first and dated 9 November 1605) shows Fawkes's signature after torture, and the image to the right shows Fawkes's signature after an eight-day period of recovery (dated 17 November 1605). Labouring under the different 'tasks', as Mol and Law would have it, of keeping himself together in two different situations, something endures, some written form of his own name – which should be understood as the *activity* of writing his name which includes but is not simply the letter and word-forms produced on the page – is *practised*, with differing but not totally differentiated results.

There is of course the 'structural' form of the 'o' in all four images above, but the form of 'o', or rather its formation, has been performed through four different modes of the same activity. Thus, the form has been *embodied* in four different though not completely distinct instances, as it has itself formed a part of the task of being-in-action. This notion of 'embodied form' acknowledges the dynamic movements and static poses articulated in time and space and experienced by the body – or rather embodied – in the processes of form. It invites askeology to consider how the practising of an exercise manipulates the body rather than thinking in purely 'structural' terms of how the body articulates it, thereby extending some concerns in the field of theatre scholarship that have focused on the 'structures' of exercise. When I write about embodied forms in this chapter, and throughout the remainder of this book, I am not simply describing a shape a body makes, or a particular contortion of that body, I am referring to the *activity* that makes up an embodied dynamic movement or pose in a given mode. I am referring to a form which, when formed, is *meaningful to a community of practitioners*.

It is partly for this reason – for the reason of meaning – that I chose to open this chapter with a written language exercise because it is clear that certain embodied activities, and the 'structural' forms with which they work and produce, are uniquely associated with practices performed together, in the collective. Like Read, Ulmer, following the literary theorist Ian Hacking, argues against any notion of an empty space as the environmental prerequisite for meaningful action to occur. Ideas, he argues, 'do not exist in a vacuum. They inhabit a social space setting.'[23] In working within the social space of training, askeological research can only talk about embodied forms if trainees and training practitioners deem them meaningful, or if they are self-evidently meaningful in certain 'settings', 'matrixes' or configuration of 'plasma'. Merleau-Ponty, whose *Phenomenology of Perception* is still providing so much impetus to contemporary performance research,[24] points out through an appropriately ethnographic (or is it touristic) example that all forms accrue and negotiate meaning within a communal context and that all forms of meaning are performed in complex matrixes of action: 'in a foreign country, I begin to understand the meaning of words through their place in a context of action, and by taking part in communal life'.[25] Here, in Merleau-Ponty's example, the word overspills its (structural) form and it becomes clear that it is formatted in collective activity even if it is 'read' in the singular. Borrowing and extending Merleau-Ponty's assertion about the forms of words, askeology takes form to refer to any activity performed in training's communal setting that enacts a particular meaning and organises the collective in which it occurs.[26]

Just as ethnography has taken language to be a primary constitutive site for investigating human cultures,[27] so too theatre training discourse has taken the 'exercise' to be the *sine qua non* of training, whether in the totalising guise of components of a 'universal system' or 'method' or in what Hodge sees as their later stage manifestation as 'principles ... made manifest through specific actor training techniques'.[28] Hodge contends that the exercises documented for each of the practitioners studied in her *Twentieth Century Actor Training* 'could be regarded as paradigmatic of [their] overall practice', in the sense that these exercises physically realise the 'core principles'[29] of a given discipline. If we can say, as Hodge suggests, that, 'some principles are fundamental, capable of transcending their [disciplinary] origins and therefore can be recognised as part of a matrix of key concepts in twentieth-century western actor training',[30] then perhaps chief among these is that exercises *do something* to the trainee, *form* them, *reform them*, re*form*at them or, perhaps more simply, trans*form* them.

The age of exercises

In a consideration of training that seeks to account for the individual and collective in performance training by seemingly viewing them as subdivisions of an actorly subjectivity, Eugenio Barba asserts, 'this daily task [training] . . . is a concrete factor in the transformation of the actor as a man, and as a group member'.[31] The 'group member' in this statement appears to refer to the ensemble (in this case the Odin Teatret) in which an actor trains and performs, and the transformation of the actor in ways that determine his/her interaction with others and the way he or she acts with them. Barba describes the training exercises used by the Odin Teatret as 'paradigms of dramaturgy'. He states that genres of performance are examples of other (more traditionally understood) paradigms of dramaturgy but these 'well contrived web[s] of actions'[32] have form and content, whereas 'exercises are pure form, dynamic developments without a plot, a story'.[33]

One such exercise is what Barba and his actors have called 'the green exercise',[34] in which I participated during a training workshop with Odin at Manchester University.[35] In this exercise two trainees work together with a length of strong ribbon or rope, each holding one end as though engaged in a tug of war. In the first phase of the exercise the two trainees play to explore the possibilities of movement enabled by the support of their partner's weight at the other end of the rope. Both find that they can, with the support of their partner at the other end, lean, crouch and reach and make new shapes with their bodies that they could not make unaided. In the next phase, the two trainees are asked to devise a brief choreography that entails three balances, held in tableau, using the support of the rope. The partners practise this sequence until they can

Figure 3 (above). Signature of Guido Fawkes on a confession made on 9 November 1605. Guido's name can be seen in a faint hand immediately above the torn bottom right corner of the document. Reprinted by permission from The National Archives, UK.

Figure 4 (right). Signature of Guido Fawkes on a confession made on 17 November 1605. Guido's full name can be seen above 'Her Majesty's State Paper Office' stamp, adjacent to the signatures of the other conspirators. Reprinted by permission from The National Archives, UK.

Figure 5 (above). 'Virtual John'. Photograph by Astor Agustsson. Reprinted by permission and with thanks.

Figure 6 (below). 'Real John'. Photograph by Glen Birchall. Reprinted by permission and with thanks.

Figure 7 (above). 'Tim the Tortoise' by Aardman Animation for Leonard Cheshire Disability 'Creature Discomforts' campaign. Reprinted by permission and with thanks to Leonard Cheshire Disability.

Figure 8 – Ian Wilding, voice of 'Tim the Tortoise'. Reprinted by permission and with thanks to Ian Wilding.

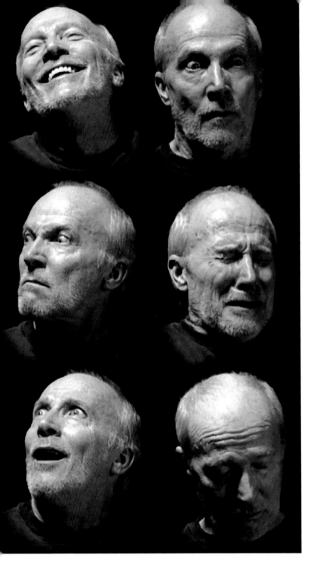

Figure 9 (left). Bill Viola, Six Heads (2000). Video on wall-mounted plasma display. Photograph by Kira Perov. Reprinted with thanks to Bill Viola and Kira Perov.

PLATE II

1

2

3

4

5

6

Figure 10 (right). 'Plate III: Joy – high spirits – love – tender feelings – devotion' taken from Charles Darwin's *The Expression of the Emotions in Man and Animals.*

both move comfortably from one balanced tableau to the next and hold each balance in a controlled fashion for a short period of time. In the final phase of the exercise, the rope is removed and the trainees have to find a way to perform their sequence without the support of their partner at the other end of the rope. The support that was coming from the partner at the other end of the rope must now be found within the body, and between the body and the floor.

The form of this exercise has a distinctly theatrical element since it culminates in the representation of a 'dramatic fiction' as if it were 'real', and in this respect the exercise has a very actorly application. Through repetition, participants develop and refine the ability to convincingly represent the absent rope, and to maintain the representation of the presence of its absence throughout the choreography. In this respect, the repeated embodying of this form has a certain skill-based application, developing the skills of the performer to act within a particularly under-stood context of theatrical performance. Is this then the alteration of training that brings about the state of impotentiality described by Agamben, the simple cultivation of skills and the increased bringing-under-control of their performance? This would appear to be what Ryzard Cieslak, the famous actor of Barba's famous mentor, Grotowski, refers to when he states, 'just as a musician has to exercise his fingers every day, so an actor has to exercise his body almost to the point of over-coming it, that is, being in complete control'.[36] Even Barba's assertion that, within the 'design of movements' or 'pattern of behaviour' in exer-cises there is some other 'imperceptible something which is worked on and guided by means of the exercise'[37] would seem to refer to an actor's theatrical skill. The three principles that, according to Jane Turner, underpin Barba's exercises – the 'alteration of balance', the 'law of oppo-sition' and 'incoherent coherence' – would appear ultimately to serve the spectatorial imperatives of a certain theatre by 'creat[ing] a quality of energy in the actor that attracts the spectator's attention'.[38] The skill of a performer in acquiring the ability to so magnetise an audience perhaps refers to what Barba calls the transformation of an actor as 'group member' – as one who trains, and more pertinently performs, with others performing a part of an extended theatrical representation. But, Barba argues, there is another application to such training exercises that might go beyond skill-acquisition and which relates to the transformation of an actor as a 'man'. There is, according to Barba, a certain personal developmental facility of formal exercises – that these structures are also pathways or 'small labyrinths that the actors' body–minds can trace and retrace'.[39]

In an article discussing the significance of exercises in an actor's dramaturgy, Barba observes that the twentieth century has been 'the age of exercises' in theatre training.[40] Interestingly, he mobilises a conception of 'exercise' to differentiate the training methodologies and techniques of Stanislavski and Meyerhold from the traditions of actor training which preceded them. Barba contends that the exercises conceived by Stanislavski and Meyerhold were 'something quite different from the training followed by students at theatre schools'[41] where trainee performers would practise fencing, ballet, singing and recitation of dramatic texts in order to assemble the skills required to perform the theatre of the day.

If Barba were merely observing that the tasks set by Stanislavksi and Meyerhold were materially different from those set in theatre schools, his insight would appear somewhat banal. If all he were saying was that instead of singing at a piano Stanislavksi's actors quietly meditated on their own emotional experiences; that instead of plieing at the bar Meyerhold's actors wriggled through a series of reflexology-inspired movements, he would really not have much of a case for distinguishing the twentieth century from any other as an 'age of exercises'. The trend that Barba is actually observing in theatre training is not just a change to the physical tasks undertaken by trainees, to their *modality*, but an alteration to or extension of the *activity* of exercises. He writes that Stanislavski, Meyerhold and their collaborators 'invented "exercises" for the *formation* of actors' [*emphasis added*].[42] Barba is adamant that the application of the exercise has a formative effect beyond teaching actors how to generate believable representations.

> Exercises teach how to work on what is visible through using repeatable forms. These forms are empty. At the beginning, they are filled with the concentration necessary for the successful execution

of each single phase. Once they have been mastered, either they die or they are filled with the capacity for improvisation.[43]

Barba contends that the 'structural' form of an exercise, such as the 'green exercise', can become something like a pedagogical tool for trainees and that repeated embodying of its form can provide the trainee with the opportunity to move from a concentrated concern with mastering the exercise towards a process of exploration by which the form becomes 'filled' again with a new purpose. In this sense, the 'structural' form becomes the template for developing experiences of embodiment and the site for exploration and cultivation of new capacities without the form of the exercise undergoing any change.

The change to the materiality of theatre training in 'the age of exercises' is significant to this project because of the change it effects in the *experience of undergoing* training. There is perhaps something in the fact that the term Barba chooses to describe this conceptual shift, 'formation', is precisely the same as that used by monasticism to denote the activity of ascetic training exercises. Perhaps Barba's borrowing of this notion of formation from Christian spiritual training is the continuation of the 'religious impulse'[44] identified by Joseph Roach in Grotowski's training practice. Academics (for example Daniel Meyer-Dinkgräfe and Jennifer Lavy) have traced the Indian and Asian spiritual and performance-based influences on Jerzy Grotowski during his studies in Moscow and his travels in central Asia.[45] In the context of Stanislavski's much-publicised interest in Eastern mysticism, this scholarship perhaps sees Grotowski as he saw himself: Stanislavski's heir. Joseph Roach's 'scientific' analysis of Grotowskian actor training argues that 'even at his most mystical, in his description of the "Holy Actor", Grotowski falls back upon the assumptions that materialistic science liberated from religious interpretations only with great difficulty in the not-too-distant past'.[46] This contention could perhaps be understood in the context of the 'enormous role' played by Roman Catholicism in Poland in the twentieth century, which, according to Polish historian Jerzy Kłoczowski, has been 'spectacularly revealed' early in the twenty-first,[47] especially with respect to Grotowski's research into 'old forms of Christianity'[48] and his tendency to speak 'as Catholics with their prelates would speak'.[49]

What formation describes for Barba and for monastics is the *deeply personally felt cultivation of the self,* and the experience of making enduring changes to the self at levels that transcend the possession of new skills acquired through the practising of tasks.[50] Put more simply, formation is more than a process of acquiring new skills; it is also a process of undergoing significant and lasting changes that affect aspects of a trainee's lived experience extending beyond what they do in training.

If one accepts that exercises have the power to instigate and support processes of formation when they are actively embodied, then one is compelled to assume one of two positions with respect to this fact: either such power is, as Barba seems to suggest, operational only within certain kinds of exercises, or conversely that it is present within all exercises as a necessary condition of what makes them exercises. It seems to me over-problematic to assume either position wholeheartedly, since in the first one would be forced to describe the necessary conditions or characteristics of an exercise that gave it formative powers (which seems to me to be practically impossible), and in the second one would have to account for why not all exercises seem to inspire formation. Paul Allain signals a possibility for askeology to reconcile these two positions by looking to individual agency in training exercises in his book on the Suzuki methods of actor training. Here he succinctly states:

> It is a mistake to believe that if you follow a method, execute it regularly and meticulously, you will become a good performer. How the individual responds to the task set and reveals him/herself through such demands is what makes any system viable.[51]

In this statement Allain describes a self-reflexive, emotional and intellectual investment apparently required of a trainee to activate formative power present within an exercise. Addressing the relationship between 'structural' form and formative processes in exercises, Allain describes the state of affairs in the 'age of the exercise':

> What is effective about [Suzuki] training is the apparent external simplicity of form, combined with the difficulty in perfecting this, which some actors have called 'impossibility'. The exercises contain an unachievable goal . . . this elision of the achievable

with the unachievable means the practice repeatedly asks the question: how far are you prepared to go?[52]

What Allain also observes here is that part of the 'structural' form of a given training exercise is always formatted in the temporal, as well as the spatial or behavioural, and so is always concerned with the body one is *doing now*. In both Allain's and Barba's descriptions there is the sense that the embodying of the exercise conducts two separate though not distinct processes. At one level there is the practical task posed by the 'structural' form, which can never be fully accomplished or its possibilities fully exhausted; and at another level there is the engagement of the trainee in response to these (im)possibilities. Barba even attempts to name these different levels practically, contending that the latter might be thought of as a 'subscore' developing out of the 'score' of the exercise. He writes:

> the value of the visible (the score) and the invisible (the subscore) generate the possibility of making them [the actors] carry on a dialogue, creating a space within the design of movements and their precision.[53]

Likewise Allain argues that the embodying of exercises in this way 'enables the participant to transgress quotidian boundaries' by actively giving to a 'pursuit of constant self-improvement'.[54] To this end, training exercises such as those developed in various forms of twentieth-century actor training facilitate enduring self-exploration and development through the repeated embodiment of forms.

The process of this development is personally felt by trainees, as is evidenced in numerous accounts of 'watershed moments' – for example Tom Nelis's revelatory experience when working with Suzuki: 'the only thing I had left was my will and this was a real revelation to me',[55] or as in Phillip Zarrilli's accounts of 'Asian disciplines of practice, including acting . . . implicitly understood to be a psychophysiological means to affecting a fundamental transformation of the individual'.[56] Zarrilli utilises South Indian martial arts exercises in the training of actors to affect personal development in much the same way the exercises of Barba and Suzuki seem to propose. The embodying of structural forms in Zarrilli's training practice is also focused on cultivating the actor as a 'man', and Zarrilli, like Allain, takes cognisance of individual agency in processes of formation.

Embodying the elephant

During an intensive three-day training workshop with Phillip Zarrilli in Kalarippayattu, a south Indian martial art, I was introduced to some of this discipline's 'poses'. Kalarippayattu poses are static 'structural' forms, which are the culmination of dynamic movement sequences.[57] Zarrilli uses these exercises in the preparation of actors to develop a state of 'awareness', which he determines as necessary for performance. As I noted in Chapter 2, Zarrilli, following A.C. Scott, calls this state of awareness 'standing still while not standing still'.[58] Zarrilli's exercises, much like Barba's, are not aimed at developing physical capacities that will be explicitly recited in performance – as would be the case for a trainee training to practise the martial art – but at fostering a certain attitude in an actor towards him or herself. One such exercise involves teaching trainee actors the Kalarippayattu 'elephant pose' in which, after a series of dynamic movements, the trainee arrives in a crouched position with feet slightly further than shoulder-width apart and forearms locked together vertically in front of the torso with thumb tips covering the nose. During the workshop series I attended, Zarrilli demonstrated the method of assuming this pose, which involved lifting the arms and dropping the pelvis in time with inhaled and exhaled breaths and concentrating focus on external points. In his article, 'The Metaphysical Studio', Zarrilli gives this definition of the active and static form of the exercise:

> The elephant pose: external gaze moves from a point of focus
> ahead, to the hands above the head and fists, and then travels
> down with the fists, to return to a point ahead.[59]

The external focus points, and the controlled breathing that support this exercise, are routed in the martial application of the pose because the awareness of the surrounding environment attunes the practitioner to sources of and for attack, while the strategic breathing ensures their readiness for action.

However, for Zarrilli, this type of training is not so much concerned with martial requirements as with developing a certain kind of embodied focus, stimulated by such martial training activities. In an article in which he describes his own experience of going to India in 1976 for a sustained period of training in Kathakali dance-drama and Kalarippayattu, Zarrilli explains how his attitude to his own body was changed. As became clear in Chapter 2, Zarrilli refers to his body before beginning training as a 'biomedical/sports body', a body in which his 'will' (which for him seems to be synonymous with 'sentience') was separate from his body and determined to master it. He suggests that his body was the body produced by Western sporting and medical practices which, he claims, see the body as 'neutral', observable and subject to will. He tells how his body struggled with Kalarippayattu training because of his attempts to force its forms into embodiment, through his desire to observe and measure results and because of his tendency to view his body in the past or future rather than the present. His claim is that over the course of many months of training he not only came to see his body differently, but also came to embody it differently: 'through the long process of repetition of basic forms of practice', he not only came to 'sense a shift in the quality of [his] relationship to [his] bodymind' but also to feel that he was 'moving from a concern with external form to awareness of the "internal" dynamic dimension of [his] psychophysiological relationship to [his] body/mind *in practice*'.[60]

In a statement that resonates with Allain's notion of 'impossibility', Zarrilli notes how important individual agency is to training: 'If training through repetition of forms is not to become an empty, habitual technique for the long-term practitioner, then an actor must commit him/herself fully to training as an ongoing *process of self-definition*' [*emphasis added*].[61] Zarrilli refers to this ongoing process as one of 're-cognise-ing' the self, which he attributes to a shift in the interrelation between body and mind. Having already outlined where askeology stands in relation to prevalent theatre training discourse on body and mind in Chapter 2, I wish to focus here not on any such shift in cognition but on how doing a different body (to recall Mol and Law) would appear to involve a self-reflexive awareness of the body-in-action. Taking on board Zarrilli's observation that, 'it is repetition per se which leads one, eventually, to the possibility of re-cognise-ing oneself through exercise',[62] I will deploy his term to help to unpick the transformation (and crucially the self-awareness and reflections upon that transformation) of trainees in relation to how they do their bodies-in-action throughout formal training.

Tom Nelis's threshold moment, documented by Paul Allain and the revelatory experiences of self-development reported by Phillip Zarrilli are not uncommon among trainee actors and performers working in disciplines that purport to operate at an 'extra-daily' or 'spiritual' level. Experiences of revelation are often to be found in accounts of undergoing training exercises practised in disciplines that operate (under) an explicitly developed conception of the human self. For example, Tamara Kohn in her anthropological study of aikido trainees and practitioners, 'The *Aikido* Body: Expressions of Group Identities and Self-Discovery in Martial Arts Training', records how many of the Aikido trainees she interviewed and interacted with felt strongly that the 'principles' of aikido – of harmonising with potentially destructive energies and redirecting them to avoid damage – were 'clarified and *taken into the body* only through repetitive and reflexive practice over many years' [*emphasis added*].[63] These principles practised on the mat of aikido *dojos* are 'simultaneously understood through a consciousness of their general applicability in the process of living from day to day'.[64] That is to say that the re-cognise-ing of self effected by formal training is not only operative during formal exercise but also affective in the everyday life experiences of trainees – with the task of keeping oneself whole.

This would resonate with Zarrilli's account of his own experience and suggest that the embodying of forms through repeated practising of formal exercises is capable of bringing about a wholesale re-cognisation of the self, not simply one restricted to the way the body is done during training times and spaces. Kohn cites examples of aikido trainees integrating the principles of harmonising, responding and redirecting into their professional and social lives as well as their creative endeavours.[65] She suggests that aikido offers its practitioners a different paradigm through which to think about themselves that pervades their lives outside the time they spend in training. Kohn observes that the personal revelations apparent in the narratives of aikido practitioners 'are genuinely felt to have emerged from the embodied experiences on the mat'[66] and that they were felt to be 'new' experiences of the self in the world rather than old ones that the aikido metaphor of blending and harmonising could slot into. The process of re-cognise-ing the self would seem to entail something more than simply holding a different attitude to one's self. If re-cognise-ing entails a wide-reaching transformation of the trainee actor as a 'man' and as a 'group member', it shares more than just a descriptive term with Christian asceticism and the exercises that formulate monastic training. Indeed, if such a tension in working practice affirms that theatre has indeed been, throughout the twentieth century (and is now in the twenty-first), in an 'age of exercises', such an 'age' is 'generational' relative to a tradition of spiritual training that is 'geological' in comparison.

Forms of praise

There are many formal exercises that must be performed during the monastic day. They are not immediately obvious to someone who, like me, undertakes to live in a monastery. In fact it took several days before I began to think about the fact that I had (without thinking) been performing these exercises. For example, to enter the choir stalls at Worth Abbey, where the monks sit during services, it is necessary to walk from the congregational area up two steps and past the altar. Suspended above the altar from steel wires reaching down from the roof is an almost life-size figure of Christ on the cross. When passing the suspended figure the monks at Worth bow. There is no rigid 'structure' to bowing and I witnessed a great range of bows from the shallow and swift to the deep and slow, bows that took place while the monk was in motion and bows that occurred after several seconds of stillness. Perhaps this variance in the precision by which this form was embodied is why I tended at first not to think about it; arriving at Worth Abbey and bringing with me embodied knowledge of my own professional training traditions consisting of precisely executed *études* and detailed *actions*, the comparatively unformalised exercises of the Abbey looked and felt like everyday behaviour.[67]

The apparent 'imprecision' of the bow is evident in a number of other monastic exercises, for example, genuflection. Genuflection is an act of reverence made by bending one knee and lowering one's body towards the ground – usually in a direction towards the figure of Christ – sometimes accompanied (as was the case in Worth) with making the sign of the cross, on the head and chest, with the right hand. Again, in this instance, the form of the genuflection is not rigid but loose, with just some few elements that must be performed. There are many other such exercises and actions ranging from the receiving of the communion wafer and chalice with the hands, or at the mouth, to the styles of kneeling for prayer. These exercises appear so structurally 'unformalised' that it is tempting to see them not as exercises at all, but almost impromptu units of everyday behaviour. They are certainly not the 'extra-daily' contortions of Odin exercises, or the exhausting exertions of Suzuki training but, nonetheless, their activity has prescribed structural forms. There is 'looseness' to their structural form when compared with the green exercise or the elephant pose in the sense that within their formal structure there is space for a significant deal of variance. Despite this, however, they have a recognisable 'form'.

These two examples of exercises from monastic training would appear to exhibit another crucial difference from the green exercise or the elephant pose in that they are necessarily practised within a given location and at specific times. Unlike the implicit sterility of the theatre-training studio that recalls the empty space where much of its performance was reported to take place, these monastic exercises are practised in explicitly formatted (plasmatic) space. As such, it is tempting to describe these exercises from the perspective of a Foucauldian analysis of timetabling which has 'no doubt' that the regulated repetitious cycles of imposed occupations in schools, prisons and hospitals are 'an old inheritance' from monastic communities.[68] Indeed the form of such timetables might constitute 'collective and obligatory rhythm[s]' which have 'passed from a *form of injunction* that measured or punctuated gestures to a *web* that constrains them or sustains them throughout their entire succession' [*emphasis added*].[69] Nicholas Ridout has narrated the view from just such a perspective on the subjectivating effects of theatre on actors (and presumably audiences) stimulated by the timetabling of urban buses and trains as well as the 'regulation of clocks and bells'[70] in theatre buildings. Perhaps, in the light of this pervasive interpretative tactic, I have chosen poor or confusing examples of monastic exercises. However, these examples will help to show that the spatial and temporal coordinates of an exercise might play a role in formatting communal work (of which re-cognise-ation is the 'new product') which is other than the alienated labour of such timetabled subjects. To circle back towards this point it is necessary to draw on another monastic exercise that is no less iconic but not so thoroughly regulated – prayer.

The spirit of exercises

If the emergence of a formational facility (or even merely formational rhetoric) in twentieth-century theatre training has made the recent past an age of exercises, then this age has a historical precedent in the development of monastic training over four millennia.[71] A range of practices runs through this tradition of asceticism from the silences of early Hindu *tapas*, or 'rigours of austerity',[72] to the 'Great Silence'[73] kept by present-day monks at Worth Abbey, and perhaps all these practices can collect under what St Ignatius (1491–1556) called 'spiritual exercises':[74]

> By this name of Spiritual Exercises is meant every way of examining one's conscience, of meditating, of contemplating, of praying vocally and mentally, and of performing all other spiritual actions ... for as strolling, walking and running are bodily exercises so every way of preparing and disposing the soul to rid itself of all disordered tendencies ... is called a spiritual exercise.[75]

The analogy St Ignatius draws from physiology to describe the scope of spiritual exercises sites him within the sixteenth-century moment of an ongoing debate within Christianity over the interrelation between body and soul.[76] St Ignatius's example of prayer as a spiritual and ascetic exercise has a central role in the development of monastic training, even though prayer may not at first appear to be as 'ascetical' as the various immolations commonly associated with monks. Prayer, unlike bowing and genuflection, is not essentially tied to a particular space or timetable. While the monastic 'liturgy of the hours', as the daily cycle of services are known, provides a timetabled structure for praise (within which prayer is a particular activity), the practice of praying is not necessarily performed in particular places or at certain times. To write about the form of 'prayer' as a spiritual exercise is a daunting task, but to consider the experience of doing-a-body in a particular 'form' of praying is perhaps more realistic here. So I now turn to a particularly well-known performance of Christian prayer – the saying of the rosary.[77]

The saying of the rosary is an iconic practice of the Catholic Church, in part because it can be said anywhere at any time. This reality carries it beyond monasteries and gives it a presence in the 'lay' world. Just as with bowing and genuflection, there is significant variance in the performance of the rosary within the parameters of its structural form. The prayers made on each bead can vary according to the person praying or the circumstances in which they come to pray and the duration of the recitation. The number of times one says the complete rosary (passes all the beads through the hands) is also contingent upon the person and their reasons for praying. Robert Llewelyn, in *A Doorway to Silence: The Contemplative Use of the Rosary*, cites a 'well known phrase' that runs, 'The beads are there for the prayers, and the prayers are there for the mysteries.'

The mysteries are the traditional focus of attention for the saying of the rosary. To explain what these are and what they mean it is necessary to describe in more detail the design of the rosary and how it is performed. A rosary chain (or chord) typically holds fifty beads in five sections of ten (a decade), separated by four 'spacer' beads and a medallion. Strung from this necklace (at the medallion) is a crucifix attached by a length of chain or cord. This is called the 'pendant', which also consists of five beads (three equidistant in the middle and two further apart) at the end of which hangs a crucifix. To say the rosary one begins by saying the Apostles' Creed, holding the crucifix.[78] One then moves to the first bead on the pendant, holding it between thumb and forefinger and says the Our Father, or Lord's Prayer.[79] On each of the next three beads on the pendant one would say the Hail Mary,[80] and on the fifth bead the Gloria.[81] One then begins the circlet by saying the Our Father on the medallion, then the Ave Maria or Hail Mary on each of the first ten beads, and concluding the decade with a Gloria on the spaced bead. The next decade follows the same pattern, but this time ignores the pendant. The saying of one round of the rosary is known as a *chaplet*. A complete saying of the rosary covers three chaplets, which allows the person in prayer to meditate on all fifteen 'mysteries'. The mysteries are essentially key points in the narrative of the birth, death, resurrection and ascension of Jesus.[82] In saying three chaplets the person in prayer meditates on one of the Joyful Mysteries on each of the five decades. On the second chaplet they will be occupied with the Sorrowful Mysteries and on the third the Glorious Mysteries. This is the traditional form of the rosary, although it is not uncommon for brief passages from scripture to be substituted for these prayers or for quite different and sometimes quite personal prayers to be said on each bead. Whatever scriptures or passages are 'said', the praying of the rosary always coordinates the physical movement of beads through fingers with the 'metaphysical' movements of meditation.[83]

As with the green exercise, there is a tension in the rosary between the skill-based element and the formational facility. St Ignatius cautioned against assuming that prayer was unlike any other bodily exercise and thus asserted that it needed to be practised and worked at in the same way. Llewelyn similarly argues that there is a necessarily physical aspect to the metaphysical activity of prayer because, as he tells his readers, if 'our prayer is to be true to our nature, we need to use material things'[84] to enact and engage spiritual activities. Llewelyn identifies five material aspects of saying the rosary that are decidedly physical and 'skill-based'.

- The beads break the time up into small elements that can be dealt with one by one.

- The pressure of the fingers on each bead is an aid to keep the mind from wandering.

- The breaking up into five decades (five sections of ten beads separated by different beads) relieves the monotony of the exercise.

- The audible repetition of the words helps to gather the attention into what is being said and done (though some wish to progress to silent recitation, and with sufficient focus the same effect is achieved).

- The beads that remain to be worked serve as an encouragement to keep going.[85]

These 'material', skill-based aspects of the structural form of the rosary serve to make the monk more skilful and practised in his prayer, capable of praying with greater economy of effort and increased meditative focus. Just as the green exercise develops the capacity to perform theatrical representations through the repeated embodiment of its structural form, so too the rosary develops the capacity for performing prayer. Like the training exercises used by the Odin, and Zarrilli, the rosary also has a formational facility that, through the repeated embodying of (more or less) simple structural forms, brings about a profound alteration that exceeds skill-based development. All these exercises appear to share the same difficult-to-describe quality: they are, at one level, simple structural forms that are repeatedly embodied, and yet at another level they would appear to induce deeply felt alterations that are reported to transcend the skill-based embodying of the structural form. It would appear that repetition, and what Allain has called 'impossibility', are central to these exercises as well as the individual agency that is asserted throughout.

Repetition, impossibility, creativity

Llewelyn argues that repeated engagement in the simple structural form of the rosary exercise is precisely what *forms* the practitioner, because it engages self-reflexive and dispositional aspects of an individual person. The repeated encounter with the 'impossibility' of completely or finally *doing* the exercise is crucial to the formational facility: 'It is just because prayer may be monotonous and boring that it provides such a splendid opportunity for patience to grow.'[86]

Llewelyn draws a straightforward distinction between 'repetition' and 'vain repetition', noting that repetition is immensely valuable if repeated activities induce formational development. An activity is, he argues, in vain only if it does not achieve the end for which it was intended. If it achieves it slowly and through frustration, it is not in vain, just difficult. He also points out that there is only repetition at all in the saying of the rosary when it is viewed at a very superficial level. Though the hands turn the beads over and over, and the prayers are said time and time again in each cycle, each bead finds the practitioner in a different state of *doing a body* in the process of training. Matthew Goulish of the theatre company Goat Island has made a similar observation about the nature of repetition in processes of learning, quite appropriately (given the example deployed at the outset of this chapter) concerned with letters:

> Take for example the process of memorising the alphabet. Is the act of recitation repetitious? . . . If all the letters are different, one could say there is no repetition. It is only at the point where a letter returns, and we recognise its return, that familiarity has occurred. But is even that a repetition? Perhaps the letter returns changed by time and events, altered by the nature of the intervening letters.[87]

Goulish contends that this is in part an issue of perception and where a viewer/reader stands relative to the letter form, phenomenologically speaking.[88] Goulish argues that the differing 'readings' – i.e. repetitive and non-repetitive – are represented by categories of *informed* and *ecstatic*, where the informed appropriately becomes associated with prior knowledge of forms and the ecstatic with 'stepping outside of familiar languages'.[89] Just as the structural form and the formational facility are bound together in the practising of training exercises, Goulish asserts that the informed and the ecstatic always coexist in the sense that 'words not only mean, but also live, and effect an irreversible change on the reader'.[90] The 'impossibility' in practising structurally simple exercises would seem to direct practitioners towards an 'ecstatic' awareness of their own practice and encourage them to resist being entirely concerned with the 'informed' perspective in repetitious practice.

Zarrilli's description of a wide-reaching 'shift in quality' is mirrored in Llewelyn's observation that the formational capacity of the rosary is not purely dispositional (as with patience) but effects wide-reaching change because, as he explains, the repeated embodiment of the rosary is also 'a little bit of death'.[91] He explains that to ask for the prayers of another is in some measure to die to oneself, because it is a renunciation of that choice which belongs to a person to pray directly for him or herself. He argues that in every act of choice some measure of the self is asserted; it does not die. In every act of submission that opportunity to assert oneself is surrendered and a little bit of dying has occurred. He argues that these little bits of dying accomplished through submission to God, Mary and the Saints prepare the individual for the death which is final. This is the 'work' of a formational exercise according to Llewelyn, not the work 'which can be displayed for all to see'[92] – implying perhaps the 'external' structural form of praying – but the work of engaging with the monotonous, the structural and letting these things act upon one. It is the patience, silence and contemplation affected by monotonous repetition of forms that is the work. 'There can be no Christian life unless it is rooted in patience',[93] advises Llewelyn, noting that it is religious 'short-hand' to say that Christians are saved by Christ's suffering, when it is actually by the patience with which his suffering was borne. 'Mere suffering can save no one,' he writes. 'Patience may be defined as the quality of life which makes suffering *creative*' [*emphasis added*].[94]

Llewelyn's notion of making suffering creative, or perhaps *suffering creatively*, resonates with Allain's assertions about individual agency in training – that it is the way one 'responds to' and 'reveals him/herself through' exercises that makes them 'viable' as formational processes. To suffer a formation, to undergo alteration, necessarily requires the assertion of individual agency. Thus the transformation experienced is not merely an alteration in an individual's powers of skill-performance but also a more far-reaching alteration that leaves them in possession of a 'new' *body-in-action*, a new way to hold the body together. In this respect the impotential developed by a trainee exists in the capacity of performing a certain skill but also in being able to do (or not do) a certain self. If this helps to describe how exercise formed individual actors, then an expansion of the analytic perspective on the exercise can perhaps also account for the formatting of a collective actor, as proposed in the previous chapter.

Collective body (of symbols)

The formal exercise has a formational facility at the collective as well as the individual level. As I suggested with the example of the letter 'o', the structural quality of a form has meaning (which is necessarily constituted in the collective even if it is read or 'produced' in the individual); but what does it mean to have meaning in the form of a training exercise, or, to continue the terms of this description, what does meaning *do*? Goulish's notion of the *informed* in the example of learning the alphabet also identifies a quality of meaning within 'familiar languages', but he goes on to explain that the informed and ecstatic intersect when the structural form is conceived of as part of an encompassing format, and in so doing can *become new*. Providing askeology with the term 'moment' to describe the format of formal exercises, Goulish writes: 'A *moment* consists of a small action in a small amount of time in a particular place. It is that action, at that time, for that amount of time, in that place' [*emphasis added*].[95] 'Moment' seems to take account of all the spatial and temporal coordinates of an activity without simply defining these as the sites and means of control over an individual. Instead Goulish emphasises that *what is done*, and the climate *in which it is done* are both elements of the (plasmatic) formatting of the activity. In a question that seems capable of inquiring into the embodying of formal exercises he asks,

> What happens when a moment repeats or nonrepeats? A *recognisable pattern* of time/place/action quality emerges . . . Maybe we can now say something new has appeared: the moment has multiplied – and through its multiplicities it has begun to accumulate meaning. [*Emphasis added.*][96]

This notion of meaning suggests a step 'outside of' familiar languages and into less familiar arrangements of meaning that is nonetheless *patterned*. Goulish suggests that the pattern of moments accumulates meaning or rather *new* meaning, which produces and organises new 'unfamiliar' languages; and in the intersection of informed and ecstatic in the repeating/non-repeating patterned moments, 'the individual meets the collective'.[97]

Sally Mackey, in her entry under the heading 'Community' in the *Performance Research* 'Lexicon' explains that anthropology and sociology have shifted from 'locating' communities geographically or topographically to conceiving of them as 'translocational'.[98] In translocation, community becomes modular or portable and 'the reality of community in people's experience thus inheres in their attachment or commitment to a common body of symbols'.[99] The kind of symbols that operate within a translocational national community may be, for example, flags which can be flown anywhere or, as Melrose suggests, dances or other performances that can be performed in many different spaces. Given what has been discussed in the previous chapter about training communities, how might formal exercises – in the light of the notion of translocation and Goulish's arguments for new meanings – format training experiences in the collective?

To expand the analytic focus on the ribbon exercise is to observe that the individually embodied form of this exercise is part of a co-embodied format. The paired trainees, literally in this case, excorporate part of their own body-in-action, spreading it out along the rope, while simultaneously incorporating a similar bodily excursion coming from the other end. In the later stages, as the 'really present' rope is replaced by the 'really performed', the excorporations and incorporations connecting these two bodies-in-action require all the more effort to hold things together. To focus the analytic lens wider still is to notice that the paired format is part of a larger activity formatted at the level of the entire group, wherein the paired format has a particular meaning for those involved. At whichever level one chooses to fix the form of the exercises (analytically speaking), it appears to operate for those involved as the kind of meaningful practice that produces, orders and distributes community relations.[100] The fact that these exercises are as transportable as any other 'symbol' helps to describe the translocational reality of training communities – that they exist when and wherever they are practised – which itself complements the expansive scale of Whitworth's 'incorporate identities' discussed in the previous chapter. Forms, embodied in exercises, produce in training communities the kind of 'unfamiliar languages' described by Goulish, the sharing in and practising together of which formats the group at an interpersonal level, just as familiar language orders more traditionally understood communities. Accordingly exercises such as those described are not only formational at the level of the individual actor, but at the level of the collective actor, too. It is by the formatting of individual actors into a collective actor through the embodied sharing of meaningful symbols that formational effects of training are able to occur.

Thinking through the examples in play in this chapter, and into the realm of monastic exercises, what Melrose, following Cohen, sees as the 'reality of community in people's lives' not only inheres in 'their attachment or commitment to a common body of symbols' but in the *practising* of these together.[101] While I was at Worth I was able to have a number of discussions with the Abbot, Christopher, and ask about how interpersonal relationships were regarded in a training discipline that seemed defined by solitude. He gave me several books to read, and some highlighted sections from various other sources, one of which was *The New Dictionary of Theology*. In the entry under 'Community' the authors state: 'The familiar Christian precept to love one's neighbour as oneself should be understood as the mandate to remain in communication with others through the exchange of signs.'[102] This, it was asserted, would not only 'perpetuate the reality of the church', but also of 'civil society' and of their 'interrelat[ion as] communities of interpretation'.[103] As Mackey explained, signs and symbols in translocational communities are not simply inert forms but embodied practices of performance, the 'exchange' of which, in the example of the monastery, is explicitly conceived as a form of communication within a formatted 'public space'.[104]

It is the process of embodying forms as an element of the experience of training that enables action, in Arendt's sense of the word, as a form of work, to occur. Training's status as a unique category of human experience comes partly from the fact that the ordered embodying of meaningful forms serves to format human togetherness and assemble and maintain communities wherein the possibility of completely new things can become an actuality. As I have already noted, Arendt in *The Human Condition* repeatedly stresses that the networks of relatedness assembled in pluralities are sustained by communication.[105] Within networks of individuals, action occurs when persons relate 'directly', which is to say without the intermediary of material things but through language. Arendt is clear in asserting that communication, particularly in the form of language, is intimately bound up in action to the extent to which it is almost unclear which is the condition of the other.

It is evident that action is dependent upon plurality, as defined in the previous chapter. Action is, in fact, the unique work-form of pluralities – and pluralities exist only through the maintenance of human interrelation, which is achieved through communication. Arendt's anthropological interest in action as an activity of the *polis*, particularly in popular resistances and uprisings, leads her quite logically to rest on language as a vital element of plural interrelation, since these events are often characterised (as in the case in her favourite example, the American Revolution) by speech-making and manifesto- or constitution-writing. Taking, as I do, Arendt's category of action and using it to explore the activities of training collectives requires a degree of 'recalibration' or rather specification in the precise terms of *communication* that can account for Goulish's 'unfamiliar languages'. Language is, of course, an essential medium through which individual group members in the collectives I have studied assemble and maintain interrelatedness and constitute themselves into pluralities capable of action. However, it is rather the unique 'unfamiliar language' of meaningful embodied forms associated with the ecstatic that provides the medium through and by which training collectives enable action. The practising of exercises *together* and the 'exchange' of these embodied forms as signs that are meaningful (to group members) entail the action of a training collective.[106] A fuller description and understanding of the newness brought about by this action can be achieved through a consideration of the iconic monastic practice of professing vows which, in the example that follows, is accessible via my experience of a 'perseverance ceremony'.

Forms of testing – perseverance

Every three months a novice must undergo a 'perseverance ceremony' conducted in the presence of the entire monastic community.[107] Before the ceremony, which concludes a period of more or less continuous testing, the novice must reread the Rule in its entirety and consider whether or not he is willing and able to live by its commands. If he is willing and able, he must ask permission in the perseverance ceremony to continue with his training. Perseverance ceremonies are usually conducted immediately before one of the daily services to minimise the disruption to the work of the community and ensure that all members will be free to attend. A monk called Anthony underwent a perseverance ceremony while I was living at Worth and a description of this ceremony will illuminate how testing is formatted within training.[108]

At 6.30 p.m. the monks gathered in the choir stalls as they would for one of the daily services, with the notable exception that Anthony and Christopher, the Abbot, sat apart from the others, directly opposite one another and approximately ten feet apart, in the open space enclosed on three sides by the choir seats. One of the monks also stood at a lectern behind Anthony and to one side of the space. Anthony sat on a small wooden stool and Christopher on a carved wooden chair, which serves in ceremonies such as this as the formal symbol of his authority as Abbot.

To begin the ceremony the monk at the lectern read aloud a passage from the *Rule of St Benedict* about the formation of a novice, the tests he must face and the duties he is expected to perform.[109] After this passage had been read in front of the whole community at a volume audible to all, Christopher asked Anthony, 'What is it you ask for?' to which he responded, 'Perseverance in the novitiate.' Christopher in turn responded to the effect that this request was granted, and went on to read aloud a statement he had written about Anthony. In this statement he congratulated Anthony on his achievements so far and advised him of what he still had to do. After hearing this, Anthony rose from his stool and went to Christopher, both men embraced, and then took their usual places for Vespers to begin.

Performance Studies has made much play of such 'rituals', reading them as either the anti-structural rites of passage first proposed by the anthropologist and ethnographer Arnold Van Gennep (1909),[110] developed by Viktor Turner (who pertinently focused on their 'form' (1969)[111] and properly absorbed into the discipline by Richard Schechner (1973)[112] or as normative performances of socially determined roles.[113] I would like to redirect the channel slightly here and divert this study away from the diametrically opposed 'suspension' and 'normalisation' motifs proposed in these analyses, associated with the object/subject–body strand of research, and outline an image of 'deceleration' to help describe how bodies-in-action come to be done differently in training.[114] This, it is hoped, will show that the form(ats) of training exercises (conceived at the collective) are decelerations within the bio-political domain of 'ordinary life' that affect decelerations of that domain, allowing it to be re-augmented and embodied in new ways.[115]

If both 'suspension' and 'normalisation' ultimately look from different angles at the *construction* of identity – 'a constructing that cannot rightfully be said to begin or end',[116] as Judith Butler has claimed – then it is appropriate that this particular consideration looks not at 'initiation' testing but at testing exercises, such as the perseverance ceremonies, that are already embedded within training processes.[117] Jon McKenzie has argued that 'testing' is essential to performative power, which increasingly views the entire world as a 'test site'.[118] For him the 'feedback loop' that guides performance is tied to evaluation, analysis and assessment.[119] His notion of testing tends towards the 'normative' analysis of performance, conceiving it at the level of data production and interpretation. Using the notion of form and format in play here, I would like to focus instead on the forms tests take and address them as particular exercises within training. Unlike either the suspension or normalisation tracks of analysis, I would like to follow Handelman and Lindquist in asserting that certain ritualised or ceremonialised body practices, such as training exercises, are not a 'modelling of lived experience . . . but a method for entering within life's vital processes and adjusting its dynamics'.[120] Handelman and Lindquist have developed a notion of 'virtuality' in ritual, which conceives of 'rites' as possessing the capacity to 'alter, change or transform the existential circumstances of persons in nonritual realities'.[121] The kind of (trans)formational process experienced in training which is reported to outlast the experience of training exercises is, I contend, the collective 'adjustment' within the dynamics of life which is effected by such deceleration as is accomplished by exercises, practised together.

Handelman and Lindquist argue that ritual, rather than performing suspension or normalisation (which would involve either halting the compositional dynamics of ordinary life, or simply performatively underlining them) *engages* the structurating processes of ordinary life in the midst of living, slowing them down and opening them up to modulation. This deceleration produces what they call the 'virtual' space of transformational rites which is thoroughly real, being a part of reality or actuality, and in which

> by entering within the particular dynamics of life by means of the virtuality of ritual, ritualists engage with positioning and structurating processes that are otherwise impossible to address in the tempo and dynamics of ordinary lived processes.[122]

The formatting of training exercises at the level of the collective produces the same 'virtuality' that Handelman and Lindquist associate with rite. It is telling that they also refer to a 'repetitive dynamic' as a key dimension in the 'slowing down' of ordinary life that takes place in virtuality, and the formation of ordinary life that is entered into and modulated by these repetitive 'virtual' formations.

> It is not so much a suspending as it is holding at bay some of the chaotic qualities of reality, thus allowing the dynamics of reality to be entered within and retuned, readjusted.[123]

This notion appears more properly to describe the formatting of interpersonal relationships in training through the practising of exercises and helps to explain the formational effects sustained by individuals as a result. Such a conception of virtuality does not place training's public 'spaces' away from or outside 'ordinary life' but as virtual spaces within it – certain decelerations of its compositional processes and readjustments of *ordinary living*. Thus training brings about new conditions of living – not out of nothing, but within living and through the structurating processes of 'ordinary life' – and organises new ways of doing-the-body.

Alan Read, in a reading of Van Gennep's three-stage model of transition in ritual, notes that during the liminal phase the ritual subject – which he points out can be both individual and corporate group – passes through a realm or dimension 'that has few, or none, of the attributes of the past or coming state'.[124] Such a liminal dimension is, as the word implies, betwixt and between the classifications of 'ordinary living' and for this reason Read asserts that the stage is not only transitional but also *potential*; not only 'going to be' but also 'what may be'.[125] In contrast, the notion of training as a 'virtual' rite, a deceleration within the classifications of 'ordinary' life, exhibits *many, if not all* of the attributes of both the past and coming state because it is simply a repetitive, slowed-down performance of them, *within them*. This is what we might call the impotentiality of training at the collective level. Far more prosaic than the ethical potential Read identifies in transition to do what *ought* to be done, this is the potential to *do again, at will*: to possess, as a corporate group, the impotential to decelerate the compositional classifications of ordinary life and readjust them, reformulate them. This does not entail the stopping, stripping down or interrupting of bio-politics that interests Read,[126] but rather allows, through deceleration as opposed to cessation, for a reassembling of them.

Structural forms of exercises are associated with skill-based proficiency in training, whereas the individually formational and the collectively formatting effects of exercises help to explain how training can effect change beyond the limited performance-ecologies of given disciplines. It is the tension between the skill proficiency associated with the subject of particular performance practices and the wide-reaching alterations experienced by trainees that stimulates the next chapter of this study, which looks at the *automatising* effects of training's virtual spaces.

6 Automatisation

Anotion of a virtual space within training would sit comfortably with a contemporary theatre demographic, which is now increasingly constituted of virtual performances.[1] Blast Theory's *Day of the Figurines*, a 'game' wherein a thousand 'players' roam a virtual town for twenty-four hours, is typical of a movement in contemporary performance practice towards technologically supported virtual performances wherein 'real' participants assume 'virtual' characters.

In this imaginary town 'virtual John' spends twenty-four hours trying to stay alive, while in the 'real' world 'real John' takes twenty-four days manoeuvring him between locations and through interaction with other characters via SMS messaging. The images in Figures 5 and 6 call attention to the troublesome agglutination of real and virtual in such performance work: 'virtual John' photographs 'real John' as 'real John' photographs him, and meanwhile in the 'real' world someone photographs 'real John' as if he were 'virtual John' or even as if he were being photographed by him. Of course 'virtual John' isn't virtual at all, he's really real, he's just really small, and his miniaturised world is a metal table in the lower levels of the Royal Festival Hall. 'Virtual John' and 'real John' are both really in the 'real world' and somewhere else in Blast Theory's software universe, is 'really virtual John' whom 'virtual John' (who represents 'real John') represents.

If that weren't enough to induce dizziness and confusion, every day in the 'real world' for 'real John' and 'virtual John' only represents one hour for 'really virtual John' almost as if his life was being lived in slow motion or mine in dog years. For every action 'real John' commits via SMS, from travelling across town, picking up and using objects and interacting with others, 'virtual John' is moved about a game board as 'really virtual John' walks, runs, rides, picks up and uses, talks and shouts. 'Virtual John' symbolically represents 'real John's' actions, as they are virtually carried out in 'really virtual John's' activity, and he oscillates, like Gulliver, between worlds composed of objects and people both bigger and smaller than those in his own. 'Virtual John's' miniaturised model town is after all embedded within the macro-world of the Festival Hall and the South Bank as it is in the improbably small world of microchip hardware and the terrifyingly large world of the internet. As I, 'real John' log on to Blast Theory's *Day of the Figurines* website to check the progress of my smaller and bigger selves, the rapid and radical adjustments of scale I am made to confront prove almost as disconcerting as the realisation that someone (and maybe more than one person) wants to hurt and possibly kill my really virtual counterpart. As I receive threatening SMS messages to my 'real' mobile phone (sometimes at *really* inconvenient times) and reports that my virtual selves are starving and wounded, I myself begin to feel really threatened – what have I signed up to here?

Late at night someone threw a VHS tape at 'virtual John' from the window of a speeding car and broke his nose, and as he composed himself he watched armed troops spread terror through town. The reality that I am a virtual character and a 'real' person, being simultaneously attacked and billed for text-messaging, has the effect of making me feel as if I am trapped within an oppressive socio-technical system, as if I were the protagonist of a Solzhenitsyn story. Like Gleb in *The First Circle*, I become conscious of the fact that while I might suffer comparatively bearable hardships, my actions might be perpetuating outer circles of oppression in which others are forced to operate, and I begin to feel the imperative to either disentangle myself from them or more fully to aggregate my fate with their own. What is more, as with the characters of Solzhenitsyn's narrative, 'the phone' takes on a new and frightening significance in my everyday life.[2]

It is clear that the computerised virtuality of performance work such as *Day of the Figurines* is a somewhat different species of the virtual than the virtuality induced through repetition of training exercises. Despite this, both introduce plasticity into 'real' lived experience by mirroring the 'real world' and opening its codes up to scrutiny. The virtual role-playing in *Day of the Figurines* might call me, as participant, to reflect on 'real-world' dilemmas and experiment with courses of action by reproducing states of affairs in micro-modelled and comparatively innocuous environments, almost as if Boal's rhetoric of 'forum' had found its literal counterpart in online chatroom debating.[3] While the dynamics of this virtuality might have a 'conscientising' effect on me and compel me to adjust certain of my 'real' actions, such virtual spaces, as with Boalian forums, maintain a no-man's-land wherein the real and the virtual are held apart and where conscious ethical decision-making can take place.[4]

The virtual spaces of training, by contrast, act as crucibles wherein compounds of 'real' and 'virtual' are dissolved and recombined, engaging and adjusting the structurating processes of the everyday not through debate or decision-making but by repetition. It is evident that for me to act in *Day of the Figurines* is for me to simultaneously set in motion a chain of both 'real' and 'virtual' consequence. The activity occurring in virtual 'deceleration', effected through repeated practising of exercises, involves a particular configuration and engagement of the unstable compound of 'real' and 'virtual', enabling a unique form of *virtually-real* action. This action marks out this practice, and the automatic performance it enables, as a meta-disciplinary process of training. Unpicking the differences between these forms of virtuality requires a precise conception of how 'reality' and 'virtuality' correspond through action.

To act

I am not the first person to observe that *to act* has both a theatrical and a definitively non-theatrical meaning and is able to describe at least two forms of *action* that, to use Robert Gordon's word 'overlap'.[5] Gordon writes that acting as *doing* in the sense of acting 'in the real world'[6] is difficult if not impossible to separate fully from acting as *pretending* in the sense of acting symbolically. This is, he maintains, because childhood role-playing informs and supports the kind of social role-playing on which society relies, but it is also the case because to act 'symbolically' is also to act 'really' – since, when an actor on stage sits down, or accepts a cream bun, they *really* sit down and *really* take the cake. Conversely, the kind of social role-playing in which things *really* get done in the *real world* relies on the symbolism of action, as so many have shown since the publication of Goffman's *The Presentation of Self in Everyday Life* (1959) and Searle's *Speech Acts: An Essay in the Philosophy of Language* (1969). In an assertion aiming for a universal description of theatrical acting and its effects in performance Gordon writes,

> All theatrical performance starts from the assumption that a performer is using her body to represent a virtual body. The actor's creation of a virtual body transforms an actual place demarcated as a playing space into a virtual place. Real time is transformed into virtual time for the duration of the performance . . . All theories of acting start from this point.[7]

In describing how a virtual world adheres to a real one, Gordon's description of the opening up of a virtual space on top of 'real' space by and during performance recalls Handelman and Lindquist's notion of the virtuality within rite. However, if acting symbolically, or theatrically, starts from the assumption of a virtual body then *really* acting in training (in preparation for acting theatrically) assumes a somewhat different virtual space.

Theatre for both actor and spectator can be deeply *affecting* in both 'positive' and 'negative' ways, as indeed most theatre critics earn their living by restating, and this capacity plays a part in the generation of the 'confusion – of attraction and repulsion, compulsion and disappointment'[8] – that Nicholas Ridout describes as a definitive experience of the modern theatre. This 'confusion' can be deeply affecting for a spectator, or indeed, *not* – as is the case in the melancholic image of the boy Marcel bitterly disappointed by a matinee, which Ridout borrows from Proust to introduce his book, *Stage Fright: Animals and Other Theatrical Problems*. That theatre can also be deeply affecting for an actor is evinced, as Ridout has shown, by the phenomenon of stage fright. The effects experienced while training to enter into this confusion as an actor, and to risk 'shaking hands, sweating palms, breathlessness, temporary paralysis, dizziness, faintness or the inability to even think'[9] are reportedly more long-lasting and stable than the melancholia or elation of a spectator.[10] If it is the assumption of a virtual, symbolic body – with an accompanying continuum of virtual time and space on-top-of the 'real' world to which Gordon refers – that separates theatrical acting from really acting, then the virtuality of training is perhaps not induced by calling attention to the 'symbolic' relevance of the 'real' in this way, but by repeatedly reciting the really symbolic. This repetition is not the recitation of a theatrical performance night after night, but the deceleration of really symbolic performances opening them up to scrutiny and modulation, just as the instant replay of a particular moment of a performance of sporting skill or criminal activity, even when not slowed down, effects a certain slow motion in which through *seeing again* one is able to *see more clearly*.

Taking a similar theme for the theatrical – the aestheticisation of the 'real' – Ridout brings Gordon's categories of *real acting* and *virtual acting* together in a way that problematises the 'assumption' from which the theatrical reportedly starts by implicating performer and spectator in what he calls 'the problem with theatre'.[11] To Gordon's description of the virtuality of the theatrical, Ridout adds the qualities of spectatorship (qualities that must be in part possessed by an actor in the act of acting), noting that 'the temporary acquisition' of an 'inability to distinguish between the real and the feigned' is the 'precondition of theatre because the willingness to take the feigned for the real is what allows theatre to entertain'.[12] Given my experiences during *Day of the Figurines*, I can add that this precondition also gives theatre the power to unnerve and disconcert.

In his reading of the image from Kleist's famous essay *Über das Marionettentheater* of a young male actor stepping out of a bath and noticing in his reflection in the mirror that he bears a strong resemblance to a Parisian statue, Ridout argues

> it is not, apparently, the young man's consciousness of his resemblance to the aesthetic object, nor yet his staging of resemblance for an audience [the older man who is reportedly watching him] so much as his *repetition* of that resemblance for an audience that destroys his graceful innocence. [*Emphasis as original.*][13]

At the behest of the older man, the young man attempts to repeat the gesture seen in the mirror, failing in such a way that, according to Kleist's narrator, 'all his charms deserted him . . . and a year later there was not a trace left in him of those qualities that had in the past so delighted the eyes of people around him'.[14] All this leaves Ridout to conclude that the problem with theatre is not doing something (or the knowledge of doing something) or even (knowingly) doing something for an audience but 'the knowledge that you are repeating something that is the problem with theatre'.[15]

And that, according to Ridout, is a pressing problem for training as well as for theatre, given that the reconciliation of the 'necessity of repetition with the equally exacting necessity of apparent spontaneity is what drove the thinking of both Diderot and Stanislavski'.[16] Both Joseph Roach[17] and Robert Gordon[18] take the nineteenth century, and more specifically the publication of Denis Diderot's *Paradoxe sur le comédien*, as a seminal point in the development of 'theories of acting' as well as a particular current in performer training where sensibility and technique are brought into opposition. Diderot's introduction of what Gordon calls 'Enlightenment standards of scientific objectivity'[19] into analyses of theatrical representation has led to the publication of nearly two centuries' worth of literature on actor training and technique. Gordon's assessment of this weight of literature – that 'most handbooks on acting aim to persuade the student that there is *one* correct method to acting . . . whereas others are unhelpful or even harmful to the student'[20] – is perhaps uncharitable in its treatment of earlier periods of theorisation of acting. His own assertion that 'today's actor should understand the relationship between the techniques being acquired in rehearsal and training and the meanings they are designed to express'[21] would appear to be as contingent on the polyvalent subject of the contemporary moment as earlier notions have been congruent with the variously constructed subjects of physiology, biology or psychology.[22]

In detailing the relationship between prevalent understandings of 'the human' in a given historical moment and the construction of 'the actor' as particular subject, Roach's influential book *The Player's Passion: Studies in the Science of Acting* has done much to show that 'conceptions of the human body drawn from physiology and psychology have dominated theories of acting from antiquity to the present'.[23] Extending into the present from the historical examples within Roach's comprehensive study, Gordon's notion of today's actor, cognisant of various performing traditions and sufficiently self-reflexive and emancipated to pick and choose between styles and manipulate his/her own performance to suit a given situation, could well describe the contemporary actor-subject. 'Today's actor', able to comprehend and exploit the 'different possibilities offered to the practitioner and the spectator by the major traditions that constitute Western theatrical performance in the new millennium',[24] is perhaps to the postmodern theatre what Richard Burbage reportedly was to the theatre of the Renaissance: a 'delightful proteus' whose 'putting off [of] himself with his clothes',[25] by managing the percolation of spirits within his seventeenth-century body, was as capable an act as the contemporary performer's flexibility and decision-making in selecting a technique to suit the given social and political demands of a performance. Gordon's rhetoric of 'today's actor' surely functions as an example of what he refers to in the writing of others as 'myth', 'justifying the principles [it] express[es]'.[26]

Gordon explains that the particular rhetoric of a given acting technique 'becomes a kind of shorthand' that can 'indicate the particular attributes and methodologies'[27] of a particular craft. These rhetorics generate an 'aesthetic vocabulary that aims to validate the artistic process it ostensibly describes',[28] the sum total and effect of which he calls 'myth'. Were Roach's analytic method brought to bear on 'today's actor' he would no doubt conclude that his/her flexibility and self-reflexivity constituted the 'skill', the repetitive development and daily exercise of which produces the wages that, according to Ridout, were elicited by 'spontaneity' in the modern theatre.[29] Recognising, thanks to Roach, that the wageworthy skill of any actor in any historical period is defined by a complex matrix of social, political and cultural factors, particularly insofar as they construct an idea(l) of the body, entails the incorporation of the developmental-repetition model of skill acquisition, defined by Ridout, within this askeological investigation. However, in the light of what has been said in the previous chapter about the qualities of formation operative in training exercises and the accounts of wide-reaching personal alterations reported by trainees, the somewhat simplistic notion of training as an apprenticeship in skill competency would not seem sufficient to describe performance training 'today'.

So, over the course of this chapter, I plan to explain the particular practices of 'automatisation' by which skills are acquired by repetition in various disciplines of training. Having done so, accepting with Goffman and Searle that it is by means of the symbolic that the real is enacted, and following McKenzie in assuming that the theatrical bleeds into the performative in the measuring of the success (or failure) with which both are elided in the accomplishment of a given (social, cultural, political – *performative*) objective, I will seek to describe how the repetitive development of a particular 'skill', or rather generation of particular conditions through training, constitutes a meta-disciplinary process of automatisation. This process is not restricted to the privileged skill of a given body of conceptions or myths of individual practices. Throughout this analysis of automatisation I will be exploring the particular 'myths' of freedom brought about by skill acquisition proposed in each discipline; and in the later stages I will explore how automatisation operates at a meta-disciplinary level with respect to positive and negative forms of freedom.

Acting freely

Unsurprisingly, given that *to act* has at least two overlapping meanings, to *act freely* can be understood in at least two ways – or posed as two different questions, the answers to which, according to a pre-eminent philosopher of freedom, Isaiah Berlin, also overlap.[30] As the different theories of acting charted by Roach demonstrate their contingency on understandings of the human body under the pressure of his analysis, so do historical conceptions of 'true freedom' show themselves to be contingent when investigated by Berlin; 'Enough manipulation with the definition of man and freedom can be made to mean whatever the manipulator wishes.'[31] In a statement that closely echoes Roach's claim that conceptions of the human body have dominated theories of acting from antiquity to the present, Berlin alludes to both ancient 'historical fact' and events from 'recent history' that have demonstrated '(if demonstration of so obvious a truth is needed) that conceptions of freedom directly derive from views of what constitutes a self, a person, a man' [*parenthesis as original*].[32]

The great variance introduced into the meaning of freedom by the kinds of manipulations alluded to by Berlin would threaten to disable freedom as a philosophical category, were it not for the fact that, as Berlin claims, there are two abiding conceptions of freedom around which variations polarise. But before I introduce Berlin's concepts of 'negative' and 'positive' freedom, it is perhaps necessary to introduce Isaiah Berlin himself (though in some circles he would fulfil the requirements of the tautological welcome for 'the man who needs no introduction').[33] The reason why Berlin's famous essay on 'Two Concepts of Liberty' (1969) is so useful in Theatre and Performance Studies' consideration of freedom is precisely because it recognises the mutability and performativity of such a 'protean word'[34] as freedom, as well as the work that it is made to do in order to *represent*. Indeed Berlin's recognition that within the 'more than two hundred senses of the word'[35] recorded by historians of ideas, two senses consistently reappear in the guise of others and would appear to bear a metaphoric resemblance to theatre's tragic-comic masks, suggesting, as does this probably unwelcome emblem, that 'positive' and 'negative' might ultimately mask the same face.[36]

Berlin's assessment of freedom in what he argues to be its two 'central' forms throughout history is invaluable here precisely because its political agenda foregrounds the interpersonal; what humans do to, for and with one another, which has been shown in the previous chapters to be as essential a concern for askeology as it is widely accepted to be for theatre.[37] It is also because, as Goffman and Searle have shown and Gordon has more recently reiterated, any consideration of how one acts or is able to act must incorporate a very 'real' dimension of political effects along with its address to any aesthetic realm; and this is precisely what Berlin provides. The notion of acting central to both Gordon and Berlin is not just to *do* (as it is with McKenzie's notion of performing) but to do *humanly within a human realm of relations*, which leads Berlin to define his concept of freedom in the negative sense thus: 'I am normally said to be free to the degree to which no man or body of men interferes with my activity.'[38] Negative freedom, in the historical traditions of philosophy that Berlin addresses, is essentially constituted by the limitation, reduction or absence of coercion or infringement placed on one human being by another or others. Berlin argues that such an individual liberal ideal of freedom would appear to be a very modern doctrine because discussions of individual liberty as a political ideal are rare in the ancient world.[39] In his consideration of the various historical versions of such a doctrine as proposed by Hobbes, Mill, Locke and others, Berlin states that such doctrines are characterised by their commitment to the protection of a sphere of negative freedom while accepting (to varying degrees) that certain limitations must be placed on the complete expansion of this sphere in order for individuals to function as and within a *polis*.

Partly because of this and partly because of the range of variables or 'magnitudes' to which it is subject, negative freedom 'is something the extent of which, in a given case, it is difficult to estimate'.[40] Nevertheless, Berlin argues that it is possible to estimate the scope of an individual's freedom provided that 'total patterns of life . . . [are] compared directly as wholes',[41] and accepting that the method by which a comparison is made and the truth of the subsequent findings of any such method will be difficult or impossible to demonstrate. It is significant that Berlin insists upon an estimation of individual freedom within a given 'ecology' even at the expense of demonstrable imprecision because this is an insistence on acknowledging the contingency of all notions of freedom upon their operational sphere.

The notion of 'positive' freedom identified by Berlin describes a sense of the term defined by 'the wish to be a subject not an object'[42] and to be 'self directed not acted upon by external nature or by other men as if I were a thing, an animal or a slave incapable of playing a human role'.[43] Berlin concedes that negative freedom, as a freedom from coercion or enslavement, is not at a 'great logical distance'[44] from a concept of positive freedom as the capacity to liberate oneself from such fetters. While his detailed analysis of the historical development of these two notions in divergent directions and their points of convergence and conflict will inform the rest of this chapter, the important point of difference to establish is the degree of self-actualisation inherent in the positive concept: that to be free in a positive sense is to be, or to be able to become, that which one would 'desire' or 'need' to be, which is quite different from simply being unaffected by the actions of others.

Sweet freedom

In a quite explicit assumption of a virtual body, Ian Wilding, a long-stay patient at the Dan yr Bryn Leonard Cheshire home in south Wales, appeared as Tim the Tortoise in a recent advertising campaign animated by Aardman to debate freedom in the social and public realm.[45]

The images in Figures 7 and 8 show the character Tim the Tortoise from the 'Creature Discomforts' advertising campaign run by the Leonard Cheshire care homes alongside Ian Wilding who provided the voice and the script for the character. In the commercial, which was broadcast on TV as well as online, Ian assumes the virtual body of Tim the Tortoise in order to tell an anecdote about going to a local shop to buy sweets for his children.

> I tend to only go to places that are accessible. Recently I've come across places which aren't, which are a bit difficult for me. I only wanted to buy some sweets for my children and I went down to the sweet shop and I couldn't get in; makes me feel a bit cross; really frustrated more than anything. I lose the will to get sweets then.[46]

The story told by Ian and Tim evinces the fact that the 'real world' is constructed to suit certain bodies, or rather individuals who can do their bodies in certain ways. The invitation to look again invites one to see that, apart from the social and professional disablement caused by a physical disability, which is supposedly mitigated by equal opportunities legislation, there is the rather more prosaic question of the ergonomics of the 'real world'.[47] The passing of the Disability Discrimination Act in 1995 (which was implemented in stages and has now been superseded by the Disability Discrimination Act 2005), requires that all businesses, including theatres, make 'reasonable adjustments' to increase access for impaired users. It highlighted the (hitherto invisible to many) obstacles that face the physically impaired within the realms of 'public' architecture. These obstacles give rise to what Hughes and Paterson in their essay on 'The Social Model of Disability and the Disappearing Body' note are 'vast tracts of space [which are] no-go areas'.[48] The response of the modern 'real' world to impairment has been what they call 'anthropemic' in denying disabled people access to sites, spaces and practices of power and privilege.[49] The tooling of the 'real world' to assist in and insist on the performance of particular kinematics is comprehensive, and providing disabled access to certain spaces, while going some way towards redressing these ergonomics, does not constitute a retooling sufficient to make this world comfortably inhabitable by the physically impaired – as Tim the Tortoise explains.

It is perhaps significant that during the latter part of the twentieth century which, as I explained in Chapter 2, some scholars have seen as characterised by a shared trend towards 'holism', Hughes and Paterson observe that, 'disabled people, in the context of a flexible post-Fordist economy' have been compelled to form themselves 'into a new social movement, and have inaugurated a struggle for emancipation from social oppression and exclusion'.[50] The late twentieth century may have been characterised by a shared belief in the 'wholeness' of the discrete body, but in the West at least the body politic has remained inherently fragmentary. While the virtual bodies of the Creature Discomforts campaign aim to generate momentum in a drive towards a 'retooling' of the 'real world', Ian's own therapeutic treatment operates an acutely 'realist' objective in the sense that rather than demanding a redesign of the real world it aims to retrain individuals so that they can perform its already designed and subsequently obligatory kinematics.

Deborah Lupton has shown in *The Imperative of Health: Public Health and the Regulated Body* that the idealised body of Western medicine is the obligatory body of such a real world, a healthy body that is also affluent (as is implicit in the assumption that it has access to nutrition and treatments). Following Lupton's reading of discourse on the body in biomedicine and epidemiology, it is evident that the 'myth', to use Gordon's term, of rehabilitative training entails a certain notion of freedom as independence associated with the healthy 'normal' body. Therapies and treatments subsequently assume, or rather ensure through diagnosis, a patient to be in possession of a deficient or diseased body or body state and, while taking into account the variance within the ideal 'norm', aim to reinstate the capabilities of the ideal body for performance in the real world.[51] Subsequently the kind of freedom that physiotherapy aims to train into recovering patients is similar to, if not identical with, the freedom of movement they enjoyed before onset of injury or disability, and as such is always oriented by the activities of the real world. Indeed the main assumption underpinning Carr and Shepherd' s 'motor learning approach'[52] is that 'regaining activities of daily living after stroke requires a relearning process that is similar to the learning process for non-impaired people'.[53]

Within this process, 'normal' movements are construed as 'free' and thought to consist of essential components, 'the invariant kinematics of an activity', which are both 'task- and context-specific'.[54] In order to regain the ability to move with 'normal' freedom, training replicates the task and context of a given movement to create functional tasks in functional settings. The therapist observes and analyses, noting the 'missing' or poorly controlled sections of the kinematics of a particular functional task, which are then practised extensively not only under the supervision of the therapist but in a range of non-supervised environments in order to promote 'carry-over' into 'real' situations.[55] Though Dean et al., in a randomised control pilot trial testing the effectiveness of task-related circuit training in improving performance of locomotive task in chronic stroke suffers,[56] found evidence for the effectiveness of such skill-based motor learning in stroke rehabilitation because of the distinctive association of freedom with 'healthy' or 'normal' bodies, most skill-acquisition studies have been done on non-impaired adults.[57] In fact most work on skill acquisition training has, perhaps unsurprisingly, been done with elite athletes and sportsmen and -women in the field of sports science research where the acquisition and exercise of a particular skill is an even more explicit objective than it is for Ridout's modern actor, and where the qualities of the 'normal' body ideal are amplified, sometimes to a grotesque degree.[58]

Delimiting and defining the kinematics of a task in the real world has an obvious parallel in the fixed ascription of the signifier–signified relationship within aesthetic gesture in performance styles such as the Peking Opera or ballet, except of course that in the everyday the focus is less on aesthetic representation and more on functionality.[59] However, in the case of sporting performance a kinematic sequence frequently maintains an aesthetic dimension alongside its functionality that directly impacts on the level of a competitive athlete's success, as is the case with figure-skating or gymnastic routines. Even in sports that do not have provision for judging aesthetic qualities within the game rules, such as football or tennis, the 'style' of a team or player may have a significant impact on the outcome of a contest. Graham White's analysis of the recitation of the 'Cruyff turn' as an aesthetic gesture by players such as Paul Gascoigne within competitive soccer games, for example, considers its effectiveness in influencing outcomes through asserting national identities within sporting contests.[60] Gascoigne's self-conscious repeat performance of this particular skill suggests that, even within the performative, the theatrical tension between doing and pretending, *really* acting and acting *symbolically* erupts and proliferates.

Within sport science much of the study of skill acquisition has come to be figured around a notion of 'automaticity'. Williams, Davids and Williams, in their book *Visual Perception and Action in Sport*, define the process of automatisation thus: 'Following extensive practice, skills can be performed "automatically" requiring restricted conscious attentional demands'.[61] This notion of 'automaticity' denotes the ease and accuracy with which an experienced practitioner can perform a specific skill in a given context on demand, without significant kinematic variance over repeated performances – the kind of performances at which Kleist's naked bather was so inexpert. Such sporting skills tend to appear in the 'overlap' between the real and virtual described by Gordon, since they are functional in the sense that they achieve physical objectives and aesthetic to the degree that these objectives are not tied into the necessary self-sustaining activities of everyday living.

Williams et al. suggest that a possible explanation for the experts' more 'polished performance could be that as a result of prolonged practice some processing activities cease to make demands on attentional resources'.[62] They use the example of a novice skier making a turn on a downhill course. They contend that as the novice becomes more proficient they are likely to stop thinking about individual parts of the turn. Instead the components of the turn will be grouped together into larger parts so that the turn in entirety becomes much more 'efficient'.[63] Moreover they note that if a skilled skier 'think(s) too much' as they practise performing a turn, they may find a consequent 'deterioration in performance'.[64] From a cognitive perspective, directing conscious attention to individual components of a task may disrupt the established motor pattern controlling the action resulting in an over-reliance on conscious feedback mechanisms or a shift towards a different mode of control altogether, leading to what they call 'paralysis by analysis'.[65]

For Williams et al. the elite performer is characterised by an ability to operate by 'subconscious mechanisms' or 'automatic processes'.[66] Their learned experience, which derives from 'extensive practice', allows them to rely on automatic processes that 'suffer no capacity limitations, are fast, parallel in nature and non-attention demanding'.[67] It is perhaps not surprising, given their analysis of the minimal time lapse and kinaesthetic variance between intention and effect in elite performers, that Williams et al. arrive at a view of the automatised performer as operating by subconscious mechanisms; but there is a certain irony in the fact that their definition of such an elite performer is, literally, a description of someone who is not paying attention.[68] Indeed the 'paralysis by analysis' that they define would seem aptly to describe the pathology of Kleist's young bather who is robbed of his skills, according to Ridout, by the problem of the knowledge that he is trying to repeat something.

It should be noted here that the minimal time lapse between intention and effect is not just a preoccupation for rehabilitative and sporting practices but also theatrical and monastic training – precisely because of the pressures of 'acting' within the associated ecologies. Within the theatrical, because of the responsibility even of the participant-spectator to be also a receiver of effects, and because of the pressure on the actor to provide these, Grotowski was motivated to write:

Unlike any other artistic practice, the actor's creation is imperative: i.e. situated within a determined lapse of time and even with a precise moment . . . An actor cannot wait for a surge of talent nor for a moment of inspiration.[69]

St Benedict, meditating on 'real world' action in community where 'intention' and 'achievement' may be similarly disaggregated and spread through a collective body, and with a similar fear about keeping important people waiting, notes:

It is, in fact, almost in one single moment that a command is uttered by the superior and the task carried to completion by the disciple, showing how much more quickly both acts are accomplished together because of their reverence for God.[70]

While the character of 'intention' and 'effect', as well as the individuals responsible for each, will be specifically determined in each performance ecology, the commitment to a minimal time lapse and minimal distortion between the two remains an ideal of efficiency in a meta-disciplinary formulation of automaticity.

Though Williams, Davids and Williams are interested in the non-attentional 'state' (which bears many of the hallmarks of the 'flow states' discussed in Chapter 2), they emphasise the need to understand the relationship between environment and the development of functional kinematics that operate within them, a relationship which 'implies that the performer and environment can best be understood as a system'.[71] They argue that the focus of study on skill acquisition 'should be on how animals typically produce a tight fit between the environment and their actions'.[72] Recognising that the constructed environment of the real world produces an ecology which specifically enables and supports non-impaired skill acquisition and performance, Robert Fawcus points out in his book on stroke rehabilitation that relearning of everyday skills must map on to the 'action schemata' of activities within this ecology;

during motor learning and relearning we are acquiring action schemata . . . If therapy is developing the acquisition of schemata or prototypical knowledge about the skill under training, then it follows that the quality of the required schemata depends largely on the variability of practice. Taken in conjunction with the plasticity of the neuromuscular system, only the faithful repetition of normal movement patterns in all relevant situations will rehabilitate sensorimotor skills effectively.[73]

Fawcus's notion of action schemata, the kinematics of an activity, recognises the ecological nature of skill and the metabolic experience of acquisition and performance, indeed Fawcus points out that, given the accord between particular ecologies and particular metabolic bodies, 'learning by means of isolated non-action-specific movement will be useless'.[74] Fawcus argues that the challenge for rehabilitation is to enable a trainee to acquire action schemata that don't easily produce what Williams et al. call a 'tight fit' with impaired bodies.

Acquiring the ability to perform certain skills automatically within a sporting event affords a practitioner a certain freedom of action within that particular ecology which, as White has explained and Paul Gascoigne has compellingly demonstrated, resonates between the real and the symbolic. The skills (re)acquired through rehabilitation training, which as Carl and Shepherd have argued are acquired through everyday learning processes, operate within a less symbolic and more functional ecology since they are associated with activities which sustain biological existence, as is ironically played out in Tim the Tortoise's sweet-buying anecdote. The freedom afforded by automaticity within an elite sporting ecology and the freedom within an ecology of the everyday are somewhat different, since in the former the 'functional' kinematics that dictate the outcome of the sporting contest are always invested with a latent aesthetic efficacy which can both transcend the game and have an impact on its outcome. The freedom made possible within an everyday ecology by skill acquisition, while undoubtedly tied into the symbolic activities of social existence (e.g. Tim the Tortoise's role as father and consumer), is, in the case of rehabilitation training, intimately associated with biological survival because of its focus on an individual's independent performance of action schemata of eating (sweets), drinking, cleansing and other activities coupled with the biological life of an organism.

While preserving these important disciplinary differences between elite sporting training and rehabilitation training, it is evident that both notions of freedom coalesce around Berlin's concept of negative freedom as a freedom from restraint or infringement within a given human ecology. The increased functional and aesthetic possibilities opened up in sporting performance by skill acquisition – memorialised in the video clip of Johan Cruyff's debut performance that metaphorically swept the 'football world' off its feet as it literally left Cruyff's opponent, Gunnar Olsson, struggling for balance – provide practitioners with the freedom to manipulate more effectively a sporting outcome by both functional and aesthetic means as they acquire the ability to perform a given skill with greater consistency.[75] The acquisition of the ability to perform such skills automatically during sporting events constitutes a negative freedom in the sense that the more effective skill-performance, and combination of skill-performances, reduce the restraints placed by opponents on an individual's influence within a given (sport) ecology. Likewise, the acquisition of the abilities to feed, clean, clothe and suchlike also constitute freedom in a negative sense because they reduce the restraints placed on an individual within an everyday ecology tooled around the independent biological and social activities of non-impaired bodies.

It is very important to be clear at this stage about precisely how Berlin's notion of political freedom is being applied within the realms of sporting performance and everyday living, particularly with respect to rehabilitation patients, given that Berlin is clear that 'mere incapacity to attain a goal is not lack of political freedom'.[76] Can an athlete's lack of skill or an individual's level of disablement truly be said to be a curtailment of their political freedom given that, as Helvetius clearly stated through an appropriately reverse-anthropomorphising analogy, 'it is not lack of freedom not to fly like an eagle or swim like a whale'?[77] Berlin is unequivocal that infringements on negative freedom can only be effected on a human by other humans and so it is necessary to have a precision understanding of the ecological reality of skill-performance in order to grasp properly the relationship between training and freedom. As Tim the Tortoise testifies, it is the very fact that the 'real world' is as artificial as the rule-governed reality of a sporting contest that results in the curtailment of the negative freedom of physically impaired actors, and if anyone should doubt the seriousness of such curtailment simply because it is testified to by a plasticine tortoise they need only reflect on how it stands between Ian and the satisfaction of his biological needs. Responsibility for the particular construction of the 'real world', and the constructed ergonomics of its attendant activities, undoubtedly lies with other humans and possibly even single individuals among them. This will be made clear when the legal penalties imposable upon individuals and organisations that do not comply with Disability Discrimination laws come into effect and the actor Mat Fraser's prediction of carnage in the wake of this legislation is fulfilled.[78] Any notion of the curtailment of the negative freedom of athletes must surely be mitigated by the fact that all implicitly accept the ergonomics of a sporting ecology simply by taking 'to the field', but the localised and manageable example of the sporting contest provides a model which, scaled up, maps directly on to the 'real world' to which it is much harder to consent and from which it is much more difficult to absent oneself.

If sports ecologies are of the same design as those of the 'real world', this is surely because they are *within* these real world ecologies, in much the same way that Gordon's notion of theatre as a virtual continuum of time and space occurs within a notionally non-virtual one. Even with an appreciation of the performativity of identity in place, it would be short-sighted to assume that the biological did not exist alongside the social, even as it is particularly 'done' by it, or that ecologies of the exemptional time/spaces of play in sport and theatre were not also biological, as has been dramatically demonstrated in lightning strikes on African football pitches and more tragically with the death of Cameroon international Mark Vivien Foe while playing in a Confederations Cup game against Columbia in France on 26 June 2003.[79] Indeed, theatrical ecologies, like their sporting counterparts, operate precisely within the overlap between the 'real' and the 'symbolic', and with a degree of self-reflexive acknowledgement of these that would appear to amplify any such consciousness in 'real' time and space. As Ridout writes, it is 'the *temporary* acquisition' of an 'inability to distinguish between the real and the feigned' that is the 'precondition ... [which] allows theatre to entertain' [*emphasis added*].[80] This temporary acquisition recalls Coleridge's oft-quoted 'willing suspension of disbelief'[81] and stands in contrast to the 'un-willed' suspension of disbelief by which Goffman first showed societies of role-playing individuals to operate.[82] How then might the freedom of actors within theatre ecologies be mapped within the social and biological ecologies of the 'real world', and what role might skill acquisition and automaticity play in theatrical performance?

Acting skilfully

I have already suggested a similarity between Roach's study of historical theories of acting and Berlin's historical study of concepts of freedom, as well as the merits of both in outlining the contingency of acting on various understandings of what it is to be human, especially with relevance to the kinds of training to which 'today's actor' is subject. The forms of actor training encountered during this project are, of course, determinedly contemporary, decisively 'today', as practised by students and professionals and predominate within Theatre and Performance Studies publishing *now*. As Campbell has argued, these contemporary trainings might sit within a broad cultural trend towards holism (even as they might be somewhat paradoxically characterised by their eclecticism or fragmentation[83]) and the source of the particular 'theatrical' tributary of this broad-flowing stream has been traced back to Antonin Artaud.[84]

Artaud's concise concluding sentence to his essay 'An Affective Athleticism' anticipates several twentieth-century body-practice developments both specifically theatrical and more broadly performative. Having explained in sparse details precisely how 'the actor' is to coordinate breath with various acupuncture pressure points to 'increase the inner density and amplitude of his feelings', Artaud summarily claims that 'the rest is achieved by screams'.[85] It is fitting that one of theatre's most famous sufferers of mental illness should find his own thoughts on the body connected to Janov's therapeutic techniques that turned a 'cry for help' into a 'primal scream', or with the psychiatric treatments proposed by R.D. Laing. Artaud's obvious dismay in realising that the affective scream was beyond the reach of French actors who 'now only know how to talk'[86] strongly connects his influential thesis on acting to a range of therapeutic techniques including both Janov's and Laing's, and referred to collectively by Dr Joy Manne as 'breathwork'.[87]

Artaud, like Laing, posited a pre-lapsarian state underlying and pre-dating the 'stifling atmosphere we live in'.[88] For Laing, the stifling atmosphere was decidedly 'real', existing in the social constraints placed on individuals that would cause them to manifest 'madness' as the quite reasonable response to the difficult and often conflicting expectations placed on them by society.[89] According to Artaud, the stifling atmosphere of 'contemporary' theatre, which as we have seen is of course embedded within 'real' ecologies, is the result of the damage wrought by psychological drama and especially the ascendancy of the written word in such an atmosphere. Against its corrupting and oppressive effects Artaud prescribes a physiological 'athleticism of the heart' that will 'rescue theatre from its human psychological prostration'.[90] Joseph Roach has shown that the contemporary psychology of figures such as Laing and our current views on acting, developed out of Artaud's appeal for an end to masterpieces, have concluded in a late-twentieth-century moment where 'we [now] believe that spontaneous feelings, if they can be located and identified, must be extracted with difficulty from beneath layers of inhibition'[91] – and it is perhaps for this reason more than any other that Artaud is widely regarded as a profound influence on some of the most written-about theatrical practice of the twentieth century – theatrical practice which has insistently denied and derided skill acquisition.[92]

Jerzy Grotowski– probably the most written-about antagonist from within this historical movement, and one who claimed to have 'studied all the major actor training methods of Europe and beyond'[93] – succinctly asserted that 'we do not want to teach the actor a predetermined set of skills or give him a "bag of tricks"'.[94] The inclusive 'we' here refers to Grotowksi's Theatre Laboratory during the 1960s when his 'Towards a Poor Theatre' essay was first published, though it might easily be read now as referring to Barba, Donnellan and others who have consciously or unconsciously adopted and adapted the principles of Grotowski's *via negativa*: 'not a collection of skills but an eradication of blocks'.[95] Of this method of actor training, which is constructed by Grotowski in opposition to the 'deductive' methods of skill acquisition, he writes:

> The education of an actor in our theatre is not a matter of teaching him something; we attempt to eliminate his organism's

resistance ... The result is freedom from the time lapse between inner impulse and outer reaction in such a way that ... impulse and reaction are concurrent.[96]

Grotowski pours scorn on deductive actor training and its focus on the accumulation of a range of skills, even likening the bag-of-tricks actor to a 'courtesan'.[97] His 'inductive' method of elimination, itself perhaps influenced by Artaud's demand for an actor to 'journey down into [his] soul in a reverse direction' and to 'delve down into his personality',[98] continues to resonate alongside it in contemporary theatrical practice and has been perhaps most explicitly taken up by the Odin Teatret.[99]

The eclecticism of the courtesan actor is manifest in the exercises of Odin training, especially the early period when 'everyone learned the same basic acrobatics, gymnastics, pantomime skills and vocal techniques',[100] but also in the later performances such as *The Book of Dances*, whose stilt-walking, instrument-playing and flag-waving was 'built from fragments of the actor's training'.[101] However, the focus on skill acquisition through training exercises came to be overcoded by a focus on an individual actor's pace and rhythm such that, according to Watson, skill acquisition now plays a 'secondary role . . . in today's training at the Odin'.[102] Eugenio Barba, in a description of Odin training as it moved towards its design 'today', de-emphasised skill acquisition, mobilising instead a rhetoric of self-discovery. He describes this as:

> a process of self-definition, a process of self-discipline which manifests itself indissolubly through physical reactions. It is not the exercise in itself that counts – for example, bending or somersaulting – but the individual's justification for his own work, a justification which although perhaps banal or difficult to explain through words, is physiologically perceptible, evident to the observer.[103]

Barba maintains that, though the training undertaken by Odin effectively prepares an actor's vocal and physical skills for performance, continual training also helps the actor to tap what he calls the 'pre-expressive'. Ian Watson contends that this idea of the pre-expressive is based upon what can be best described as the 'deconstruction and reconstruction of the body in Eastern performance training' – that is, 'using training to break the normal patterns of behaviour in order to discover a cohesive physical and vocal grammar of performance that engages the body differently from our daily activities and speech'.[104] Such a training does not just involve acquiring new skills but also involves examining and exploring the self to find what Barba calls an actor's own 'personal temperature' – their own rhythm, boundaries, abilities, that which makes them unique as a performer within an ecology of the 'pre-expressive'.

I have already indicated that delimiting and defining the kinematics of a task in the real world has a parallel in the fixed ascription of signifier–signified relationship within aesthetic lexica of performance styles such as Peking Opera. Gordon writes that disciplinary trainings for perform-ance forms with fixed signifier–signified relationships (ballet in his illustrative example) are characterised by the focus on skill acquisition, which results in automaticity. However, Gordon notes that, while the formation of particular skill competency affords a performer a potency within a given ecology, this also results in a 'deformation of the body', meaning that as a performer's 'kinaesthetic potential is formed . . . his training render[s] his body virtually unable to dance in any other way'.[105] While such deformation is necessary for the negative freedom of a per-former within such a specific theatre ecology, the very ecological specifi-city of formation/deformation would logically inhibit the flexibility of 'today's actor' to select between and adopt different kinaesthetic styles, unless there existed what Hodge has called 'principles' of performance training 'capable of transcending their origins'.[106] It is precisely a shared belief in such transcendental principles that unites post-Artaud practi-tioners such as Grotowski and Barba and constructs the myths of their training practice in antagonism to skill acquisition.

The kinds of performance generated by Barba and the Odin training, while at times reliant upon skill competency, cannot be said to operate by a codex of signifier–signified relationships, given that the production of meaning would seem to be less 'linear' than in forms of performance that operate by such predetermined axes of meaning-production. This is typified by 'The Director's' comment in Barba's essay on *The Book of Dances*: 'People seeing *The Book of Dances* sometimes say: "If that meant anything I didn't understand it. But one thing is obvious: there was violence".[107] The opening up of realms of meaning-making in such performance that would appear to rely little on 'understanding' in any conclusive (or perhaps simply, narrative) sense, but wherein certain meaning-constructions are 'obvious', seems very difficult to explain without making recourse to a 'pre-cultural' realm of experience, since all 'linear' relationships are assuredly produced within a specific culture. Indeed, such a realm derives from and supports Barba's notion of the 'pre-expressive', just as, as Grotowski was fond of quoting: 'Each technique leads to a metaphysics.'[108] The transposition into theatre ecologies of skills developed in the 'green exercise' outlined in the previous chapter are somewhat harder to map than the transposition of ballet poses or Peking Opera movements into their own performance ecologies, or even eating and drinking kinematics into ecologies of the real world, given that the 'real' and 'virtual' dimensions of such skills fine away even less neatly into 'functional' or 'symbolic', 'real' or 'virtual' categories in 'pre-expressive' performance forms. However, the freedom afforded a theatrical performer as a result of their training in contemporary practice such as this does align with 'negative' forms of the concept.

Watson appears to suggest that 'extra-daily' training might produce a 'grammar' of performance skills which, rather than being 'pre-expressive', would be merely 'non-ordinary', and thus their effect on audiences might rely on generating interest in the same way as a magician or a contortionist, whose skills *appear* to transcend 'real'-world ecologies even as they operate within them. These non-ordinary vocal and physical techniques might render the ordinary *non-ordinary* and particularly sensitise an audience to the daily, just as Brecht's famous *Verfremdungseffekt* makes 'the familiar strange'. Viewed from the angle proposed by Watson's analogy to certain Eastern training techniques, a grammar of extra-daily skills might bear more resemblance to a fixed codex of signifier–signified relationships even as it eschews linear 'meanings' in favour of generalised impressions or effects. The accumulation of a range of 'extra-daily' skills, while constructed within a myth critical of skill acquisition, might still be directed towards the kind of skill-based negative freedom that Grotowski called 'freedom from the time lapse between inner impulse and outer reaction', but where, unlike in other performance ecologies, the reaction is not a linear, functional or symbolic outcome but an 'alienating' effect.

To take the notion of the 'pre-expressive' a bit deeper and on its own terms, even with the range of problems associated with defining what any expressive statement could be 'before' culture, this tradition of training operates another differently calibrated notion of negative freedom, in that it is associated with inducing a particular state in the performer wherein they are 'liberated' from the restraints and restrictions of everyday expression. Watson writes that 'the most obvious aim of [the Odin's] daily discipline . . . is to maintain the actor's *performance conditioning*' [*emphasis added*], which for Watson relates to the pre-expressive and the expressive as well as the more quotidian necessity of the rehearsal process.[109] Performance conditioning might sound oddly like the kind of thing one might expect a racehorse to undergo, particularly since the implicit notion of 'conditions of performance' would suggest a more delimited ecology of play than might be anticipated in such 'pre-expressive' theatre. Carreri, one of the Odin's actors, gives some definition to this state by asserting, 'I keep training in order to be ready to respond, to be able to meet the demands of the new performance'.[110] If the lower-case 'n' of 'new' here were to be beefed up to an upper-case 'N', then Carreri might well be echoing Gordon's ambition for 'today's actor' capable of understanding and applying a range of theatrical techniques to suit a given performance. Seeing as she would seem to be referring to new productions rather than new performance styles, perhaps the conditioning achieved by 'keep[ing] training' refers to something more like the state described by Grotowski as a 'passive readiness to realise an active role, a state in which one does not "want to do" but rather "resigns from not doing"',[111] more recently translated by Phillip Zarrilli as 'standing still while not standing still'.[112] It might seem to some that, in the climate of today's theatre (I am presuming that this would be the natural habitat of today's actor), freedom is not so much characterised by the automaticity of a particular skill (unlike yesterday's theatre[113]) – but by the flexibility to acquire and select between a range of skills, which as the experiments of Grotowski's inheritors, Barba and Brook, have shown, may entail what Watson has called 'negotiating cultures'.[114]

Barba's notion of the 'pre-expressive' is predicated upon an ecology of a *really-real* world that pre-exists the artificiality of all cultural ecologies and achieves a 'tight fit' with an independent 'transcultural physiology'.[115] Watson et al. argue that acquiring such a physiology of the pre-expressive entails:

> acquiring through training . . . certain bodily tensions and oppositions, certain ways of moving, vocalising and gesturing [that] leads performers to their 'extra-daily' bodies, their special nonordinary performing bodies.[116]

It is perhaps only in such a contemporary climate, wherein such an ability is said to transcend cultures, that Gordon's depiction of today's actor as an emancipated consumer of performance styles doesn't seem either absurd or piratical, and where the claims of post-Artaud practitioners for an uninhibited performance-conditioned actor find any traction. To bracket the myth of the pre-expressive or pre-cultural and all of their attendant debates for a moment, to speak of a 'state' in which one is free to act within a given ecology is to describe a condition of negative freedom entirely commensurate with the automatic performances of elite athletes and the non-impaired; yet a unique feature of skill acquisition training during 'the age of exercises' is an insistence on 'positive' effects.

Grotowski's commitment to the self-revelatory nature of the *via negativa* contains the implicit assumption that there is an underlying self to be revealed underneath various layers of inhibition. This idea is directly transposed into Barba's notions of the extra-daily and pre-expressive in the assertion that there exists before and underneath the everydayness of culture a universal expressive ecology that a self (all selves) can access through training. A belief in a transcendent self and a commitment to accessing or recovering it draws on particular versions of the positive concept of freedom as manifest in practices often overtly hostile to extensive 'negative' liberties, such as religious training and in what Jack Clay has called the 'self-use systems'[117] of body practice of the twentieth century.[118] These self-use systems have arisen during the 'broad cultural trend' towards holism identified by Campbell and have, throughout the twentieth century, become increasingly integrated in the professional theatre trainings also partaking in this trend.[119]

Self-use systems, such as those designed by F.M. Alexander, operate particular body ideals, and the potential for embodying these is latent within all individuals precisely because they are characterised by 'normal, organically correct self-use'.[120] The myth of these self-use training practices is constructed around the assertion that, while all individuals possess the latent potential for 'correct self-use', most are subject to 'the eccentricities of their own habitual behaviour, movement and speech'.[121] It is precisely through the strict limitation of an individual's negative freedom to act as they wish or as their various social roles and environments compel them to move and talk, that they are able to attain the more fully positive freedom associated with correct self-use. Being able to self-actualise one's own latent 'correct' body ideal constitutes a manifestation of positive freedom which, as with so many manifestations of the concept, is reliant upon the restriction and limitation of an individual's negative liberty. In the case of these self-use systems an individual is prevented from moving 'incorrectly' with the promise that 'correct' self-use will constitute a more genuine freedom of movement.

Berlin clearly recognises the paradox of such a model in his study in forms of freedom. He argues that any system that lays claim to an 'essential self' must negotiate between the self-realisation of the individual and his/her enslavement, since the proponents of such a system are 'in a position to ignore the actual wishes of men or societies to bully, oppress, torture in the name, and on behalf of their "real" selves"'.[122] Clearly there is a difference of magnitude, if not also of character, between any such 'oppression' in voluntary participation in self-use systems and the state-based oppression of a tyrant. It might seem overly 'serious' to be connecting the coercion of a physical therapy to Berlin's examples of state-based oppression. If we take Berlin's advice and compare 'total patterns of life . . . directly as wholes' we surely couldn't fail to conclude that the voluntary participant in self-use training is more free even in a negative sense than Gleb Nerzhin in *The First Circle*, for instance. Nonetheless, such self-use systems might provide 'miniaturised' models embedded within the macro-model of 'real-world' situations in much the same way as have the exemptional spaces of theatre and sport – a quality with which Blast Theory's *Day of the Figurines* makes much play. This being so, the example of religious training provides a 'model' wherein the micro and the macro (and their appropriate scales of seriousness) are more completely coagulated, and one whose particular myth has been overtly appropriated for theatre by the most influential post-Artaud practitioner.

Monastic techniques

Following Foucault, Richard Marsden notes that the monastery has spawned many transformative institutions and practices because it is 'the ideal-typical enclosure ... [and] source of many contemporary organisational techniques'.[123] It is characteristic of the eclecticism of Grotowski's work that while he replicated the Bohr Institute of Physics in his Theatre Laboratory (for which the Bohr Institute provided 'a model illustrating a certain type of activity'[124]), he was also utilising 'organisational techniques' and religious rhetoric from decidedly non-scientific traditions of human-investigation.[125] Both the initial relative isolation of the Theatre Laboratory and the disciplined nature of the activity that occurred in this isolation, later identified by Robert Findlay,[126] appear to replicate aspects of monastic withdrawal (*anchoresis*) and strictly controlled activities (*horarum*), for example.[127] Grotowski's insistence that actors under his direction engage in daily training recalls the daily timetabling of activities in a monastery that deliberately and conspicuously place strict limits on an individual's negative freedom.[128] Indeed, the author and Benedictine monk Terrence Kardong notes that 'the modern mentality that prizes individual rights and freedom', in a definitively negative sense, will not find Benedict's verses on obedience and denial 'very congenial'.[129] The freedom that is attained through such restrictions of an individual's negative liberty is, like other practices discussed here, tied into a belief in a transcendent self, and in this context Kardong claims that Benedict 'radicalises obedience' because through negative restraint the individual achieves 'freedom and full loving confidence in Christ'.[130] It is precisely because the freedom achieved through monastic training is associated with the transcendental spiritual dimension of Christ that it is mapped into a 'real' world ecology of restraint and denial.[131] However, the consequences of this are perhaps not so straightforwardly translated into the paradox identified by Berlin.

I have already suggested that Grotowski's particular brand of religious rhetoric might be associated with his Polish upbringing as well as with his adventures into Eastern religious practices. In his essay on the 'Deconstruction of the Body in Indian Asceticism', Patrick Olivelle exposes certain trends within asceticism, and Indian asceticism in particular, that position it alongside the self-use systems being popularised during the development of Grotowski's practice. Olivelle argues that there is a tension inherent within asceticism whereby 'creation' rubs up against 'deconstruction' in a process of ascetic transformation, with the body of biological material and latent transcendent capacity separating from the body as social construct. He argues that 'ascetic creation' is in actuality 'a deconstruction of the socially created body',[132] and as such 'the ascetic deconstruction of the body has to be located . . . within the socially constructed correspondence between the two bodies – the physical and the social'.[133] Part of the myth of ascetic traditions of training, among which we might locate both the *via negativa* and the pre-expressive, involves the systematic disaggregation of an 'essential self' from a social self or selves, such that the underlying and universal non-social self is revealed.

Patricia Cox-Miller, in a reading of the 'Aesthetics of Asceticism' that incorporates Eastern and Western traditions and accounts for this disaggregation of the terms of the 'real' and the 'virtual', provides a meta-description of asceticism as various 'attempts to control the play of the body as a signifier; it attempts to reimagine how the body can be read and what it can say'.[134] Cox-Miller's meta-definition of ascetic training would seem to speak to Gordon's version of the assumption of a virtual body in a very direct address that tackles the fact that the point from which all theories of acting reportedly start is unstable and difficult to control, and yet all theories of *actor training* might initiate with the very intention of stabilising and managing this volatility. Cox-Miller is not alone in reading asceticism as a curiously paradoxical process whereby the very embodiment of social roles is overtly challenged even as these are practically reconfigured, or as Averil Cameron puts it:

The self-consciousness of asceticism itself embodies an act of self-creation that possesses its own aesthetics; it transcends the natural and resembles an act of literary or artistic creation.[135]

Asceticism has a certain paradoxical element in that it is a process whereby the essential self (associated with the 'real') is separated from the social self (associated with the 'virtual') only to produce a new compound of the two. This process 'scales up' from the individual into the macro as it is rendered in what Kalistos Ware calls a 'pattern' in the personal biographies of famous ascetics whereby 'a flight [is] followed by a return'.[136]

The results of configuring a 'real' self as the antithetical counterpart of a virtual, social one has arguably produced at certain periods throughout monastic history a 'dichotomous model of human composition',[137] and situated asceticism in a battleground between the rational, dominant, transcendent component and the irrational, desirous and destructive element which acts for the transcendental like 'a prison or a mechanistic object in space'.[138] Within such a context, negative restrictions placed on the liberty of individuals through religious training are justifiable in so far as they only adversely affect the mechanistic object and in so doing emancipate the essential self.[139]

While this state of affairs, a realisation of Berlin's paradox, may be congruent with certain distinct periods in Western monastic history, as Cox-Miller has argued, it is not applicable to early Christian asceticism and neither is it applicable to contemporary Benedictine monastic practice.[140] Cox-Miller argues that 'in the Christian asceticism of late antiquity, the body was perceived to be problematic not because it was a body but because it was not a body of plenitude'.[141] It is rather an inheritance of the comparison between what Vernant called the 'dim body' of humanity and the 'dazzling body'[142] of the gods for Greeks of the archaic period – a human–divine comparison rather than a interiorly human division – that leads to the body being viewed with despair and disgust in later periods.

Although certain Christian theologians embraced the dichotomous version of a Platonic view of the human, they could not consign the body to status as restrictive envelope if they were to give affirmation to the value of human creation recorded in the book of Genesis, which Cox-Miller observes was 'one of the central texts for anthropological speculation'.[143]

Thus, when the body was altered by various practices of 'mutilation', 'this was not because of its sheer materiality as part of the physical world, but rather because it functioned as a signifier of a lack that was not only spiritual but also corporeal'.[144]

The idea that the various negative restrictions placed on individuals undergoing ascetic training might have less to do with the domination of the social self by the essential self and more with the transformation of the body and its signifying capabilities would appear to draw a line across religious and rehabilitative training, as well as the post-Artaud tradition of theatrical practice, and constitute freedom of action in a positive sense.

It is clear that negative freedom can in actuality be indifferent to oppression, and much ascetic practice finds itself in a solipsistic endgame of what Berlin calls 'retreat to the inner citadel'.[145] Schopenhauer's conception of asceticism as a training in self-mastery of will is characteristic of such a retreat,[146] as is the more phlegmatic consideration of conditions within the citadel of Solzhenitsyn's prisoner Bobynnin (to whom I felt an increasing affinity during my participation in *Day of the Figurines*).

> I've got nothing, see. Nothing! . . . you only have power over
> people so long as you don't take everything away from them. But
> when you've robbed a man of everything he's no longer in your
> power – he's free again.[147]

Alexander Solzhenitsyn's novels, including *The First Circle*, in which Bobynnin castigates the 'Minister of State Security' for his unintentionally ineffective oppressive policies, constitute a body of work that variously depicts the conditions by which individuals experience the forcible disaggregation of their 'real' selves from their social bodies. As I have already indicated, following Berlin, to conclude, as Bobynnin does, that the results of state-based oppression might not be of a different species to those of voluntary asceticism even if they are of a different magnitude, is potentially dangerous because it fails to recognise differences between 'total patterns of life'. Bobynnin's argument faithfully retraces the steps of a dichotomous model of self and reasserts the primacy of the 'essential' in the correspondence between the spiritual and the social, the 'real' and the 'virtual', but it also points towards the meta-disciplinary askeological process developing out of asceticism which seeks to control the play of the body as a signifier because it, at least implicitly, recognises the potential for certain practices to separate and reaggregate the 'real' and 'virtual', so that the self no longer acts as a signifier of a lack, but of a unity.

It is perhaps only the ability *voluntarily* to control the transformation of one's 'virtually-real' self that sets training apart from discipline or state-based oppression, but it is nonetheless the conscious and deliberate engaging of processes of real–virtual aggregation, and the wilful deceleration of these processes and redetermination of the correspondence between real and virtual through repetitive practice, that enables trainees to transform themselves at the levels of personal experiences and social existence. Indeed, in the conclusion of *Day of the Figurines*, as night falls on the virtual town and I am once again disaggregated from my virtual and really-virtual selves, I am strangely recompleted. My troublesome aggregation with my virtual selves that has disturbed my 'real' life as text-message reports of chaos interjected within it, is ended and the lacuna that had begun to open between what I was 'really' doing and what I was only 'virtually' bringing about closes up. My phone now looks innocuous again and no longer represents the *lack* which I myself had come to signify as I struggled and failed to hold my selves together and maintain a sovereign realm of freedom for all of them.

While I may struggle to hold my selves together within the particular ecology of *Day of the Figurines* I can, of course, as I can with other such exemptional spaces of play, exempt myself from the various oppressions of these ecologies even if I cannot satisfactorily overcome them. However, as has been shown by White and Fawcus, such play-ecologies are embedded within a 'real world', and as Tim the Tortoise has already explained, it is near impossible and almost completely undesirable to opt out of this particular ecology. The example of rehabilitation makes clear that training, even as it conducts processes of automatisation constructed in response to the particular restrictions of specific exemptional ecologies, is also, by the same token, disintegrating and reaggregating real and virtual as it reconfigures both social subjectivity and its overlapping counterpart, self-identity in the 'real world'.

7 What is called training?

As was clear at the outset of this book, understanding training would involve formulating an appropriate question about it. Formulating the question, 'What is called training?' entailed the provision of a framework, which I called 'askeology', that would allow this question to be engaged and enable the activities it addressed to be meaningfully explored. It is perhaps fitting that the consequences of naming should raise some concerns in a book which has had to respond to a certain imperative to anonymise or rename those who have participated in it, and that in conclusion I might be impelled to consider what is at stake in the name 'askeology'.[1]

It's tough living with the wrong name. That's the gist of the lesson taught by one of the better-known artefacts belonging to 'the theatre' – Act Two, Scene Two, of *Romeo and Juliet*, or 'the balcony scene', as it is more often known. The balcony scene, along with the two-dimensional graveyards and battlements of Hamlet's Denmark and especially the 'Usurper's Court' and the set-painted forests of Arden, where the action of *As You Like It* takes place, have connected theatre to itself and to worlds beyond the stage. Questions posed in these scenographic environments about the nature of identity, mortality, corporeality and especially *performativity* have secured Shakespeare's ownership of the dramaturgical metaphor – 'all the world's a stage' – which has been appropriated by disciplines as diverse as sociology and marine biology.[2] Romeo and Juliet seem assured that performances of Capulet and Montague identity can be easily exchanged and as the transformational proposition of the balcony scene has been inflected and augmented to realign theatre with the innumerable contexts in which it operates, from Brecht's Romeo-as-Landlord to Grande Otelo's black male Juliet-in-drag, still it remains in each context a dialogue about *naming*.[3]

The young lovers, recognising that the obstacle to their courtship lies in the very names they bear, debate various strategies of un-naming from denying a father to writing the offending title on a piece of paper, only to tear it up before finally resolving to marry – an iconic transformational practice that involves a person, traditionally a woman, taking a new name. The magnitude of their delusion in believing that marriage will smoothly reconcile the antagonism in their names is compounded by Friar Lawrence's assurance that the plan can 'Turn your households' rancour to pure love',[4] which sets in motion the narrative of one of the most famous tragedies of the English stage. That neither the Friar nor the Nurse, as confidants to the two lovers, raises a protest against the un-naming plan only serves to conceal the quite foreseeable consequences of the partnership and the reality that possession of the wrong name is seldom easily relinquished. I know of no better response to Juliet's oft-quoted question, 'What's in a name?', posed from the balcony to a garden she believes to be empty, than that supplied by a famously rancorous vigilante who is himself, like Romeo, skulking in the shrubbery below, the unfortunate bearer of the wrong name.

Johnny Cash's 'Boy Named Sue' has probably given the most evocative testament to the tribulations of bearing the 'wrong' name, as well as perhaps the most powerful expression of the impulse to acquire the right one, which is undoubtedly, for him, tied into the experience of *being who I really am*.[5] Sue tells his listener that his father abandoned him aged three, leaving behind little to cherish, including Sue's inappropriate name. Throughout his childhood Sue endures the taunts of boys and the giggling of girls and becomes an embittered fighter, ready with a fist to answer any slight. At times throughout the song Sue can't even bring himself to say his own name, and ultimately he vows to hunt down and kill his father in retribution for giving him such an unsuitable name.[6] Even as the lyric concludes and Sue is reconciled with his father he still can't quite bring himself to associate with his gender-bending moniker and determines to call his own son *anything* but Sue.

While the 'imaginatively' named children of the rich and famous may have 'Boy Named Sue' childhoods, it seems more likely that, among peers also named after city suburbs, space hardware or fruit and veg, these individuals are untouched by the violence, embarrassment and shame that haunts Sue throughout life. It becomes clear through Cash's lyric that Sue is not the *wrong* name to own, but is, like the name Montague worn in a Capulet garden, a hard name to own in a particular environment. This is in fact the very reason Sue's errant father gives for naming him thus; after an epic and near patricidal fight, Sue's father, finally beaten to the draw, and smiling at Sue, points out that Sue's victory in the contest is a direct consequence of all the practice he got defending himself from his childhood tormentors.[7] Accepting that his naming strategy may have backfired on him even as it achieved its desired objective, Sue's father argues that, before killing him, Sue should at least thank him for the role he has played in making Sue such a formidable opponent.

The consequences of naming are not of course limited to theatrical or lyrical narratives, but are uniquely felt in the range of training disciplines that inform this project. Name-giving is integrally linked to creation throughout the Bible, and responsibility for it is relinquished to the human domain early on and only fully reclaimed in the final book of Revelation. By Chapter 2 of Genesis, Adam, who would appear to have acquired his name from the Ur-creation of the earth,[8] assumes the task of naming all living creatures, an activity which, in effect, defines their fate because, 'whatsoever Adam called every living creature, that *was* the name thereof' [*emphasis as original*].[9] Much of the controversy generated around the historical figure of Jesus, and certainly those particular controversies that lead directly to his trial and subsequent execution, issue from his insistent application of a new taxonomy wherein existing phenomena acquire new names.[10] Given the significance of name-giving to the religious narrative and the impact it has in the realm of human relations, 'the revelation' that the Holy Spirit will *rename* those who overcome earthly trials reclaims the responsibility of name-giving from humankind (which has struggled to manage its consequences) and restores it to the spiritual plain;

And I will give him a white stone, and in the stone a new name written, which no man knoweth saving he that receiveth it.[11]

The significance attached to name-giving in the books of the Bible is reflected in Christian practices of baptism and (most pertinently to this study) in the monastic practice by which postulants become novices through the taking of a new 'religious' or 'monastic' name.[12]

Naming also plays an important role in rehabilitation training, where the diagnostic naming of a condition also fixes the clinical identity of the patient. This is probably nowhere better exemplified than in the medical term 'ictus' or 'stroke', deriving from the Latin *icere* meaning 'to strike', which quite literally identifies sufferers as those who have been *struck down*. The history of physiotherapeutic medicine in the West, as of performance, is closely associated with the term *chorea*, deriving from the Greek word *khoreia* meaning 'to dance'. Chorea has, since at least the Middle Ages, and possibly right back to the third century, been used to isolate a particular pathology, the symptoms of which are characterised by the seemingly involuntary movement of the limbs.[13]

Medicine operates through an ever-expanding lexicon of terms, each naming a previously unnamed constellation of symptoms and producing a new disease. The existence of a disease is, Deleuze has argued, generated in the instance of its naming and the measure of the eradication of diseases such as, for example, smallpox, is perhaps to be found in the decreased usage of the term and even in the decreasing awareness of what it entails.[14] Indeed, Deleuze shows that the process of naming in medicine is, at a certain level, indistinguishable from the naming done in 'critical' or artistic creation; and in his analysis of the writings of the Marquis de Sade and Leopold Sacher-Masoch he has much to say about the naming of diseases by clinicians and its association with 'critical' artistic creation. In 'Mystique et Masochisme', which provides the text of a brief interview with Deleuze on the subject of his *Masochism: An Interpretation of Coldness and Cruelty*, he argues that symptomology occupies 'a sort of neutral point, a limit point, premedical or submedical, belonging as much to art as medicine'.[15] Unlike the attendant medical fields of etiology and therapeutics, which look respectively at the causes of disease and application of treatments, symptomology is 'almost on the exterior of medicine, at a neutral point, a zero point, where artists and philosophers and physicians and patients can meet one another'.[16] To the congregation of popular figures accumulating in this chapter – from Romeo and Juliet to Adam and Sue – I might add the historical figure of St Vitus, who as patron saint to both actors and epileptics and an individual associated with both medicine and dance, personifies just such a 'meeting point'.[17]

Deleuze writes that it is the capacity to regroup signs – undoing existing aggregations of symptoms, and establishing new, 'profoundly original clinical pictures[s]'[18] – that, in the act of naming, provides a meeting place for art and medicine.[19] This project is, in many ways, like the disciplines it studies (and especially the theatre and performance discipline from where it departed), fixated with naming, and, just as is the case for the ('real' and 'virtual') characters within these disciplines, there is a need for it to acquire the right name. I suggested at the outset that, unlike Read's 'showciology', askeology was an existing discipline in search of a name and having arrived again at the question posed in my introductory chapter by analysis of a series of other newly named processes, it is appropriate to assess how fitting a name it has acquired, and what the consequences of its acquisition are likely to be. As Deleuze has shown, in encountering what he calls the 'phantasys' of living, there is the potential to work up an original view of the world by connecting and combining 'symptoms' to form a clinical image. He has also suggested, through his analysis of the term sadomasochism and its relatedness to the lives and writings of de Sade and Sacher-Masoch, that the usefulness of such a clinical image might reside in its coherence and irreducibility, since in the case of the word 'sadomasochism' this term turns out to be a 'semio-logical howler':

> what appeared to be a common 'sign' linking the two perversions turned out on investigation to be in the nature of a mere syndrome which could be broken down into irreducibly specific symptoms of one or the other inquiry.[20]

The attempts made throughout this book to organise the 'symptoms' of training respond directly to Watson's observation, quoted at the outset, that, 'training is a generic term that means different things to different people'[21] and were motivated by a dissatisfaction with the low level of isolation in a symptomology that satisfied itself with such statements. It is not my contention that the clinical image of askeology presented herein is completely irreducible – no attempt to produce such an image for 'performance' and 'theatre' has proved authoritative and any such 'definition' would probably not be desirable[22] – but rather that there is a value to and a need for a coherent clinical image to emerge before other investigative work can get properly under way.

This is not to say that Theatre and Performance Studies must postpone analyses of the various 'generic' applications of the term training until they can say what the word is being used to describe, but that they will ultimately, like the star-crossed lovers, be forced to bear any consequences attendant on failure to accept what is at stake in a name. Providing a name and an isolation of a meta-disciplinary category of training is, after all, not only a matter of closing the chasm opened in self-identity as a result of having the wrong name, or no name, but of filling the void where first philosophies should be. Whether or not the name 'askeology' is ill-fated and whether it will be able to play happily with other studies and sciences or have to struggle to 'be who I really am' remains to be seen. At least with the company of showciology it will have an equally idiotic-ally named playmate and within the still-forming environment of the no less absurdly titled 'PS' may, in fact, fit right in.

Whether the name will survive a generation in a way the 'Sue' is destined not to and be taken up by other scholars also remains to be seen, but the term 'askeology' has not been constructed, like celebrity child monikers, to conform to fashions or, like Sue, to toughen up a discipline, but to give a name to a phenomenon that has otherwise been nameless. Having no name is, as 'The Man with No Name' in both his Eastern and Western appearances has shown, even more perilous and estranging than having the wrong one.[23] There is just as much at stake in the name askeology as there is in Montague, Capulet or Sue and things worth struggling for even if ultimately not worth dying over.

A second image

Just as this book has been prompted by the inadequacies of a particular clinical view and motivated to provide another to sit alongside it, much of the analysis of this book has been conducted through the co-location of two images of the same phenomena, be it Guido Fawkes's signature during and after torture, Ian Wilding and Tim the Tortoise or 'real' and 'virtual' John. It seems fitting that these couplings should now be confronted by their archetype. The generation of a coherent clinical image is perhaps most commonly associated with processes of training in the production and publication of 'before' and 'after' images. In a culture which Alphonso Lingis has shown to be alternately enthralled and repulsed by body changes, these images have come to fascinate.[24] The transformation that finds itself somewhat simplistically and perhaps overly visually documented in this archetypal pairing is, as the prevalence of such images reveals, a highly privileged experience. Contrasting the glorification of such a transformational experience in magazines and on TV screens, Sparks, Batey and Brown, in their study of a bodybuilder retired through injury, have shown just how profound the psychological effect can be when the conditions of 'before' are juxtaposed by those experienced in the 'aftermath' of physical degeneration.[25]

In the territory shared by painting and performance, Bill Viola's video artworks have activated the static 'before and after' images to meditate on and record a process of transformation in a way that resists the simple binarisation of aesthetic images and allows an exploration of the social, emotional and political stakes wagered in the process. In my version of this archetypal pairing (see Figures 9 and 10), where 'critical' is juxtaposed by 'clinical', a still photograph of Bill Viola's Six Heads provides an image both historically and figuratively 'after' those reproduced by Charles Darwin in his earlier study of expression. Darwin's image itself was one that was produced 'before' by a man in the process of developing a completely new clinical image of the body. Darwin's reproduction of Duchenne's photographic image of the electrically stimulated muscles of a patient suffering facial anaesthesia (extreme right column) are presented here alongside the 'unaffected' expressions of three young girls.

As technologies for understanding emotion and expression, perhaps Bill Viola's moving image provides a more 'irreducible' account than Darwin's photographic plates, and thus perhaps a more 'complete' appreciation of the face and emotion than does Duchenne's battery-operated man.

The development of Duchenne's clinical view of neurology is a prime example of what Deleuze described as the 'isolation' (as opposed to 'invention'[26]) of a clinical view characterised here by the fact that diseases frequently acquire the name of the doctor who first identifies their irreducible symptoms. Duchenne's isolating of the neurological system has given rise not only to *Duchenne's Muscular Dystrophy* but also to the chromosomal model of a human via the possession of the *DMD* gene.[27]

While something of the value of a clinical view may reside in its coherence and irreducibility, its *use* may exist, as Deleuze has suggested, in its provision of a meeting place for artists, philosophers, physicians and patients. To put it another way and to say it specifically about training, askeology might provide somewhere for all of us who suffer alteration to gather and think and talk about that experience. It is, of course, only in the provision of such a space now, in the production of this book, as the isolation of training begins to take on a coherent image, that those who have been involved get the proper 'right of reply'. As Deleuze writes, etiology and therapeutics *precede from* symptomology. If, to speak through the medical example, diagnosis is the necessary prelude to prognosis, to speak for the sub-medical, the development of a coherent clinical view is the precondition of effective action both in the 'practical' mode of training and the 'reflective' modes by which we think and talk about this experience. The clinical view proposed by askeology, by bringing the critical imperatives of Performance Studies to bear on a field of Theatre Studies – 'training' – which to date has not been exposed to these imperatives, offers new ways of understanding, thinking and talking about training as well as a different sensitivity with which to practise it.

'A' for 'askeology'

Given the current interest among theatre and performance scholars in archives and curatorial practices, which would seem to reveal an implicit interest in classification as much as documentation, the current climate provides ideal environs in which to reflect on how the development of original clinical views impacts upon the organisation of and access to knowledge. Duchenne's experiments produced a clinical model of 'neurology' that connected the electrical discourse of current and voltage with the biological discourse of flesh and bone, and in so doing gave engineers and physicians a language with which to speak to one another about a shared phenomenon. Without collapsing the specificity of the individual studies of electrics and medicine, Duchenne contributed towards a clinical view of humankind and its world as an ecology ruled by the agitation and movement of charged particles. His experiments with the aesthetic effects of his new technology and his decision to codify these through relation to famous characters of the English stage, as well as Charles Darwin's subsequent decision to evoke these experiments in his study of human and animal expression, admitted theatre scholars also to his new domain and invited them to join a discussion.[28]

To stay in the 'safe and sound' (if disconcertingly quiet) space of the archive for a little longer, it is for this reason that Duchenne's 'album', and works containing his ideas and images, can be found archived under medicine, theatre, biology, photography and other subject headings. Indeed the tone of Duchenne's address to his readers, and his subdivision of his text into 'scientific' and 'aesthetic' sections, suggests that he anticipated a catholic readership consisting of artists, actors and 'the general public' as well as physicians. To recall the model of expression instituted by Diderot and taken up by Duchenne, the fact that his *Mechanism of Human Facial Expression* is shelved and cross-referenced under a number of subject headings is not only its inherent effect but also an *outward expression* of it; and if askeology too straddles the classificatory divisions of the archive, then it is because it also provides a clinical view whose irreducible characteristics underlie and emerge within a range of human practices. If askeology can provide a domain and a language through which differently situated voices can speak together and to one another, its use might also reside, as with Law's version of multi-voiced storytelling, in its capacity to open up novel questions.[29]

'P' for 'performance'

The emergence of a category of human experience (or rather the emergence of a clinical view of a category of human experience) that cuts across classificatory boundaries in the same way that neurology's nervous system runs across the organs and tissues of the body's sub-systems and facilitates the formulation of novel questions about human activity has a strong precedent in the emergence of the Performance Studies framework. Michel Foucault's Francocentric prophecy that the twentieth century would belong to a fellow Parisian and be regarded as Deleuzian[30] has perhaps been oddly fulfilled in Jon McKenzie's seemingly conflicting assertion that it has in fact been *performative*.[31] The development of the clinical view of an individual self and its social world, and more recently of the technological realm that seems poised fully to envelop both as *performative*, in opening up a new and quite vast clinical domain has also prompted original and diverse questions, including those asked about training in this study. McKenzie's 'isolation' of the performative (and thus not-Deleuzian) century, even as it rebuffs Foucault's claim, apparently confirms it because it is a supreme example of the sub-medical process itself 'isolated' by Deleuze.

Given the comparative youth of the discipline of Performance Studies and the possibility that its infancy may be on the cusp of adolescence, or possibly in the throes of a mid-life crisis, now would seem like an appropriate time for it to take notice of those things that are closest to it, having been initially stimulated by its inquisitiveness to make distant exploratory forays.[32] To carry the ageing metaphor a bit further: if, as Jacques Lacan has argued, each child comes only relatively late on to recognise itself as an individual self through a confrontation with mirrors, and traces its own physical and psychic borders somewhat later than those of external terrains, then this period of Performance Studies development may indeed be characterised by what Ridout has called 'the return of theatre'.[33] For all its analytical preoccupations with the transformations occurring during rites of passage and surgical procedures, it might seem remiss that a discipline of performance has not yet thought about the rather less 'dramatic' and rather more 'theatrical' alterations effected before someone gets up on stage. If the self-reflection of mirroring provides a certain opportunity for the reclassification of the image, then the Performance Studies framework brought to bear on theatrical models of training provides the kind of 'reflection' described by Michael Taussig whereby an entity (in this case, theatre) will be made to see 'itself mirrored in the eyes and handiwork of others'.[34]

It is in the meta-disciplinary character of training that the example of theatre has already undergone such a reflection in the rehabilitative example of drama therapy and that the monastic, as it encounters the various sites in which its organisational principles have been taken up, finds itself in a veritable hall of mirrors. It is perhaps only on the shared ground of askeology that actors, monastics, therapists and patients can become properly 'absorbed' in their own practices by seeing them through the lenses of each other's. It is in this climate where the fallacy of mastery of one's own practices (which entails mastery of oneself) gives way to an entrance into the practices of others and the possibility of newly attuned and self-aware practice.[35] The isolation of a clinical view of askeology is as much within the province of Performance Studies as it is an image of it, providing a fresh basis for the formulation of novel questions centred on 'training' that might intersect with those being asked about 'theatre' or 'performance'. While the enquiries into vocation, obedience, formation and automatisation prompted by the monastic, theatrical and rehabilitative are examples of such novel questions, they are, no doubt, not the limit of them.

To sharpen up the image of askeology's clinical view of training it is perhaps necessary to consider how the original image it has produced could sit alongside the 'generic' one that was already in place. This may be something like the comparison that is elicited by the before and after pairings in so far as it may trace out some of the concerns this clinical view of training shares with the existing 'generic' image, as well as those it has rejected. It may reiterate the results of this change of focus and some of the novel questions stimulated by it. In so doing I direct your attention to what has happened *between* my engagement with the generic image of training in my introductory chapter and the isolation of the clinical view of askeology, just as the 'before' and 'after' couplet, like so many second-act set changes, invites one to think about what has taken place in the interval. So this final chapter draws together the meta-disciplinary processes isolated in the preceding chapters and attempts to choreograph them into a coherent, if necessarily provisional view of training. Recalling the sub-medical process described by Deleuze and highlighted in my first chapter, this concluding chapter takes stock of the uses of askeology and considers what might be at stake in instating an isolation of training and giving it a name.

Askeology has arrived at a provisional image of training as sets of experiences, guided by a specific imperative, felt as a personal call. The relational conditions of the calling of vocation support and maintain the interpersonal networks in which training takes place. These interpersonal relationships provide the conditions for a form of work as *action* to take place; and training is, in a sense, characterised partly by the systematic frequency with which it is able to provide the conditions for action. Training groups share certain relational dynamics with performance, but the levels of organisation, or consociation, assemble a collective agency that overspills the spatial and temporal boundaries of the performance situation. The formatting of groups through their repeated shared prac-tising of exercises enables trainees to engage and decelerate structurating and subjectivating processes and re-form not only their performance capabilities but also their own social and physical selves. Suffering such alterations involves the acquisition of skills, which is accomplished by inducing 'negative' restrictions within particular performance ecologies. A trainee's repeated and continuing involvement in these activities, sus-tained by their own sense of vocation, evokes the conditions of 'positive' freedom whereby they are also able to engage continually in their own self-actualisation.

This clinical view generated by askeology suggests that the relationship between training and performance, as meta-disciplinary categories of activity, needs to be understood as more extensive and complicated than disciplinary views allow. Rather than amounting to a set of preparatory procedures, training shares many key traits with performance as it is now understood. It too is a relational phenomenon, but one wherein the tem-porarily assembled aesthetics of relations are extended over time and space and support and sustain conditions for action. Because these relational dynamics are repeatedly rehearsed, motivated by the imperative to training, they are able to achieve a 'consociative' agglutination of individual agencies more extensive than that which is found in the interrupting or exemptional situations of theatre. Training, like theatrical performance, occupies a certain virtual space but, unlike theatre, this virtual is not 'artificial'. The imaginational transformation of an 'actual place' into a 'virtual place'[36] or the imaginative conditions that allow us 'to take the feigned for the real'[37] and provide, according to Robert Gordon, the 'start point' or, as Nicholas Ridout has it, the 'precondition' of theatre are quite different to the virtuality induced by repetition in training. Here the 'real' is not overwritten or held at bay but separated and recombined with the 'social' in the alteration of the self. Ridout's newly invigorated 'precondition' of theatre redefines the beliefs that are said to be suspended in performance, much as analyses of the suspended liminal states of rites of passage provide a conceptual model of ritual. However, unlike ritual, training's virtual spaces don't *hold up* but *slow down* the structurating and subjectivating processes of living. The connections between the social and physical elements of self-identity are tested and redetermined in training as trainees undergo radical alterations to their capabilities and their own sense of themselves in the world.

Training, like performance, is deeply affecting but its effects are not attained in ethical or intellectual forums but through the radical suffering-of-alteration to what an individual can do, and *not do*. Askeology, through its investigations into becoming impotential, is able to explain how an expert becomes expert, and what role they play in performance because, if the objects of theatre are 'measured, not for their potential to act, but for their impotential to be realised',[38] one particular object – the trained performer – is the only object that can properly control their ability to disappoint. Where performance may manipulate signification by controlling the play of surfaces, training's repeated efforts to 'control the play of the body as signifier'[39] within and beyond the performance event indicates that the impotential of the trained performer transcends the parameters of disappointment in theatre and other performance ecologies. Isolating these key characteristics of training through investigations in a range of disciplinary practices secures a meeting place for practitioners from these disciplines and provides them with a language of provisional terminology through which to share their experiences.

Reflecting on what askeology has achieved highlights what has happened between my initial posing of the question, 'What is called training?' and this final chapter. This book shares some of the aims of Bill Viola's video paintings in showing that if, as the 'before and after' pairing suggests, where one arrives at needs to be put in the context of where one started from, the conditions 'after' also need to be understood through considering what happens *between* now and 'before'. It is of course on this continuum that training operates; always between and in relation to various *becomings*. The juxtaposition of before and after and its function in calling our attention to what is between is quite uniquely evident in the bell-ringing, light-dimming and curtain-pulling routines of the theatre auditorium and operates within what Bert O. States has called 'the realm of formal beginnings and endings whereby we punctuate the events of social life and rescue them from the indifferent drift of time'.[40] Training, too, marks endings in complex formalised ceremonies such as the monastic perseverance ceremony as well as in smaller-scale organised routines such as the ribbon exercise; and in the ritualised practices for the scientific recording of data during rehabilitative training these terminal points are reorganised as beginnings and training becomes sub-divided into so many 'events'.

Training, like other 'social events', including theatre, would seem to want to force our attention on what is *between* beginnings and endings precisely by highlighting these and thus resist the treatment of the passage of time as if it were indifferent. But unlike theatre, even with its interminable curtain call, training, at the meta-disciplinary level of process, resists all attempts to formalise endings even as its disciplinary exercises are concluded in readiness to be begun again. The continuing promise of self-actualisation inherent in the positive freedom associated with formation, obedience and vocation recalls the path of the Moebius strip, which introduces Lyotard's libidinal economy and informs his 'postmodern condition' from which, as B.E. Ellis's notorious *American Psycho* finds, there is no escape. The Moebius strip is, of course, associated in Lyotard's *Libidinal Economy* with the libidinal skin that has neither inside nor outside. The characteristic of this strip that interests here is not its inner/outer relationship but its beginning/ending dynamic. The experience of living at the end of meta-narratives, or at least with incredulity towards them, announced elsewhere in Lyotard's *The Postmodern Condition*, has been critically isolated in Ellis's character, Patrick Bateman, who is not ignorant of but incredulous to categories of right and wrong, good and evil, and who, in a fittingly Moebian twist, finds at the end of the narrative that 'this is not an exit'.[41]

I have already explained that the ordering of the chapters of this book does not reflect a linear passage through training even as it might tentatively hypothesise that some aspects of vocation may 'come first', but rather that these processes, and probably others, persist throughout training even as they are at times more deliberately foregrounded and at other times made to recede from focus. That secular institutionalised trainings may mark a terminus for the organisational principles that, historically speaking, were begun in the monastery is itself represented in the 'event' of this book beginning, as it did, its discussion of meta-disciplinary processes with the example of monastic vocation and concluding here by returning to the same site.

The daily liturgy is perhaps the first and certainly the most systematic and thorough attempt to resist the indifferent drift of time. The recurrence of its 'events' on a continuum mirrors, and in the case of the monastic quite literally overcodes, the repetition of exercises on a developmental passage of formation. That the daily liturgy of the monastery is modelled on a human life – through the womblike silence of the night, to the 'first words' at Matins and the committal back to silence at Compline – as it repeatedly occurs within one life, draws our attention most starkly to the indifference of time, which is really time's indifference to the lives lived within it, and suggests that our efforts to construct 'events' might be, in part, directed at assembling a social life that can outlast the private one.[42] That institutionalised training's Ur-site might also be the first site of coherent and conspicuous human resistance to time's indifference to life indicates that training, even as it demarcates events, is especially cognisant of the preciousness of what happens between 'before' and 'after', and it is in keeping with the object of its study that askeology too should wish to resist . . . for as long as is possible . . . ever bringing things to a complete . . . and definitive . . . end.

Postscript

If the references I made throughout the body of this book to songs, books and films as well as theatre and performance orient it within a historical and critical context, then the allusion that follows perhaps establishes one final 'performative' point of reference for my writing: Dave Eggers's seminal novel *A Heartbreaking Work of Staggering Genius* concludes, or perhaps begins, with a section entitled 'Mistakes We Knew We Were Making'. The ambiguity over whether or not this section opens or closes the novel, or should be consulted as a reference source through-out, exists primarily because it is published upside down and back to front, meaning that the reader must re-orient the novel turning it through 180 degrees on its vertical axis and opening the back cover as a front cover in order to read it. This gives the artefact of the book a curious symmetry and effectively removes any back cover, prompting the reader to decide which front cover should be opened first. In 'Mistakes We Knew We Were Making' Eggers reveals to the reader all the inaccuracies, in-adequacies, omissions, embellishments and weaknesses of the main narrative – or at least enough to make a reader believe that the list is exhaustive and in plausible enough detail for readers to accept the details as genuine.

That this list is back to front and upside down is only an element of the presentation, since the text also shrinks and enlarges and is sometimes altogether supplanted by a drawing or an image. Eggers's insistence on a mistake-making 'we' recalls not only the author and his brother, who provide the central characters of the book, but also implicates the reader in the production of the work. The title 'Mistakes We Knew We Were Making' recalls the 'deliberate mistake' that alert readers and viewers – those familiar with what should and should not appear on the page, stage or screen – are expected to identify, and situates the work within a formal tradition that it is in the process of reforming. In a contemporary moment where theatre performances such as Forced Entertainment's *First Night* have, as Ridout has claimed, taken articulating an anxiety about their own form as a central subject matter,[1] Eggers's formal innovation feels at home among a cross-disciplinary body of work that has been called post-modern. Eggers has, perhaps more fruitfully than a lot of writing loosely referred to as 'performative', succeeded in situating whatever we might call his 'working' (the 'work of an author') within his 'work' (his book) and turned the deficiencies of such working into the formal foundations of the work. 'Mistakes We Knew We Were Making' is not so much a testament to an anxiety over the form of creative production as a self-conscious awareness of the causes of such an anxiety and a deliberate multiplication of these anxieties effectively to nullify them.

Given that the formal constraints on a novel have probably always been more relaxed than those placed on a research-led monograph, this might not be the place for an Eggerian manoeuvre even if *now* might be the time in which one is called for. While such research-led writing might be undergoing a slow process of reformation in the context of 'practice-based' research, it remains incumbent upon an author to produce an Eggerian-type list, even if he or she is ultimately dissuaded from pro-ducing it in such an appositely 'performative' manner. Subsequently this section cannot be ʇuoɹɟ oʇ ʞɔɐq or too small and difficult to read, but while it provides an account of the deficiencies of this particular research and the further work that it leaves (and enables) to be done, it is also self-aware of the weaknesses produced by the formal restraints placed on research and is responding to the need for any discursive and analytic writing to be at least as sensitive to the conditions of its historical moment as the practices it studies during this moment.

I explained at the outset that the selection of practices I have parti-cipated in during the research for this book does not place a limit on those that should be included in askeology. The absence of other practices is itself significant in upholding the resolute exclusivity of certain training groups and allowing their self-imposed exclusion from this study to form a part of it. I would suggest that by way of assessing the irreducibility of the various processes studied in the third, fourth, fifth and sixth chapters of this book a valuable contribution towards the isolation of training in the study of askeology could be made simply by investigating a larger range of practices. As Deleuze indicates, these 'further observations' would not produce a *better* image of training but one whose operational context was larger and more inclusive. While the methods of meta-disciplinary analysis practised in askeology invite such further investigations, they also propose encounters with other forms of training that might operate different interpersonal dynamics and might therefore need to be investigated differently – for example, the roles of trainer and trainee which, though differently constructed, are operational within all of the disciplines under investigation here.

Much fruitful work could no doubt be done looking at practices with less formalised or institutionalised interpersonal dynamics, given that there is evidently a strong current of independence inherent in vocation and running 'beneath the surface' of social interactions during training. Against the increasingly prevalent trend in sports training for the 'scouting' of ever younger 'talent' and the systematic admittance (and frequent rejection) of future athletes on to organised programmes of training there appear the heroic narratives of sporting figures who, often in conditions of poverty, successfully self-train and come to dominate a sport in which the other participants have 'benefited' from organised and institutionally based training. These heroic accounts represent a largely 'independent' version of the 'collective' phenomenon of training. Rubbing up alongside Sartre's 'virtual' character, 'the self-taught man' who shares a library with the dilettante Antoine Roquentin, is Rancière's very 'real' ignorant schoolmaster Joseph Jacotot, himself one member in a historical crowd of autodidacts.[2] The phenomenon of autodidacticism in the arts, where standards of excellence in a given field can be subjectively defined, is evident in the archetypal character of the self-taught musician, writer or actor whose particular condition of genius has, as Steve Connor has shown, been interwoven with madness in the modern age.[3] Even the model of monasticism that has provided so many other institutions with an interpersonal framework and sets of organisational principles is, historically speaking, the product of an initially solitary and autodidactic process.[4] Even as this book has drawn on these histories insofar as they have contributed towards the growth of interpersonal training models, it has not sought to trace individual 'case histories' in training across any great period of time, A future research project which might now be prompted by this book could entail consideration of the effects of vocation, formation, automatisation and especially obedience in the auto-training of the self-taught, though a different methodology would have to be developed to support such investigations given that a participatory one would not seem appropriate or sufficient.

Some examples of practices that might be investigated could be found through accessing the scouting procedures of professional sporting clubs or by speaking with individuals who live in cultures where disease and disability are even more heavily stigmatised than in the UK and where, as a result of social exclusion, individuals have self-taught functionality and perhaps even recovery.[5] Accepting that autodidacticism deserves a voice within askeology also entails the acknowledgement that those who plateau or pause during training and those who 'drop out' altogether should also be accommodated at the meeting place of askeology.

This book, prompted largely by the experiences of individuals I have encountered during my research, has in its consideration of training processes assumed a certain kind of trainee. While the conception of this trainee is catholic in the sense that it includes a range of ages, genders and abilities, it does not as yet incorporate those who participate in training but with little effect. Individuals who might be included in askeology's clinical view of training could range from monks who break their vows, to patients who fail to regain motility and actors who, despite years of often costly training, spend most of their professional life out of work.[6] The withdrawal from training, or the failure to achieve desired performance abilities despite participation in training, represented in the case histories of such individuals could help to deepen appreciations of training processes and widen understanding of their effects.

Speaking about such experiences is made difficult partly because there are evidently other factors besides training in play – the theological question of belief, the biological and genetic limits placed on recovery and the market forces of an economy saturated with supply and comparatively limited in demand. Nonetheless, as individuals who could at some time or in some sense be described as trainees the inclusion of those who pause or stop training, or whose training in one sense 'fails' them, may help to sharpen in further study the image of training developed here.

The rejection of training in certain practices of performance, the more generalised contemporary trend in theatre towards a characteristic of both juvenile and geriatric 'amateurism' identified by Adrian Kear in work such as Victoria Theatre's *Ubung* (2002) and Pina Bausch's *Kontaktoff* (2002) also provides examples through which to study the denunciation of training by performance practitioners.[7] The performances of Goat Island – the dance company who couldn't dance and have now stopped dancing – have also furnished contemporary theatre with an amateurish aesthetic that does not operate via means of the 'non-competent' appearance of the very young or the very old and deliberately avoids the somewhat condescending fascination of an audience in the achievements of the seemingly incapable (which, within a restricted realm, still concerns itself with the virtuoso[8]). That performance in its postmodern moment may make play of the conditions of amateurism within what Kear has called a 'tightly orchestrated *mise-en-scène*,'[9] might prove only that the professionalism of the virtuoso has taken on a new dimension, but investigation of this trend alongside 'non-theatrical' examples of disjuncture between training and performance, or the performances of those who have not trained or who withdraw from training, could be an important project for askeology in the future and one that, like the phenomenon of autodidacticism, needs to be mentioned in this book before it concludes.

Before finally drawing the curtain, it is necessary to mention the amateur, the failure and the autodidact and to suggest that these might provide fresh frontiers for askeological research, but it is perhaps also appropriate to make a statement about what future research askeology may enable in areas of study beyond training. While askeology's primary contribution to the various disciplines it engages is in the provision of a space and a language to speak within it, the approaches used to isolate training might also offer something to both Theatre and Performance Studies more generally – for example, through the application of its ecological model of how we *do* our bodies.

It is more than a happy coincidence for askeology that the influential psychologist and theorist of perception J.J. Gibson developed many of his ideas while helping to train aeroplane pilots during the Second World War. Gibson quickly determined that both the success and safety of a flight-training programme was dependent upon reliable depth perception in the trainee, especially during landing and takeoff, and yet he found that tests based on pictorial cues to depth and exercises designed to capitalise on depth information were unsuccessful in preparing pilots for flight.[10] From the 1950s onwards, Gibson focused on 'surfaces' in place of a conception of 'depth' or 'space' in his development of an *ecological* model of perception, grounding perception theory in an appropriately literal manner by emphasising the terrain over which the gaze moves.

Gazing, or *the gaze,* has been a primary focus of Performance Studies since precisely the time Richard Schechner published his now famous *Performance Theory* (1976) one year after Laura Mulvey's no less famous article 'Visual Pleasure and Narrative Cinema', which made clear the 'split between active/male and passive/female'[11] inherent in narrative spectacles. Mulvey's cinematic gaze has provided Theatre and Performance Study with perhaps the most obviously accessible critique of spectatorial perception, and one that reassuringly belies the commonly held belief that 'cinema killed the theatre', insofar as it rejuvenated discourse around theatre while also reflecting the concerns of a particular moment in Performance Studies. That the active/male and the passive/female might reflect the actor–audience dynamic of the *theatron* – a dynamic unwanted by performance in its 'first moment' which was, according to Ridout, 'defined [by] the emergence of theatrical or other practices that explicitly reject, oppose, expose or move beyond the framework of theatre'[12] – might go some way towards explaining why Mulvey's gaze has enjoyed a prominent position in theatre criticism and analysis.

Blau, a quite prolific writer on the gaze in theatre, has offered a notion of 'gradients of the gaze' that 'move from a state of beholding, or contemplation to one of stupefaction',[13] while insisting that, despite the various angles from which one may look at it, 'the body, despite all subject (and sexual) positions, is not so transformable as our ideas about it'.[14] Recognising the perils of trying to use Blau's statement on *ideas about the body* to open up into a particular statement *about bodies* (and at the risk of being accused of merely confirming the veracity of his point), I would like to rephrase it a little to say, 'our ideas about the body, and all its subjectivated positions, are not as transformable as our bodies themselves'. It is perhaps disingenuous of me to redirect Blau's critique of the transformational claims made specifically in the practices of Stelarc and Orlan in this way; I do not want to get involved in arguing for what 'the body' could be if it weren't constructed as this or that particular body, but I am asserting that if, as Blau would seem to be suggesting, some discrete form of body persists through a range of body practices, then the characteristic of any such discrete body is a state of constant transformation. Thus to gaze on this body will require a properly ecological model of perception. It is hoped that as performance, and the study that accompanies it, moves through its third moment and into a fourth, askeology's focus on how bodies are *done* and the effects of *doing them differently* restores the imperative of an ecological model of the body and of gazing on it which can, by adding to the passive/active gaze, shift questions away from subject-construction or how to 'carve the joint' between body and mind, and towards enquiries about how we *do* ourselves in different environments.

One specifically theatrical example of the application of this shift in focus could perhaps (appropriately) be found in investigations of theatre audiences by resisting historical precedents that focus on the socio-economic organisation of the auditorium or the objectifying effects of the spectatorial gaze.[15] These analytic approaches must, after all, assume a certain complicity or acquiescence on behalf of the spectator in the operations of the auditorium, because if stratified pricing of theatre seats or the proximical dimensions of spectation *produce* certain subjects, analyses of these operations *assume* the subjects are either ignorant of their subjectivation or powerless in the face of it. Reflecting on how we do our bodies could enable a focus on how auditoria might produce certain spectators, not through simple enforcement of accepted codes of conduct but through the spectators' struggles to remain whole against the forces that might impel them to fall apart in such environs – forces apparent in the generalised 'side effects'[16] of embarrassment, corpsing and fiasco identified by Ridout as well as in some of the more spectacular riots that have accompanied many now-famous theatrical events. In its conceptualisation of embodiment as a metabolic experience, askeology might stimulate enquiries beyond the field of training and propose some different ways of thinking about 'bringing down the house'.

Notes

Introduction

1 See Carole Zucker, *In the Company of Actors: Reflections on the Craft of Acting*, for further anecdotal evidence of the centrality of vocational training to professional success in 'the theatre'.

2 The National Council of Drama Training is a partnership of employers in theatre, broadcast and media industries and employee representatives. The NCDT is an accrediting body for training providers.

3 Ridout, N.P., *Stage Fright: Animals and Other Theatrical Problems*, Cambridge: Cambridge University Press, 2006, p. 41.

4 The aesthetic of asceticism can be seen within the passive submission to the will of others and the acts of self-inflicted violence which characterise Abramovic's 'Rhythm' series of the 1970s. This ascetic aesthetic is also in evidence in Hsieh's anchoritic *One Year Performances*, especially 'Cage Piece'.

5 Watson, I., *Performer Training: Developments Across Cultures*, London; New York, NY: Routledge, 2001, p. 1.

6 I am alluding here to the taxonomical interests of the discipline of Theatre Studies which can be traced back through the output of modern scholars such as Raymond Williams in his 1976 work *Key Words: A Vocabulary of Culture and Society* and to the writings of ancient critics such as Plato (in *The Republic*) and Aristotle (in *Poetics*).

7 Allsopp and Williams, 'On Form/Yet to Come', *Performance Research*, Vol. 10, No. 2, 2005, p. iii.

8 Foucault addressed himself to monastic training as a form (in one sense the archetypal form) of discipline in his work *Discipline and Punish: The Birth of the Prison*. This approach to analysing the 'institutionalising' effects of training can be seen to influence contemporary scholarship, for example in Simon Shepherd's 'The Institution of Training', *Performance Research*, Vol. 14, No. 2, 2009, pp. 5–15.

Chapter 1

1   Fogelin, R.J., *Wittgenstein*, London: Routledge, 1987, p. 121.
2   Ibid., p. 31.
3   Ibid.
4   Wittgenstein, L., *Philosophical Investigations*, Oxford: Blackwell, 1953, p. 3.
5   Barker, G.P., and Hacker, S.H., *An Analytical Commentary on Wittgenstein's Philosophical Investigations*, Oxford: Blackwell, 1983, p. 128.
6   Watson, I., *Performer Training: Developments Across Cultures*, London; New York, NY: Routledge, p. 1.
7   Gustafson argues that several of Wittgenstein's critics (such as Picher) are wrong to assume that he identifies word-meaning and word-use because things identified, rightly or wrongly, must be of the same type, and 'use' and 'meaning' are not. If Wittgenstein were making what Gustafson calls 'a typical move' of identification by identifying the meaning of a word with use of that word, he would be compelled to explain a 'type or category to which meaning and use both belong' and it is precisely because he doesn't that his argument is so novel. (See Gustafson, 'On Pitcher's Account of Investigations 43', *Philosophy and Phenomenological Research*, Vol. 28, 1967–1968, pp. 252–258.) Rather than pursuing this process of identification, Gustafson argues that Wittgenstein shows that meaning does not exist separately from use in a way that makes the two terms identifiable by reference to an external category, but that meaning *is* use (in the sense that the only existence meaning has) it is constructed in the wider context in which a word is used, or, as Wittgenstein puts it, paraphrasing Frege, 'a word [has] meaning only as part of a sentence' (see Fogelin, op. cit., p. 121).
8   Deleuze, G., in Smith, D.W., and Greco, M.A. (eds), *Giles Deleuze: Essays Critical and Clinical*, London: Verso, 1997, p. xix.
9   Ibid., xiv.
10 See Deleuze, G., *Nietzsche and Philosophy*, London: Continuum, 2006.
11 Jean Khalfa has undertaken a much more thorough comparison of Wittgenstein and Deleuze than I am offering. He has argued that in Wittgenstein there is an idea which 'almost approaches that of a single "ground"' underlying the multiplicity of language games that resembles Deleuze's ultimate plane of immanence which 'varies and becomes specific in a thousand sheets' (see Khalfa, J., *Introduction to the Philosophy of Giles Deleuze*, London: Continuum, 2003, p. 20). What is pertinent here is that, as Wittgenstein shows, generic usage does not preclude definitive understanding of a term and that Deleuze has proposed *a* method for isolating any such meaning.
12 Allsopp and Williams, 'On Form / Yet to Come', *Performance Research*, Vol. 10, No. 2, 2005, p. iii.
13 For a study of the early applications of the term, especially in religious settings, see Dressler, H., *The Usage of Askeo and Its Cognates in Greek Documents AD 100*, Whitefish, MT: Kessinger Publishing, 2006.
14 For a fuller explication of the ancient Greek socio-cultural context of asceticism, see Jaeger, W., *Paidiea: The Ideals of Greek Culture Vol. 1: Archaic Greece, the Mind of Athens*, Oxford: Oxford University Press, 1968. For a range of essays defining and describing the 'ascetic impulse', see 'Part Two: Origins and Meanings of

Asceticism', in Wimbrush, V.L., and Valantasis, R. (eds), *Asceticism*, Oxford: Oxford University Press, 1995, pp. 31–125.

15   For a discussion of the absorption of the secular term *askesis* into religious discourse, and subsequent philosophical response to the Christian 'ascetical' way of life, see Nola, R., *Rescuing Reason: A Critique of Anti-rationalist Views of Science and Knowledge*, Berlin: Springer, 2003, p. 505.

16   By 'holy' here I am, of course, referring to Grotowski's (1968) and Brook's (1968) application of the term to an actor and a theatre respectively.

17   Hodge, A., *Twentieth Century Actor Training*, London; New York, NY: Routledge, 2000, p. 1.

18   By 'discipline' I refer to particular practices of performance training. For example, the discipline of Suzuki's techniques for performance training, or the discipline of training on a rehabilitation ward after stroke. This should not be confused with Foucault's use of 'discipline' to describe the 'means of correct training' (through observation, judgement and examination) to produce the subject of this formation of power (Foucault, M., *Discipline and Punish: The Birth of the Prison*, London: Penguin, 1991 [1977], p. 170).

19   Ulmer, G., *Applied Grammatology: Post(e)-Pedagogy from Jacques Derrida to Joseph Beuys*, Baltimore, MD: Johns Hopkins University Press, 2005, p. xxii.

20   A 'character' from Forced Entertainment's *Emmanuelle Enchanted* (1992).

21   Read, A., *Theatre, Intimacy and Engagement: The Last Human Venue*, Basingstoke; New York: Palgrave Macmillan, 2008, p. 22.

22   Ibid., p. 23.

23   Ibid., p. 25.

24   The centrality of this conceit to askeological research is related to Read's use of Latour's metaphor of 'plasma' for the conditions in which relations are assembled – conditions typified by their always-already organised status and the co-embedding of objects and entities this entails.

25   Read, A., op. cit., 2008, p. 25.

26   See Melrose, S., 'Practice', in 'A Lexicon', *Performance Research*, Vol. 11, 2006, pp. 99–103.

27   Ibid., p. 99.

28   Ibid., p. 102.

29   See Knowles, A., 'Process', in 'A Lexicon', *Performance Research*, Vol. 11, 2006, p. 105.

30   Melrose argues that these intimations are 'properly ancient' because *practice* understood as such is other than *idea/ideal* in the sense of an antagonism between the contemplative and active life (op. cit., p. 99).

31   Read, A., op. cit., 2008, pp. 29–30. Read is responding to Thompson and Schechner's 'rallying cry' that Social Theatre can 'carry this banner [of Performance Studies] into practice by going into hospitals, prisons and war zones and prove that performance itself is a method for understanding what goes on there' (see Schechner, R., and Thompson, J., 'Why Social Theatre?', in *TDR: The Drama Review*, Vol. 48, No. 3, 2004, pp. 15–16).

32   Read, A., op. cit., 2008, p. 25.

33   Aristotle, trans. Hett, W.S., *Aristotle in Twenty-Three Volumes, Volume 8: The Soul, Parva Naturalia, On Breath*, Cambridge, MA: Harvard University Press, 1986, p. 98.

34 The notion of 'environmental' experiences of suffering beginning to emerge here will become important to the 'ecological' conception of the body that I will develop shortly, and should be born in mind especially in the penultimate chapter, 'Automatisation', during my discussion of 'positive' and 'negative' accounts of freedom.

35 See Rubenson, S., 'Christian Asceticism and the Emergence of the Monastic Tradition', in Wimbrush, V. L., and Valantasis, R. (eds), *Asceticism*, Oxford: Oxford University Press, 1995, pp. 49–58.

36 Miner, E., *Comparative Poetics*, Princeton, NJ: Princeton University Press, 1990, p. 51.

37 McLeish, K., trans., *Aristotle: Poetics*, London: Nick Hern Books, 1998, pp. x–xi.

38 See Miller, A., '*Death of a Salesman*: A Modern Tragedy?' in Brandt, W.G., *Modern Theories of Drama: A Selection of Writings on Drama and Theatre 1840–1990*, 1998, pp. 106–115.

39 I am referring here to a notion of 'discipline' as advanced in Foucault's *Discipline and Punish*.

40 Heraclitus, trans. Hillman, J., *Fragments*, London: Penguin, 2003, p. xv.

41 Schechner and Thompson, op. cit., 2004, p. 15.

42 McKenzie, J., *Perform or Else: From Discipline to Performance*, London; New York: Routledge, 2001, p. 4.

43 Carlson, M., *Performance: A Critical Introduction*, London; New York: Routledge, 1996, p. 5.

44 McKenzie, J., op. cit., 2001, p. 53.

45 Agamben, G., *Potentialities: Collected Essays in Philosophy*, Palo Alto, CA: Stanford University Press, 1999, p. 179.

46 Read, A., op. cit., 2008, p. 1.

47 Aristotle, in Agamben, G., op. cit., 1999, p. 184.

48 Zarrilli, P.B., 'Negotiating Performance Epistemologies: Knowledges "about", "in" and "for"', in *Studies in Theatre and Performance*, Vol. 22, 2001, p. 36.

49 Ibid.

50 Loukes, R., 'Tracing Bodies: Researching Psychophysical Training for Performance through Practice', *Performance Research*, Vol. 8, No. 4, 2003, p. 58.

51 I would be quick to note here that to define certain materials as constituting a corpus of knowledge 'surrounding' training is the kind of manoeuvre that can only ever be accomplished 'perspectivally', since what 'surrounds' training, from my perspective, may well be a combination of other people's experiences and reflections on their own development *within* training.

52 See Heradland, Pike and Harris, *Emics and Etics: The Insider/Outsider Debate*, Thousand Oaks, CA: Sage, 1990.

53 Zarrilli, P.B., op. cit., 2001, p. 34.

54 Grosz, in Loukes, R., op. cit., 2003, p. 57.

55 Loukes, R., op. cit., 2003, p. 57.

56 Ibid., p. 58.

57 Metraux, in Loukes, R., op. cit., 2003, p. 58.

58 Kohn, T., 'The Aikido Body: Expressions of Group Identities and Self Discoveries in Martial Arts Training', in Dyck, N., and Archetti, E.P., *Sport, Dance and Embodied Identities*, Oxford: Berg, 2003, p. 142.

59 Ibid., pp. 142–143.

60 Participatory research over a twenty-year period in India has reportedly informed Zarrilli's *When the Body Becomes All Eyes: Paradigms, Discourses and Practices in Kalarippayattu, a South Indian Martial Art*, Oxford: Oxford University Press, 1998.

61 Allain, P., *Gardzienice: Polish Theatre in Transition*, London; New York, NY: Routledge, 1997, p. 5.

62 Allain's *The Art of Stillness: The Theatre Practice of Tadashi Suzuki* combines his observations of a demonstration by Suzuki in Toga in 1999 with a two-week workshop with Ellen Lauren of SITI in Vicenza, Italy, in 1995. Allain also participated in and watched training led by several practitioners with backgrounds in SCOT, SITI or Frank during his research for the book. As director of the British Grotowski Project, Allain has facilitated a range of workshops with students of Grotowski, and developed a 'multi-modal' international conference designed to bring academics, practitioners and their practices together (British Grotowski Project, 2008).

63 Schechner drew on Turner's theories in two collaborative works: *Between Theater and Anthropology* (1985) and *The Future of Ritual* (1993).

64 It should be clear that the application of this anthropological method is especially appropriate to my 'meta-disciplinary' project, given that anthropological methodologies such as participant-observation are employed not only by those investigating theatre trainings but also dance (Royce, A.P., *The Anthropology of Dance*, 2000), sport (Dyck, N., and Archetti, E.P., *Sport, Dance and Embodied Identities*, 2003), martial arts (Jones, D.E., *Combat, Ritual and Performance: Anthropology of Martial Arts*, 2002), sickness, illness and recovery (Good, B., *Medicine, Rationality and Experience: An Anthropological Perspective*, 1994) and a range of other embodied practices.

65 Law, J., 'Making a Mess with Method', Centre for Science Studies, Lancaster University, 2003, p. 11.

66 Read, A., op. cit., 2008, pp. 31–32.

67 On the problem of 'context' Read cites Latour on the 'impossibility of staying in one of the two sites for a long period' (Latour, in Read, A., op. cit., p. 32).

68 Read, A., op. cit., 2008, p. 121.

69 See Foucault's *Discipline and Punish* and *The Birth of the Clinic*.

70 Auerbach, E., trans. Trask, W.R., *Mimesis: The Representation of Reality in Western Literature*, Princeton, NJ: Princeton University Press, 1953, p. 14.

71 Gallagher, C., and Greenblatt, S., *Practising New Historicism*, Chicago, IL: Chicago University Press, 2000, p. 35.

72 Ibid.

73 Mullaney, S., *The Place of the Stage: Power, Play and License in Renaissance England*, Ann Arbor, MI: University of Michigan Press, 1995, p. 27.

74 Ibid., p. 26.

75 'The Theatre' here refers to both theatrical activity and The Theatre, constructed by James Burbage in 1576, which provided the model for the subsequent playhouses such as The Rose and The Globe that serve as *ansatzpunkte* for Peggy Phelan in her consideration of the cultural landscapes of late-twentieth-century London – see Phelan, P., 'Playing Dead in Stone, or When is a Rose Not a Rose?', in Diamond, E. (ed.), *Performance and Cultural Politics*, London; New York, NY: Routledge, 1996, pp. 65–89.

76 'Zarrilli', University of Exeter homepage, 2008.

77 Read, A., op. cit., 2008, p. 283.

78 Allain, P., *The Art of Stillness: The Theatre Practice of Tadashi Suzuki*, London: Methuen, 2002, p. 99.

79 Read, A., *Theatre and Everyday Life*, London; New York, NY: Routledge, 1995, p. 23.

80 Read, A., op. cit., 2008, p. 38.

81 Auerbach, E., op. cit., 1953, pp. 548–549.

82 Ibid., p. 549.

83 Ibid.

84 Auerbach, E., trans. Said, M.E., 'Philogogy and Weltliteratur', in *Centennial Review*, Vol. 13, 1969, p. 8.

85 Law, J., op. cit., 2003, p. 7.

86 Auerbach, E., op. cit., 1953, p. 325.

87 Wellek, R., 'Review of *Mimesis*', in *Kenyon Review*, Vol. 16, 1954, p. 300.

88 Law, J., op. cit., 2003, p. 10.

89 Ibid., p. 10.

90 Ibid., p. 3.

91 Ibid., p. 9.

92 Auerbach, E., trans. Said, M.E., op. cit., 1969, p. 8.

93 Blau, H., *The Eye of Prey: Subversion of the Postmodern*, Ann Arbor, MI: University of Michigan Press, 1987, p. 171.

94 Ridout, N., *Stage Fright: Animals and Other Theatrical Problems*, Cambridge: Cambridge University Press, 2006, p. 94.

95 Schechner, R., *Performance Theory*, London; New York: Routledge, 2003, p. 22.

96 McKenzie, J., *Perform or Else: From Discipline to Performance*, London; New York, NY: Routledge, 2001, p. 4.

97 Ibid., p. 18.

98 Ibid., p. 19.

99 Chaudhuri, U., 'Zoo Stories: "Boundary Work" in Theatre History', in Worthen, W.B., and Holland, P. (eds), *Theorizing Practice: Redefining Theatre History*, Basingstoke: Palgrave Macmillan, 2003, p. 136.

100 The duck in Theatre Razi and the horse in Societas Raffaello Sanzio's performance work inspire Ridout's investigations into animals on stage in *Stage Fright: Animals and Other Theatreical Problems*, while Societas Raffaello Sanzio's infant and animal performers inform Read's book *Theatre, Intimacy and Engagement: The Last Human Venue*. The lion provides a reference to the 'animal acts' that interest both John Stokes's article, 'Lion Griefs: The Wild Animal Act as Theatre', *New Theatre Quarterly* (2004) and the articles which make up an edition of *Performance Research*, 'On Animals' (2000).

101 Goldrup, T., *Growing up on Set: Interviews with 39 Former Child Actors of Classic Film and Television*, Jefferson, NC: McFarland, 2002, p. 264.

102 Ibid., p. 1.

103 Scruton, R., *Animal Rights and Wrongs*, London: Demos, 1998, p. 59.

104 Ibid., p. 60.

105 Ibid.

106 ANT's project to map 'material' relations between things and 'semiotic' relations between concepts in the description of social phenomena takes a methodological

lead from Garfinkel's arguments in *Studies in Ethnomethodology*, the 'central recommendation' of which is that the activities whereby members produce and organise settings for everyday affairs are identical with members' procedures for rendering those settings accountable. (See Garfinkel 1984.)

107 Read, A., op. cit., 2008, p. 7.
108 Gottsegen, M.G., *The Political Thought of Hannah Arendt*, Albany, NJ: SUNY Press, 1994, p. 51.
109 Read, A., op. cit., 2008, p. 27.
110 Arendt, H., *The Human Condition*, Chicago, IL: University of Chicago Press, 1958, p. 7.

Chapter 2

1   Ridout, N., *Stage Fright: Animals and Other Theatrical Problems*, Cambridge: Cambridge University Press, 2006, p. 5.
2   Gordon, R., *The Purpose of Playing: Modern Acting Theories in Perspective*, Ann Arbor, MI: University of Michigan Press, 2006, p. 286.
3   Scheer, E., *Antonin Artaud: A Critical Reader*, London; New York, NY: Routledge, 2004, p. 81.
4   Rose, M., *Parody: Ancient, Modern and Postmodern*, Cambridge: Cambridge University Press, 1994, pp. 267–268.
5   See Zurbrugg and Stelarc, in Huxley and Witts (eds), *The Twentieth Century Performance Reader*, London; New York, NY: Routledge, 2002, p. 397.
6   See Loukes, R., 'Tracing Bodies: Researching Psychophysical Training for Performance through Practice' (2003), for a consideration of the 'psycho-physical' nature of training; Merlin, B., *Beyond Stanislavski: The Psycho-physical Approach to Actor Training*, for a description of the 'components – body, mind and emotion – [that] are part of psycho-physical mechanism that makes up the actor' (London: Nick Hern Books, 2001, pp. 4–5); and Gordon, R., op. cit., 2006, for discussion of acting teachers, such as Copeau, and their 'serious[ness] in the aim of cultivating their students' wholeness of body, mind and feelings', pp. 127–128.
7   For examples see Zarrilli, P.B., 'The Metaphysical Studio' (2002), 'Acting "at the Nerve Ends": Beckett, Blau, and the Necessary' (1997), as well as his articles and introductions to the various sections in his edited collections, *Acting (re)Considered: Theories and Practices* (1995) and *Acting (re)Considered: A Theoretical and Practical Guide* (2002).
8   Zarrilli, P.B., '"On the Edge of a Breath, Looking": Cultivating the Actor's Bodymind through Asian Martial/Meditative Arts', in Zarrilli, P.B. (ed.), *Acting (re)Considered: A Theoretical and Practical Guide*, New York; London: Routledge, 2002, p. 190.
9   For examples see, respectively, Loukes, R., 'How to be "Deadly": The "Natural" Body in Contemporary Training and Performance' (2007), and Bloch et al., 'Effector Patterns of Basic Emotion: A Psychophysiological Method for Training Actors', in Zarrilli, P.B. (ed.), op. cit., 2002.
10 Zarrilli, P.B., *Psychophysical Acting: An Intercultural Approach after Stanislavski*, London; New York, NY: Routledge, 2009, p. 38.

11 Ibid., p. 13.
12 Patterson, S., and Crane, T., *History of the Mind–Body Problem*, London; New York, NY: Routledge, 2000, p. 5.
13 Ibid., p. 95.
14 Ibid., p. 79.
15 Shaner, in Zarrilli, P.B., '"On the Edge of a Breath, Looking": Cultivating the Actor's Bodymind through Asian Martial/Meditative Arts' in Zarrilli, P.B. (ed.), *Acting (re)Considered: A Theoretical and Practical Guide*, New York, NY; London: Routledge, 2002, p. 190.
16 Ibid.
17 Burnyeat, in Patterson and Crane, op. cit., 2000, p. 77.
18 McDowell, in Patterson and Crane, ibid.
19 Zarrilli, P.B., op. cit., 2002, p. 195.
20 Ibid.
21 Ibid., p. 185.
22 Ibid.
23 Ibid., p. 195.
24 Descartes, R., in Cottingham, J., Stoothoff, R., and Murdoch, D., *The Philosophical Writings of Descartes*, 2 volumes, Cambridge: Cambridge University Press, 1984, p. 106.
25 Watson, R., *Cogito Ergo Sum: The Life of René Decartes*, Boston, MA: David R. Godine, 2002, p. 15.
26 See Zarrilli, P.B., op. cit., 2002, p. 195, and Zarrilli, P.B., op.cit., 2009, p. 38.
27 Yuaso, trans. Nagatomo, S., in Zarrilli, P.B., op. cit., 2002, p. 195.
28 Ibid., p. 191.
29 Zarrilli, P.B., op. cit., 2009, p. 85.
30 Ibid., p. 181. Zarrilli is borrowing this phrase from A.C. Scott, a practitioner of Wu-style *t'ai chi ch'uan*, via Robert Benedetti's essay, 'What We Need to Learn from the Asian Actor', *Educational Theatre Journal*, Vol. 25, 1973, p. 463.
31 Ibid., p. 182.
32 Jackson and Csikszentmihalyi in Weinberg, R.S., and Gould, D., *Foundations of Sports Psychology*, Champaign, IL: Human Kinetics Publishing, 2006, pp. 147–148.
33 Zarrilli, P.B., op. cit., 2002, pp. 183–186.
34 Weinberg and Gould, op. cit., 2006, p. 148.
35 Zarrilli, P.B., op. cit., 2002, p. 183.
36 Ibid., p. 182.
37 Ibid., p. 183.
38 Carlstedt, R.A., *Critical Moments During Competition: A Mind–Body Model of Sports Performance When It Counts the Most*, Oxford: Psychology Press, 2004, p. 24.
39 Ibid., pp. 24–25.
40 Ibid., p. 10.
41 See Zarrilli, P.B., op. cit., 2002, p. 182, and Zarrilli, P.B., op. cit., 2009, p. 23.
42 Zarrilli, P.B., op. cit., 2002, p. 183.
43 For examples see Yasuo, trans. Nagatomo and Kasulis, *The Body: Toward an Eastern Mind–Body Theory*, Albany, NY: State University of New York Press, 1987; Nagatomo, 'An Asian Perspective on Mind–Body', *Journal of Philosophy and Medicine*, Vol. 21, 1996, pp. 436–439, 1996; and Nagatomo, 'An Eastern Concept of the Body: Yuasa's Body-Scheme', in Sheets-Johnstone, 1992.

44 Patterson and Crane, op. cit., p. 70.

45 Gordon, R., *The Purpose of Playing: Modern Theories of Acting in Perspective*, Ann Arbor, MI: University of Michigan Press, 2006, p. 22.

46 See Campbell, P., *The Body in Performance*, London; New York, NY: Routledge, 2001, p. 10.

47 Gregson, N.H., Drees, W.B., and Gorman, U., *The Human Person in Science and Theology*, London: Clark, 2000, p. 47.

48 de Waal, E., *Rule of St Benedict: Introduction and Commentary*, Chester: Gracewing Publishing, 1990, p. xvii.

49 deWaal, E., *Seeking God: The Way of St Benedict*, Norwich: SCM Canterbury Press, 1999, p. 73.

50 Duncan, G., in French, S., and Sim, J. (eds), *Physiotherapy: A Psychosocial Approach*, New York, NY: Elsevier, 2004, p. 122.

51 See Viala and Masson-Sekine, *Butoh: Shades of Darkness*, Clarendon, VT: Tuttle Publishing, 1988; and Fraleigh, *Dancing into Darkness*, Pittsburgh, PA: University of Pittsburgh Press, 1999.

52 See Suzuki, T., Rimmer, T., *The Way of Acting: The Theatre Writings of Tadashi Suzuki*, New York: Theatre Communications Group, 1986; Allain, P., *The Art of Stillness: Theatre Practice of Tadashi Suzuki*, London: Methuen, 2002; and Potter, N., *Movement for Actors*, New York, NY: Allworth Communications, 2002.

53 See Schechner, R., and Appel, W., *By Means of Performance*, Cambridge: Cambridge University Press, 1990; and Zarrilli, P.B. (ed.), *Acting (re)Considered: Theories and Practices*, London; New York, NY: Routledge 1995; *When the Body Becomes All Eyes: Paradigms, Discourses and Practices of Power in Kalarippayattu, a South Indian Martial Art*, Oxford: Oxford University Press, 1998.

54 In his study, *Cinemas of the Black Diaspora: Diversity, Dependence and Oppositionality* (Detroit, MI: Wayne State University Press, 1995, p. 74), Michael Martin describes the Quarup as a 'joyous death ritual' celebrated by Amazonians, but for a brief description of the celebrations see Christopher Hampton's 'A Note on the Quarup' in his *Savages*, London: Faber & Faber, 1974, pp. 17–18.

55 Hampton, *Savages*, op. cit., 1974, Scene 19.

56 See Corry, 'Ethnocide: A Report from Columbia', RAI News, *Anthropology Today*, Vol. 6, Jan/Feb 1975, pp. 1–2. Note that Corry uses the term 'tribe' to denote the various groups, reserving 'ethnic' to describe the differences between Indian and 'white'.

57 Ibid.

58 Ibid.

59 Ibid.

60 Mair, L., 'Ethnocide', in RAI News, *Anthropolgy Today*, Vol. 7, 1975, pp. 4–5.

61 Ibid.

62 Ibid.

63 Benthall, J. (ed.), *The Best of Anthropology Today*, London; New York, NY: Routledge, 2002, p. 52.

64 Zarrilli, P.B., '"On the Edge of a Breath, Looking": Cultivating the Actor's Bodymind through Asian Martial/Meditative Arts', in Zarrilli, P.B. (ed.), *Acting (re)Considered: A Theoretical and Practical Guide*, New York, NY; London: Routledge, 2002, p. 185.

65 Schechner, R., *Performance Theory*, London; New York, NY: Routledge, 2003, p. 30.

66 Ibid.

67 Ibid., p. 31, layout as original.

68 Blocker, J., *What the Body Cost: Desire, History and Performance*, Minneapolis, MN: University of Minnesota Press, 2004, p. 24.

69 Schneider, R., *The Explicit Body in Performance*, London; New York, NY: Routledge, 1973, p. 131.

70 Campbell, P., op. cit., 2001, p. 10.

71 Zarrilli, P.B., op. cit., 1995, p. xvi.

72 Read, A., *Theatre and Everyday Life*, London; New York, NY: Routledge, 1993, p. 5.

73 Read, A., *Theatre, Intimacy and Engagement: The Last Human Venue*, Basingstoke; New York, NY: Palgrave Macmillan, 2008, p. 77.

74 Campbell, P., op. cit., 2001, p. 27.

75 See Boal's 'The Function of the Actor', in *Games for Actors and Non-Actors*, 2002, for his concept of the 'spect-actor'.

76 Read's notion of 'witness' is allied to a performance politics 'understood as the constant care and attention required to maintain the efficacy of groups as collectives' wherein 'the witness participates continuously in the maintenance of what is under way' (Read, op. cit., 2008, p. 44).

77 Campbell, P., op. cit., 2001, p. 32.

78 See Hables Gray, C., 'In Defence of Prefigurative Art: The Aesthetics and Ethics of Orlan and Stelarc', in Zylinska, J. (ed.), *The Cyborg Experiments: Extensions of the Body in the Media Age*, London: Continuum, 2002, pp. 181–193.

79 Appelby, J., 'Planned Obsolescence: Flying into the Future with Stelarc', in Zylinska, J. (ed.), op. cit., 2002, p. 101.

80 Schechner, R., op. cit., 2003, p. 31, layout as original.

81 Sarup, M., and Raja, T., *Identity, Culture and the Postmodern World*, Edinburgh: Edinburgh University Press, 1996, p. 97.

82 Eagleton, T., *After Theory*, London: Allen Lane, 2003, p. 22.

83 I am thinking here of Forced Entertainment in particular, but also Goat Island, the New York City Players and numerous others.

84 See Fuchs, E., *The Death of Character: Perspectives on Theatre after Modernism*, Bloomington, IN: Indiana University Press, 1996.

85 Zarrilli, P.B., op. cit., 2002, p. 182.

86 This directly recalls Bernard Williams's description of politics in *The Sense of the Past: Essays in the History of Philosophy*, 2006, and cited by Read, op. cit., 2008, p. 26.

87 It is important to note that this particular allegorical point of departure is not taken from my own research but from a paper by John Law, from whom I am appropriating this 'allegorical' method.

88 Interview with Miriam T— in Mol, A., and Law, J., *Embodied Action, Enacted Bodies: The Example of Hypoglycaemia*, Centre for Science Studies, Lancaster University, 2004, p. 7.

89 Sullivan, M., 'In What Sense is Contemporary Medicine Dualistic?', *Culture, Medicine and Psychiatry*, Vol. 10, 1986, p. 344. Such a notion is necessarily 'modern' according to Foucault, who suggests that this dualism was invented in the early nineteenth century where an epistemic shift occurs from a conception of disease as *occupying* the body to one where it is a *condition* of the body. In

such an episteme the pathological gaze takes over, subjecting the body to the senses of the pathologist most sharply identified with the eye. See *The Birth of the Clinic: An Archaeology of Medical Perception*.

90 Zarrilli, P.B., op. cit., 2002, p. 16.
91 Mol, A., and Law, J., op. cit., 2004, pp. 1–2.
92 Ibid., p. 3.
93 Ibid., p. 7.
94 Ibid., p. 10.
95 See Ehrlich, A., and Schroeder, C.L., *Medical Terminology for Health Professionals*, Stamford, CT: Cengage Learning, 2004, p. 225.
96 Merleau-Ponty, M., trans. Smith, C., *Phenomenology of Perception*, London; New York, NY: Routledge, 2002 (1945), p. 173.
97 Betz Hull, M., *The Hidden Philosophy of Hannah Arendt*, London; New York, NY: Routledge, 2002, p. 159.
98 Husserl, E., trans. Sheehan, T., and Palmer, R.E., *Psychological and Transcendental Phenomenology and the Confrontation with Heidegger 1927–1931*, Dodrecht: Kluwer, 1997, p. 498.
99 Gadamer, H.-G., 'The Nature of Things and the Language of Things', in Linge, D. (ed.), *Philosophical Hermenuetics*, Berkeley, CA: University of California Press, 1977, pp. 77–78.
100 Levinas, E., trans. Lingis, A., *Totality and Infinity: An Essay on Exteriority*, Pittsburgh, PA: Duquesne University Press, 1969, p. 77.
101 See Gibson, J.J., *The Ecological Approach to Visual Perception*, Boston, MA: Houghton Mifflin Harcourt, 1979.
102 Welton, M., 'Once More with Feeling', *Performance Research: On Theatre*, Vol. 10, No. 1, 2005, p. 110.
103 Chemero, A., 'Radical Empiricism through the Ages', review of Harry Heft's *Ecological Psychology in Contexts: James Gibson, Roger Barker, and the Legacy of William James' Radical Empiricism*, in *Contemporary Psychology*, Vol. 48, 2003, pp. 18–20, cited in Welton, M., op. cit., p. 11.
104 Zarrilli, P.B., op. cit., 2009, p. 49.
105 Ibid., p. 4.
106 Ibid.
107 Moran, D., *An Introduction to Phenomenology*, London; New York, NY: Routledge, 2000, p. 393.
108 Merleau-Ponty, M., trans. Smith, C., *Phenomenology of Perception*, London: Routledge and Kegan Paul, 1962, p. 203.
109 Ibid., p. 471.
110 Zarrilli, P.B., op. cit., 2009, p. 49.
111 Mol, A., and Law, J., op. cit., 2004, p. 2.
112 *PING BODY* by Stelarc, first performed 10 April 1996 at Arts Space, Sydney, Australia.
113 Ibid., p. 10.
114 Read has devoted a section of his recent work, *Theatre, Intimacy and Engagement: The Last Human Venue* to 'fur' (op. cit., 2008, pp. 152–157) wherein he articulates, following Julia Emberly, that fur has a 'cultural politics with values which circulate around not just its commodity nature, as luxury good, article of trade,

but also its investment within libidinal desire' (p. 153), which he traces through the appearance of animals in the theatre of Societas Raffaelo Sanzio (pp. 169, 164–166). Ridout also builds a section of his text *Stage Fright: Animals and Other Theatrical Problems* around 'the animal on stage', including the 'accidental' appearance of a 'mouse in the house' (op. cit., 2006, p. 96).

115 See Ridout, N.P., op. cit., 2006, pp. 96–100.
116 Bourriaud, N., trans. Pleasance, S. and Woods, F., *Relational Aesthetics*, Dijon: Presses du Réel, 2002, p. 15.
117 Ridout, N.P., op. cit., 2006, p. 131.
118 Brian McHale has argued that the collapse of hierarchical distinctions between high and low, distinctions properly instituted during the modernist period, is 'one of the most potent and attractive myths of postmodern culture' ('Science Fiction', in Bertens, H., *International Postmodernism: Theory and Literary Practice*, Amsterdam: John Benjamins, 1997, p. 236). Contemporary performance, such as *The World in Pictures* (2006) by Forced Entertainment, devised and presented in this cultural climate, has made much play in this collapse by staging the 'high' narratives of creation, evolution and history through the 'low' media of pop concerts, stand-up and children's games, and has played a role in a movement 'from acting to performance' that motivates Philip Auslander's landmark edited collection, *From Acting to Performance: Essays in Modernism and Postmodernism* (1997).
119 See Derrida, J., trans. Spivak, G.C., *Of Grammatology*, Baltimore, MD: Johns Hopkins University Press, 1976.
120 There is a congruence between the politics of the theatron and the politics of the academy where, as Read has put it, 'the old saw dividing practice and theory, the capacity of the performer set against the incapacity of the spectator' has helped to maintain 'a set of preordained positions that in fact suit those empowered enough to preach them and to practise them' (Read, A., op. cit., 2008, p. 179).
121 Bourriaud, N., op. cit., 2002, p. 58.
122 Bruno Latour has done much to show that the relational dynamics of performance are (re)assembled in the matrixing of actors who are 'not simply the hapless bearers of symbolic projection' (Latour, B., *Reassembling the Social*, Oxford: Oxford University Press, 2005, p. 10). Read, extending the claims of Latour's Actor-Network Theory, has done much to show that this performative matrixing has serious political dimensions in a theatre of 'reassociation' of the 'objects and subjects, things and humans' that were sundered by the work of modernity (Read, A., op. cit., 2008, p. 41).
123 Bayly, S., 'What State am I in? Or How to be a Spectator', in Kelleher, J., and Ridout, N.P., *Contemporary Theatres in Europe: A Critical Companion*, London; New York, NY: Routledge, 2006, pp. 206–207.
124 Read, A., op. cit., 2008, p. 27.
125 Reinelt, J., 'Foreword from "Across the Pond"', in Kelleher, J. and Ridout, N.P., op. cit., 2006, p. xvii.
126 Bayly, S., in Kelleher, J., and Ridout, N.P., op. cit., 2006, p. 201.
127 Robbins, J. (ed.), *Is It Righteous to Be?: Interviews with Immanuel Levinas*, Stanford, CA: Stanford University Press, 2001, p. 12.
128 See Ajzenstat, O., 'Levinas vs Levinas: Hebrew, Greek and Linguistic Justice', *Philosophy and Rhetoric*, Vol. 38, No. 2, 2005, pp. 145–158.

129 Vanhoozer, K.J., *The Drama of Doctrine: A Canonical-Linguistic Approach to Christian Theology*, Westminster: John Knox Press, 2005, p. 269.
130 Rendell, J., *Art and Architecture: A Place Between*, London: I.B. Tauris, 2006, p. 147.

Chapter 3

1 The names of the groundskeeper and the two postulants have been changed out of respect for the privacy of these individuals.
2 The Rule of St Benedict was probably written around AD 540 and formalised into a single authoritative manuscript in the ninth century by Charlemagne, who wished to standardise the practices in the monasteries of his Empire. The 'Codex' of 914, held at the St Gall library, is believed to be the oldest copy in existence, although the 'Oxford Hatton' manuscript contests its status. The original manuscript was written in Low Latin and it has been translated from this into numerous languages.
3 Benedict, 'Rule of St Benedict', in Marret-Crosby, A. (ed.), *The Benedictine Handbook*, Norwich: Canterbury Press, 2003, p. 10.
4 SLS, 2001, p. 21.
5 Benedict, in Marret-Crosby, A., op. cit., 2003, p. 80.
6 Ibid.
7 Gregorian chant is a form of monophonic singing with eight scalar modes. The daily office is sung in English at Worth and draws on a broader range of tones developed from the eight Gregorian tones by composers such as Joseph Gelineau, Dom Gregory Murray and Dom Laurence Bevenot. An example of this singing can be heard on the audio CD *Chants for Benedict* (1994). For a fuller account of the development of contemporary psalm-singing see Apel, W., B;oomington, *Gregorian Chants: History and Criticism*, Bloomington, IN: Indiana University Press, 1990.
8 Cochran, L., *The Sense of Vocation: A Study of Career and Life Development*, Albany, NY: SUNY Press, 1990, p. vii.
9 Mill, J.S., in Cochran, L., op. cit., 1990, p. 2.
10 Lazreg, M., *Torture and the Twilight of Empire: From Algiers to Baghdad*, Princeton, NJ: Princeton University Press, 2008, p. 120.
11 See Skeat, W.W., *A Concise Etymological Dictionary of the English Language*, New York, NY: Cosimo, 2005, p. 644.
12 For a translation of the Epistle of Philemon in the New Testament, see Barth, M., trans. Blanke, H., *The Letter to Philemon: A New Translation with Commentary*, Grand Rapids, MI: Eerdmans, 2000, p. 237.
13 See Holl, K., 'The History of the Word Vocation (*Beruf*)', *Review and Expositor*, Vol. 55, 1958, pp. 126–154; and for a full explication of the development of a Lutheran notion of vocation, see Weber, M., trans. Parson, T., *The Protestant Ethic and the Spirit of Capitalism*, Chelmsford, MA: Courier Dover, 2003 (1958), pp. 79–95.
14 For a detailed account of the early expansion of Christian communities, see Esler, P.F., 'Part III: Community Formation and Maintenance', in *The Early Christian World*, London: Routledge, 2004, pp. 295–316.

15 See Esler, P.F., ibid., p. 580. For further details of developments in monastic living contributed by Anthony (251–356) and Pachomius (286–346) see, Knowles, *From Pachomius to Ignatius: A Study in the Constitutional History of Religious Orders*, Oxford: Clarendon Press, 1996.

16 À Kempis reads the life of Christ thus, as both a real biography and an allegory for divinity, in his *The Imitation of Christ*, first published in Latin in 1418.

17 Samuel is woken from sleep three times while resting in a church. He mistakes the voices for the voice of a priest. Realising that Samuel is hearing a voice other than his own, the priest instructs him to wait to be called again and to answer, 'Speak Lord for thy servant heareth.' When Samuel is called again the Lord tells him, 'Behold I will do a thing in Israel, at which both the ears of everyone that heareth shall tingle' (KJV, I Sam. 3:4–12).

18 Elijah is told to expect the Lord by an angel, and as high winds, earthquakes and fires assail him he doesn't perceive the Lord until he hears 'a still small voice'. Hearing this, Elijah recognises the Lord; he stands at the entrance of a cave and 'there came a voice unto him, and said, what doest thou here Elijah?' (KJV, Kings 1:11–14).

19 KJV, John 10:3–4. The Gospel of St Matthew appears to suggest that all present at Jesus's baptism in Jordan by John the Baptist hear a voice as he emerges from the water, saying, 'This is my beloved son, in whom I am well pleased' (KJV, Matthew 3:17).

20 Stokes, J., 'Lion Griefs: The Wild Animal Act as Theatre', *New Theatre Quarterly*, Vol. 20, No. 2, 2000, p. 151.

21 Greenslade, S.L., *The Cambridge History of the Bible: Volume 3, The West from Reformation to the Present Day*, Cambridge: Cambridge University Press, 1975, p. 515.

22 KJV, Coll. 1:18.

23 For Paul the international congregation becomes the body of Christ just as Christ's body becomes the church in cruciform architecture. One of the earliest examples of such architecture, Qal'a Sim'an or the Church of St Simeon in Syria, embodies a Christ not only on the cross but at the moment of death: the east basilica of the cruciform is longer (further from the centre of the cruciform) and more elaborate than the west because Christ's head reputedly fell to the left as he died. For discussion of other anthropomorphic features of church architecture see 'The Body and Sacred Buildings', in Feuerstein's *Biomorphic Architecture: Human and Animal Forms in Architecture*, New York, NY: Axel Menges, 2002, pp. 81–95.

24 For an account of '*langue*', see Harris, R., *Reading Saussure: A Critical Commentary on the Cours de Linguistique generale*, London: Duckworth, 1987, p. 210.

25 For discussion of the range and use of metaphor, allegory and parable in the Bible, see Lockyer, H., *All the Parables of the Bible*, Grand Rapids, MI: Zondervan, 1988.

26 Llewelyn, R., *A Doorway to Silence: The Contemplative Use of the Rosary*, Norwich: Darton, Longman & Todd, 1986, p. 14.

27 Benedict in Marret-Crosby (ed.), op. cit., 2003, p. 24.

28 Ibid., p. 15.

29   SLS, 2001, p. 6.
30   Ibid.
31   Ibid., p. 8.
32   See Andrews et al., 'The Rate of Recovery from Stroke – and Its Measurement', *International Journal of Rehabilitation Medicine*, Vol. 3, 1981, pp. 155–161; also Skillbeck et al., 'Recovery after Stroke', *Journal of Neurology, Neurosurgery and Psychiatry*, Vol. 46, 1983, pp. 5–8; and Olsen, T.S., 'Arm and Leg Paresis as Outcome Predictors in Stroke Rehabilitation', *Stroke*, Vol. 21, 1990, pp. 247–251.
33   See Bobath, B., *Adult Hemiplegia: Evaluation and Treatment*, Oxford: Heinemann, 1990.
34   See Lennon, S., 'The Bobath Concept: A Critical Review of the Theoretical Assumptions that Guide Physiotherapy Practice in Stroke Rehabilitation', *Physical Therapy Review*, Vol. 1, No.1, 1996, pp. 35–45.
35   OED.
36   See Skeat, W.W., *A Concise Etymological Dictionary of the English Language*, New York, NY: Cosimo, 2005, p. 256.
37   Barba, E., in Turner, J., *Eugenio Barba*, London: Routledge, 2004, p. 107.
38   Foucault, M., in Lupton, D., *The Imperative of Health: Public Health and the Regulated Body*, Thousand Oaks, CA: Sage, 1995, p. 1.
39   Lingis, A., *The Imperative*, Bloomington, IN: Indiana University Press, 1998, p. 3.
40   Ibid., p. 2.
41   Ibid.
42   Ibid., p. 135.
43   Ibid., p. 136.
44   Hale, L.A., and Eales, C.J., 'Recovery of Walking Function in Stroke Patients after Minimal Rehabilitation', *Physiotherapy Research International*, Vol. 3, 1998, p. 194.
45   Punt, T.D., 'No Success Like Failure: Walking Late after Stroke, Case Report', *Physiotherapy*, Vol. 86, No. 11, 1999, p. 564.
46   Ibid., p. 566.
47   Nancy, J.-L., *Being, Singular, Plural*, Palo Alto, CA: Stanford University Press, 2000, p. xvi.
48   For Heidegger, *Dasein* represents the fact that a human being cannot be anything other than a being existent 'in'; a being among other things. To be human is to be embedded in a tangible everyday world and it is on this collective experience that Nancy focuses his attention.
49   See Durkheim, E., *The Division of Labour in Our Society*, Glencoe: The Free Press, 1947.
50   Nisbet, in Cohen, R., and Kennedy, P.M., *Global Sociology*, New York, NY: NYU Press, 2000, p. 375.
51   See Mackey, S., 'A Lexicon', *Performance Research*, Vol. 11, No. 3, 2006, p. 26. Sullivan also assesses the damaging effects of the 'assumption' that 'one natural characteristic will take precedence over others' in the '(supposed) primordial bond' that certain feminist writers claim to be 'shared' by women *in general* (Sullivan, N., *A Critical Introduction to Queer Theory*, Edinburgh: Edinburgh University Press, 2001, pp. 138–139).
52   Stokes, J., 'Lion Griefs: The Wild Animal Act as Theatre', *New Theatre Quarterly*, Vol. 20, No. 2, 2004, p. 152.

53　It is vital to note here that the ascribing of 'primordial' sharing could be produced 'out of' the notion of community being developed here as a consequence of the status of the group within, and in relation to, other socio-cultural institutions.

54　Mackey, S., op. cit., 2006, p. 27.

55　Ibid. Mackey develops this notion out of work by the anthropologists Rapport and Amit, who claim that attachment to a community should be seen as 'an achievement not an ascription'; thus 'the existence of communities is deemed an expression of free negotiations between individuals' (Amit, V., and Rapport, N., *The Trouble with Community: Anthropological Reflections in Movement*, London: Pluto Press, 2002, p. 9). In this conceptualisation of community, Rapport accounts for both the efforts of individuals to 'metabolise' themselves within a group, and also the 'negotiation' that will be both the setting and the product of such work.

56　Mackey, S., op. cit., 2006, p. 27.

57　Rapport in Amit, V., and Rapport, N., op. cit., 2002, p. 9.

58　Delanty, G., *Communities*, London: Routledge, 2003, p. 188.

59　There is disagreement over this, some choosing to point to 'communus' as a pairing of together (*cum*) and one (*unus*) which might help to explain why, by the time it appeared in English, the meaning of 'common' was in contradistinction to 'togetherness'. For example, common lands or the commons or even commoners contrasted with the nobility and their lands and thus 'common' came to mean 'ordinary' or 'vulgar'. This could be why, in contrast with 'common', 'community' has only favourable connotations and does not have an antithetical counterpart. See Shepard, G.J., and Rothenbuhler, E.W., *Communication and Community*, Laurence Erlbaum, 2001, p. 263, for examples of historical usage of the word 'community'.

60　Phelan, S., *Getting Specific: Postmodern Lesbian Politics*, Minneapolis, MN; London: University of Minnesota Press, 1994, p. 77.

61　Learmans, R., 'A Lexicon', *Performance Research*, Vol. 11, No. 3, 2006, p. 24.

62　Ibid.

63　See Learmans, op. cit., 2006, p. 24, and Luhmann, N., trans. Baecker, D., *Social Systems*, Palo Alto, CA: Stanford University Press, 1995.

64　Learmans, R., op. cit., 2006, p. 24.

65　In 1983 the sociologist Charles Cooley suggested in his book *Human Nature and Social Order* that 'all normal humans' have a natural affinity for community, and the primary factor inhibiting the formation and continuation of communities was not personal choice or even commitment as such, but that they were difficult to *organise*. One year later, in his work *The Constitution of Society: Outline of the Theory of Structuration*, the social theorist Anthony Giddens incorporated Cooley's idea into his notion of 'structuration' as the organisational process that ordered and reproduced *systems*, which are social entities, or 'reproduced relations between actors or collectives'. Though 'structures', for Giddens, and after him Poole and Hirokawa (1996), Myers and Oetzel (2003), are made up of rules and norms, they are both the 'medium and outcome of action' (see Poole, M.S., Hirokawa, R.Y., *Communication and Group Decision Making*, Thousand Oaks, CA: Sage, 1996, p. 117), because they are continually being 'produced and reproduced as a result of interaction' (see Shepherd et al., *Communication As . . . Perspectives on Social Theory*, Thousand Oaks, CA: Sage

Publications, 2006, p. 145). In this respect the social organisation of groups, such as consociations, is both the product and the medium for communication to the extent to which the existence of the consociation is reliant upon interactive communication between its members.

66 Both of these constitute imperatives, but following Lingis's assertion of the need to describe encounters with the imperative separately, the use of 'directive' and 'incentive' is here intended to draw out the different characteristics identified by Weber in the two historical phenomena.

67 Weber, M., trans. Parsons, T., *The Protestant Ethic and the Spirit of Capitalism*, Chelmsford, MA: Courier Dover, 2003 (1958), p. 181.

68 The historical account of the 'secularisation' of vocation that follows here is necessarily concise. See Weber (op. cit., 2003, pp. 79–95) for a fuller explication of the process by analysis of contemporaneous sources.

69 Holl, K., 'The History of the Word Vocation (*Beruf*)', *Review and Expositor*, Vol. 55, 1958, pp. 19–22.

70 KJV, Gen. 1:2–3.

71 KJV, Gen. 1:27–28.

72 Lingis, op. cit., 1998, p. 179.

73 KJV, Gen. 3:17–19.

74 See McTaggart, L., in Marret-Crosby, A. (ed.), *The Benedictine Handbook*, Norwich: Canterbury Press, 2003, p. 117. The length of this book precludes a fuller discussion of ascetic traditions, but it is important to contextualise the manoeuvre described by McTaggart with regard to Benedictine monasticism, given that it is this traditions of asceticism that underlies this chapter. Benedict coined the phrase 'idleness is the enemy of the soul' in Chapter 48 of his Rule, which he devotes to advising on how monks should work. Work is the only practice which Benedict explicitly describes as monastic in the entire Rule: thus, 'They will really be in the best monastic tradition if the community is supported by the work of their own hands.' The tradition of desert monasticism to which he refers, like McTaggart, views work not as a punishment but as a penance, because of its redemptive and reconciliatory capacity.

75 Luther's effect on secular notions of vocation is wrapped up in his translations of the New Testament. Understanding precisely how the particular concept of work he unleashes on laymen developed requires a detailed knowledge of Luther's translations of the term 'vocation' and his interpretation of Paul and John's use of *klesis* in the New Testament. In order fully to understand Weber's history of a Lutheran conception of vocation in secular work, it is necessary to know something about Pauline and Johannine usage of *klesis* and its translation into 'vocation' by Tertullian and subsequently *Beruf* by Luther. I have tried to give an indication of the etymology of these three terms as well as their usage but for an authoritative study of the translation of *klesis* in St Paul, see Barth's translation of the *Letter to Philemon with Commentary: A New Translation with Commentary*, Grand Rapids, MI: Eerdmans, 2000.

76 Smith, A., *An Inquiry into the Nature and Causes of the Wealth of Nations*, Cambridge, MA: Harvard University Press, 2005 (1776), p. 2.

77 Ibid., p. 3.

78 Ibid., p. 6.

79 Ibid.

80 Marx, K., in O'Malley, J. (ed.), *Marx: Early Political Writing*, Cambridge: Cambridge University Press, 1994, p. 96.

81 Ibid.

82 Ibid. p. 95.

83 Ibid.

84 Ibid., p. 96.

85 Ibid.

86 It should be quite clear that I am in no way suggesting a consciously theological conception of work in Marx's theories of alienation. The antagonism towards religion and the Church in Marx's thinking is well known, but it should be understood that my invocation of the two biblical images of work help to figure two conceptions of the function and experience of work and so help to explain how the separate elements of religious vocation have historically entered secular theories of labour. It should also be made clear that the justification for 'happiness' and 'self-expression' in Marx is not that work is an originally divine capability but rather a distinctively human one; 'since human nature is the true community of men, those who produce thereby confirm their nature, human community and social being . . . To say that man is alienated from himself is to say that the society of this alienated man is the caricature of his real community' (see Marx, K., in Nancy, J.-L., op. cit., 2000, p. 1).

87 This will be more comprehensively discussed in Chapter 5.

88 Arendt, H., *The Human Condition*, Chicago, IL: Chicago University Press, 1958, p. 151.

89 Arendt, H., in Birmingham, P., *Hannah Arendt and Human Rights: The Predicament of Common Responsibility*, Bloomington IN: Indiana University Press, 2006, p. 72.

90 Arendt, H., op. cit., 1958, pp. 7–8.

91 See Birmingham, P., op. cit., 2006, p. 73.

92 Arendt, H., op. cit., 1958, pp. 7–8.

93 See Arendt, H., ibid., pp. 178–179, 184–186, 199–200.

94 Arendt, H., in Benhabib, S., *The Reluctant Modernism of Hannah Arendt*, Lanham, MD: Rowman & Littlefield, 2003, p. 199.

95 Ibid.

96 Ibid., p. 99.

97 Arendt's concept of 'public space' is left suspended here, but it will be reanimated and developed in the next chapter and throughout the book. The claim that Arendt *doesn't* make, according to Benhabib, is obviously the very claim of J.L. Austin and John Searle's 'speech acts'. It is essential that the 'linguistic structure' of action as a form of work is not confused with the action *caused* by certain pronouncements.

Chapter 4

1 Abse, D., *Ash on a Young Man's Sleeve*, London: Vallentine-Mitchell, 1971 (1954), p. 20.

2 Ibid.

3 Ibid.

4 Ibid., p. 22.
5 Statistics taken from the Stroke Association, 2010.
6 See Milgram, S., *Obedience to Authority: An Experimental View*, New York: Harper & Row, 1974.
7 Ibid., p. 123.
8 Ibid., p. xii.
9 Ibid., p. 133.
10 Abse, D., *The Dogs of Pavlov*, London: Vallentine-Mitchell, 1973, p. 27.
11 Ibid., p. 22.
12 Ibid.
13 Milgram, S., in Abse, D., op. cit., 1973, p. 42.
14 Ibid., p. 40.
15 Ibid., p. 44.
16 Ibid., p. 41.
17 See Prentice in Postmes, T., Jetten, J. (eds), *Individuality and the Group*, Thousand Oaks, CA: Pine Forge Press, 2006, p. 39.
18 It is of some interest that R.A. Nye, in his *The Origins of Crowd Psychology: Gustave LeBon and the Crisis of Democracy in the Third Republic* (1975), argues that LeBon's ideas may actually have influenced Hitler, whose own beliefs resonated with LeBon's emphasis on racial factors in crowd situations. In this respect LeBon's text feeds directly into the debate between Abse and Milgram because it goes some way towards addressing Milgram's question about Eichmann.
19 For Diener, deindividuation is not a psychological state but a set of relationships among situations, emotional states and behavioural responses.
20 See Diener, E., 'Deindividuation: The Absence of Self-awareness and Self-regulation in Group Members', in Paulus, P.B. (ed.), *Psychology of Group Influence*, Hillsdale, NJ: Erlbaum, 1980; and Prentice-Dunn, S., and Rogers, R.W., 'Effects of Public and Private Awareness on Deindividuation and Aggression', *Journal of Personality and Psychology*, Vol. 43, 1982, pp. 503–513, for examples.
21 Postmes, T., and Spears, R., 'Deindividuation and Antinormative Behaviour: A Meta-analysis', *Psychological Bulletin*, Vol. 123, 1998, p. 253.
22 This note is intended to amplify the difference between 'holding' a role and 'playing' a role with respect to the understanding of embodiment engaged by this book. 'Holding' a role focuses our attention on the subject position of the individual and subsequently their 'place' within institutionally organised entities; 'playing' a role, by contrast, focuses on what an individual 'does' within a social unit – how, through incorporation and excorporation, they come to do their metabolic body-in-action.
23 Lindsay, S., *Handbook of Applied Dog Behaviour and Training*, Oxford: Blackwell, 2005, p. 4.
24 Ibid., pp. 4–5.
25 Giddens, A., *Sociology*, Cambridge: Polity Press, 2006, p. 163.
26 Ibid.
27 See Skeat, W.W., *A Concise Etymological Dictionary of the English Language*, New York, NY: Cosimo, 2005, p. 354.
28 Lingis, A., *The Imperative*, Bloomington, IN: Indiana University Press, 1998, p. 3.

29   Lingis repeats this phrase twice, once in his introduction (ibid., p. 3) and again in his explanation of Kantian philosophy (p. 180).

30   In showing how the imperative is conducted through thought and into ordered relationships between 'the surface effects of the world', of which the thinking subject is one, Lingis explains, that, 'Thought formulates relationships that comprehensively retain the concept that represents what is passing here . . . With its concepts and relationships, thought establishes order'. Succinctly, he demonstrates that, 'The imperative commands thought to order' (ibid.).

31   Ibid.

32   Ibid., p. 1.

33   Ibid., p. 2.

34   Ridout, N.P., *Stage Fright: Animals and Other Theatrical Problems*, Cambridge: Cambridge University Press, 2006, p. 1.

35   Theatre Training Initiative was established in London in 2000, as a registered, not-for-profit company producing workshops and creative development events for theatre, dance and performing artists. The Directors are Frances Barbe, Lukas Angelini and Melanie Wynnyard.

36   It is important to understand, as I hope will become evident through the discussion of collective action that will follow, that the 'unification' of a group of individuals into a collective does not entail the disruption of their own individuality such that it would interrupt the distinctness of individuals and destroy plurality. As in contemporary understandings of social identity deindividuation, it is understood that individuals do not *lose* any sense of self but rather *acquire* an image of self as a member of a group.

37   Fraleigh, S.H., *Dancing into Darkness*, Pittsburgh, PA: University of Pittsburgh Press, 1999, p. 177.

38   Ibid.

39   Different Butoh practitioners practise the 'Butoh walk', if there is such a thing, very differently. In addition to working with Katsura Kan between 18 and 21 May 2006, I have taken part in a much longer Butoh workshop series with Marie-Gabrielle Rotie, a Butoh dancer and teacher. I mention this here only to note that Rotie's attitude to walking (and certainly to teaching walking) was very different to Kan's in that it was more explicitly technical as well as pointedly differentiated from my own 'normal' walk. Despite the differences between Kan and Rotie's attitude towards walking in Butoh, both appear to be invested in this aspect of Butoh dance. In addition to these experiences of Butoh walking, I took part in a workshop session (lasting approximately three hours) with Fran Barbe at 'The Changing Body: The Bodymind in Contemporary Training and Performance' symposium, Exeter, in January 2006. Fran Barbe is a Butoh dancer, choreographer and movement coach and her workshop also consisted of walking 'exercises' and compositional work structured around walking.

40   Whitworth, J., 'Translating Theologies of the Body: SITI'S Physical Theatre: Training and Corporeal Ideology', *Performance Research*, Vol. 8, No. 2, 2003, p. 24.

41   Whitworth points out that Suzuki training was developed using elements of Japanese Kabuki and Noh theatre (ibid., p. 23). Fraleigh also notes the influence of Noh and Kabuki on Butoh as well as similarities between Butoh performance and these traditional Japanese styles (op. cit., 1999, pp. 81–82, 105, 171–172).

42   Whitworth, J., op. cit., 2003, p. 23.

43 Ibid., p. 21.

44 Ibid., p. 25.

45 Ibid.

46 Ibid.

47 Ibid., p. 24.

48 Pitches, J., 'Tracing/Training Rebellion: Object Work in Meyerhold's Biomechanics', *Performance Research*, Vol. 12, No. 4, 2008, p. 100.

49 Ibid.

50 It seems reasonable to assume that, in the context of group activities, Pitches is using 'unarticulated' to mean 'without speech' as opposed to 'not consisting of joined segments'.

51 Bourriaud, N., trans. Pleasance, S. and Woods, F., *Relational Aesthetics*, Dijon: Presses du Réel, 2002, p. 15.

52 Allsopp, R.,'On Form/Yet to Come', *Performance Research*, Vol. 10, No. 2, 2005, p. 2. Allsopp dates this trend back to George Bataille's (1929) definition of *informe* and his focus on the task words perform in given contexts, as opposed to their meaning. He traces this development through J.L. Austin's (1961) speech acts and the performativity of language as well as through Tadeusz Kantor's (1965) 'Informal Theatre Definitions'.

53 Ibid., p. 1.

54 Latour, B., in Read, A., *Theatre Intimacy and Engagement: The Last Human Venue*, Basingstoke; New York, NY: Palgrave Macmillan, 2008, p. 41.

55 Read, A., op cit., 2008, p. 44.

56 Badiou, A., in Hallward, P., *Badiou: A Subject to Truth*, Minneapolis, MN: University of Minnesota Press, 2003, p. 94.

57 Hallward, P., op. cit., 2003, p. 94.

58 Ibid.

59 Badiou, A., trans. Feltham, O., *Being and Event*, London: Continuum, 1988, p. 33.

60 Whitworth, J., op. cit., 2003, p. 25.

61 Ibid.

62 Ibid., p. 27.

63 Whitworth spends only one paragraph discussing the relevance of branding with respect to incorporate identity, focusing on the company logo: 'The company's name itself emblazoned on students' T-shirts, asks one to think about twenty-first-century demands of corporate marketing that is necessary to keep non-profit, experimental theatre alive in the commercial environment of American theatre . . . SITI training is its own phenomenon, its own product for marketing' (op. cit., 2003, p. 27). This aspect of 'identity' is played out in a discourse of brand recognition alongside other logos and is tied to the 'phenomenon' of SITI.

64 Ibid.

65 LeBon, G., *The Crowd*, Ottawa: Xinware Corporation, 2007, p. 94.

66 Ibid.

67 Ibid.

68 See Weber, M., *Economy and Society*, Vol. 1, Berkeley, CA: University of California Press, 1978 (1914), p. 4. Max Weber refutes collective responsibility on the grounds that 1) groups cannot form psychological intentions and thus cannot take rational or purposeful action; and 2) that it is practically

impossible to distinguish collective actions from identical actions performed by many persons. The influence of Max Weber's classical methodological individualism in ascribing agency purely to the individual on Western juridical systems is significant and can perhaps best be traced to his 1954 work, *Max Weber on Law in Economy and Society*. See 'The Specific and Peculiar Rationalism of Modern Law' (Boucock, G., *In the Grip of Freedom: Law and Modernity in Max Weber*, Toronto: Toronto University Press, 2000, pp. 44–45); 'Individual Autonomy and Formal Legal Rationality' (pp. 54–59); and 'Formal Legal Rationality Verses Individual Autonomy' (pp. 65–67).

69   The philosopher David Cooper, in his article 'Collective Responsibility' (*Philosophy*, 1968), uses this legal reality to support his assertion of the (coherent) existence of collective action. He observes that even outside penal systems we frequently assign blame to groups, an assertion taken a step further by Peter French, who contends in his book, *Individual and Collective Responsibility* (1998), that there are certain intentional actions that can only be taken by groups. He asserts that there is a 'class' of predicate that simply cannot be true of individuals, such as 'disbanded', 'elected a president', or (somewhat ironically in this instance) 'passed a law'.

70   Jackson, B., *The Battle for Orgreave*, Brighton: Vanson Wardle, 1986, p. 37.

71   See Figgis, M., *The Battle of Orgreave*, ArtAngel, 2001.

72   Lynne Pearce shows in her reading of Bakhtin's notion of carnival that 'carnival must ultimately be considered a *conservative* social/aesthetic force, in that it permits a "topsy-turvydom" for a limited spell only, after which the social order in necessarily restored' [*emphasis as in original*], in Waugh, P. (ed.), *Literary Theory and Criticism: An Oxford Guide*, Oxford: Oxford University Press, 2006, p. 230.

73   The sum of £160 refers to the fee volunteers were paid for taking part in Deller's re-enactment.

74   Names have been changed to protect identities.

75   A technician on a physiotherapy ward is a trained but not medically qualified therapist.

76   Davis, Rosen and Donman, in Bogousslavsky, J. (ed.), *Acute Stroke Treatment*, London: Informa Health Care Publishers, 2003, p. 8.

77   D'Esposito, in Schiffer, R.B., Roa, M.R., and Fogel, B.S. (eds), *Neuropsychiatry*, Haggerston, MD: Lippencott, Williams & Wilkins, 2003, p. 335.

78   Ibid., p. 328.

79   Pitches, J., op. cit., 2007, p. 102.

80   Pitches quotes heavily from Nick Worrall's chapter, 'Meyerhold's "Magnanimous Cuckold"', in Schneider and Cody's *Re:direction: A Theoretical and Practical Guide*. This quotation from Gvozdev is taken from Worrall's chapter and cited in Pitches, J., op. cit., 2007, p. 102.

81   Pitches, J., ibid.

82   Ibid., p. 100.

83   Allsopp, R., op. cit., 2005, p. 2.

84   Ridout, N.P., *Stage Fright*, Cambridge: Cambridge University Press, 2006, p. 97.

85   Ibid., p. 96.

86   Ibid., pp. 96–97.

87   Admittedly the lack of a question mark in the title of this conference would
     suggest that the substance of its name was more instructive than inquisitive, but
     this was belied not only by the approach adopted by the range of practitioners,
     theoreticians and academics present but also by the titles of various of the sessions:
     'When does acting begin?', 'Am I bovvered?' and 'What can the puppets teach the
     actor?', for example.

88   Latour, B., *Reassembing the Social*, Oxford: Oxford University Press, 2005, p. 137.

89   In *Theatre, Intimacy and Engagement: The Last Human Venue*, Alan Read
     commends Kelleher and Ridout's *The Theatre of Societas Raffaello Sanzio* (2007)
     and their descriptions of 'Tragedia Endogonidia' as one of several exemplary
     texts by the authors in a more generalised movement towards inversion of the
     academic hierarchy in which descriptions should be outside something called
     'academic analysis'. *Theatre, Intimacy and Engagement: The Last Human Venue*,
     with its range of 'weak examples' and its commitment to 'thick description', is of
     course also an exemplary text in this movement.

90   The particular notion of acting I am referring to here is that which has been
     described by Daniel Smith as an 'ancient hylomorphic model', 'which conceived
     of the artistic task as the imposition of form upon matter' – see 'Deleuze's
     Theory of Sensation: Overcoming the Kantian Duality', in Patton, P. (ed.),
     Deleuze: A Critical Reader, Oxford: Blackwell, 1996, p. 43. Accepting rhetorical
     differences in the descriptions of acting practice, Smith's model encompasses a
     range of ancient and non-ancient practices in which the actor, as 'master', is
     conceived of as the artistic agent of the artwork. This notion can be seen
     imprinted on the Stanislavskian actor – 'It takes a great artist to convey great
     feeling . . . Without profound mastery of his art an actor cannot carry over to the
     spectator either the idea, theme or living content of the play' (Stanislavski, K., *An
     Actor's Handbook*, London: Methuen, 1990, p. 11) – as well as actors of
     contemporary 'psychophysiological method': 'The phenomenon of acting can be
     characterised as a particular form of behaviour produced at will by an actor in
     order to transmit gnostic and emotional information to an audience' – see
     Bloch, Orthous and Santibanez, 'Effector Patterns of Basic Emotions: A
     Psychophysiological Method for Training Actors', in Zarrilli, P.B. (ed.), *Acting
     (re)Considered: A Theoretical and Practical Guide*, London; New York: Routledge,
     2002, p. 219.

91   As discussed in note 69, Peter French uses linguistic analysis to argue for the
     coherence of collective action: 'There is a class of predicate that cannot be true
     of individuals, that can only be true of collectives. Examples of such predicates
     abound . . . and include "disbanded" (most uses of), "lost the football game",
     "elected a president", and "passed an amendment" (French, P., op. cit., 1998, p. 37).
     Clearly the charge of 'rioting', heard by Bernard Jackson after his involvement at
     Orgreave, would fall into French's class of predicate, although in this chapter I
     focus less on linguistic arguments for collective action and more on the work of
     those thinkers such as May, Velleman and Gilbert who rely on social and relational
     theory. This is because consideration of interpersonal relationships is central to
     the notion of obedience as interaction with others, and also because relationality
     is now thoroughly related to a field of aesthetics. I would however wish to signal
     the worth of such linguistic analyses of blaming attitudes in theatre particularly
     with respect to the 'theatrical problems', which Ridout refers to as 'mutual

predicaments' – corpsing and fiasco – in *Stage Fright: Animals and Other Theatrical Problems.*

92 Though later methodological individualists such as J.R.S. Downie (1969), J. Naverson (2002) and Angela Corlett (2001), following the evidence-based agenda set by Weber and Lewis, cite the problems with collective responsibility given that groups do not have mental lives in the same way as individuals, they seem willing to acknowledge the possibility of collective action in a number of practical examples.

93 Corlett, A., 'Collective Moral Responsibility', *Journal of Social Philosophy*, Vol. 32, 2001, p. 575.

94 See Gilbert, M., *On Social Facts*, New York, NY: Routledge, 1989, and *Sociality and Responsibility*, Lanhan, MD: Rowman & Littlefield, 2000.

95 Gilbert, M., op. cit., 2000, p. 22.

96 See Velleman, J.D., 'How to Share an Intention', in *Philosophy and Phenomenological Research*, Vol. 57, 1997, pp. 29–50.

97 Whitworth, J., op. cit., 2003, p. 25.

98 See May, L., *The Morality of Groups*, Notre Dame IN: University of Notre Dame Press, 1987, p. 55.

99 This of course draws a distinction between the subject-body of the institution and the metabolic-body or body-in-action embodied in practice.

100 Whitworth, J., op. cit., 2003, p. 24.

101 Ibid., p. 27.

102 See Tuomela, R., 'Actions by Collectives' in *Philosophical Perspectives*, Vol. 3, 1989, p. 494. Tuomela's approach to collectives recalls Thomas Hobbes's effort to create a collective subject in the guise of his Leviathan. Hobbes attempted to justify sovereignty, and that the authority of the English crown posited a higher authority in the community. The will and action of the Leviathan came to be the will and actions of its/his subjects as a result of them having transferred their own agency to it/him. This, for Hobbes, was the only kind of exchange that could enable social life to function at the level of political states, where the Leviathan's own subjectivity not only represented but also was indivisible from the subjectivities of state-members. At least one contemporary defender of collective responsibility makes reference to Hobbes's *Leviathan* (see Copp, D., 'Hobbes on Artificial Persons and Collective Actions', *Philosophical Review*, Vol. 89, No. 4, 1980, pp. 579–606), but the concept is generally thought to be too authoritarian for capturing collective will/agency.

103 It is of some interest that Tuomela (like LeBon before him) singles out crowds as appropriate sites of collective responsibility, even though they do not exhibit the kinds of organised relational structure that May argues to be essential to collective acting: 'Crowds and rioters . . . are without much or any structure (and division of tasks and activities) . . . But they can be said to act in virtue of their members' action . . . Thus in a riot the members of a collective typically perform their destructive actions as members of a collective without acting on its behalf' (see Tuomela, R., 'Actions by Collectives', in *Philosophical Perspectives*, Vol. 3, 1989, p. 476).

104 Whitworth, J., op. cit., 2003, p. 27.

105 Read, A., op. cit., 2008, p. 45. Read follows Latour in figuring the medium in which the relations of theatre and performance occur (relations which in Read's

showciology include non-human 'distances, volumes and surfaces') as plasma – as an as yet 'unformatted' phenomenon.

106 Law, J. and Callon, M., 'On Qualculation, Agency and Otherness', Centre for Science Studies, Lancaster University, 2003, p. 13.

107 Ibid. Offering an example designed to explain both relationality and the 'newness' made possible by it, Law and Callon draw on 'the loss of selfhood in a collective, a group' during Quaker worship (p. 5), and assert that, 'The workings of the Holy Spirit depend on the arrangement of the room' (p. 13).

108 Ibid., p. 11.

109 Ibid., p. 12.

110 Ibid.

111 In July 2008, police were called to break up a water fight organised on the social networking site Facebook, after several participants – who were reportedly armed with knives – escalated the level of conflict. Nine men were arrested and paramedics took three children to hospital, where they were treated for broken bones. The children had been thrown when the horses they were riding were spooked by the disturbance (Sky News: 'Water Fight in Hyde Park', 2008). The first 'flashmob' – an internet-organised collective 'party' in a public space – reputedly took place in the rug section of Macy's department store in New York in June 2001, and since this time the number of 'flash' phenomena and instances of 'mobbing' have increased, sometimes, as with the Hyde Park water fight, with destructive consequences (CNN News: 'Flashmob to Lynch Mob', 2008).

112 Arendt, H., in Birmingham, P., *Hannah Arendt and Human Rights: The Predicament of Common Responsibility*, Bloomington, IN: Indiana University Press, 2006, p. 70.

113 I accept, with Law and Callon, that networked spaces always involve non-human entities including, but not only, in the respect to which humans relate to these. However, given the promises made by participant observation to speak with others and not on their behalf, this discussion of collectivity necessarily narrows focus to explore the human interpersonal dimensions of the collective actor.

114 Arendt, H., in Birmingham, P., op. cit., 2006, p. 70.

115 Bio-politics is the name Foucault gives to the power exerted on humans as a group, rather than the anatamo-politics exerted on each of them as an individual body. It is thus a form of politics entailing the 'administration of processes of life' (see Dean, M., *Governmentality: Power and Rule in Modern Society*, Thousand Oaks, CA: Sage, 1999, p. 98).

116 Benhabib, in Hinchman, L.P., *Hannah Arendt: Critical Essays*, Albany, NY: SUNY, 1994, p. 129.

117 Ibid.

118 Adrian Kear's article, 'Troublesome Amateurs: Theatre, Ethics and the Labour of Mimesis', in *Performance Research* traces this history through Plato's distinction between 'mimesis as a labour of production and as a mode of consumption' (2005, p. 30) through Aristotle's figuration of mimesis as a 'productive principle governed by poesis' (p. 32) and into Adorno's argument that 'a human being only becomes human at all by imitating' (Adorno, in Kear, 2005, p. 26), and Lacoue-Labarthe's notion of 'demiurgy' showing that 'the essence of mimesis is not imitation but production' (Lacoue-Labarthe, in Kear, 2005, p. 31).

Chapter 5

1   Stanislavski is understood to have kept notebooks of all his performances, from his first at the age of fourteen, in which he recorded his impressions of his performances, meditated on the causes of difficulties in performance and sketched out possible solutions (see Benedetti, J., *Stanislavski: An Introduction*, London; New York, NY: Routledge). Quintillian's *Institutio* was designed as a series of guidebooks to educate especially promising youths towards the goal of eloquence which was, according to Joseph Roach, 'the most highly esteemed attainment of ancient public life' (*The Player's Passion: Studies in the Science of Acting*, Newark, DE: University of Delaware Press, 1985, p. 23). Book 6, for example, is concerned with imparting the 'secret principles' of using pathos to elicit sympathy from an audience.

2   Allsopp, R., 'On Form/Yet to Come', *Performance Research*, Vol. 10, No. 2, 2005, p. ii.

3   KJV, John 1:1.

4   KJV, Gen. 1:2.

5   For the purpose of this analogy, the 'Research Degrees Board: Application to Register for a Higher Degree by Research' (or form 'RDB 2'), from which the images are taken is one quite literally 'formal' example of PhD regulation.

6   Heidegger, M., trans. Schuwer, A., and Rojcewicz, R., *Parmenides*, Bloomington, IN: Indiana University Press, 1992, pp. 80–81.

7   Goffman, E., *Stigma: Notes on the Management of Spoiled Identity*, London: Simon & Schuster, 1963, p. 1.

8   Plato, trans. Allen, R.E., *The Republic*, London: Yale University Press, 2006, p. 93.

9   Detainee P, an Algerian who reportedly has no hands, was one of the last eight foreign nationals held without trial under the 2001 Anti-Terrorism, Crime and Security Act, charged with being an associate of an Algerian terror groups (BBC News: 'Detainee P', 2008).

10 Young, in Rothenburg, J., and Clay, S., *A Book of the Book: Some Works and Projections about the Book and Writing*, New York: Granary Books, 2000, pp. 25, 49.

11 Allsopp, R., op. cit., 2005, p. 2.

12 I am thinking here about 'body language' as a certain materiality for spoken language that complements the breath.

13 Read, A., *Theatre Intimacy and Engagement: The Last Human Venue*, Basingstoke; New York, NY: Palgrave Macmillan, 2008, p. 45.

14 Brook, P., *The Empty Space*, London: Penguin Books, 1990 (1968), p. 11.

15 Allsopp, R., op. cit., 2005, p. 1.

16 Ridout, N.P., *Stage Fright: Animals and Other Theatrical Problems*, Cambridge: Cambridge University Press, 2006, p. 7.

17 Hodge, A., *Twentieth Century Actor Training*, London; New York, NY: Routledge, 2000, p. 2.

18 Ridout, N.P., op. cit., 2006, p. 7.

19 Hejinian, L., 'The Rejection of Closure' in Hejinian, L. (ed.), *The Language of Inquiry*, Berkeley, CA: University of California Press, 2000 (1983), p. 47.

20 Ignace Gelb coined the term grammatology in his 1952 book, *A Study of Writing*, to refer to the scientific study of writing systems. Derrida's *De La Grammatologie* (*Of Grammatology*, 1967) adopts and adapts Gelb's term to show that the ways

in which ideas are written decisively affects knowledge. Gregory Ulmer's *Applied Grammatology: Post(e) Pedagogy from Jacques Derrida to Joseph Beuys* (1985) picks up this lineage and processes it through analysis of a range of media technologies studying the 'apparatus' of grammar across a range of its modes. Ulmer's approach in particular can be related to the discussion of Connor's attitudes to writing later in this chapter, in describing a history of grammatology.

21 Connor, S., *Modernism and the Writing Hand*, an embellished transcript of a paper given at 'Modernism and the Technology of Writing' conference, Institute of English Studies, University of London, 26 March 1999, p. 2 (see Internet resources).

22 Hejinian has argued that *intention* is integrally linked to form, and that intention may actually provide the 'structural' framework for form/s of writing: 'The act of writing is a process of improvisation within a framework (form) of intention' (Hejinian, L., 'The Language of Inquiry', Academy of American Poets, 2000). (See Internet resources.)

23 Hacking in Ulmer, G., *Electronic Monuments*, Minneapolis, MN: University of Minnesota Press, 2005, p. xx. Ulmer, like Hacking, adopts the term 'matrix' rather than 'plasma' for this effective milieu, that 'with which an idea, a concept or kind, is formed' (ibid.).

24 Paul Allain explains the influence of *The Phenomenology of Perception* on Suzuki's theatre practice by furthering 'notions of performance as self-encounter and self-revelation before others' (see *The Art of Stillness: The Theatre Practice of Tadashi Suzuki*, London: Methuen Drama, 2000, p. 18). These notions of performance have proved to be guiding principles for much of Performance Studies, including the training research of Zarrilli, Loukes and others, which inform this book.

25 Merleau-Ponty, M., *Phenomenology of Perception*, London; New York, NY: Routledge, 2002 (1945), p. 208.

26 This notion of form recalls Deleuze and Guattari's 'order-words' upon which subjectification depends. These order-words 'function by conjugating a certain socially defined action with a statement that effectively accomplishes it' (see Goodchild, P., *Deleuze and Guattari: An Introduction to the Politics of Desire*, Thousand Oaks, CA: Sage, 1996, pp. 152–153).

27 See Roberts, Byram, Barro, Jordan and Street's *Language Learners as Ethnographers*, Tonowanda, NY: Multilingual matters, 2000, for a novel take on the relationship between language and ethnography that problematises the assumption that language and dialect can provide a source of ethnographic insight.

28 Hodge, A., op. cit., 2000, p. 8.

29 Ibid.

30 Ibid.

31 Barba, E., in Huxley, M. and Witts, N., *The Twentieth Century Performance Reader*, London; New York, NY: Routledge, 2002, p. 42.

32 Ibid.

33 Ibid.

34 One of Barba's actors explained that the exercise was given this name purely because the ribbons first used were green in colour.

35 This workshop took place at the Alsager Campus of Manchester University on 4 November 2005.

36   Cieslak, R., interviewed by Torzecka, M., in 'Running to Touch the Horizon', *New Theatre Quarterly*, Vol. 8, No. 3, 1992, p. 261.

37   Barba, E., trans. Fowler, R., *The Paper Canoe: A Guide to Theatre Anthropology*, London; New York, NY: Routledge, 1995, p. 51.

38   See Turner, J., *Eugenio Barba*, London: Routledge, 2004, p. 50. The principles described the varying attempt of Odin training to encourage a trainee to put his/her body into positions they would not normally inhabit and engage muscles in ways that they would not be engaged in the course of daily living. In this respect they refer to what Barba has called 'hot' or 'extra-daily' behaviour, and which Turner describes as the product of a 'transformation in the body'.

39   Barba, E., 'An Amulet Made of Memory', in Zarrilli, P.B. (ed.), *Acting (re)Considered: A Theoretical and Practical Guide*, London; New York, NY: Routledge, 2002, p. 101.

40   Ibid., p. 100.

41   Ibid.

42   Ibid.

43   Ibid., p. 101.

44   Roach, J., *The Player's Passion: Studies in the Science of Acting*, Ann Arbor, MI: University of Michigan Press, 1993, p. 225.

45   See Meyer-Dinkgräfe, D., *Approaches to Acting, Past and Present*, London: Continuum, 2006, pp. 74–80; and Lavy, J., 'Theoretical Foundations of Grotowski's Total Act, Via Negativa and Conjuctio Opposortium', *The Journal of Religion and Theatre*, Vol. 4, No. 2, 2005, p. 175.

46   Roach, J., op. cit., 1993, p. 225.

47   Kłoczowksi, J., *A History of Polish Christianity*, Cambridge: Cambridge University Press, 2000, p. xxx.

48   Wolford, L., and Schechner, R. (eds), *The Grotowski Sourcebook*, New York, NY: Routledge, 1997, p. 476.

49   Ibid., p. 155.

50   Dykstra's description of the wide-reaching effects formation – 'The faith community has formative power in the lives of people. It can nurture their faith and give shape to the quality and character of their spirits' – reflects what he calls a 'general consensus . . . among religious educators at the present time' – see Dykstra, C., in Astley, Francis and Crowder (eds), *Theological Perspectives on Christian Formation: A Reader on Theology*, Chester: Gracewing Publishing, 1996, p. 252.

51   Allain, P., *The Art of Stillness: Theatre Practice of Tadashi Suzuki*, London: Methuen Drama, 2002, p. 98.

52   Ibid., p. 124.

53   Barba, E., in Zarrilli, P.B., op. cit., 2002, p. 104.

54   Allain, P., op. cit., 2002, p. 124.

55   Nelis, T., in ibid.

56   Zarrilli, P.B., 'Introduction', *Acting (re)Considered: A Theoretical and Practical Guide*, London; New York, NY: Routledge, 2002, p. 95.

57   While these poses are in one sense 'static', as combat poses they entail the 'active' readiness of the practitioner, who remains 'ready to act' from a static position by maintaining muscular tensions and sensory focus.

58 See, Zarrilli, P.B., '"On the Edge of a Breath, Looking: Cultivating the Actor's Bodymind through Asian Martial/Meditiation Arts', in Zarrilli, P.B., op. cit., 2002, p. 181. Robert Benedetti records A.C. Scott as having referred to 'standing still while not standing still', and contends that the goals of any 'serious actor training' is to discover 'stillness at the centre' (in Zarrilli, P.B., ibid).

59 Zarrilli, P.B., 'The Metaphysical Studio', *TDR: The Drama Review*, Vol. 46, No. 2, 2002, p. 150.

60 Zarrilli, P.B., op. cit., 2002, pp. 183–184.

61 Ibid., p. 188.

62 Ibid., p. 190.

63 Kohn, T., 'The *Aikido* Body: Expressions of Group Identity and Self-Discovery in Martial Arts Training', in Dyck, N., and Archetti, E.P. (eds), *Sport, Dance and Embodied Identities*, Oxford: Berg, 2003, p. 144.

64 Ibid.

65 Kohn cites numerous examples from various areas of daily life including one trainee's story of 'blending' with the reality of her father's death; Dobson's 'infamous' story of aikido being used to subdue a drunken man on a train; and an account from an aikido practitioner named Marcus who applied aikido principles to his verbally abusive boss.

66 Ibid., p. 145.

67 The reference here is to the Meyerholdian traditions of physical exercises in actor training and the Stanislavskian legacy of constructing detailed, intellectualised, psychological coordinates for playing a role.

68 Foucault, M., trans. Sheridan, A., *Discipline and Punish: The Birth of the Prison*, London: Penguin, 1991 (1977), p. 149.

69 Ibid., pp. 152–153.

70 Ridout, N.P., *Stage Fright: Animals and Other Theatrical Problems*, Cambridge: Cambridge University Press, 2006, p. 42.

71 This statement refers to monasticism in its broadest sense, not merely Christian monasticism (dating back to the fourth century B.C.) or Benedictine monasticism (Benedict's Rule dates back to the sixth century, but the 'monastic revival' it sparked is usually dated to the tenth).

72 See De Dreuille, M., *From East to West: A History of Monasticism*, Herefordshire: Gracewing; New York, NY: Crossroads,1999.

73 Keeping the 'Great Silence' is a monastic tradition honoured at Worth Abbey whereby the entire community refrain from speech in the interval of time between Compline, the last service of the day, usually at about 9 p.m., and Matins, the first service, which takes place at 6.20 a.m.

74 Phillip and Carol Zaleski, in their work, *Prayer: A History* (2005), discuss the centrality of exercises of prayer to historical practices of monasticism.

75 Ignatius Loyola, trans. Fr Mullen, *The Spiritual Exercises of St Ignatius Loyola*, New York, NY: Cosimo, 2007, p. 3.

76 St Ignatius writes of 'the compound of body and soul' in a complex description that considers man's place on earth as soul 'imprisoned' in the body and this 'compound' 'exiled amongst brute beasts' (trans. Mullen, op. cit., 2007, p. 36). St Ignatius's particular conception of body and soul resonates with Llewelyn's present-day conception typified in his statement, 'without entirely understanding

the relation between body and soul that causes (the) special connection between thought and some mechanical activity, we know that it exists . . . We are not pure spirit but composite beings made of spirit *and* matter' (see *A Doorway to Silence: The Contemplative Use of the Rosary*, Norwich: Darton, Longman & Hodge, 1986, p. 31).

77 I have elected to use the example of the rosary because of its specific relevance to monasticism. Robert Llewelyn, the chaplain of the Julian Shrine at Norwich, in his book about saying the rosary suggests that the rosary represents 'a little Office'. The 'big' Office that it represents is the daily cycle of services a priest or nun must perform, and consequently the representational aspect of the rosary makes it a particularly apposite exercise to explore in seeking to describe monastic training.

78 In English: 'I believe in God the Father, Almighty, Maker of heaven and earth, and in Jesus Christ, his only begotten Son, our Lord, Who was conceived by the Holy Ghost, born of the Virgin Mary, suffered under Pontius Pilate; was crucified, dead and buried: He descended into hell, the third day he rose again from the dead, He ascended into heaven, and sits at the right hand of God the Father Almighty, from thence He shall come to judge the quick and the dead. I believe in the Holy Ghost, I believe in the Holy Catholic Church, the communion of saints, the forgiveness of sins, the resurrection of the body, and the life everlasting. Amen.'

79 In English: 'Our Father, Who art in Heaven, Hallowed be Thy name, Thy kingdom come, Thy will be done on earth as it is in heaven. Give us this day our daily bread and forgive us our trespasses as we forgive those who trespass against us, lead us not into temptation, but deliver us from evil, amen.'

80 'In English: 'Hail Mary, full of Grace, the Lord is with thee. Blessed art thou among women, and blessed is the fruit of thy womb, Jesus. Holy Mary, Mother of God, pray for us sinners now, and at the hour of our death. Amen.'

81 In English: 'Glory be to the Father, and to the Son and to the Holy Ghost. As it was in the beginning, is now and ever shall be, world without end. Amen.' N.B. The Gloria is often referred to as the 'Glory Be', but I use 'Gloria' here in conformity with Robert Llewelyn.

82 The fifteen 'points' are divided into three groups of five: the Joyful Mysteries, the Sorrowful Mysteries and the Glorious Mysteries. To give an example, the five points within the Sorrowful Mysteries are, the agony in the Garden of Gethsemane (KJV, Luke 22:39–46), the flogging (KJV, Mark 15:15), the crowning with thorns (KJV, Mark 15:16–20), the carrying of the cross (KJV, John 19:16–17), the Crucifixion (KJV, John 19:18–30).

83 While it is not possible to give a definitive meaning for 'meditation' here, it is important to say that in this context meditation most definitely does not mean discursive or analytical thought. Though meditation is different from intellectual thought or imagination, Allain would appear to be describing a similarly formatted activity to the rosary when he writes that in Suzuki exercises, 'the external form is fixed but the *imaginative focus* is not proscribed' [*emphasis added*] (Allain, op. cit., 2002, p. 96).

84 Llewelyn, R., *A Doorway to Silence: The Contemplative Use of the Rosary*, Norwich: Darton, Longman & Hodge, 1986, p. 31.

85 Ibid.

86   Ibid., p. ix.
87   Goulish, M., *39 Microlectures in Proximity of Performance*, London; New York, NY: Routledge, 2000, p. 33.
88   Simply stated, Goulish poses the question of 'ownership' from the perspectives of informed and ecstatic: 'Does one see the repeating/non-repeating moment as occurring *inside of* or *outside of* a language?' (Goulish, op. cit., 2000, p. 33).
89   Ibid., p. 34.
90   Ibid.
91   Llewelyn, R., op. cit., 1986, p. 24.
92   Ibid., p. 4.
93   Ibid., p. ix.
94   Ibid.
95   Goulish, M., op. cit., 2000, p. 32.
96   Ibid.
97   Ibid., p. 37.
98   Mackey, S., 'Community', *Performance Research*, Vol. 11, No. 3, 2006, p. 25.
99   Cohen, in Mackey, S., ibid.
100 It should be noted that exercises practised in solitude, such as the rosary can be, might in a certain sense dwell more explicitly in the realm of the relational conditions of vocation that underlie interpersonal organisation.
101 'Together' here of course refers to the form of togetherness enjoyed by translocational communities, not 'together' in the reductive spatial or temporal sense of more traditionally understood notions of community.
102 See Komonchack, J.A., Collins, M., and Lane, D.A. (eds), *The New Dictionary of Theology*, New York: Glazier, 1987, p. 217. It seems noteworthy that in two separate texts from two separate 'fields' the same themes should emerge under the heading of 'community'. Melrose's citation of Cohen's notion of attachment to a common 'set of symbols' and Komonchack et al.'s arguments for a commitment to exchanging signs both appear to identify communication of particularly meaningful signs/symbols as the defining characteristic of community.
103 Ibid.
104 Within the specific example of monasticism, this thought should send the reader back to Esler's observations about the formation and maintenance of early Christian communities in Chapter 3, where a notion of calling (as a specific kind of communication) acts to produce and structurate Christian communities.
105 Arendt, H., *The Human Condition*, Chicago, IL: University of Chicago Press, 1958, pp. 178–179, 184–186, 199–200.
106 It may be important to note here that the development of a novel 'language' of gestures is, of course, not unique to training. One only has to look to political movements, members' clubs and social institutions to witness the practising of peculiarly meaningful embodied signs. It should be clear that what sets the language of embodied forms exchanged in training contexts apart from these other instances of interrelation is the fact that the practising of these forms does not *just* perform symbolic representative functions within a group (as may be the case with forms of deference or greeting, such as salutes), but that they bring about the alterations unique to training by forming the individual actor and formatting the collective.
107 This is a slight simplification. Father Thomas gave me the figure of three

months, though a closer reading of the regulations in *School for the Lord's Service: Stages of Monastic Growth* revealed that a Novice Master's reports on a novice are submitted to the Abbot and council at three-month intervals (see Declaration 71). According to the *Rule of St Benedict*, the intervals between perseverance testing are suggested as being two months, six months and four months, though this is probably a fairly arbitrary division intended to show that at least one year should elapse in the novitiate.

108 Anthony's ceremony was conducted at 6.30 p.m., just before Vespers on 3 September 2005.

109 This passage is taken from a section of the *Rule of St Benedict* entitled 'Reception of candidates for the community'.

110 Van Gennep, A., trans. Vizedom, M., and Caffee G.L., *The Rites of Passage*, London; New York, NY: Routledge, 2004 (1909), pp. 1–26.

111 Turner, V., *The Ritual Process: Structure and Anti-Structure*, Piscataway, NJ: Aldine, 1995 (1969), p. 94.

112 Schechner, R., *Performance Theory*, London; New York, NY: Routledge, 2003 (1973), pp. 112–170.

113 See Butler, J., *Gender Trouble: Feminism and the Subversion of Identity*, London; New York, NY: Routledge, 1990. See also this work in context in McCann, C.R., and Kim, S.-K., *Feminist Theory Reader: Local and Global Perspectives*, London: Routledge, 2002, pp. 415–428. Peggy Phelan and Jill Lane have characterised this division as 'the paradox of the liminal-norm', which they describe as the fact that 'Liminality can be theorised not only in terms of a time/space of anti-structural play, but also in terms of a time/space of structural normalisation' (see *The Ends of Performance*, New York, NY: New York University Press, 1998, p. 223).

114 While I recognise that 'acceleration' would be the correct term to use here because of its capacity to denote increases and decreases in speed, I resort to the slightly awkward 'deceleration' in order to disambiguate the pace of this phenomenon and ensure that it is understood as a 'slowing down'.

115 I use the notion of a bio-political 'domain' here to describe the plasmatic conditions of 'ordinary life' in any given setting, conditions in which training operates and engages.

116 See Butler, J., op. cit., 1990, p. 43.

117 The extent to which initiation ceremonies should be, or can be, analysed as *initiating* rather than adapting or reorganising provides the backdrop to a significant debate in anthropology and ethnography (see Bell, C., *Ritual Perspectives and Dimensions*, Oxford: Oxford University Press, 1997, pp. 53–58). Contention over this issue, in the specific case of religious ceremonies, is modelled on the differences between male and female experiences of liminality – see Bynum, C.W., 'Women's Stories, Women's Symbols: A Critique of Victor Turner's Theories of Liminality', in Moore and Reynolds (eds), *Anthropology and the Study of Religion*, Chicago, IL: Centre for the Scientific Study of Religion, 1991, pp. 105–125.

118 McKenzie, J., *Perform or Else: From Discipline to Performance*, London; New York, NY: Routledge, 2001, p. 114.

119 Ibid., p. 108.

120 Handelman, D., and Lindquist, G., *Ritual in Its Own Right: The Dynamics of Transformation*, Oxford: Berghahn Books, 2005, p. 48.

121 Ibid. Handelman and Lindquist acknowledge that this notion of 'virtuality' builds on Deleuze and Guatarri's notion of virtuality, which they describe as 'a descent into processes of the really real' (p. 48). It seems to me that the key point taken from Deleuze and Guatarri's notion of virtuality is that we oscillate between the 'real' and the 'really real' or 'virtual' so that both are inscribed within one another. Because of this, 'virtual' rites are *within* the 'actual' or the 'real' and can 'really' affect lived conditions.

122 Ibid., p. 48.

123 Ibid.

124 Read, A., *Theatre, Intimacy and Engagement: The Last Human Venue*, Basingstoke; New York, NY: Palgrave Macmillan, 2008, p. 154.

125 Ibid.

126 Ibid., p. 8.

Chapter 6

1 I am thinking here not only of Stelarc's *PING* performances but also of the appearance online of video footage of performances by Societas Raffaello Sanzio on websites such as YouTube.com (Societas Rafaello Sanzio 'YouTube', 2008), as well as the use of online profile and social networking sites, such as Myspace, by theatre companies including Forced Entertainment (Forced Entertainment, 'Myspace', 2008).

2 There are numerous references to the malevolence of the telephone under Stalin's dictatorship in *The First Circle*, ranging from fears that one's voice can be identified down the line to the reality that messages received on the phone could result in one being spirited away from one's daily affairs instantly, and possibly permanently. Ultimately, Gelb discovers, merely looking at a telephone might call attention to one's 'guilt'.

3 Indeed several of the SMS messages I receive use multi-choice options to force me to take decisions by sending message of reply containing certain letters, for example, '03:45AM, IT'S GETTING SCARY: MORE TROOPS, ARMED, TERRIFIED, JUMPY. DO YOU A): MEEKLY TURN AWAY B): ASK WHAT'S GOING ON C): HURL A BEER BOTTLE?'

4 'Conscientisation' denotes the concept of empowerment effected by a dynamic of reflection and action whereby oppressive structures can be exposed and disassembled. This concept is usually attributed to Freire and his *Pedagogy of the Oppressed* (1970). Its particular relevance here is in its extension and transposition by Boal from the realms of pedagogy to a theatre which, Read has argued, 'announces a premature end to the constant process of collective, performative politics' (*Theatre, Intimacy and Engagement: The Last Human Venue*, Basingstoke; New York, NY: Palgrave Macmillan, 2008, p. 44). I can, on the basis of my experiences as a participant in the work of the Boalian theatre company *Cardboard Citizens*, agree with Read and also note that, apart from any announced end attendant upon the 'solution' found through forum, such 'theatre of the oppressed' also exhibits a conscious disintegration of the 'real' and the 'virtual' during forum that facilitates a cycle of reflection and action wherein processes of reality and virtuality are mutually exclusive.

5   Gordon, R., *The Purpose of Playing: Modern Theories of Acting in Perspective*, Ann Arbor, MI: University of Michigan Press, 2006, p. 1.

6   Ibid.

7   Ibid., p. 2.

8   Ridout, N.P., *Stage Fright: Animals and Other Theatrical Problems*, Cambridge: Cambridge University Press, 2006, p. 3.

9   Ibid., p. 53.

10 Here I am contrasting the enduring formative effects experienced during performance training, discussed in the previous chapter, with the transient effects of theatre on Proust's Marcel. A few pages after the 'bitter disappointment' that initiates Ridout's study, Marcel reports that, despite the immediate let-down of Berma's performance, his 'interest in Berma's acting had continued to grow ever since the fall of the curtain' until upon reflection he concludes, 'No; I have not been disappointed!' See Proust, M., trans. Moncrieff, S., *The Remembrance of Things Past Vol. 1*, Hertfordshire: Wordsworth Editions, 2006 (1922), p. 428.

11 Ridout, N.P., op. cit., 2006, p. 19.

12 Ibid., p. 22.

13 Ibid., p. 19.

14 Kleist, in Ridout, N.P., op. cit., 2006, p. 19.

15 Ridout, N.P., op. cit., 2006, p. 19.

16 Ibid., p. 20. This problem with the theatrical leads to a central theme of Ridout's book, namely that the activities required of a modern performer are like those of any other worker – 'the repetitive development of a skill and its daily exercise for wages' (p. 19) – and this undermines the bourgeois ideal of the artist whose work is supposed to be spontaneously creative.

17 Roach, J., *The Player's Passion: Studies in the Science of Acting*, Newark, DE: University of Delaware Press, 1985, pp. 116–160.

18 Gordon, R., op. cit., 2006, p. 12.

19 Ibid.

20 Ibid., p. 2.

21 Ibid., pp. 2–3.

22 Roach's 'study in the science of acting' charts historical formulations of the physical basis of emotion such as these alongside developments in practices of theatrical representation, taking these historical formulations to be constructions based on differently understood conceptions of 'the nature of the body, its structure, its inner and outer dynamics and its relationship to the larger world' (op. cit., 1985, p. 11).

23 Roach, J., op. cit., 1985, p. 11.

24 Gordon, R., op. cit., 2006, p. 3.

25 Flecknoe, 1664, in Roach, J., op. cit., 1985, p. 41.

26 Gordon, R., op. cit., 2006, p. 5.

27 Ibid.

28 Ibid.

29 Ridout, N.P., op. cit., 2006, p. 20.

30 In his essay 'Two Concepts of Liberty', Berlin poses two questions in order to outline the concerns of positive and negative senses of freedom. The first is concerned with the area within which a person or group of persons is able to act

without interference from other persons. The second asks about the source of control that allows a person to act as they wish. While Berlin maintains, 'the two questions are clearly different', he acknowledges 'the answers may overlap' ('Two Concepts of Liberty', in *Four Essays on Liberty*, Oxford: Oxford University Press, 1969, pp. 121–122).

31 Ibid., p. 134.

32 Ibid., p. 34.

33 My use here of the image of the stage announcer and my allusion to the conventions of his (conventionally 'his') performance is not intended to theatricalise Berlin so as to incorporate him more easily into this study, but to point out the particular theatrical history of his essay, and the very 'real' and very 'symbolic' action that was its context: Berlin's essay was presented by him as his Inaugural Lecture for the Chichele Chair of Social and Political Theory, delivered – which is to say, performed – at the University of Oxford on 31 October 1958.

34 Berlin, op. cit., 1969, p. 121.

35 Ibid.

36 This formal resemblance between positive and negative versions of freedom and the 'happy' and 'sad' masks of tragedy and comedy is pertinent to the understanding of automatisation being developed in this chapter, which relates to the combination of 'real' and 'virtual' in the ipseity of identity. For Simon Bayly in his 'theatre-philosophy', the masks of tragedy and comedy do not 'stand for' humour and pathos but 'for a philosophical physiology of the composure and de-composure of being, the making and un-making of so-called "identity"' (Bayly, S., *A Pathognomy of Performance: Theatre, Philosophy and the Ethics of Interruption*, doctoral thesis, University of Surrey, 2002, p. 67).

37 Alan Read is just one writer who recognises the interest of Performance Studies in theatre's ontological *a priori* – its *liveness* – and one who is in the process of redirecting or recalibrating this interest towards theatre's *life* in an attempt to root theatre firmly within the ethical and political. For further discussions in this area see Matthews, J., and Torevell, D. (eds), *A Life of Ethics and Performance*, Newcastle upon Tyne: Cambridge Scholars Press, 2011.

38 Berlin, I., op. cit., 1969, p. 121.

39 Ibid., p. 129.

40 Ibid., p. 130. The 'magnitudes' proposed by Berlin that are associated with the estimation of the extent of negative freedom are: 'a) How many possibilities are open to me (although the method of counting these can never be more than impressionistic; . . . b) How easy or difficult each of these possibilities is to actualise; c) How important in my plan of life, given my character and circumstances, these possibilities are when compared with each other; d) how far they are closed and opened by deliberate human acts; [and] e) what value not merely the agent but the general sentiment of the society in which he lives, puts on the various possibilities'.

41 Ibid.

42 Ibid., p. 131.

43 Ibid. In this statement we see the anthropocentric quality of freedom that will resurface shortly through discussion of an anthropomorphised Tortoise in the case of rehabilitation training, and which here appears to tie freedom directly to

Berlin's 'self, human, man' triad, in contradistinction to the notionally non-human animal, slave, object.

44 Ibid.

45 Ian suffers with multiple sclerosis which, unlike stroke, is a degenerative condition. This means that Ian's treatment is primarily palliative. Despite this fact, Ian does undergo certain rehabilitative training exercises which aim, like those associated with stroke recovery outlined in the previous chapter, to sustain and where possible improve functional motility, thereby maintaining and increasing Ian's independence. It is with this aspect of therapeutic training that this section is concerned. The skill-acquisition exercises discussed in this section take the same form as the stretching exercises described in the previous chapter with the addition of occupational task-based specificity – for example, stretching the muscles of the arm and controlling their extension and contraction becomes involved in the task of reaching for a cup and guiding it to the lips.

46 Creature Discomforts, 2008.

47 By 'real world' in this context I am referring to the social world, which is topo-graphically and architecturally constructed by socio-cultural forces and can in this respect be differentiated from the digitised, virtual world that nonetheless exists within and alongside it.

48 Hughes and Paterson, in Blaikie, A. (ed.), *The Body: Critical Concepts in Sociology*, London: Routledge, 2003, p. 146.

49 The impact of this legislation on theatres in particular indicates the position they occupy as what Hughes and Paterson call a site of power or privilege. The actor and disability campaigner Matt Fraser argued this case in *Dail* (Disability Arts in London) magazine after an interview with the BBC in which he contended that London theatres in particular would 'have to be sued' before they relinquished such status. 'Let the carnage begin,' he pronounced, 'and hopefully in two years' time we'll be able to go to the theatre' (*Dail*, 2004, p. 4).

50 Hughes and Paterson, in Blaikie, A., op. cit., 2003, p. 146.

51 Lois Magner, in her *History of Medicine*, has noted this primacy of symptom-ology within contemporary and historical practices of medicine (see *History of Medicine*, New York, NY: Marcel Dekker, 1992, pp. 335–371).

52 See, Carr, J.H., and Shepherd, R.B., *A Motor Learning Model for Stroke*, Oxford: Butterworth Heinemann, 1987; Carr, J.H., and Shepherd, R.B., 'A Motor Learning Model for Stroke Rehabilitation', *Physiotherapy*, Vol. 75, 1989, pp. 372–380; Carr, J.H., and Shepherd, R.B., *Stroke Rehabilitation: Guidelines for Exercise and Training to Optimize Motor Skill*, Oxford: Butterworth Heinemann, 2003.

53 In Barnes, Dobkin and Bogousslavsky (eds), *Recovery After Stroke*, Cambridge: Cambridge University Press, 2005, p. 229.

54 Ibid.

55 The operation of what Foucault, in *Discipline and Punish: The Birth of the Prison*, trans. Sheridan, London: Penguin, 2003 (1963), p. 61, called the 'great myth of the free gaze' that 'traverses a sick body [and] attains the truth' (p. 72) is as essential to this process as any other clinical treatment. What is particularly interesting about this treatment is the emphasis placed on 'carry-over' by the focus on functional settings that replicate or are the same as those of the 'real world'.

56 Dean, C., Richards, C., and Malouin, F., 'Task Related Circuit Training Improves Performance of Locomotor Tasks in Chronic Stroke: A Randomised Control Pilot Trial', *Archives of Physical and Medical Rehabilitation*, Vol. 81, 2000, pp. 409–417.

57 For examples see, Schmidt, R.A., and Lee, T.D., *Motor Control and Learning: A Behavioural Emphasis*, Champaign, IL: Human Kinetics, 1999; and Magill, R.A., *Motor Learning: Concepts and Applications*, Madison, WI: Brown and Benchmark, 2001.

58 Alphonso Lingis discusses the 'grotesque' musculature 'built in the rituals of the body builders' cult' at some length in *Foreign Bodies* (New York, NY; London: Routledge, 1994, p. 37).

59 Robert Gordon describes the 'relationship between kinesic signifier and its signified' in Peking Opera (op. cit., 2006, p. 298).

60 See White, G., 'The Cruyff Turn: Performance in the Cultural Memory of International Soccer', *Sport in Society*, Vol. 10, No. 2, 2007, pp. 256–267.

61 Williams, A.M., Davids, K., and Williams, J.G., *Visual Perception and Action in Sport*, London: E & FN Spon, 1999, p. 43.

62 Ibid.

63 Ibid.

64 Ibid.

65 Ibid.

66 Ibid.

67 Ibid.

68 Williams et al. point out that, from a cognitive psychology perspective, 'attention' can be understood to refer to at least three different processes: 'selective attention', whereby we focus our attention on this thing, and not that; 'divided attention', whereby we are able to distribute our attention across a number of attention-demanding stimuli; and attention understood as a state of 'alertness' or readiness. They suggest that a performer's conciousness of their application of these processes is in inverse proportion to their attainment of a given effect.

69 Grotowksi, J., in Drain, R. (ed.), *Twentieth Century Theatre: A Source Book*, London: Routledge, 1995, p. 277.

70 Benedict, 'The Rule', in Marret-Crosby, A. (ed.), *The Benedictine Sourcebook*, Norwich: Canterbury Press, 2003, p. 24.

71 Williams, Davids, and Williams, op. cit., 1999, p. 194.

72 Ibid., pp. 194–195.

73 Fawcus, R., *Stroke Rehabilitation: A Collaborative Approach*, Oxford: Blackwell, 2000, p. 76.

74 Ibid.

75 It is telling that, as White documents, the Englishman Paul Gascoigne should go on to employ the Cruyff turn against two of Cruyff's fellow countrymen, thereby utilising this particular skill not only 'functionally' to evade his opponents but also symbolically to 'play' with them, or make play out of them in a way that asserted the waning influence of the Dutch national team and the ascension of the English team on the stage of world football. While, as White has argued, Gascoigne's performance has a psychological effect during the contest which impacts on both participants and crowd members, it is also the case that skill

innovation is rapidly absorbed within a particular ecology in such a way that failure to acquire innovated skills results in negative infringements on a practitioner's freedom. McMorris has documented in his *Acquisition and Performance of Sports Skills* that, 'despite the fact that this way of turning [the Cruyff turn] had never been seen before, by the beginning of the next English soccer season players in every standard from the First Division (now the Premiership) to local parks players were using the "Cruyff turn". This was only six weeks later' (2004, p. 174), and those who had not acquired the skill struggled to control their own influence on a game.

76 Berlin, I., op. cit., 1969, p. 122.

77 Ibid., p. 122. The zoomorphism (or perhaps inverted anthropomorphising) is appropriate because, as Giorgio Agamben has shown, the 'anthropological machine' 'functions by animalising the human, by isolating the non-human within the human' (trans. Attell, K., *The Open: Man and Animal*, Palo Alto, CA: Stanford University Press, 2004, p. 36). In this context, this entails excluding the freedom of non-sentient beings (animals) from human conceptions of the concept of freedom, such that the properly (free) human is uniquely self-conscious. Berlin is clear that conceptions of freedom are produced alongside that which 'constitutes a self, a person, a [hu]man' (op. cit., 1969, p. 134), which is in distinction to that which is definitively non-human because both positive and negative senses of the concept derive from a self-consciousness and self-identification – both of which have been constructed as absent in animals.

78 Part III, Section 25, 'Enforcement Remedies and Procedure', of the Disability Discrimination Act 1995 makes clear that claims will be brought against individual persons for failure to comply with this act, which will lead to County Court or Sheriff Court hearings (Disability Discrimination Acts 1995 and 2005).

79 Lightning struck a football pitch during a Premier League match in Johannesburg on Saturday 24, 1998 leaving players from both teams – the Jomo Cosmos and the Moroka Swallows – writhing on the grass holding their ears and their eyes. Reports of similar incidents with more dramatic consequences came from the Democratic Republic of Congo in the same year when the Kinshasa daily newspaper *L'Avenir* reported that lightning had struck a football match in the eastern region of Kasai, although civil conflict prevented official confirmation. The collapse and death of Mark Vivien Foe, along with these incidents, pays tragic testament to the failure of exemptional time/spaces of play to exempt participants from biological imperatives, a state of affairs that finds itself reflected in the famous death of Molière after collapsing on stage during a performance in the title role of the Hypochondriac.

80 Ridout, N.P., op. cit., 2006, p. 22.

81 Coleridge, S.T. (1817), in Foakes, R.A. (ed.), *Coleridge's Criticism of Shakespeare*, London: Continuum, 1989, p. 36.

82 See Goffman, E., *The Presentation of Self in Everyday Life*, New York, NY: Doubleday, 1959.

83 Neither the eclecticism of Grotowksi's training practice, incorporating influences from Kathakali, Peking Opera, Noh Theatre and Hatha Yoga, nor the fragmentation of 'today's actor', working within no particular tradition and yet with every tradition, contradicts the holistic view of the human being. Indeed,

there may even be a relationship between the commitment to the 'wholeness' of the individual and to the 'one-ness' of all human practice.

84 Alison Hodge, for example, regards Artaud's writings as 'a significant reference point for many in the second half of the twentieth century' (see 'Antonin Artaud', in *Twentieth Century Actor Training*, London; New York, NY: Routledge, 2000, p. 6).

85 Artaud, A., 'An Affective Athleticism', in *The Theatre and Its Double*, Montreuil; London; New York, NY: Calder, 1999 (1970), p. 93.

86 Ibid.

87 Manne, J., *Soul Therapy*, Berkeley, CA: North Atlantic Books, 1997.

88 Artaud, A., 'No More Masterpieces', in *The Theatre and Its Double*, op. cit., 1999 (1970), p. 93.

89 See Laing, R.D., *The Divided Self: An Existential Study in Sanity and Madness*, London; New York, NY: Routledge, 1999 (1960).

90 Artaud, A., op. cit., 1999 (1970), p. 68.

91 Roach, J., op. cit., 1985, p. 218.

92 Hamilton describes Artaud as a 'pivotal character' in twentieth-century theatre history and Grotowski as 'the most influential of the figures heeding Artaud's call' (*The Art of Theatre*, Oxford: Blackwell Publishing, 2007, p. 7). Apart from the evidence of Artaud's influence on Grotowski's theatrical practice (see Esslin, M., *Artaud: The Man and His Work*, London: Calder, 1976, p. 92), Grotowski's writings on Artaud in 1969 may serve as a single example demonstrating his awareness of Artaud's ideas, along with his problems with them (see Meyer-Dinkgraefe, D., *Approaches to Acting, Past and Present*, London: Continuum International Publishing Group, 2006, p. 71). Gordon lists among the numerous figures and groups he claims to have been influenced or motivated by Artaud, and who might also be said to be antagonistic to conceptions of training as a skill acquisition process, Hijikata and other Butoh artists as well as the performance artists of Happenings in the United States during the 1960s (op. cit., 2006, p. 391).

93 Grotowski, J., *Towards a Poor Theatre*, London: Methuen, 1991 (1968), p. 16.

94 Ibid. Although, as Gordon and others have noted, Grotowski claimed to have no knowledge of Artaud until 1964, 'his poor theatre manifested itself in structures of ceremonial enactment that evoked Artaudian ideals of performance' (Gordon, R., op. cit., 2006, p. 287).

95 Grotowski, J., op. cit., 1991 (1968), p. 17. The rest of this section will focus on Barba and Odin training in particular, but the trend identified in this tradition of theatre practice is explicitly evident in the writing of practitioners such as Declan Donnellan, for whom the *via negativa* has provided both a rhetoric for his training practice – 'We can be taught how not to block our natural instinct to act' (*The Actor and the Target*, London: Nick Hern Books, 2002, p. 2) – and as a paradigm in which to work: 'Rather than claim that "x" is a more talented actor than "y", it is more accurate to say that "x" is less blocked than "y"' (p. 6).

96 Grotowski, J., op. cit., 1991 (1968), p. 16.

97 Ibid., p. 35.

98 Artaud, A., op. cit., 1999 (1970), pp. 90–91.

99 Barba has discussed his 'period of [theatrical] apprenticeship' (*Beyond the Floating Islands*, New York: PAJ Publications, 1986, p. 239) with Grotowski many

times, and the 'debt [owed] to Barba's mentor', particularly evident in his training practice has been identified by many, including Ian Watson (in Hodge, A., op. cit., 2000, p. 214).

100 Watson, I., in Hodge, A. (ed.), op. cit., 2000, p. 212.
101 Ibid., p. 224.
102 Ibid., pp. 214, 219.
103 Barba, E., op. cit., 1986, p. 56.
104 Watson, I., in Hodge, A. (ed.), op. cit., 2000, p. 219.
105 Gordon, R., op. cit., 2006, p. 343. Williams et al. observe precisely the same phenomena, noting that automatised skills 'are difficult to modify once they have been learned' (op. cit., 1999, p. 43).
106 Hodge, A. (ed.), op. cit., 2000, p. 8.
107 Watson, I., *Negotiating Cultures: Eugenio Barba and the Intercultural Debate*, Manchester: Manchester University Press, 2002, p. 137. 'The Director' is one of the 'characters' who narrates a dialogue on this production in the article 'Theatre Presence: Sea Lanes, Sardinia 1975', in Ian Watson, *Negotiating Cultures: Eugenio Barba and the Intercultural Debate* (pp. 128–141).
108 Sartre, in Grotowski, J., op. cit., 1991 (1968), p. 18.
109 Watson, I., in Hodge, A. (ed.), op. cit., 2000, p. 219.
110 Carreri, 1985 interview with Ian Watson quoted in Hodge, A. (ed.), op. cit., 2000, p. 220.
111 Grotowski, J., op cit., 1991 (1968), p. 17.
112 At this point I refer the reader back to the discussion in Chapter 2 on 'standing still while not standing still' and 'flow states' in performance.
113 This notion of automaticity in a sample of 'yesterday's theatre' refers to what Roach has argued to be an erroneous justification of 'a symbolic style of acting on the Elizabethan stage' (op. cit., 1985, p. 34). Citing Bulwer's famous *Chirologia*, Roach demonstrates how the real and the virtual dimensions of acting adhered in Elizabethan performance because Bulwer and his contemporaries believed that the fixed signified–signifier relationships played out in the *Natural Language of the Hand* were traceable to universal biological operations in which 'art hath no hand' (in Roach, J., ibid., p. 34).
114 According to Ian Watson, Barba draws on a conception of the 'pre-cultural . . . an all-inclusive dimension of human expression that eclipses or subtends culture' to motivate and justify his idea of the pre-expressive and the 'cultural pluralism' of his company's work (Watson, I., op. cit., 2002, pp. 3–4).
115 Barba, E., and Savarese, N., *A Dictionary of Theatre Anthropology: The Secret Art of the Performer*, London; New York, NY: Routledge, 1991, p. 118.
116 Watson, I., *Towards a Third Theatre: Eugenio Barba and the Odin Teatret*, London; New York, NY: Routledge, 1993, p. xi.
117 Clay, J., 'Self-use in Actor Training', *TDR: The Drama Review*, Vol. 16, No. 1, 1972, pp. 16–22.
118 Indeed, Barba's connection to Alexander's self-use system is particularly evident in his insistence on the origins of 'real actions', that generate a change in perception in the spectator, in the spine (Watson, I., in Hodge, A., op. cit., 2000, p. 222) which is a particular focus of Alexander's therapy (see Claire, T., *Bodywork*, Laguna Beach, CA: Basic Health Publications, 2006, pp. 59–70).

119 This is evidenced in numerous journal and monograph publications, including Nicole Potter's *Movement for Actors* (2002), a chapter of which is devoted to 'Alexander Technique and the Integrated Actor: Applying the Principles of the Alexander Technique to Actor Preparation'. According to Potter, 'leading actor-training institutions' (p. 65) such as the Juilliard School of Performing Arts, Dell'Arte School of Movement and the Royal Academy of Dramatic Arts all recognise the 'relevance' of Alexander technique to actor training and have incorporated its teaching into their training programmes.

120 Clay, J., op. cit., 1972, p. 16.

121 Ibid.

122 Berlin, I., op. cit., 1969, p. 132.

123 Marsden, R., *The Nature of Capital: Marx after Foucault*, London; New York, NY: Routledge, 1999, p. 159.

124 Grotowski, J., in Drain, R., op. cit., 1995, p. 277.

125 Two examples of such techniques are *anchoresis*, which refers to the monastic practice of 'withdrawal' or anchoritism, and *horarum*, deriving from the Greek word *hora*, meaning 'hour', which refers to the timetabling of daily activities within a monastery.

126 Findlay, R., 'Grotowski's Laboratory Theatre: Dissolution and Diaspora', in Wolford, L., and Schechner, R. (eds), *The Grotowski Sourcebook*, New York, NY; London: Routledge, 1997, p. 174.

127 Description of the strictly controlled exercises and routines of Grotowski's training practice can be found in his own writing, especially *Towards a Poor Theatre*, and some scholars have commented on the 'ceremonial' elements of the work undertaken by his actors (Gordon, R., op. cit., 2006, p. 287). In an interview with *Performance Arts Journal*, Susan Sontag also discusses the 'hermeticism' of Artaud and Grotowski and asserts her belief that such withdrawal might have been prompted for both by their shared belief 'in the reality of evil' (Sontag, S., and Poague, L.A., *Conversations with Susan Sontag*, Jackson, MS: University of Mississippi Press, 1995, p. 80). It is hoped that using Foucault's project to show how the monastery has provided a model for other institutions, makes clear the connections not only between monastic living and Grotowskian training but also more generally between monastic 'techniques' and the range of techniques practised in post-Artaud actor training.

128 According to Kumiega, Grotowksi asserted that Stanislavski's primary legacy to the profession of acting was his emphasis on the need for daily training (*The Theatre of Grotowski*, London: Methuen, 1987, p. 110); and Wolford observes that in her experiences with Grotowski's Objective Drama programme at the University of California-Irvine between 1989 and 1992, as well as in her observations of training at the Workcentre of Jerzy Grotowski and Thomas Richards in Pontedera between 1986 and 2000, 'Grotowski consistently upheld this mandate, requiring the actors under his direction to engage in regular physical and vocal training' (in Hodge, A., op. cit., 2000, p. 198).

129 Kardong, T., *Benedict's Rule: A Translation and Commentary*, Collegeville, MN: Liturgical Press, 1996, p. 478.

130 Ibid., p. 572. It should be clear that while this discussion of monastic obedience tracks back to Chapter 4, the particular understanding of obedience used by

Kardong here is a more traditional version of the concept associated with conformity to commands that carry with them a threat of punishment.

131 John Dillon, in his article 'Rejecting the Body, Refining the Body: Some Remarks on the Development of Platonist Asceticism', observes that the archetypal practices of restraint and denial can be traced back through the historical development of Western traditions of asceticism to Plato's *Phaedo* and to implied conceptualisations of the relationship between body and soul. For the 'dualist' tradition, Dillon argues that one interpretation of the word *phroura* in Socrates' statement, 'We men are *en tini phrourai* and one ought not to release oneself from this or run away,' led to the development, through the hermeneutics of Xenocrates, of a 'world-negating' version of asceticism – in Wimbush, Valantasis and Byron (eds), 1995, p. 81. This version, he explains, is also associated with a Pythagorean dictum, known to Plato, that for the soul the body (*soma*) is a tomb (*sema*) which translates into an image in Xenocrates of human beings as 'condemned to imprisonment in mortal bodies on this earth, but who may free themselves and attain happiness after death by the practice of strict ascetic practices'. Dillon also explains that *phroura*, as well as meaning 'prison', can also mean 'guard post', and it is through this interpretation that a 'world-affirming' conception of asceticism develops that views restraint and denial as associated not with rejection of the world but a 'refining of the body, to make it a worthy, or at least non-injurious receptacle of the soul'. This tradition, in which the body-in-the-world is threatened but redeemable, and capable of redemption only through particular interaction with its environment, is not subject to a mind–body dualism but a worldly–divine dichotomy.

132 Olivelle, P., in Wimbush, V.L., and Valantasis, R. (eds), *Asceticism*, Oxford: Oxford University Press, 1995, p. 188.

133 Ibid., pp. 188–189.

134 Cox-Miller, in Wimbush, V.L., and Valantasis, R. (eds), op. cit., 1995, p. 286.

135 Cameron, A., in ibid., p. 153. Extending the notion of artistic creation, Cameron and Harpham have been influential in arguing that Christian ascetic life in particular became like a text, constructed by the shared aesthetics of its partici-pants and produced for others to read. Following Cameron and Harpham, Elizabeth Castelli has extended the notion that interplay between 'real' and 'virtual' has uniquely supported asceticism even as it explicitly claims to disintegrate the two: 'The biographies and autobiographies that constituted the major narrative formulation of early Christian asceticism were texts which transformed their subjects into texts themselves, exemplars with whom readers were called in mimetic relation' (in Wimbush,V.L., and Valantasis, R., op. cit., 1995, p. 179).

136 Ware, K., in ibid., p. 4. This pattern is produced by the ascetic practices of *anachoresis* or withdrawal from the human, social world, which characterises the attempt to disaggregate the essential self from its social counterpart evident in the major ascetic traditions. In this way, Ware argues, the flight into literal and metaphorical deserts is not 'world-denying but world-affirming' (p. 5) in cases where the ascetic reintroduces themselves (and their discoveries) into the social world by making themselves available to others. Ware contends that 'this pattern – of flight followed by a return – recurs repeatedly in the course of monastic history'.

137 Cox-Miller, P., in ibid., p. 281.

138 Ibid.

139 At this point I refer the reader back to Xenocrates' interpretation of Platonic asceticism.

140 As an illustrative example of the decidedly non-dichotomous conception of the individual in Benedictine spirituality, Kardong, in his commentary on the Rule of St Benedict, notes instances where Benedict drops contemporaneous phrases such as *pro anima* ('on behalf of your soul') 'to preclude a dualist interpretation' of the human person (Kardong, T., op. cit., 1996, p. 83).

141 Cox-Miller, P., in Wimbush, V.L., and Valantasis, R., op. cit., 1995, pp. 281–282.

142 According to Vernant, the body 'is an entirely problematic notion' that must be defined by the 'functions it assumes and the forms it takes on' in a given culture – in Feher, Nadaf and Tazir (eds), *Fragments for a History of the Human Body*, New York, NY: Zone, 1989, pp. 1–20.

143 Cox-Miller, P., in Wimbush, V.L., and Valantasis, R., op. cit., 1995, p. 282.

144 Ibid.

145 Berlin, I., op. cit., 1969, p. 135.

146 Arthur Schopenhauer's famous consideration of asceticism in *The World as Will and Representation* (trans. Payne, F.E.J., New York: Courier Dover, 1966), offers a treatment of asceticism which is particularly commensurate with Buddhism, but indicates the central concerns of ascetic living for many religious traditions. Schopenhauer contends that 'all suffering is simply nothing but unfulfilled and thwarted willing' (p. 361), even physical pain, seeing as the body is nothing but the will itself made object. If life is full of unfulfilled willing and this is the cause of suffering one is faced with two options. First, one could attempt to satisfy the will – Schopenhauer notes here, though, that apart from the fact that this is practically untenable, to satisfy one's will actually has the effect of escalating the intensity of willing, making the task of satisfying it increasingly harder; second, one could try to stop willing. Schopenhauer argues that the way to diminish willing is *not* to give the will what it wants. Schopenhauer calls this asceticism in a 'narrow sense' and proposes it as the one adequate solution to the central problem of suffering.

147 Solzhenitsyn, A.I., trans. Whitney, T.P., *The First Circle*, Evanston, IL: Northwestern University Press, 1997 (1968), p. 83.

Chapter 7

1 Names have been changed throughout this work to protect privacy. Ian Wilding has given permission for his name to be used, and names of monks have been altered in cases where their identity is known in the public domain. Joshua and Damian are not examples of such a case and the Groundskeeper, Felton, has acquired his name from the Old English, meaning, 'settlement on the field'.

2 Trevino, in his book *Goffman's Legacy*, credits Erving Goffman with introducing the dramaturgical metaphor to the social sciences (New York, NY: Rowman & Littlefield, 2003, p. 18), while Alan Read has discussed Cousteau's appropriation of this metaphor to explain the behaviour of cephalopods specifically, as well as the more general subject of 'unaddressed expressive phenomena' (*Theatre Intimacy*

and Engagement: The Last Human Venue, Basingstoke; New York, NY: Palgrave Macmillan, 2008, p. 112) in animal behaviour.

3   For this particular (and other) 'multicultural' appropriations of Shakespeare, see Robert Stam's discussion of the Brazilian film *Chanchadas,* starring Grande Otelo – 'Multiculturalism and the Neoconservatives', in McClintock, Mufti and Shohat (eds), *Dangerous Liaisons: Gender, Nation and Postcolonial Perspectives,* Minneapolis, MN: University of Minnesota Press, 1997, p. 192. For 'Romeo-as-Landlord' see Brecht's '"The Servants", a scene to be played between Act II Scene I and Act II Scene II', in 'BB's Rehearsal Scenes: Estranging Shakespeare', *TDR: The Drama Review,* Vol. 12, No. 1, 1967–68, pp. 108–111.

4   *Complete Works* II, III, p. 1077.

5   This song was written by Shel Silverstein (see following note), but popularised by Johnny Cash.

6   Silverstein, S., 'Boy Named Sue', performed by Cash, J., *Johnny Cash at San Quentin,* Columbia Records, 1969.

7   Ibid.

8   The name Adam in the Old Testament would appear to derive from the Hebrew word *adamah,* which refers to the red colour of soil, and relates the creation of Adam to the creation the earth – to the dust from which he is made. See Freedman, D.N., Myers, A.C., and Beck, A.B., *Eerdman's Dictionary of the Bible,* Grand Rapids, MI: Eerdmans, 2000, pp. 18–19.

9   KJV, Gen. 2:19.

10 An oft-quoted example of this is Jesus overturning the tables of the money-lenders: having done so, and having been asked by the crowd for a sign of his authority, Jesus answers, 'Destroy this temple, and in three days I will raise it up' (KJV, John 2:19). The assembly is incredulous and remind him that the temple took forty-six years to construct, but John advises his reader that 'he spake of the temple of his body' (KJV, John 2:21) which would be resurrected after crucifixion. According to Matthew, at his crucifixion Jesus is mocked by the crowd, who have also failed, according to the biblical narrative, to interpret this remark: 'They that passed by reviled him, wagging their heads, and saying, Thou that destroyest the temple, and buildest it in three days, save thyself.' It is ultimately Jesus's adoption of the name 'Messiah' that leads to his crucifixion; in the narrative of Jesus's death Pilate, who can find no cause to execute him, is manipulated by the chief priests, who invoke a law prohibiting the adoption of such a title (KJV, John 19:7) and threaten rebellion if Jesus is not punished for his crime.

11 KJV, Rev. 2:17.

12 Anthropological studies dating back to Van Gennep's influential *The Rites of Passage* (1909) have identified the significance of adopting a new name to transformational processes, as well as securing an individual identity and status within a group. Atwell's article, 'A Benedictine Who's Who', records the names taken by a range of Benedictine monks throughout history and explores the reasoning behind a selection of these – in Marret-Crosby, A. (ed.), *The Benedictine Handbook,* Norwich: Canterbury Press, 2003, pp. 226–229.

13 Haubrich, W.S., *Medical Meanings: A Glossary of Word Origins,* Philadelphia, PA: APC Press, 2003, p. 48. Hecker, Babington and Caius describe the 'dancing mania' (see *The Epidemics of the Middle Ages,* Delaware: Trubner, 1859, p. 84)

associated with chorea in the Middle Ages, and Midlefort records that St Vitus' 'dancing mania' was in the sixteenth century especially associated with the legs and with hopping and jumping (see *A History of Madness in Sixteenth Century Germany*, Palo Alto, CA: Stanford University Press, 2000, pp. 32–33).

14 The Dhalem workshop on 'The Eradication of Infectious Disease', 1997, marked the twentieth anniversary of the eradication of smallpox and concluded, following the evaluation of the International Task Force for Disease Eradication 1993, that of eighty potential candidate-diseases for eradication six were eradicable (Dowdle and Hopkins, 1998). Chapter 4, 'Smallpox', and its sub-headed questions such as, 'What is smallpox?' 'How is smallpox spread?' and 'What are the symptoms of smallpox?' in Senator Bill Frist MD's book *When Every Moment Counts: What You Need to Know about Bioterrorism* (2002) suggests that the reintroduction of smallpox will be accompanied, or rather prefigured by increased understanding of the term.

15 Deleuze, G., trans. McNeil, J., *Masochism: An Interpretation of Coldness and Cruelty*, New York, NY: Braziller, 1971, pp. 12–13.

16 Ibid.

17 The name St Vitus has, since A.D. 300, undergone a gradual disaggregation from the phenomena of chorea, the latter stages of which were achieved in the wake of Duchenne's publication and Doctor George Huntington's successful isolation of Huntington's Chorea or Huntington's Disease in 1872 – see Bates, G.B., Harper, P.S., Jones, L., *Huntington's Disease*, Oxford: Oxford University Press, 2002.

18 Deleuze, G., trans. McNeil, J., op. cit., 1971, p. 15.

19 Deleuze argues that the basis common to literary creation and symptomology is 'the phantasy (le phantasme)' and the difference between the two arises in the kind of *work* that is performed on the phantasy' [*emphasis as original*], the former artistic and the later pathological (ibid., p. 13).

20 Deleuze, G., trans. McNeil, J., *Masochism*, New York, NY: Zone Books, 1991, p. 134.

21 Watson, I., *Performer Training: Developments Across Cultures*, London; New York, NY: Routledge, 2001, p. 1.

22 I refer the reader back to Marvin Carlson's comment on the dangers of 'seeking some overarching semantic field' for performance cited with reference to my own project in my introductory chapter.

23 In both Kurosawa's *Yojimbo* (1961) and Leone's 'Dollars Trilogy' – *A Fist Full of Dollars* (1964), *For a Few Dollars More* (1965) and *The Good, the Bad and the Ugly* (1966) – the central protagonist is a nameless figure referred to only by pseudonyms and nicknames – a dangerous and socially marginalised character. The 'Man with No Name' poses serious threats to the organisation of the social groups in which he appears, disrupting and undermining their codes and organisation often through violence while he himself appears as a 'not-complete' human; mostly silent and with malfunctional, unused or deliberately hidden limbs.

24 Lingis, A., *Foreign Bodies*, New York; London: Routledge, 1994, p. 29.

25 Sparkes, Batey and Brown's paper, *The Muscled Self and Its Aftermath: A Life History Study and an Elite Black, Male Bodybuilder* for *Autobiography Journal* (2005), details the profound social and psychological effects on 'Jessenka' (not his real name), a professional bodybuilder who is in injured in a car accident.

They trace the effects of 'losing muscle and losing self' (p. 147) on Jessenka's particular trajectory of 'becoming black again' (p. 151).

26 In Smith and Greco's commentary on the writing of Gilles Deleuze they discuss the range of diseases, including Parkinson's, Roger's and Alzheimer's, which elucidate this 'isolation' thesis (See *Gilles Deleuze: Essays Critical and Clinical*, London: Verso, 1997, p. xvi).

27 The DMD gene codes for the protein dystrophin and is located on the x chromosome. Dystrophin provides structural stability to the dystroglycan complex and mutation in the DMD gene affects the coding of dystrophin. causing the onset of progressive muscle weakness and other symptoms associated with Duchenne Muscular Dystrophy (See Anderson and Bushby, *Muscular Dystrophy: Methods and Protocols, Methods in Molecular Medicine*, Totowa, NJ: Humana Press, 2001, p. 111).

28 In the 'aesthetic' section of Duchenne's *The Mechanism of the Human Facial Expression*, Lady Macbeth is the subject of several plates that depict the electrical agitation of the face in a female patient such that she is made to represent Shakespeare's character at certain key moments (some of them invented by Duchenne) during the play (see Duchenne, G.-B., trans. Cuthbertson, R.A., *The Mechanism of Human Facial Expression*, Cambridge: Cambridge University Press, 1990, p. 127–128 and plates 82, 83, 84).

29 Law, J., *Making a Mess with Method*, Centre for Science Studies, Lancaster University, 2003, p. 11.

30 Foucault's famous remark at the beginning of 'Theatrum Philosophicum' is cited by Eleanor Kauffman as an example of the 'delirium of praise' and the very style of his praising of Deleuze is contrasted with Deleuze's own more quietly and calmly reserved praise of Foucault. Kauffman states, as is probably already quite clear, the concept of a 'Deleuzian century' cannot practically be recuperated, but argues that in their (differently expressed) praise for one another 'the difference between one thinker and the other is no longer measurable in terms of one distinct person versus another', so that what arises, in a form that recalls the 'irreducibility' inherent in Deleuze's notion of a clinical view, is 'a variable multiplicity of articulations of the Same' (see *The Delirium of Praise: Bataille, Blanchot, Deleuze, Foucault, Klossowski*, Baltimore, MD: Johns Hopkins University Press, 2001, p. 122).

31 McKenzie contends that, much as the eighteenth and nineteenth centuries were modelled on the particular arrangement of 'discipline' (*Perform or Else: From Discipline to Performance*, London; New York, NY: Routledge, 2001, p. 17), the last half of the twentieth century has been characterised by the emergence of various senses of 'performance' (p. 22). He suggests that this stratum of knowledge will overcode and replace discipline and 'profoundly shape our understanding of twenty-first-century structures of power and knowledge' (p. i).

32 My human ageing analogy is prompted by Ridout's identification of three 'moments' in the historiography of performance that I have already mentioned, and especially the contemporary 'return of theatre' after the inclusion of 'distant' practices, e.g. 'from snake rituals, to park ranger presentations'. See *Stage Fright: Animals and Other Theatrical Problems*, Cambridge: Cambridge University Press, 2006, p. 5.

33　Ibid. Coward and Ellis have shown that such an encounter with (an image of) the self is necessary not only for self-identification but also for the entrance into economies of interactive exchange, because 'mechanisms of the imagery . . . are at the basis of the ideological fixing of the subject in identifications and positions of exchange in the symbolic' (*Language and Materialism: Developments in Semiology and the Theory of the Subject*, London; New York, NY: Routledge, 1977, p. 111). Their argument that 'the subject able to signify is produced as a result of a process of acquiring a position in which the image of the mirror phase is a part' helps to define the 'coming of age' of Performance Studies, as described above, through a process of (as Ridout has suggested) 'returning' to look/think/ · act again on its theatrical infancy (Ridout, N.P., op. cit., 2006, p. 5).

34　Taussig, M., *Mimesis and Alterity: A Particular History of the Senses*, New York, NY: London: Routledge, 1993, p. 236. Taussig uses an anthropological example to represent this form of reflection whereby the West is mirrored in the handiwork of 'Others' and 'the interpreting self is itself grafted into the object of study', and 'the self enters into the alter against which the alter is defined and sustained'.

35　Taussig refers to the experience of 'absorption' documented by Captain FitzRoy of HMS *Beagle* on witnessing the encounters of 'Third World' others with 'matters familiar to civilised men'. He suggests that this condition of absorption arises as a result of seeing one's own practices reflected back to one by or through another, a process in which 'First World' and 'Other Worlds' 'mirror, interlock and rupture each other's alterity' (ibid., p. 236). The meta-disciplinary encounter stimulated by askeology, in producing a clinical 'realm' in which a range of practitioners can meet and share practice, also provides the conditions for such absorption.

36　Gordon, R., *The Purpose of Playing: Modern Acting Theories in Perspective*, Ann Arbor, MI: University of Michigan Press, 2006, p. 2.

37　Ridout, N.P., op. cit., 2006, p. 22.

38　Read, A., *Theatre Intimacy and Engagement: The Last Human Venue*, Basingstoke; New York, NY: Palgrave Macmillan, 2008, p. 4.

39　Cox-Miller, P., in Wimbush, V.L., and Valantasis, R. (eds), *Asceticism*, Oxford: Oxford University, 1995, p. 282.

40　States, B.O., in Ridout, N.P., op. cit., 2006, p. 162.

41　See Ellis, B.E., *American Psycho*, London: Picador, 1991, p. 384.

42　That this liturgy itself is an 'event' within the seasonal *horarum* of the year draws our attention to the question of scale involved in the construction of events.

Postscript

1　Ridout, N.P., *Stage Fright: Animals and Other Theatrical Problems*, Cambridge: Cambridge University Press, 2006, p. 7.

2　'The self-taught man' is a character in Jean-Paul Sartre's *Nausea* (1969), often encountered by the protagonist Roquentin reading books in the library. Ranciere's *The Ignorant Schoolmaster: Five Lessons in Intellectual Emancipation* (1991) analyses the work of Joseph Jacotot, an exiled French schoolteacher who found that he could teach subjects that he himself knew nothing about.

3 See Connor, S., *Beside Himself: Glenn Gould and the Prospects of Performance*, text of a talk broadcast on BBC Radio 3, 4 November 1999.

4 David Knowles is not the first to note that 'Monasticism, as its etymology (*uovoc* – alone) suggests, began with an individual's retirement from the world' (see *From Pachomius to Ignatius: A Study in the Constitutional History of Religious Orders*, Oxford: Clarendon Press, 1966, p. 2).

5 The research territory of Hale and Eales's study of recovery in stroke patients after early discharge from Baragwanath Hospital South Africa provides a potential starting point for such further investigations (see 'Recovery of Walking Function in Stroke Patients after Minimal Rehabilitation', *Physiotherapy Research International*, 1998).

6 According to Lyn Gardner, it will not be hard to find such out-of-work actors given that theirs is a profession in which '80 per cent earn less than £10,000 a year' (see 'Not Puppets but Thinking Actors', *Guardian*, 15 July 2008).

7 Kear, A., 'Troublesome Amateurs: Theatre, Ethics and the Labour of Mimesis', *Performance Research*, Vol. 10, No. 1, 2005, pp. 26–46.

8 With reference to this phenomenon, Newson reflects on his own responses when auditioning the (then) sixty-four-year-old dancer Diana Payne-Myers who performed in DV8 *Strange Fish*. He recalls that 'the danger you often have is with older dancers, some who are in their fifties and you say, "My God, aren't they incredible."' Newson notes that such 'incredible' performers can produce a 'spectacle' on stage that centres not on what they do but on their capability to do something at a certain age (see Lonsdale, J., 'Ancestral and Authorial Voices in Lloyd Newson DV8's *Strange Fish*', *New Theatre Quarterly*, Vol. 20, pp. 117–126).

9 Kear, A., op. cit., 2005, p. 28.

10 See Bruce, V., Green, P.R., and Georgeson, M.A., *Visual Perception: Physiology, Psychology and Ecology*, Oxford: Psychology Press, 2003, p. 302.

11 Mulvey, L., 'Visual Pleasure and Narrative Cinema', *Screen*, Vol. 16, No. 3, Autumn 1975, pp. 6–18.

12 Ridout, N.P., op. cit., 2006, p. 5.

13 Blau, H., *Nothing in Itself: Complexions of Fashion*, Bloomington, IN: Indiana University Press, 1999, p. 9.

14 Ibid., p. 221.

15 I offer as one example of this precedent Herbert Blau's *The Audience*, which can be seen to privilege what is 'seen' and describes a 'delirium of seeing', tracing the dizzying effects of 'watchers watching the watcher watch' (Albany, NY: Johns Hopkins University Press, 1990, p. 7).

16 Ridout, N.P., op. cit., 2006, p. 160.

Bibliography

Abbreviations

'Complete Works' – Shakespeare, W., with biographical and general introduction by Sisson, C.J., *The Complete Works of William Shakespeare*, London: Odhams Press, 1954

'KJV' – *The Holy Bible: King James Version*, London: Collins, 1931

'*Mimesis*' – Auerbach, E., trans. Trask, W.R., *Mimesis: The Representation of Reality in Western Literature*, Princeton, NJ: Princeton University Press, 1953

'SLS' – The English Benedictine Congregation, *School for the Lord's Service: Stages of Monastic Growth*, printed for private use by the General Chapter and used with permission, 2001

Full-length works and articles in books

Aarsbergen-Ligtvoet, C., *Isaiah Berlin: A Value Pluralist and Humanist View of Human Nature and the Meaning of Life*, Amsterdam: Rodopi Press, 2006

Abse, D., *Ash on a Young Man's Sleeve*, London: Vallentine-Mitchell, 1971 (1954)

———, *The Dogs of Pavlov*, London: Vallentine-Mitchell, 1973

Adler, Patricia A., and Adler, P., 'Observational Techniques', in Denzin, N., and Lincoln, Y.S. (eds), *Handbook of Qualitative Research*, Newbury Park, CA: Sage, 1994

Agamben, Giorgio, *Potentialities: Collected Essays in Philosophy*, Palo Alto, CA: Stanford University Press, 1999

———, trans. Attell, K., *The Open: Man and Animal*, Palo Alto, CA: Stanford University Press, 2004

À Kempis, T., trans. Knox, R., *The Imitation of Christ*, San Francisco, CA: Ignatius Press, 2005 (1418)

Albert, M.L., *Human Neuropsychology*, New York: John Wiley, 1978

Allain, Paul, *Gardzienice: Polish Theatre in Transition*, London; New York: Routledge, 1997

————, *The Art of Stillness: Theatre Practice of Tadashi Suzuki*, London: Methuen, 2002

Amit, V., *Realizing Community: Concepts, Social Relationships and Sentiments*, London: Routledge, 2002

————, and Rapport, N., *The Trouble with Community: Anthropological Reflections in Movement*, London: Pluto Press, 2002

Anderson, L.V.B., and Bushby, K.M.D., *Muscular Dystrophy: Methods and Protocols* (*Methods in Molecular Medicine*), Totowa, NJ: Humana Press, 2001

Apel, W., *Gregorian Chants: History and Criticism*, Bloomington, IN: Indiana University Press, 1990

Arendt, H., *The Human Condition*, Chicago, IL: University of Chicago Press, 1958

————, trans. Winston, C., Winston, R., and Weissberg, L., *Rachel Varnhagen: The Life of a Jewess*, Baltimore, MD: Johns Hopkins University Press, 1997

Aristotle, trans. Hett, W.S., *Aristotle in Twenty-Three Volumes, Vol 8: On the Soul, Parva Naturalia, On Breath*, Cambridge, MA: Harvard University Press, 1986

————, trans. McLeish, K., *Poetics*, London: Nick Hern Books, 1998

Artaud, A., *The Theatre and Its Double*, Montreuil; London; New York: Calder, 1999 (1970)

Astley, Francis, and Crowder (eds), *Theological Perspectives on Christian Formation: A Reader on Theology*, Chester: Gracewing Publishing, 1996

Auerbach, E., trans. Trask, W.R., *Mimesis: The Representation of Reality in Western Literature*, Princeton NJ: Princeton University Press, 1953

Augustine, *The Confessions of St Augustine*, Peabody, MA: Hendrickson, 2004

Auslander, P., *From Acting to Performance: Essays in Modernism and Postmodernism*, London: Routledge, 1997

Badiou, A., trans. Feltham, O., *Being and Event*, London: Continuum, 1998

Barba, E., *Beyond the Floating Islands*, New York: PAJ Publications, 1986

————, and Savarese, N., *A Dictionary of Theatre Anthropology: The Secret Art of the Performer*, London; New York: Routledge, 1991

————, trans. Fowler, R., *The Paper Canoe: A Guide to Theatre Anthropology*, London; New York: Routledge, 1995

————, 'An Amulet Made of Memory: The Significance of Memory in an Actor's Dramaturgy', in Zarrilli, P.B. (ed.), *Acting (Re)considered: a Theoretical and Practical Guide*, London; New York: Routledge, 2002, pp. 99–106

Barker, G.P., and Hacker, S.H., *An Analytical Commentary on Wittgenstein's Philosophical Investigations*, Oxford: Blackwell, 1983

Barnes, M.P., Dobkin, B.H, and Bogousslavsky, J., *Recovery After Stroke*, Cambridge: Cambridge University Press, 2005

Barrett, Mark, *Crossing*, Harrisburg, PA: Morehouse Publishing, 2002

Barth, M., trans. Blanke, H., *The Letter to Philemon: A New Translation with Commentary*, Grand Rapids, MI: W.B. Eerdmans, 2000

Bates, G.B., Harper, P.S., and Jones, L., *Huntington's Disease*, Oxford: Oxford University Press, 2002

Bayly, S., *A Pathognomy of Performance: Theatre, Philosophy and the Ethics of Interruption*, unpublished doctoral thesis, 2002

————, 'What State am I in? Or How to be a Spectator', in Kelleher, J., and Ridout, N.P., *Contemporary Theatres in Europe: A Critical Companion*, London; New York: Routledge, 2006, pp. 199–212

Becker, Howard, S., *Problem of Inference and Proof in Participant Observation*, New York: Irvington Publishing, 1993

Bell, C., *Ritual Perspectives and Dimensions*, Oxford: Oxford University Press, 1997

Betz Hull, M., *The Hidden Philosophy of Hannah Arendt*, London; New York: Routledge, 1997

Benedetti, J., *Stanislavski: An Introduction*, London; New York: Routledge, 1988

Benhabib, S., *The Reluctant Modernism of Hannah Arendt*, Lanham, MD: Rowman & Littlefield, 2004 (2003)

Benthall, J., *The Best of Anthropology Today*, London; New York: Routledge, 2002

Berlin, I., *Four Essays on Liberty*, Oxford: Oxford University Press, 1990

Birmingham, P., 1969, *Hannah Arendt and Human Rights: The Predicament of Common Responsibility*, Bloomington, IN: Indiana University Press, 2006

Blaikie, A. (ed.), *The Body: Critical Concepts in Sociology*, London: Routledge, 2003

Blau, H., *The Eye of Prey: Subversions of the Postmodern*, Ann Arbor, MI: University of Michigan Press, 1987

———, *The Audience*, Albany, NI: Johns Hopkins University Press, 1990

———, *Nothing in Itself: Complexions of Fashion*, Bloomington, IN: Indiana University Press, 1999

Bloch, S., Orthous, P., and Santibañez-H. G., 'Effector Patterns of Basic Emotion: A Psychophysiological Method for Training Actors', in Zarrilli, P.B. (ed.), *Acting (re)Considered: A Theoretical and Practical Guide*, London; New York: Routledge, 2002, pp. 219–241

Blocker, J., *What the Body Cost: Desire, History and Performance*, Minneapolis, MN: University of Minnesota Press, 2004

Boal, A., and Jackson, A., *Games for Actors and Non-actors*, London; New York: Routledge, 2002

Bobath, B., *Adult Hemiplegia: Evaluation and Treatment*, Oxford: Heinemann, 1990

Bogdan, Robert, *Participant Observation in Organizational Settings*. Syracuse, NY: Syracuse University Press, 1972

Bogousslavsky, J. (ed.), *Acute Stroke Treatment*, London: Informa Health Care Publishers, 2003

Boucock, G., *In the Grip of Freedom: Law and Modernity in Max Weber*, Toronto: Toronto University Press, 2000

Bourriaud, N., trans. Pleasance, S., and Woods, F., *Relational Aesthetics*, Dijon: Presses du Réel, 2002

Brandt, G.W., *Modern Theories of Drama: A Selection of Writings on Drama and Theatre, 1840–1990*, Oxford: Oxford University Press, 1998

Brecht, B., *Poems, Part Three 1939–1956*, London: Eyre Methuen, 1976

Brook, P., *The Empty Space*, London: Penguin Books, 1990 (1968)

Brooman, S., and Legge, D., *Law Relating to Animals*, London; Sydney: Cavendish Publishing, 1997

Bruce, V., Green, P.R., and Georgeson, M.A., *Visual Perception: Physiology, Psychology and Ecology*, Oxford: Psychology Press, 2003

Bruyn, Severyn, *The Human Perspective in Sociology: The Methodology of Participant Observation*, Englewood Cliffs, NJ: Prentice-Hall, 1966

Butler, J., *Gender Trouble: Feminism and the Subversion of Identity*, London; New York: Routledge, 1990

Bynum, C.W., 'Women's Stories, Women's Symbols: A Critique of Victor Turner's

Theories of Liminality', in Moore and Reynolds (eds), *Anthropology and the Study of Religion*, Chicago, IL: Centre for the Scientific Study of Religion, 1991

Callon, Michel, 'The Sociology of an Actor-Network: The Case of the Electric Vehicle', in Callon M., Law, J., and Rip, A. (eds), *Mapping the Dynamics of Science and Technology: Sociology of Science in the Real World*, London: Macmillan, 1986

Campbell, P., *The Body in Performance*, London; New York: Routledge, 2001

Carlson, M., *Performance: A Critical Introduction*, London; New York: Routledge, 2004 (1996)

Carlstedt, R.A., *Critical Moments During Competition: A Mind–Body Model of Sports Performance When It Counts the Most*, Oxford: Psychology Press, 2004

Carr, J.H., and Shepherd, R.B., *A Motor Learning Model for Stroke*, Oxford: Butterworth Heinemann, 1987

———, *Stroke Rehabilitation: Guidelines for Exercise and Training to Optimize Motor Skill*, Oxford: Butterworth Heinemann, 2003

Chaudhuri, U., 'Zoo Stories: "Boundary Work" in Theatre History', in *Theorizing Practice: Redefining Theatre History*, in Worthen, W.B., and Holland, P. (eds), Basingstoke: Palgrave Macmillan, 2003

Claire, T., *Bodywork*, Laguna Beach, CA: Basic Health Publications, 2006

Clark, K, and Holquist, M., *Mikhail Bakhtin*, Cambridge, MA: Harvard University Press, 1984

Cochran, L., *The Sense of Vocation: A Study of Career and Life Development*, Albany, NY: SUNY Press, 1990

Cohen, R., and Kennedy, P.M., *Global Sociology*, New York: NYU Press, 2000

Coleridge, S.T., ed. Foakes, R.A., *Coleridge's Criticism of Shakespeare*, London: Continuum, 1989 (1817)

Conquergood, D., *I am a Shaman: A Hmong Life Story with Ethnographic Commentary*, Evanston, IL: Northwestern University Press, 1989

Cooley, C.H., *Human Nature and the Social Order*, Piscataway, NJ: Transaction Publications, 1983

Cottingham, J., Stoothoff, R., and Murdoch, D., *The Philosophical Writings of Descartes*, 2 volumes, Cambridge: Cambridge University Press, 1984

Coward, R., and Ellis, J., *Language and Materialism: Developments in Semiology and the Theory of the Subject*, London; New York: Routledge, 1977

Crowley, M., *Dying Words: The Last Moments of Writers and Philosophers*, Amsterdam: Rodopi Press, 2000

Dean, M., *Governmentality: Power and Rule in Modern Society*, Thousand Oaks, CA: Sage, 1999

De Dreuille, M., *From East to West: A History of Monasticism*, Chester: Gracewing Publishing, 1999

Delanty, G., *Communities*, London: Routledge, 2003

Deleuze, G., trans. McNeil, J., *Masochism: An Interpretation of Coldness and Cruelty*, New York: Braziller, 1971

———, trans. McNeil, J., *Masochism*, New York: Zone Books, 1991 (1967)

———, Smith D.W., and Greco, M.A. (eds), *Gilles Deleuze, Essays Critical and Clinical*, London: Verso, 1997

———, trans. Tomlinson, H., *Nietzsche and Philosophy*, London: Continuum, 2006

Demastes, W., *Staging Consciousness: Theatre and the Materialization of the Mind*, Ann Abor, MI: University of Michigan Press, 2002

Derrida, J., *De Le Grammatolgie*, Paris: Editions de Minuit, 1967
———, trans. Spivak, G.C., *Of Grammatology*, Baltimore, MD: Johns Hopkins University Press, 1976
De Waal, E., *Rule of St. Benedict: Introduction and Commentary*, Chester: Gracewing Publishing, 1990
———, *Seeking God: The Way of St Benedict*, Norwich: SCM Canterbury Press, 1999
Diamond, E. (ed.), *Performance and Cultural Politics*, London; New York: Routledge, 1996
Diener, E., 'Deindividuation: The Absence of Self Awareness and Self Regulation in Group Members', in Paulus, P.B. (ed.), *Psychology of Group Influence*, Hillsdale, NJ: Erlbaum, 1980
Donnellan, D., *The Actor and the Target*, London: Nick Hern Books, 2002
Dowdle and Hopkins, *The Eradication of Infectious Diseases: Report on the Dhalem Workshop*, Hoboken, NJ: John Wiley, 1998
Drain, R. (ed.), *Twentieth-Century Theatre: A Source Book*, London: Routledge, 1995
Dressler, H., *The Usage of Askeo and Its Cognates in Greek Documents AD 100*, Whitefish, MT: Kessinger, 2006
Duchenne, G.B., trans. Cuthbertson, R.A., *The Mechanism of Human Facial Expression*, Cambridge: Cambridge University Press, 1990
Durkheim, Emile, *The Division of Labour in Our Society*, Glencoe: The Free Press, 1947
———, trans. Halls, W.D., *The Rules of Sociological Method*, New York: Free Press, 1992 (1895)
Dyck, N., and Archetti, E.P., *Sport, Dance and Embodied Identities*, Oxford: Berg Publishers, 2003
Eagleton, T., *After Theory*, London: Allen Lane, 2003
Eggers, D., *A Heartbreaking Work of Staggering Genius*, London: Picador, 2000
Ellis, B.E., *American Psycho*, London: Picador, 1991
Engleman, P., trans. Furtmuller, L., *Letters from Ludwig Wittgenstein*, Oxford: Blackwell, 1967
Esler, P.F., *The Early Christian World*, London: Routledge, 2004
Esslin, M., *Artaud: The Man and His Work*, London: John Calder, 1976
Eysneck, M.W., *Psychology: An International Perspective*, Oxford: Psychology Press, 2004
Fawcus, R., *Stroke Rehabilitation: A Collaborative Approach*, Oxford: Blackwell, 2000
Feher, Nadaf and Tazir (eds), *Fragments for a History of the Human Body*, New York: Zone, 1989
Feuerstein, G., *Biomorphic Architecture: Human and Animal Forms in Architecture*, New York: Axel Menges, 2002
Findlay, R., 'Grotowski's Laboratory Theatre: Dissolution and Diaspora', in Wolford, L., and Schechner, R. (eds), *The Grotowski Sourcebook*, New York; London: Routledge, 1997, pp. 172–189
Fine, B., and Millar, R., *Policing the Miners' Strike*, London: Lawrence & Wishart, 1985
Fogelin, R.J., *Wittgenstein*, London: Routledge, 1995
Foucault, M., trans. Sheridan, A.M., *The Birth of the Clinic: An Archaeology of Medical Perception*, London: Routledge, 2003 (1963)
———, trans. Sheridan, A., *Discipline and Punish: The Birth of the Prison*, London: Penguin, 1991 (1977)

Fraleigh, Sondra Horton, *Dancing into Darkness*, Pittsburgh, PA: University of Pittsburgh Press, 1999

Freedman, D.N., Myers, A.C., and Beck, A.B., *Eerdman's Dictionary of the Bible*, Grand Rapids, MI: Eerdmans Publishing

Freire, P., trans. Ramos, M.B., *Pedagogy of the Oppressed*, London: Penguin Books, 1993 (1970)

French, P.A., *Individual and Collective Responsibility*, Cambridge, MA: Schenkman Books, 1998

French, S., and Sim, J., *Physiotherapy: A Psychosocial Approach*, New York: Elsevier Health Sciences, 2004

Frist, W., *When Every Moment Counts: What You Need to Know about Bioterrorism*, Lanham, MD: Rowman & Littlefield, 2002

Fuchs, E., *The Death of Character: Perspectives on Theatre after Modernism*, Bloomington, IN: Indiana University Press, 1996

Gadamer, H.G., 'The Nature of Things and the Language of Things', in *Philosophical Hermenuetics*, ed. Linge, D., Berkeley, CA: University of California Press, 1977

Gallagher, C., and Greenblatt, S., *Practising New Historicism*, Chicago, IL: University of Chicago Press, 2000

Garfinkel, H., *Studies in Ethnomethodology*, Oxford: Blackwell, 1984 (1967)

Gaus, G.F., *Political Concepts and Political Theories*, Jackson, TN: Westview Press, 2000

Gelb, I., *A Study of Writing*, London: Routledge & Kegan Paul, 1952

Gibson, J.J., *The Ecological Approach to Visual Perception*, Boston, MA: Houghton Mifflin Harcourt, 1979

Giddens, Anthony, *The Constitution of Society. Outline of the Theory of Structuration.* Cambridge: Polity Press, 1984

————, *Sociology*, Cambridge: Polity Press, 2006

Gilbert, M., *On Social Facts*, New York: Routledge, 1989

————, *Sociality and Responsibility*, Lahnman, MD: Rowman & Littlefield, 2000

Gillmean, L.M., *John Osborne: A Reading of His Life and Work*, London; New York: Routledge, 2002

Goffman, E., *The Presentation of Self in Everyday Life*, New York: Doubleday, 1959

————, *Asylums: Essays on the Social Situation of Mental Patients and Other Inmates*, Peterborough: Anchor Books, 1961

————, *Stigma: Notes on the Management of Spoiled Identity*, London: Simon & Schuster, 1963

————, *Stigma: Notes on the Management of Spoiled Identity*, New York: Touchstone, 1986

Goldrup, T., *Growing up on the Set: Interviews with 39 Former Child Actors of Classic Film and Television*, Jefferson, NC: McFarland Publishing, 2002

Good, B., *Medicine, Rationality and Experience: An Anthropological Perspective* Cambridge: Cambridge University Press, 1994

Goodchild, P., *Deleuze and Guattari: An Introduction to the Politics of Desire*, Thousand Oaks, CA: Sage Publications, 1996

Gordon, R., *The Purpose of Playing: Modern Acting Theories in Perspective*, Ann Arbor, MI: University of Michigan Press, 2006

Gottsegen, M.G., *The Political Thought of Hannah Arendt*, Albany, NY: SUNY Press, 1994

Goulish, M., *39 Microlectures in Proximity of Performance*, London; New York: Routledge, 2000

Gregson, N.H., Drees, W.B., and Gorman, U., *The Human Person in Science and Theology*, London: T&T Clark Publishing, 2000

Greenslade, S.L., *The Cambridge History of the Bible: Volume 3, The West from Reformation to the Present Day*, Cambridge: Cambridge University Press, 1975

Grotowski, J., *Towards a Poor Theatre*, London: Methuen, 1991 (1968)

Hables, Gray, C., 'In Defence of Prefigurative Art: The Aesthetics and Ethics of Orlan and Stelarc', in *The Cyborg Experiments: Extensions of the Body, the Media Age*, Zylinska, J. (ed.), London: Continuum, 2002, pp. 181–193

Hadot, P., *Philosophy as a Way of Life: Spiritual Exercises from Socrates to Foucault*, Oxford: Blackwell, 1995

Hallward, P., *Badiou: A Subject to Truth*, Minneapolis, MN: University of Minnesota Press, 2003

Hamilton, J.R., *The Art of Theatre*, Oxford: Blackwell, 2007

Hampton, C., *Savages*, London: Faber & Faber, 1974

Handleman, D., and Lindquist, G., *Ritual in Its Own Right: The Dynamics of Transformation*, Oxford: Berghahn Books, 2005

Harper, D., *On the Authority of the Image, Visual Methods at the Crossroads*, in Denzin, N., and Lincon, Y. (eds), *Handbook of Qualitative Research*, Newbury Park, CA: Sage, 1994

Harris, R., *Reading Saussure: A Critical Commmentary on the Cours de Linguistique Generale*, London: Duckworth, 1987

Haubrich, W.S., *Medical Meanings: A Glossary of Word Origins*, Philadelphia, PA: APC Press, 2003

Haynes, D., *The Vocation of the Artist*, Cambridge: Cambridge University Press, 1997

Headland, T.N., Pike, T.L., and Harris, M., *Emics and Etics: The Insider/Outsider Debate*, Thousand Oaks, CA: Sage, 1990

Heberman, Pace, Pallen, Shahans and Wynne, *The Catholic Encyclopaedia: An International Work of Reference*, Reading, MA: Robert Appleton, 1919

Hecker, J.F.C., Babington, B.G., and Caius, J., *The Epidemics of the Middle Ages*, Delaware: Trubner Press, 1859

Heidegger, M., trans. Glenn Gray, J.,*What is Called Thinking?*, New York: Harper & Row, 1968

———, trans. Schuwer, A., and Rojcewicz, R., *Parmenides*, Bloomington, IN: Indiana University Press, 1992

Hejinian, L., 'The Rejection of Closure', in Hejinian, L. (ed.), *The Language of Inquiry*, Berkeley, CA: University of California Press, 2000 (1983)

Heraclitus, trans. Hillman, J., *Fragments*, London: Penguin

Hinchman, L.P., *Hannah Arendt: Critical Essays*, Albany, NY: SUNY Press, 1994

Hobbes, T., *Leviathan*, New York: Penguin, 1968 (1651)

Hodge, A., *Twentieth Century Actor Training*, London: Routledge, 2000

Holl, K., *Gesammelte Aufsatze zur Kirchengeschichte: Vol 3*, Tubingham: Mohr, 1928

Hoskin, K., 'Foucault under Examination: The Crypo-Educationalist Unmasked', in Ball, S.J. (ed.), *Foucault and Education: Disciplines and Knowledge*, London; New York: Routledge, 1990

Huxley, M., and Witts, N., *The Twentieth Century Performance Reader*, London; New York: Routledge, 2002

Ignatius Loyola, trans. Mullan, F., *The Spiritual Exercises of St Ignatius Loyola*, New York: Cosimo, 2007 (1522–1524)

Jackson, B., *The Battle for Orgreave*, Brighton: Vanson Wardle Publishing, 1986

Jaeger, W., trans. Hignet, G., *Paideia: The Ideals of Greek Culture Vol 1: Archaic Greece The Mind of Athens*, Oxford: Oxford University Press, 1948

———, *Paidiea: The Ideals of Greek Culture*, Oxford: Oxford University Press, 1986

Jones, D., 'The Genealogy of the Urban Schoolteacher', in Ball S.J. (ed.), *Foucault and Education: Disciplines and Knowledge*, London; New York: Routledge, 1990

Jones, D. E., *Combat, Ritual and Performance: Anthropology of Martial Arts*, Westport, CT: Praeger, 2002

Jones, T., *Modern Political Thinkers and Ideas: An Historical Introduction*, London: Routledge, 2002

———, *The Individual and the Political Order*, Lanham, MD: Rowman & Littlefield, 2007

Jorgensen, Danny, L., *Participant Observation: A Methodology for Human Studies (Applied Social Research Methods, Vol. 15)*, Thousand Oaks, CA: Sage, 1993

Kardong, T., *Benedict's Rule: A Translation and Commentary*, Collegeville, MN: Liturgical Press, 1996

Kauffman, E., *The Delirium of Praise: Bataille, Blanchot, Deleuze, Foucault, Klossowski*, Baltimore, MD: Johns Hopkins University Press, 2001

Kelleher, J., and Ridout, N. (eds), *Contemporary Theatres in Europe*, London: Routledge, 2006

———, Ridout, N., Castelluci, C., Castelluci, R., and Guidi, C., *The Theatre of Societas Raffaello Sanzio*, London: Routledge, 2007

Khalfa, J., *Introduction to the Philosophy of Gilles Deleuze*, London: Continuum, 2003

Kleine, Donna, C., *Dominion and Wealth: A Critical Analysis of Karl Marx Theory*, Berlin: Germany: Springer Publishers, 1987

Knowles, D., *From Pachomius to Ignatius: A Study in the Constitutional History of Religious Orders*, Oxford: Clarendon Press, 1966

Kłoczowski, J.A., *History of Polish Christianity*, Cambridge: Cambridge University Press, 2000

Kohn, T., 'The Aikido Body: Expressions of Group Identities and Self Discoveries in Martial Arts Training', in Dyck, N., and Archetti, E.P., *Sport, Dance and Embodied Identities*, Oxford: Berg, 2003, pp. 139–157

Komonchack, J.A., Collins, M., and Lane, D.A., *The New Dictionary of Theology*, New York: Michael Glazier, 1987

Koppett, K., *Training Using Drama*, London: Kogan Page, 2003

Kumiega, J., *The Theatre of Grotowski*, London: Methuen, 1987

Laing, R.D., *The Divided Self: An Existential Study in Sanity and Madness*, London; New York: Routledge, 1999 (1960)

Latour, B., *Science in Action: How to Follow Scientists and Engineers Through Society*, Milton Keynes: Open University Press, 1987

———, *Reassembing the Social*, Oxford: Oxford University Press, 2005

Lauria, A.R., *Higher Cortical Function in Man*, New York: Basic Books, 1966

Law, J., 'Technology and Heterogeneous Engineering: The Case of Portuguese Expansion', in Bijker, W.E., Hughes, T.P., and Pinch, T.J. (eds), *The Social Construction of Technological Systems: New Directions in the Sociology and History of Technology*, Cambridge, MA: MIT Press, 1987

Lawson-Tancred, H., *De Anima: On the Soul*, London: Penguin, 1986
Lazreg, M., *Torture and the Twilight of Empire: From Algiers to Baghdad*, Princeton, NJ: Princeton University Press, 2008
Le Bon, G., *The Crowd*, Ottawa, Ontario: Xinware Corporation, 2007 (1895)
———, *The Crowd*, Edison, NJ: Transaction Publishers, 1995
Leder, D., *The Absent Body*, Chicago, IL: University of Chicago Press, 1990
Levinas, E., trans. Lingis, A., *Totality and Infinity: An Essay on Exteriority*, Pittsburgh, PA: Duquesne University Press, 1969
Lezak, M., *Neuropsychological Assessment*, New York: Oxford Press, 1995
Lindsey, S., *Handbook of Applied Dog Behaviour and Training*, Oxford: Blackwell, 2005
Lingis, A., *Foreign Bodies*, New York; London: Routledge, 1994
———, *The Imperative*, Bloomington, IN: Indiana University Press, 1998
Llewelyn, R., *A Doorway to Silence: The Contemplative Use of the Rosary*, Norwich: Darton, Longman & Todd, 1986
Lockyer, H., *All the Parables in the Bible*, Grand Rapids, MI: Zondervan Publishing, 1988
Luhmann, N., trans. Baecker, D., *Social Systems*, Palo Alto, CA: Stanford University Press, 1995
Lupton, D., *The Imperative of Health: Public Health and the Regulated Body*, Thousand Oaks, CA: Sage, 1995
Lyotard, J.F., *The Postmodern Condition: A Report on Knowledge*, Minneapolis, MN: University of Minnesota Press, 1984
———, *Libidinal Economy*, London: Continuum, 2001
Magill, R.A., *Motor Learning: Concepts and Applications*, Madison, WI: Brown & Benchmark, 2004
Magner, L.N., *A History of Medicine*, New York: Marcel Dekker, 1992
Manne, J., *Soul Therapy*, Berkeley, CA: North Atlantic Books, 1997
Marret-Crosby, A. (ed.), *The Benedictine Handbook*, Norwich: Canterbury Press, 1999
Marret-Crosby, D. and A., and Wright, T., *Doing Business with Benedict: The Rule of St. Benedict and Business Management – A Conversation*, London: Continuum, 2003
Marsden, R., *The Nature of Capital: Marx after Foucault*, London; New York: Routledge, 2003
Marshall, J.D., 'Foucault and Educational Research', in Ball S.J. (ed.), *Foucault and Education: Disciplines and Knowledge*, London; New York: Routledge, 1990
Martin, M., *Cinemas of the Black Diaspora: Diversity, Dependence and Oppositionality*, Detroit, MI: Wayne State University Press, 1995
Marvin, H., and Johnson, O., *Cultural Anthropology*, Upper Saddle River, NJ: Pearson Higher Education, 2006
Marx, K., ed. O'Malley, J., *Marx: Early Political Writing*, Cambridge: Cambridge University Press, 1994
———, and Engels, F., 'Comments on James Mill's Eléments d'économie politique', in *Collected Works Vol. 3*, New York; London: International Publishers, 1975
Marx, W.K., *Martial Arts Therapy*, Blountsville, AL: Fifth Estate, 2005
Maxine Sheets-Johnstone, M. (ed.), *Giving the Body Its Due*, Albany, NY: SUNY Press, 2005
May, L., *The Morality of Groups*, Notre Dame, IN: University of Notre Dame Press, 1987

Merleau-Ponty, M., trans. Smith, C., *Phenomenology of Perception*, London; New York: Routledge, 2002 (1945)

————, *Phenomenology of Perception*, London: Routledge & Kegan Paul, 1962

Meyer-Dinkgräfe, D., *Approaches to Acting, Past and Present*, London: Continuum, 2006

McCann, C.R., and Kim, S.-K., *Feminist Theory Reader: Local and Global Perspectives*, London: Routledge, 2002

McClintock, Mufti and Shohat (eds), *Dangerous Liaisons: Gender, Nation and Postcolonial Perspectives*, Minneapolis, MN: University of Minnesota Press, 1997

McDonnell, D., *Theories of Discourse: An Introduction*, Oxford: Blackwell, 1986

McHale, B., 'Science Fiction', in Bertens, H. (ed.), *International Postmodernism: Theory and Literary Practice*, Amsterdam: John Benjamins, 1997, pp. 235–243

McKenzie, J., *Perform or Else: From Disciplne to Performance*, London; New York: Routledge, 2001

McMorris, T., *Acquisition and Performance of Sports Skills*, Hoboken, NJ: John Wiley, 2004

Merlin, B., *Beyond Stanislavski: The Psycho-physical Approach to Actor Training*, London: Nick Hern Books, 2001

Midlefort, H.C.E., *A History of Madness in Sixteenth Century Germany*, Palo Alto, CA: Stanford University Press, 2000

Milgram, S., *Obedience to Authority: An Experimental View*, New York: Harper & Row, 1974

Miner, E., *Comparative Poetics*, Princeton, NJ: Princeton University Press, 1990

Mol, A., *The Body Multiple: Ontology in Medical Practice*, Durham, NC: Duke University Press, 1990

Montgomery, K., *How Doctors Think: Clinical Judgment and the Practice of Medicine*, Oxford: Oxford University Press, 2006

Mullaney, S., *The Place of the Stage: Power, Play and License in Renaissance England*, Ann Arbor, MI: University of Michigan Press, 1995

Nancy, J.L., *Being, Singular, Plural*, Palo Alto, CA: Stanford University Press, 2003

Nola, R., *Rescuing Reason: A Critique of Anti-Rationalist Views of Science and Knowledge*, Berlin: Springer, 2000

Nye, R.A., *The Origins of Crowd Psychology: Gustave Le Bon and the Crisis of Democracy in the Third Republic*, Beverly Hills, CA: Sage, 1975

Onions, C.T., Friedrichsen, G.W.S., and Burchfield, R.W. (eds), *Oxford Dictionary of English Etymology*, Oxford: Clarendon Press, 1966

Patterson, S., and Crane, T., *History of the Mind–Body Problem*, London; New York: Routledge, 2000

Patton, P. (ed.), *Deleuze: A Critical Reader*, Oxford: Blackwell, 1996

Phelan, P., 'Playing Dead in Stone or When is a Rose Not a Rose?', in Diamond, E. (ed.), *Performance and Cultural Politics*, London; New York: Routledge, 1996, pp. 65–89

————, and Lane, J., *The Ends of Performance*, New York: New York University Press, 1998

Phelan, S., *Getting Specific: Postmodern Lesbian Politics*, Minneapolis, MN; London: University of Minnesota Press, 1994

Pike, Kenneth, L., *Mystery of Culture Contacts, Historical Reconstruction and Text Analysis: An EMIC Approach*, Washington, DC: Georgetown University Press, 1995

Plato, trans. Allen, R.E., *The Republic*, London: Yale University Press, 2006

Poole, M.S., and Hirokawa, R.Y., *Communication and Group Decision Making*, Thousand Oaks, CA: Sage, 1996

Porter, S. B., *Tidy's Physiotherapy*, Oxford: Elsevier, 2003

Postmes, T., and Jetten, J., *Individuality and the Group*, Thousand Oaks, CA: Pine Forge Press, 2006

Potter, N., *Movement for Actors*, New York: Allworth Communications, 2002

Power, E.J., *A Legacy of Learning: A History of Western Education*, New York State University of New York Press, 1991

Proust, M., trans. Scott Moncreiff, C.K., *The Remembrance of Things Past, Vol. 1*, Hertfordshire: Wordsworth Editions, 2006 (1922)

Read, A., *Theatre and Everyday Life: An Ethics of Performance*, London; New York: Routledge, 1993

————, *Theatre, Intimacy and Engagement: The Last Human Venue*, Basingstoke; New York: Palgrave Macmillan, 2008

Reinelt, J., 'Foreword from "Across the Pond"', in Kelleher, J., and Ridout, N.P., *Contemporary Theatres in Europe: A Critical Companion*, London; New York: Routledge, 2006, p. xiv

Rendell, J., *Art and Architecture: A Place Between*, London: I.B. Tauris, 2006

Ridout, N.P., *Stage Fright: Animal and Other Theatrical Problems*, Cambridge: Cambridge University Press, 2006

Roach, J., *The Player's Passion: Studies in the Science of Acting*, Newark, DE: University of Delaware Press, 1985; Ann Arbor, MI: University of Michigan Press, 1993

Robbins, J. (ed.), *Is It Righteous to Be?: Interviews with Immanuel Levinas*, Stanford, CA: Stanford University Press, 2001

Roberts, Byram, Barro, Jordan and Street, *Language Learners as Ethnographers*, Tonowanda, NY: Multilingual Matters, 2000

Rose, M., *Parody: Ancient, Modern and Postmodern*, Cambridge: Cambridge University Press, 1993

Rothenburg, J., and Clay, S., *A Book of the Book: Some Works and Projections about the Book and Writing*, New York: Granary Books, 2000

Royce, A.P., *The Anthropology of Dance*, Hampshire, England: Dance Books, 2000

Rudé, G., *The Crowd in History: 1730–1848*, New York: John Wiley, 1964

Sartre, J.-P., trans. Barnes, H.E., *Being and Nothingness: An Essay on Phenomenological Ontology*, London: Methuen, 1958

Sarup, M., and Raja, T., *Identity, Culture and the Postmodern World*, Edinburgh: Edinburgh University Press, 1996

Schechner, R., *Essays on Performance Theory 1970–1976*, New York: Drama Book Specialists, 1977

————, *Performance Studies: An Introduction*, London; New York: Routledge, 2002

————, *Performance Theory*, London; New York: Routledge, 2003

————, and Turner, V., *Between Theatre and Anthropology*, Philadelphia, PA: University of Pennsylvania Press, 1985

Schechner, R., and Appel, W., *By Means of Performance*, Cambridge: Cambridge University Press, 1990

————, and Turner, V., *The Future of Ritual*, London; New York: Routledge, 1993

Scheer, E., *Antonin Artaud: A Critical Reader*, London; New York: Routledge, 2004

Schiffer, R.B., Roa, M.R., and Fogel, B.S. (eds), *Neuropsychiatry*, Haggerston, MD: Lippencott, Williams and Wilkins, 2003

Schmidt, R., and Lee, T.D., *Motor Control and Learning: A Behavioural Emphasis*, Champaign, IL: Human Kinetics, 1999

Schneider, R., *The Explicit Body in Performance*, London; New York: Routledge, 1997

Schopenhauer, A., trans. Payne, F.E.J., *The World as Will and Representation*, New York: Courier Dover Publications, 1966

Scruton, R., *Animal Rights and Wrongs*, London: Demos, 1998

Searle, J.R., *Speech Acts: An Essay in the Philosophy of Language*, Cambridge: Cambridge University Press, 1969

Shepherd, D. (ed.), *Bakhtin: Carnival and Other Subjects*, New York: Rodopi Press, 1993

Shepherd, G.S., and Rothenbuhler, E.W., *Communication and Community*, Mahwah, NJ: Lawrence Erlbaum, 2001

Shepherd, J., St. John, J., and Striphas, T.G. (eds), *Communication as Perspectives on Social Theory*, Thousand Oaks, CA: Sage Publications, 2006

Skeat, W.W., *A Concise Etymological Dictionary of the English Language*, New York: Cosimo, 2005

Smith, A., *An Inquiry into the Nature and Causes of the Wealth of Nations*, Cambridge, MA: Harvard University Press, 2005 (1776)

Smith, D.W., 'Deleuze's Theory of Sensation: Overcoming the Kantian Duality', in Patton, P. (ed.), *Deleuze: A Critical Reader*, Oxford: Blackwell, 1996, pp. 29–57

———, and Greco, M.A., *Essays Critical and Clinical*, London: Verso, 1997

Solzhenitsyn, A.I., trans. Whitney, T.P., *The First Circle*, Evanston, IL: Northwestern University Press, 1997 (1963)

Sontag, S., and Poague, L.A., *Conversations with Susan Sontag*, Jackson, MS: University of Mississippi Press, 1995

Stam, R., 'Multiculturalism and the Neoconservatives', in McClintock, Mufti and Shohat (eds), *Dangerous Liaisons: Gender, Nation and Postcolonial Perspectives*, Minneapolis, MN: University of Minnesota Press, 1997

Stanislavski, K., *An Actor's Handbook*, London: Methuen, 1990 (1924)

Steiner, G., *Heidegger*, Sussex: Harvester Press, 1978

Stoller, P., *Sensuous Scholarship: Contemporary Ethnography*, Philadelphia, PA: University of Pennsylvania Press, 1997

Stone, J.R., *The Routledge Dictionary of Latin Quotations*, London; New York: Routledge, 2004

Sullivan, N., *A Critical Introduction to Queer Theory*, Edinburgh: Edinburgh University Press, 2001

Suzuki, T., trans. Rimmer, T., *The Way of Acting: The Theatre Writings of Tadashi Suzuki*, New York: Theatre Communications Group, 1986

Taussig, M., *Mimesis and Alterity: A Particular History of the Senses*, New York; London: Routledge, 1993

Townsend, D., and Taylor, A., *The Tongue of the Fathers*, Philadelphia, PA: University of Pennsylvania Press, 1998

Trevino, J., *Goffman's Legacy*, New York: Rowman & Littlefield, 2003

Turner, J., *Eugenio Barba*, London: Routledge, 2004

Turner, R., and Killian, L., *Collective Behaviour*, Engelwood Cliffs, NJ: Prentice Hall, 1972

Turner, V., *The Anthropology of Performance*, New York: PAJ Publications, 1988

————, *The Ritual Process: Structure and Anti-Structure*, Piscataway, NJ: Aldine Transactions, 1995

Ulmer, G., *Applied Grammatology: Post(e)-Pedagogy from Jacques Derrida to Joseph Beuys*, Baltimore, MD: Johns Hopkins University Press, 1985

————, *Electronic Monuments*, Minneapolis, MN: University of Minnesota Press, 2005

Van Gennep, A., trans. Vizedom, M., and Caffee, G.L., *The Rites of Passage*, London; New York: Routledge, 2004 (1909)

Vanhoozer, K.J., *The Drama of Doctrine: A Canonical-Linguistic Approach to Christian Theology*, Westminster: John Knox Press, 2005

Viala, J., and Masson-Sekine, N., *Butoh: Shades of Darkness*, Clarendon, VT: Tuttle Publishing, 1988

Warnock, M., *Existentialism*, Oxford: Oxford University Press, 1970

Warwick University, Organizational Behaviour Staff, *Organizational Behaviour*, London: Routledge, 2000

Watson, I., *Towards a Third Theatre: Eugenio Barba and the Odin Teatret*, London; New York: Routledge, 1993

————, *Performer Training: Developments Across Cultures*, London; New York: Routledge, 2001

————, *Negotiating Cultures: Eugenio Barba and the Intercultural Debate*, Manchester: Manchester University Press, 2002

Watson, R., *Cogito Ergo Sum: The Life of René Descartes*, Boston, MA: David R. Godine, 2002

Waugh, P., *Literary Theory and Criticism: An Oxford Guide*, Oxford: Oxford University Press, 2006

Weber, M., *Economy and Society Vol. I*, Berkeley, CA: University of California Press, 1978 (1914)

————, trans. Parson, T., *The Protestant Ethic and the Spirit of Capitalism*, Chelmsford, MA: Courier Dover Publications, 2003 (1958)

————, *The Vocation Essays*, Indianapolis, IN: Hackett, 2004

Weinberg, R.S., Gould, D., *Foundations of Sport Psychology*, Champaign, IL: Human Kinetics Publishing, 2006

Whitehead, A.N., *The Aims of Education*, London: Ernest Benn, 1929

Willem, J., *International Postmodernism: Theory and Literary Practice*, Amsterdam: John Benjamins Publishing, 1997

Williams, A.M., Davids, K., and Williams, J.G., *Visual Perception and Action in Sport*, London: E and FN Spon, 1999

Wimbush, V.L., and Valantasis, R. (eds), *Asceticism*, Oxford: Oxford University Press, 1995

Winnicott, D.W., *Holding and Interpretation: Fragment of an Analysis*, Jackson, TN: Grove Press, 1987

Wittgenstein, L., trans. Ogden, C.K., *Tractatus Logico-Philosophicus*, London; New York: Routledge, 1981 (1921)

————, *Philosophical Investigations*, Oxford: Blackwell, 2001 (1953)

Wolford, L., and Schechner R. (eds), *The Grotowski Sourcebook*, New York: Routledge, 1997

Worrall, N., 'Meyerhold's "Magnanimous Cuckold"', in Schneider, R., and Cody, G. (eds), *Re:direction: A Theoretical and Practical Guide*, London, Routledge, 2002 (1973)

Yasuo, Y., trans. Nagatomo, S., and Kasulis, T.P., *The Body: Toward an Eastern Mind–Body Theory*, Albany, NY: SUNY Press, 1987

Zaleski, P., and C., *Prayer: A History*, Boston, MA: Houghton Mifflin, 2005

Zarrilli, P.B. (ed.), *Acting (re)Considered: Theories and Practices*, London; New York: Routledge, 1995

———, *When the Body Becomes All Eyes: Paradigms, Discourses and Practices of Power in Kalarippayattu, a South Indian Martial Art*, Oxford: Oxford University Press, 1998

———, '"On the Edge of a Breath, Looking": Cultivating the Actor's Bodymind through Asian Martial/Meditative Arts', in Zarrilli, P.B. (ed.), *Acting (re)Considered: A Theoretical and Practical Guide*, New York; London: Routledge, 2002, pp. 181–200

———, *Psychophysical Acting: An Intercultural Approach after Stanislavski*, London; New York: Routledge, 2008

Zimbardo, P.G., *The Stanford Prison Experiment: A Simulation Study of the Psychology of a Prison*, Phillip G. Zimbardo, 1971

Zylinska, J., *The Cyborg Experiments: Extensions of the Body in the Media Age*, London: Continuum, 2002

Conference papers and articles in journals

Ajzenstat, O., 'Levinas vs Levinas: Hebrew, Greek and Linguistic Justice', *Philosophy and Rhetoric*, Vol. 38, No. 2, 2005, pp. 145–158

Allsopp, R., 'On Form/Yet to Come', *Performance Research*, Vol. 10, No. 2, 2005, pp. 1–4

Amit, V. 'Unimagined Communities: Distinguishing between Categories and Consociations of Community', at 'Civic Centre: Reclaiming the Right to Performance', Roehampton University, 13 April 2003

Andrews, K., Brocklehurst, J.C., Richards, B., and Laycock, P.J., 'The Rate of Recovery from Stroke – and Its Measurement', *International Journal of Rehabilitation Medicine*, Vol. 3, 1981, pp. 155–161

Auerbach, E., trans. M., and E. Said, 'Philology and Weltliteratur', *Centennial Review*, Vol. 13, 1969, pp. 1–17

Barker, S., 'The Alexander Technique: An Acting Approach', *Theatre Topics*, Vol. 12, No. 1, 2002, pp. 35–48

Benedetti, R., 'What We Need to Learn from the Asian Actor', *Educational Theatre Journal*, Vol. 25, 1973, pp. 463–468

Bohannon, R.W., Horton, M.G., and Wikholm, J.B., 'Importance of Four Variables, Walking to Patients of Stroke', *International Journal of Rehabilitation Research*, Vol. 14, 1991, pp. 246–250

Bratman, M. (1993) 'Shared Intentions', *Ethics*, Vol. 104, 1993, pp. 97–103

Brecht, B., 'BB's Rehearsal Scenes: Estranging Shakespeare', *TDR, The Drama Review*, Bertolt Brecht, Vol. 12, No. 1, 1967–1968, pp. 108–111

Carr, J.H., and Shepherd, R.B., 'A Motor Learning Model for Stroke Rehabilitation', *Physiotherapy*, Vol. 75, 1989, pp. 372–380

Chemero, A., 'Radical Empiricism through the Ages', *Contemporary Psychology*, Vol. 48, 2003, pp. 18–20

Cieslak, R., interviewed by Torzecka, M., 'Running to Touch the Horizon', *New Theatre Quarterly*, Vol. 8, No. 31, 1992, pp. 261–263

Clay, J., 'Self-use, Actor Training', *TDR, The Drama Review*, Vol. 16, No. 1, 1972, pp. 16–22

Cooper, D.E., 'Collective Responsibility', *Philosophy*, Vol. 43, 1968, pp. 248–268

Copp, D., 'Hobbes on Artificial Persons and Collective Actions', *Philosophical Review*, Vol. 89, No. 4, 1980, pp. 579–606

Corlett, A., 'Collective Moral Responsibility', *Journal of Social Philosophy*, Vol. 32, 2001, pp. 573–584

Corry, S., 'Ethnocide: A Report from Columbia', RAI News, *Anthropology Today*, Vol. 6, Jan/Feb 1975, pp. 1–2

Dean, C., Richards, C., Malouin, F., et al., 'Task Related Circuit Training Improves Performance of Locomotor Tasks, Chronic Stroke: A Randomised Control Pilot Trial', *Archives of Physical and Medical Rehabilitation*, Vol. 81, 2000, pp. 409–417

Deleuze, G., 'Mystique et Masochisme', *La Quinzaine Litteraire*, Vol. 25, 1967, pp. 12–13

Downie, J.R.S., 'Collective Responsibility', *Philosophy*, Vol. 44, 1969, pp. 66–69

Festinger, Pepitone and Newcomb, 'Some Consequences of Deindividuation: A Group', *Journal of Abnormal and Social Psychology*, Vol. 47, 1952, pp. 382–389

Goldie, P.A., Matyas, T.A., and Evans, O.M., 'Deficit and Change, Gait Velocity During Rehabilitation after Stroke', *Archives of Physical Medicine and Rehabilitation*, Vol. 77, 1996, pp. 1074–1082

Gustafson, D., 'On Pitcher's Account of Investigations, 43', *Philosophy and Phenomenological Research*, Vol. 28, 1967–68, pp. 252–258

Hale, L.A., and Eales, C.J., 'Recovery of Walking Function, Stroke Patients after Minimal Rehabilitation', *Physiotherapy Research International*, Vol. 3, 1998, pp. 194–205

Holl, K., 'The History of the Word Vocation (*Beruf*)', *Review and Expositor*, Vol. 55, 1958, pp. 126–154

Innes, A.M., and Chudley, A.E., 'Woodrow Wilson, Woody Guthrie and Huntington's Disease', *Clinical Genetics*, Vol. 61, No. 4, 2002, pp. 263–266

Kear, A., 'Troublesome Amateurs: Theatre, Ethics and the Labour of Mimesis', *Performance Research*, Vol. 10, No. 1, 2005, pp. 26–46

Lavy, J., 'Theoretical Foundations of Grotowski's Total Act, Via Negativa and Conjuctio Opposortium', *The Journal of Religion and Theatre*, Vol. 4, No. 2, 2005, pp. 175–188

Law, J., 'Notes on the Theory of Actor-Network: Ordering, Strategy and Heterogeneity', *Systems Practice*, Vol. 5, 1992, pp. 379–393

Learmans, R., 'Communication', *Performance Research*, Vol. 11, No. 3, 2006, pp. 23–25

Lennon, S., 'The Bobath Concept: A Critical Review of the Theoretical Assumptions that Guide Physiotherapy Practice, Stroke Rehabilitation', *Physical Therapy Review*, Vol. 1, No. 1, 1996, pp. 35–45

Lewis, H.D., 'Collective Responsibility', *Philosophy*, Vol. 24, 1948, pp. 3–18

Lonsdale, J., 'Ancestral and Authorial Voices: Lloyd Newson DV8's Strange Fish', *New Theatre Quarterly*, Vol. 20, 2004, pp. 117–126

Loukes, R., 'Tracing Bodies: Researching Psychophysical Training for Performance Through Practice', *Performance Research*, Vol. 8, No. 4, 2003, pp. 54–61

————, 'How to be "Deadly": The "Natural" Body, Contemporary Training and Performance', *Contemporary Theatre Review*, Vol. 17, No. 2, 2007, pp. 50–58

Mackey, S., 'Community', *Performance Research*, Vol. 11, No. 3, 2006, pp. 25–29

Mair, L., 'Ethnocide', RAI News, *Anthropology Today*, Vol. 7, 1975, pp. 4–5

Mulvey, L., 'Visual Pleasure and Narrative Cinema', *Screen*, Vol. 16, No. 3, Autumn, 1975, pp. 6–18

Myers, K.K., and Oetzel, J.G., 'Exploring the Dimensions of Organizational Assimilation: Creating and Validating a Measure', *Communication Quarterly*, Vol. 51, 2003, pp. 438–457

Nagatomo, S., 'An East Asian Perspective on Mind–Body', *The Journal of Philosophy and Medicine*, Vol. 21, 1996, pp. 439–466

Naverson, J., 'Collective Responsibility', *Journal of Ethics*, Vol. 6, 2002, pp. 179–186

Olsen, T.S., 'Arm and Leg Paresis as Outcome Predictors, Stroke Rehabilitation', *Stroke*, Vol. 21, 1990, pp. 247–251

Pitches, J., 'Tracing/Training Rebellion: Object Work, Meyerhold's Biomechanics', *Performance Research*, Vol. 12, No. 4, December 2008, pp. 97–103

Postmes, T., and Spears, R., 'Deindividuation and Antinormative Behaviour: A Meta-Analysis', *Psychological Bulletin*, Vol. 123, 1998, pp. 238–259

Prentice-Dunn, S., and Rogers, R.W., 'Effects of Public and Priavte Awareness on Deindividuation and Aggression', *Journal of Personality and Psychology*, Vol. 43, 1982, pp. 503–513

Punt, T.D., 'No Success Like Failure: Walking Late After Stroke, Case Report', *Physiotherapy*, Vol. 86, No. 11, 2000, pp. 563–566

Read, A. (ed.), *Performance Research*, 'On Animals', Vol. 2, No. 5, 2000

Schechner, R., and Thompson, J., 'Why "Social Theatre"?', *TDR, The Drama Review*, Vol. 48, No. 3, 2004, pp. 15–16

Skillbeck, C.E., Wade, D.T., Hewer, R.L., and Wood, V.A., 'Recovery after Stroke', *Journal of Neurology, Neurosurgery and Psychiatry*, Vol. 46, 1983, pp. 5–8

Sparkes, A., Batey, J., and Brown, D., 'The Muscled Self and Its Aftermath: A Life History Study of an Elite Black, Male Bodybuilder', *Autobiography Journal*, Vol. 13, 2005, pp. 131–161

Stokes, J., 'Lion Griefs: The Wild Animal Act as Theatre', *New Theatre Quarterly*, Vol. 20, No. 2, 2004, pp. 138–154

Sullivan, M., 'In What Sense is Contemporary Medicine Dualistic?', *Culture, Medicine and Psychiatry*, Vol. 10, 1986, pp. 341–350

Tuomela, R., 'Actions by Collectives', *Philosophical Perspectives*, Vol. 3, 1989, pp. 471–496

Velleman, J.D., 'How to Share an Intention', *Philosophy and Phenomenological Research*, Vol. 57, 1997, pp. 29–50

Wellek, R., 'Review of *Mimesis*', *Kenyon Review*, Vol. 16, 1954, pp. 299–307

Welton, M., 'Once More with Feeling', *Performance Research: On Theatre*, Vol. 10, No. 1, 2005, pp. 100–112

White, G., 'The Cruyff Turn: Performance, the Cultural Memory of International Soccer', *Sport, Society*, Vol. 10, No. 2, 2007, pp. 256–267

Whitworth, J., 'Translating Theologies of the Body: SITI'S Physical Theatre Training and Corporeal Ideology', *Performance Research*, Vol. 8, No. 2, 2003, pp. 21–27

Zarrilli, P.B., 'Acting at the Nerve Ends: Beckett, Blau, and the Necessary', *Theatre Topics*, Vol. 7, No. 2, 1997, pp. 103–116

————, 'Negotiating Performance Epistemologies: Knowledges "about", "in" and "for"', *Studies, Theatre and Performance*, Vol. 21, 2001, pp. 31–46

————, 'The Metaphysical Studio', *TDR: The Drama Review*, Vol. 46, No. 2, 2002, pp. 157–169

Filmography

Cameron J., *Terminator 2: Judgment Day*, Canal + Production, 1991

Figgis, M., *The Battle of Orgreave*, Artangel Production, 2001

Kurosawa, A., *Yojimbo*, Kurosawa Production Company, 1961

Leone, S., The 'Dollars Trilogy': *A Fist Full of Dollars*, 1964; *For a Few Dollars More*, 1965; and *The Good, the Bad and the Ugly*, 1966, MGM Entertainment

Miller, G., and Ogilvie, G., *Mad Max 3: Beyond Thunderdome*, Kennedy Miller Productions, 1985

Discography

Benedictine Monks of Worth Abbey, *Chants for Benedict*, Herald AV Publications, 1994

Silverstein, S., performed by Cash, J., 'Boy Named Sue', originally released on *Johnny Cash at San Quentin*, Columbia Records, remastered and re-released as *At San Quentin, 1969*, Sony Records, 2000

Internet resources

BBC News, 'Detainee P' <www.news.bbc.co.uk/1/hi/uk/4101751.stm>, 2008, accessed 10/08/2008

BBC News Africa <www.bbc.co.uk/1/hi/world/africa/203137.stm>, 2008, accessed 04/07/2008

British Grotowski Project <www.britishgrotowski.co.uk>, 2008, accessed 01/03/2008

CNN News, 'Flashmob to Lynch Mob' <www.cnn.com/, 2007/2008, TECH/06/04/flashmob.lynchmob/>, accessed 10/08/2008

Connor, S., 'Beside Himself: Glenn Gould and the Prospects of Performance', text of a talk broadcast on BBC Radio 3 <www.bbk.ac.uk/english/skc/gould.htm>, 4 November, 1999, accessed 01/03/2008

————, 'Modernism and the Writing Hand', an 'amplified version' of a paper given at 'Modernism and the Technology of Writing' conference, <www.stevenconnor.com/modhand.htm>, 26 March 1999, accessed 01/03/2008

Creature Discomforts <www.creaturediscomforts.org>, 2008, accessed 10/08/2008

Dail, magazine <www.ldaf.org/images/dail/dial-184web%20v2.pdf>, 2008, accessed 10/08/2008

Disability Discrimination Acts <www.opsi.gov.uk/acts/acts1995/ukpga_19950050_en_1>, and <www.opsi.gov.uk/acts/acts2005 /pdf/kpga 2005 0013_en.pdf>, 1995 and 2005, accessed 10/08/2008

Forced Entertainment, 'myspace' <profile.myspace.com/index. cfm?fuseaction=user.viewprofile&friendid=196106347>, 2008, accessed 10/08/2008

Gardner, L., 'Not Puppets but Thinking Actors', *Guardian* <www.guardian.co.uk/education/2008/jul/15/highereducation.uk1>, 15 July 2008, accessed 04/07/2008

Hejinian, L., 'The Language of Inquiry', from Academy of American Poets, <www.poets.org/viewmedia.php/prmMID/16195>, 2000, accessed 04/03/2008

Law, J., *Making a Mess with Method*, published by Centre for Science Studies, Lancaster University <www.lancs.ac.uk/fass/sociology/papers/law-making-a-mess-with-method.pdf>, 2003, accessed 10/08/2008

————, and, Callon, M., 'On Qualculation, Agency and Otherness', published by Centre for Science Studies, Lancaster University <www.lancs.ac.uk/fass /sociology/papers/callon-law-qualculation-agency-otherness.pdf>, 2003

————, and Mol, A.-M., *Embodied Action Enacted Bodies: The Example of Hypoglycaemia*, published by Centre for Science Studies, Lancaster University <www.lancs.ac.uk/fass/sociology/papers/mol-law-embodied-action.pdf>, 2004, accessed 10/08/2008

Sky News, 'Water Fight in Hyde Park' <news.sky.com/skynews /Home /UK-News/Water-Fight-In-Hyde-Park-London-Turns-Violent-Police-Arrest-Nine-Men/Article/200807415061698>, 2008, accessed 10/08/2008

Societas Rafaello Sanzio, youtube <www.youtube.com/watch ?v=1NZ5pMUbnwY>, 2008, accessed 10/08/2008

Stroke Association <www.stroke.org.uk/about_us/index.html>, 2008, accessed 11/09/2008

Times, The, 'International Olympic Committee Probe', <www.timesonline.co.uk /tol/sport/olympics/article4583174.ece>, 2008, accessed 04/07/2008

'Zarrilli', University of Exeter, homepage, <www.spa.ex.ac.uk, /drama/staff/kalari/zarrilli.html>, 2008, accessed 10/08/2008

Index

Methuen Drama is the leading publisher of titles on all aspects of Theatre, both on stage and behind the scenes.

Methuen Drama publishes plays and anthologies from classic and contemporary playwrights, a wide range of practical and reference texts to support students of drama, literature and media, and instructive titles on professional practice.

New and recent titles from Methuen Drama:

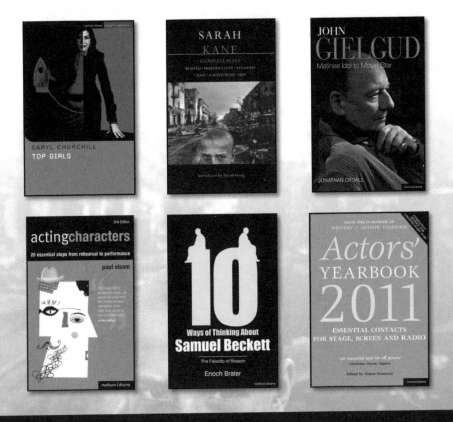

Media Practice from Methuen Drama

Performance Books from Methuen Drama